6

CLAMP

TRANSLATED AND ADAPTED BY
William Flanagan

LETTERED BY
Dana Hayward

Published in the United Kingdom by Tanoshimi in 2006

1 3 5 7 9 10 8 6 4 2

First published in serialization and subsequently published in book form by
Kodansha Ltd, Tokyo in 2004.

Published by arrangement with Kodansha Ltd., Tokyo and with Del Rey,
an imprint of Random House Inc., New York

Tanoshimi
Random House, 20 Vauxhall Bridge Road,
London, SW1V 2SA

www.tanoshimi.tv
www.randomhouse.co.uk

Addresses for companies within The Random House Group Limited can be found at:
www.randomhouse.co.uk

Random House Group Limited Reg. No. 954009

A CIP catalogue record for this book is available from the British Library

ISBN 9780099504948 (from Jan 2007)
ISBN 0 09 950494 4

The Random House Group Limited makes every effort to ensure that the papers used in its books
are made from trees that have been legally sourced from well-managed and credibly certified
forests. Our paper procurement policy can be found at: www.randomhouse.co.uk/paper.htm

Printed and bound in Germany by GGP Media GmbH, Pößneck

Translated and adapted by William Flanagan
Lettered by Dana Hayward

Contents

Honorifics Explained

Throughout the Tanoshimi Manga books, you will find Japanese honorifics left intact in the translations. For those not familiar with how the Japanese use honorifics and, more important, how they differ from English honorifics, we present this brief overview.

Politeness has always been a critical facet of Japanese culture. Ever since the feudal era, when Japan was a highly stratified society, use of honorifics — which can be defined as polite speech that indicates relationship or status — has played an essential role in the Japanese language. When addressing someone in Japanese, an honorific usually takes the form of a suffix attached to one's name (example: "Asuna-san"), or as a title at the end of one's name or in place of the name itself (example: "Negi-sensei," or simply "Sensei!").

Honorifics can be expressions of respect or endearment. In the context of manga and anime, honorifics give insight into the nature of the relationship between characters. Many translations into English leave out these important honorifics, and therefore distort the "feel" of the original Japanese. Because Japanese honorifics contain nuances that English honorifics lack, it is our policy at Tanoshimi not to translate them. Here, instead, is a guide to some of the honorifics you may encounter in Tanoshimi Manga.

-san: This is the most common honorific, and is equivalent to Mr., Miss, Ms., Mrs., etc. It is the all-purpose honorific and can be used in any situation where politeness is required.

-sama: This is one level higher than "-san." It is used to confer great respect.

-dono: This comes from the word "tono," which means "lord." It is an even higher level than "-sama" and confers utmost respect.

-kun: This suffix is used at the end of boys' names to express familiarity or endearment. It is also sometimes used by men among friends, or when addressing someone younger or of a lower station.

-chan: This is used to express endearment, mostly toward girls. It is also used for little boys, pets, and even among lovers. It gives a sense of childish cuteness.

Bozu: This is an informal way to refer to a boy, similar to the English term "kid".

Sempai/Senpai: This title suggests that the addressee is one's senior in a group or organization. It is most often used in a school setting, where underclassmen refer to their upperclassmen as "sempai." It can also be used in the workplace, such as when a newer employee addresses an employee who has seniority in the company.

Kohai: This is the opposite of "sempai," and is used toward underclassmen in school or newcomers in the workplace. It connotes that the addressee is of lower station.

Sensei: Literally meaning "one who has come before," this title is used for teachers, doctors, or masters of any profession or art.

-[blank]: Usually forgotten in these lists, but perhaps the most significant difference between Japanese and English. The lack of honorific means that the speaker has permission to address the person in a very intimate way. Usually, only family, spouses, or very close friends have this kind of permission. Known as *yobisute*, it can be gratifying when someone who has earned the intimacy starts to call one by one's name without an honorific. But when that intimacy hasn't been earned, it can also be very insulting.

Tsubasa crosses over with *xxxHOLiC*. Although it isn't necessary to read *xxxHOLiC* to understand the events in *Tsubasa*, you'll get to see the same events from different perspectives if you read both!

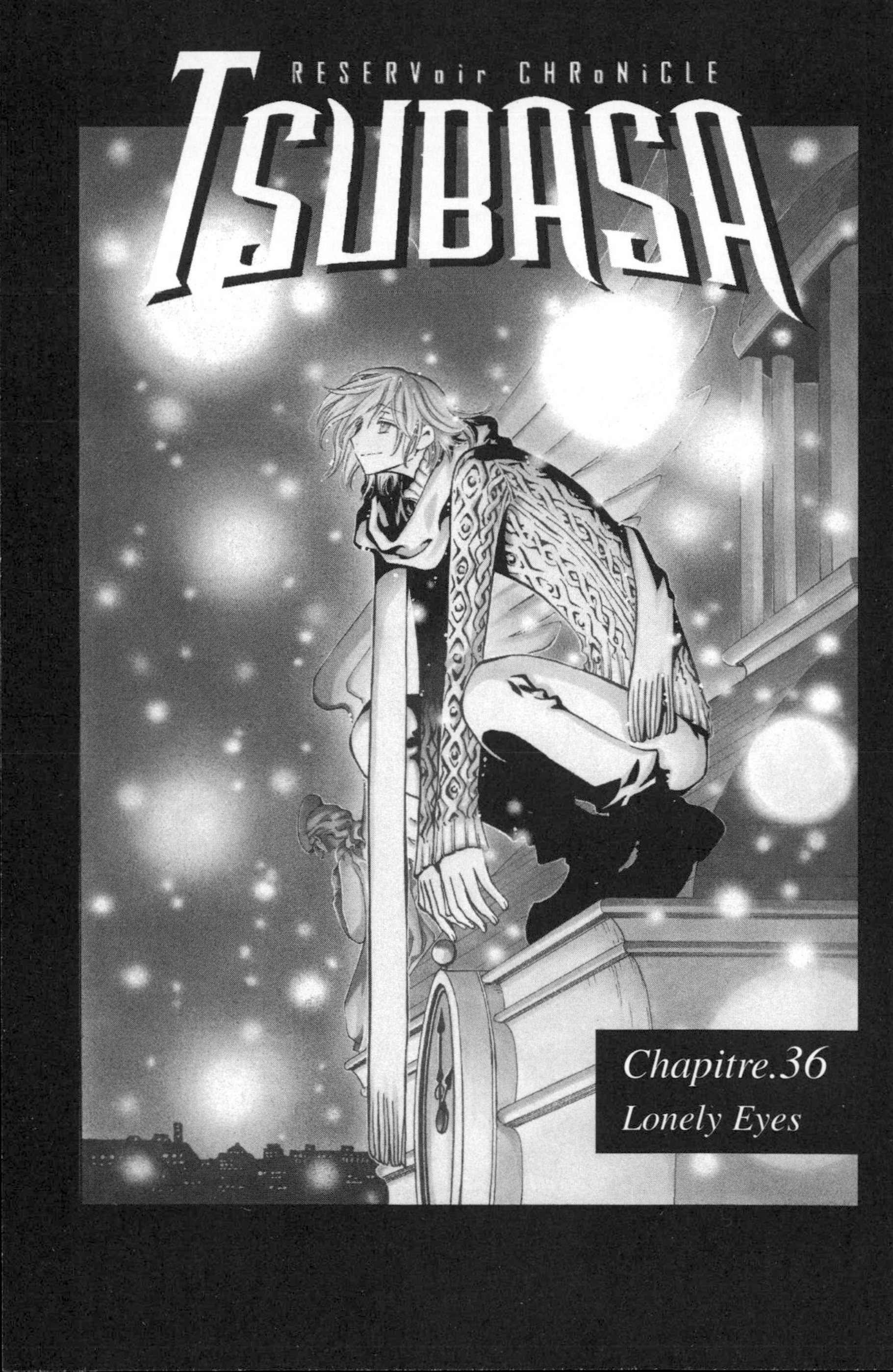
RESERVoir CHRoNiCLE
TSUBASA
Chapitre.36
Lonely Eyes

ツバサ

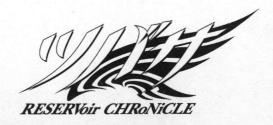

RESERVoir CHRoNiCLE

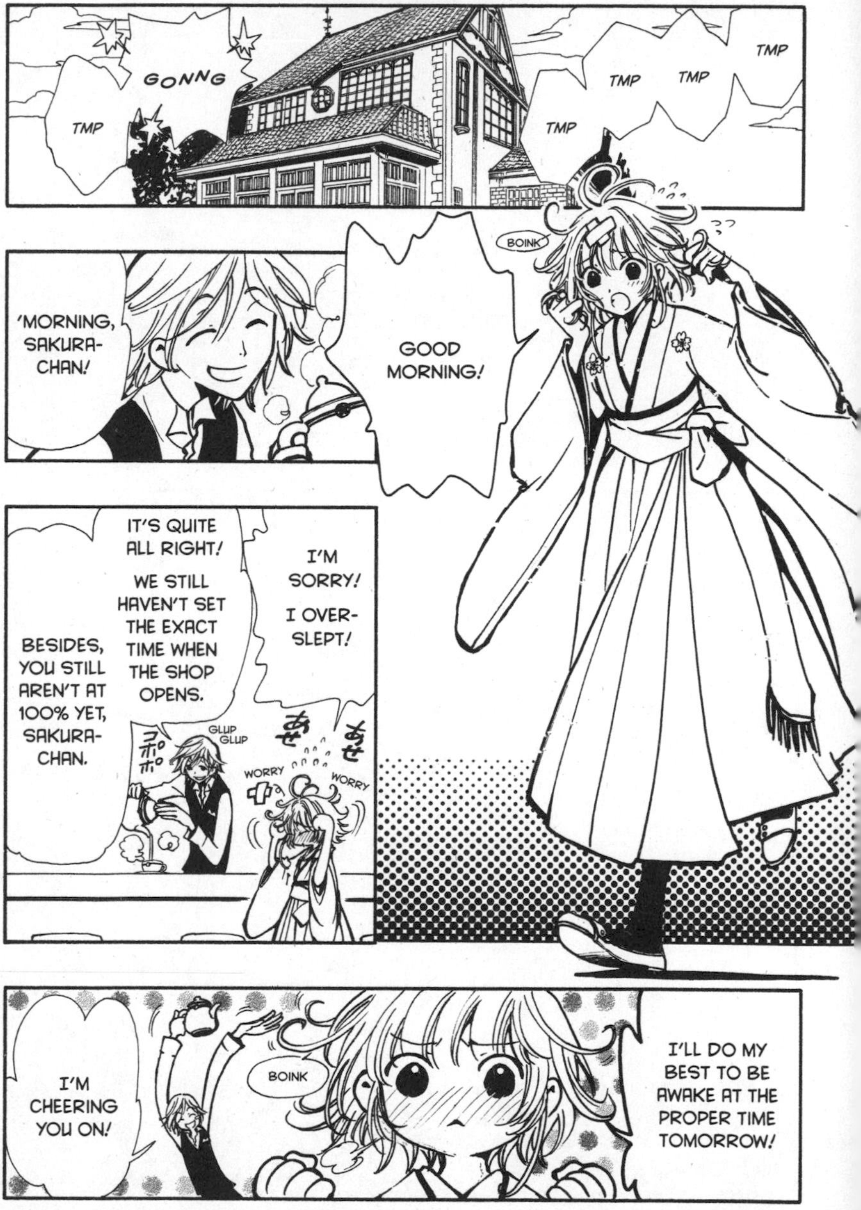
TMP
TMP
TMP
TMP
GONNG
TMP
BOINK
GOOD MORNING!
'MORNING, SAKURA-CHAN!
I'M SORRY! I OVER-SLEPT!
あせ
あせ
WORRY
WORRY
IT'S QUITE ALL RIGHT! WE STILL HAVEN'T SET THE EXACT TIME WHEN THE SHOP OPENS.
GLUP GLUP
BESIDES, YOU STILL AREN'T AT 100% YET, SAKURA-CHAN.
I'LL DO MY BEST TO BE AWAKE AT THE PROPER TIME TOMORROW!
BOINK
I'M CHEERING YOU ON!

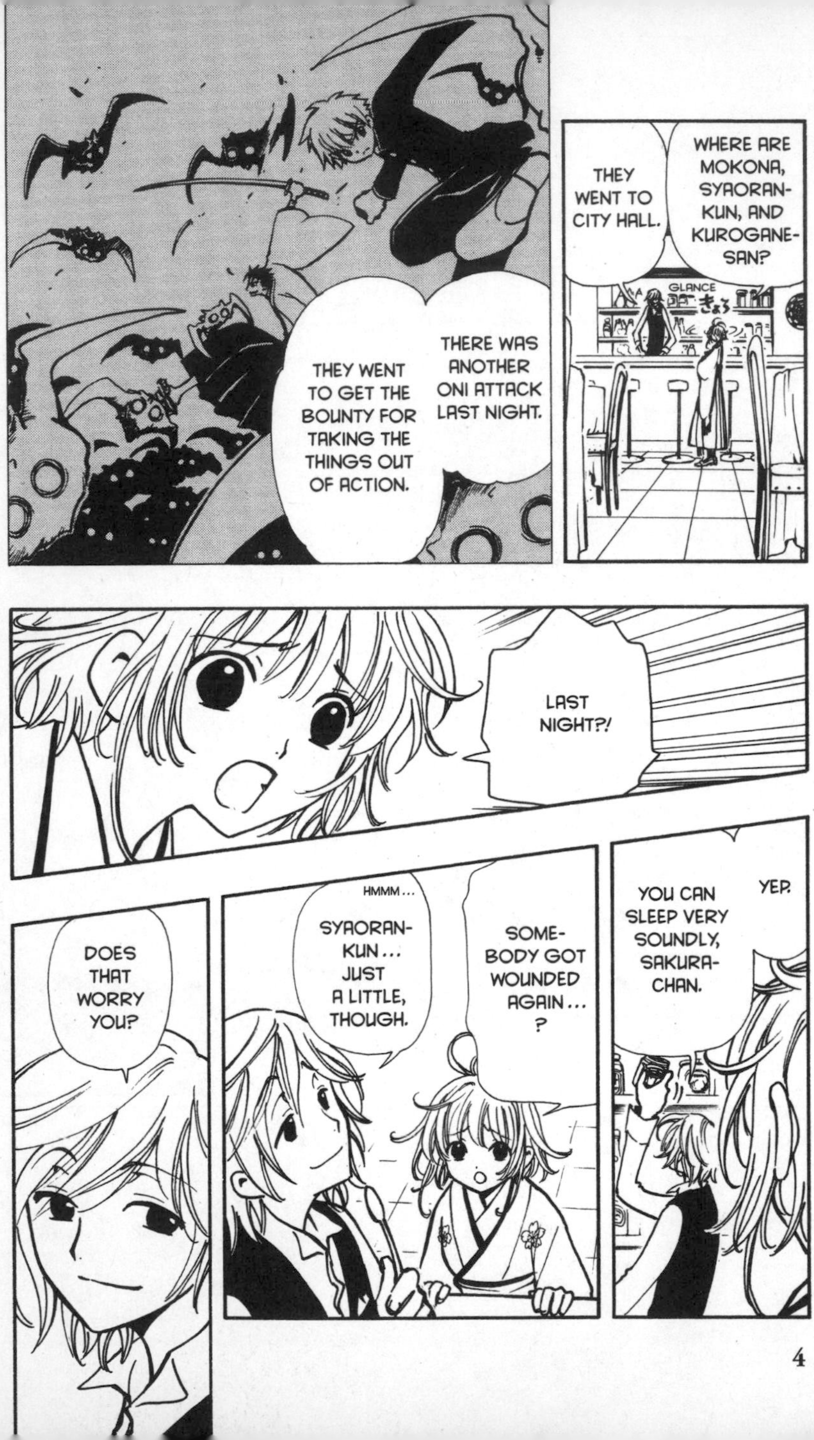
WHERE ARE MOKONA, SYAORAN-KUN, AND KUROGANE-SAN?
THEY WENT TO CITY HALL.
GLANCE
THERE WAS ANOTHER ONI ATTACK LAST NIGHT.
THEY WENT TO GET THE BOUNTY FOR TAKING THE THINGS OUT OF ACTION.
LAST NIGHT?!
YEP.
YOU CAN SLEEP VERY SOUNDLY, SAKURA-CHAN.
SOMEBODY GOT WOUNDED AGAIN...?
HMMM...
SYAORAN-KUN... JUST A LITTLE, THOUGH.
DOES THAT WORRY YOU?

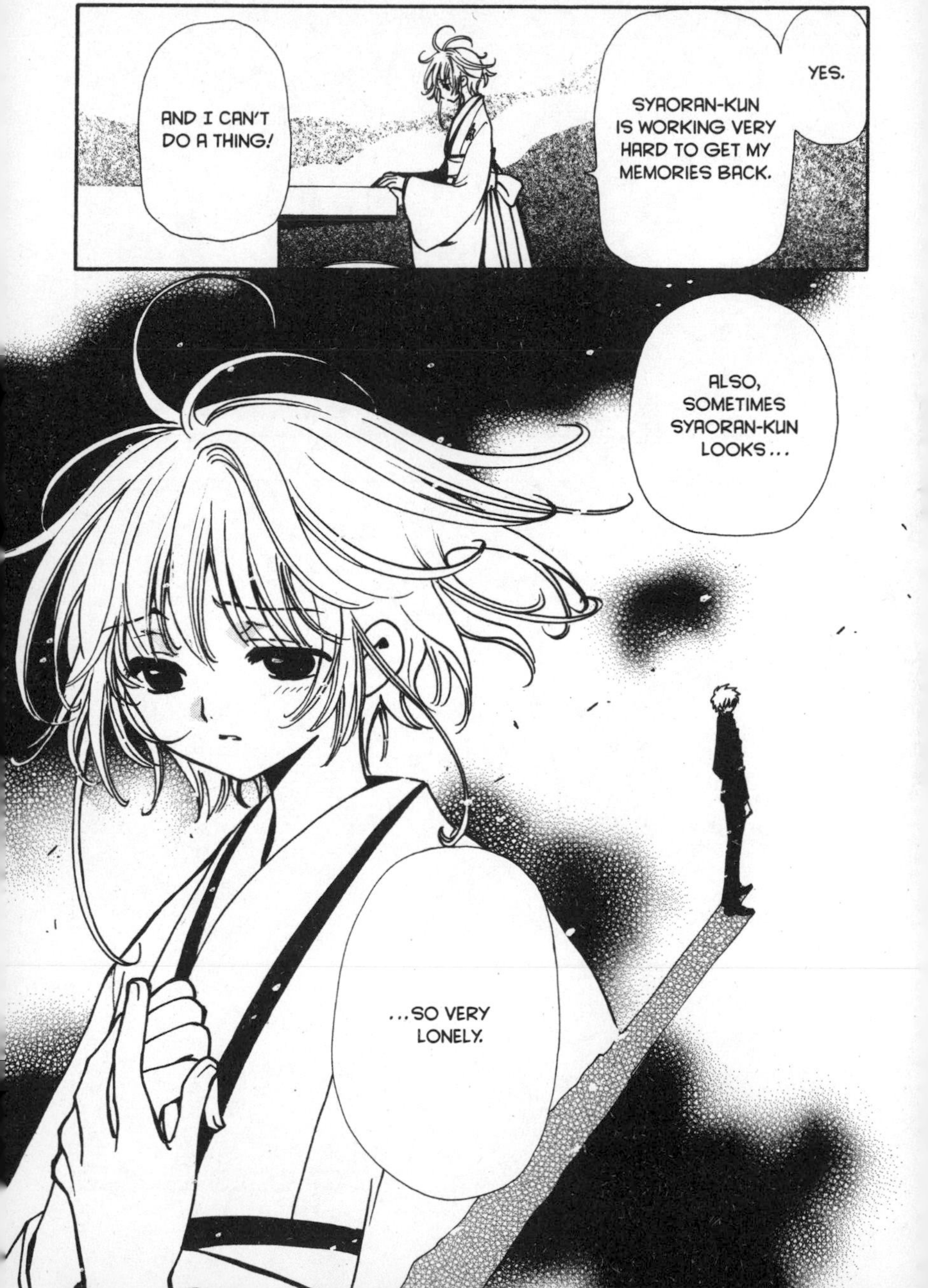
YES.
SYAORAN-KUN IS WORKING VERY HARD TO GET MY MEMORIES BACK.
AND I CAN'T DO A THING!
ALSO, SOMETIMES SYAORAN-KUN LOOKS...
...SO VERY LONELY.

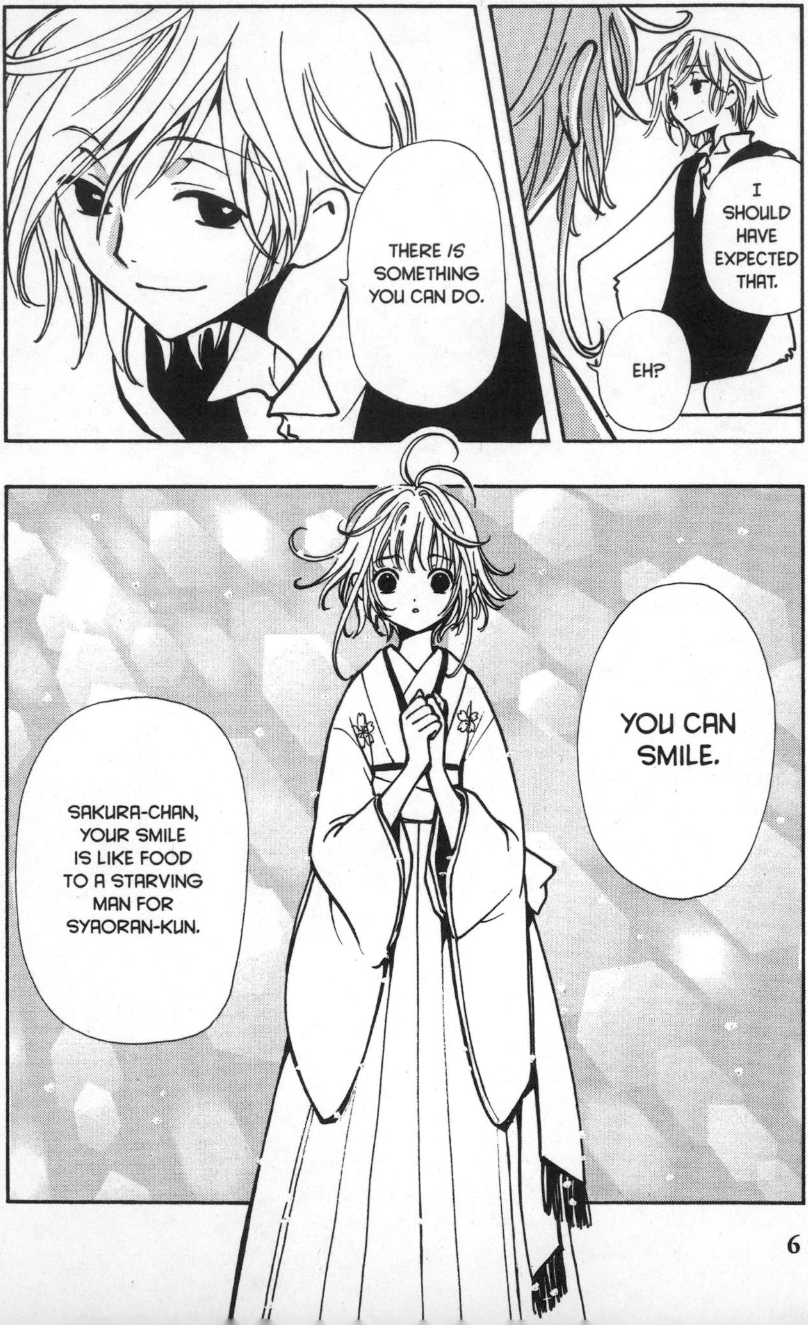
I SHOULD HAVE EXPECTED THAT.
EH?
THERE IS SOMETHING YOU CAN DO.
YOU CAN SMILE.
SAKURA-CHAN, YOUR SMILE IS LIKE FOOD TO A STARVING MAN FOR SYAORAN-KUN.

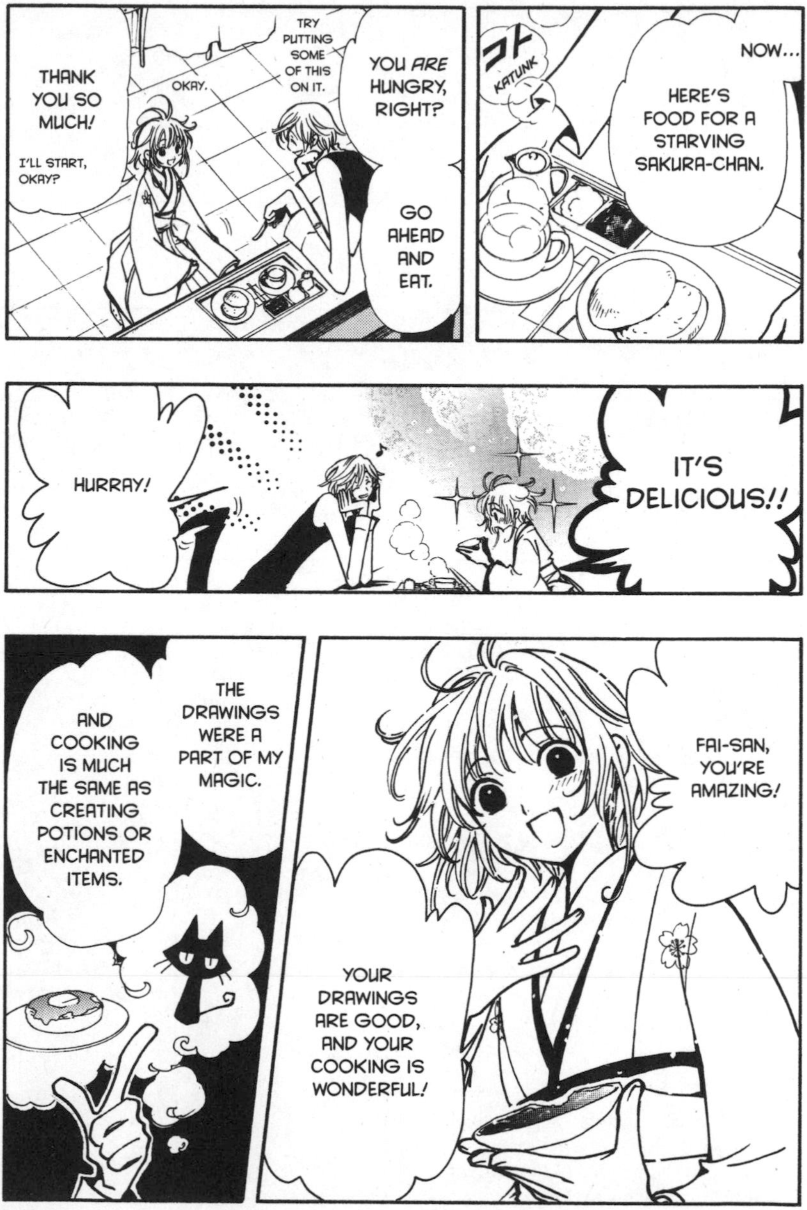
NOW...
HERE'S FOOD FOR A STARVING SAKURA-CHAN.
KATUNK
YOU *ARE* HUNGRY, RIGHT?
GO AHEAD AND EAT.
TRY PUTTING SOME OF THIS ON IT.
OKAY.
THANK YOU SO MUCH!
I'LL START, OKAY?
IT'S DELICIOUS!!
HURRAY!
FAI-SAN, YOU'RE AMAZING!
YOUR DRAWINGS ARE GOOD, AND YOUR COOKING IS WONDERFUL!
THE DRAWINGS WERE A PART OF MY MAGIC.
AND COOKING IS MUCH THE SAME AS CREATING POTIONS OR ENCHANTED ITEMS.

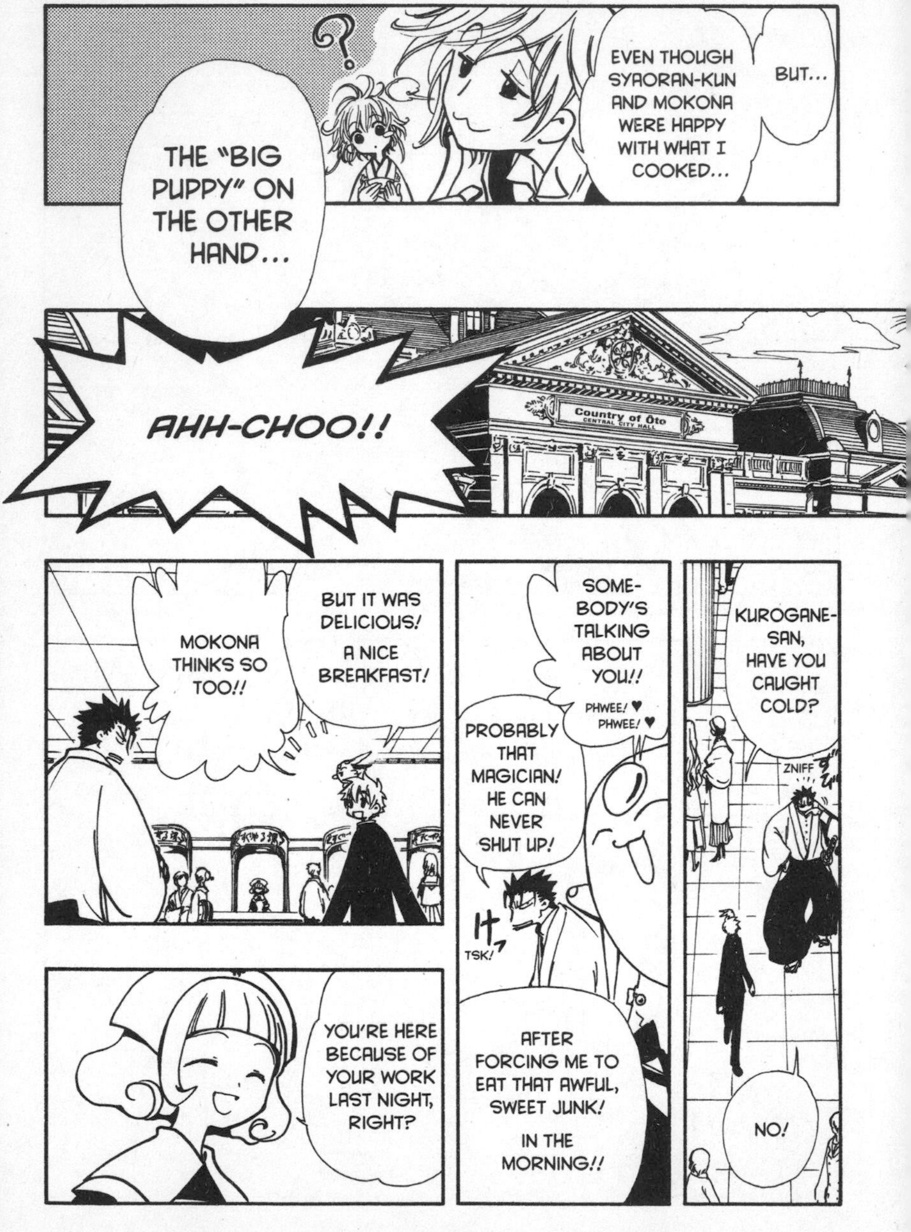
BUT...
EVEN THOUGH SYAORAN-KUN AND MOKONA WERE HAPPY WITH WHAT I COOKED...
THE "BIG PUPPY" ON THE OTHER HAND...
Country of Ōto CENTRAL CITY HALL
AHH-CHOO!!
KUROGANE-SAN, HAVE YOU CAUGHT COLD?
ZNIFF
NO!
SOME-BODY'S TALKING ABOUT YOU!!
PHWEE! ♥ PHWEE! ♥
PROBABLY THAT MAGICIAN! HE CAN NEVER SHUT UP!
TSK!
AFTER FORCING ME TO EAT THAT AWFUL, SWEET JUNK!
IN THE MORNING!!
BUT IT WAS DELICIOUS! A NICE BREAKFAST!
MOKONA THINKS SO TOO!!
YOU'RE HERE BECAUSE OF YOUR WORK LAST NIGHT, RIGHT?

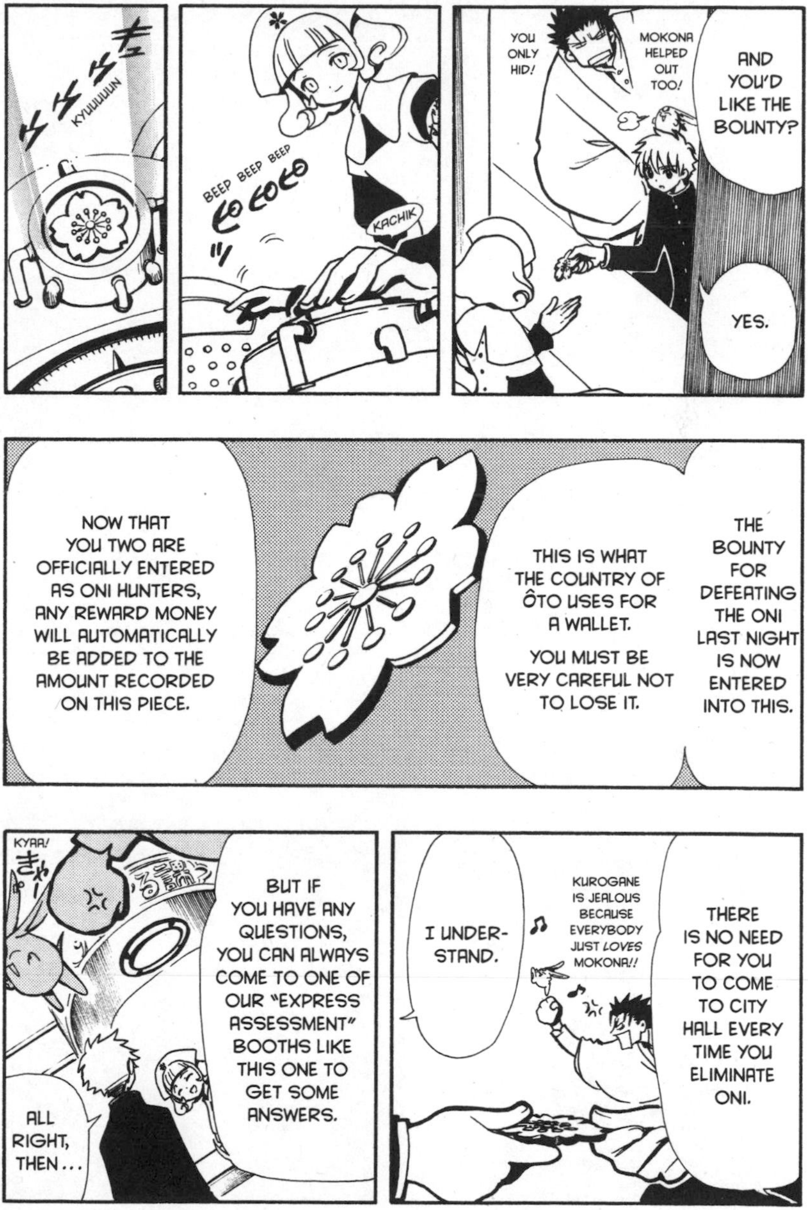
AND YOU'D LIKE THE BOUNTY?
MOKONA HELPED OUT TOO!
YOU ONLY HID!
YES.
BEEP BEEP BEEP
KACHIK
KYUUUUUN
THE BOUNTY FOR DEFEATING THE ONI LAST NIGHT IS NOW ENTERED INTO THIS.
THIS IS WHAT THE COUNTRY OF ÔTO USES FOR A WALLET.
YOU MUST BE VERY CAREFUL NOT TO LOSE IT.
NOW THAT YOU TWO ARE OFFICIALLY ENTERED AS ONI HUNTERS, ANY REWARD MONEY WILL AUTOMATICALLY BE ADDED TO THE AMOUNT RECORDED ON THIS PIECE.
THERE IS NO NEED FOR YOU TO COME TO CITY HALL EVERY TIME YOU ELIMINATE ONI.
KUROGANE IS JEALOUS BECAUSE EVERYBODY JUST *LOVES* MOKONA!!
I UNDER-STAND.
BUT IF YOU HAVE ANY QUESTIONS, YOU CAN ALWAYS COME TO ONE OF OUR "EXPRESS ASSESSMENT" BOOTHS LIKE THIS ONE TO GET SOME ANSWERS.
KYAA!
ALL RIGHT, THEN...

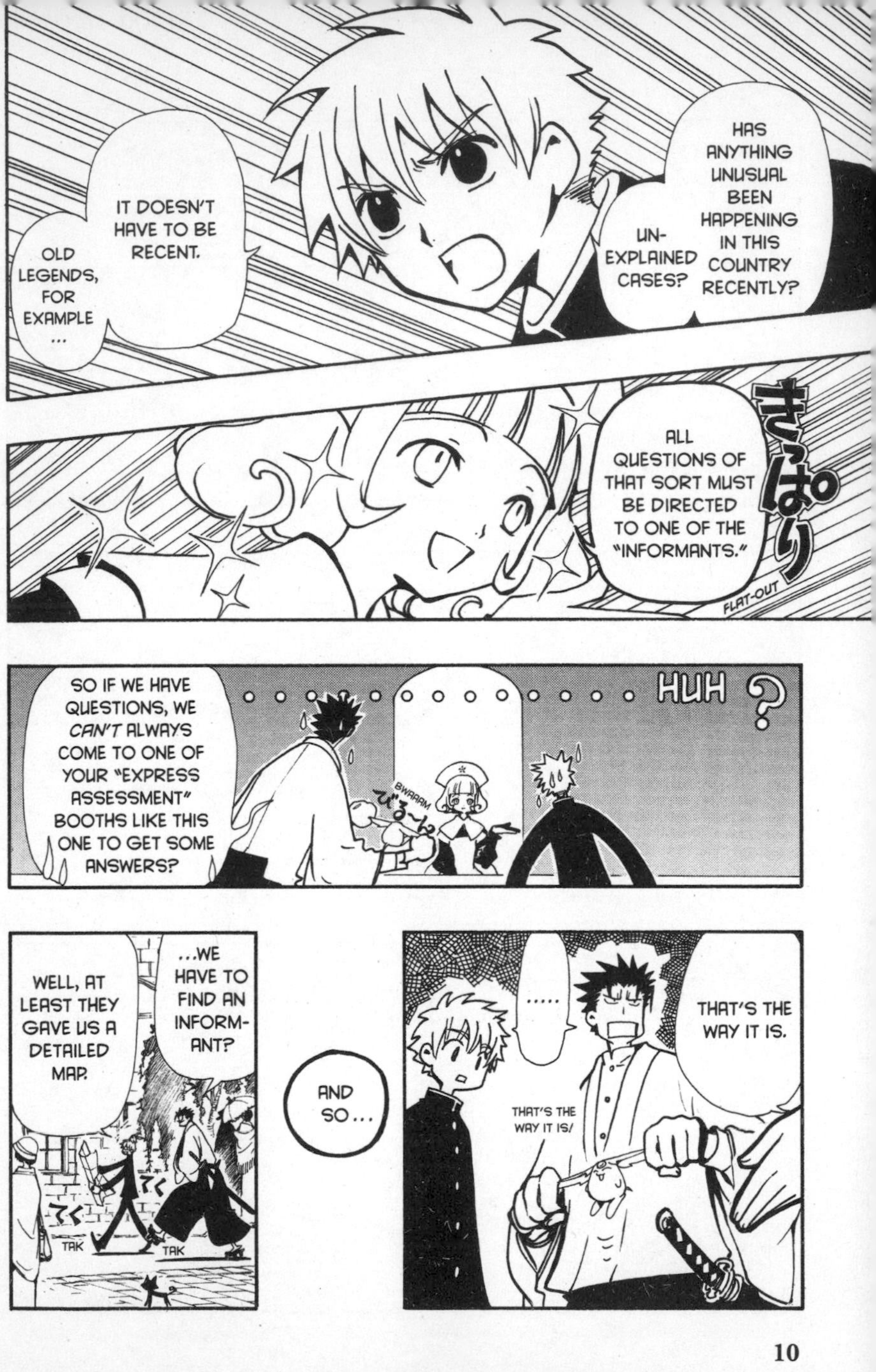
HAS ANYTHING UNUSUAL BEEN HAPPENING IN THIS COUNTRY RECENTLY?
UN-EXPLAINED CASES?
IT DOESN'T HAVE TO BE RECENT.
OLD LEGENDS, FOR EXAMPLE ...
きっぱり
FLAT-OUT
ALL QUESTIONS OF THAT SORT MUST BE DIRECTED TO ONE OF THE "INFORMANTS."
HUH ?
BWAAAM
びる〜ん
SO IF WE HAVE QUESTIONS, WE *CAN'T* ALWAYS COME TO ONE OF YOUR "EXPRESS ASSESSMENT" BOOTHS LIKE THIS ONE TO GET SOME ANSWERS?
THAT'S THE WAY IT IS.
THAT'S THE WAY IT IS!
.....
AND SO...
...WE HAVE TO FIND AN INFORM-ANT?
WELL, AT LEAST THEY GAVE US A DETAILED MAP.
てく
てく
TAK
TAK

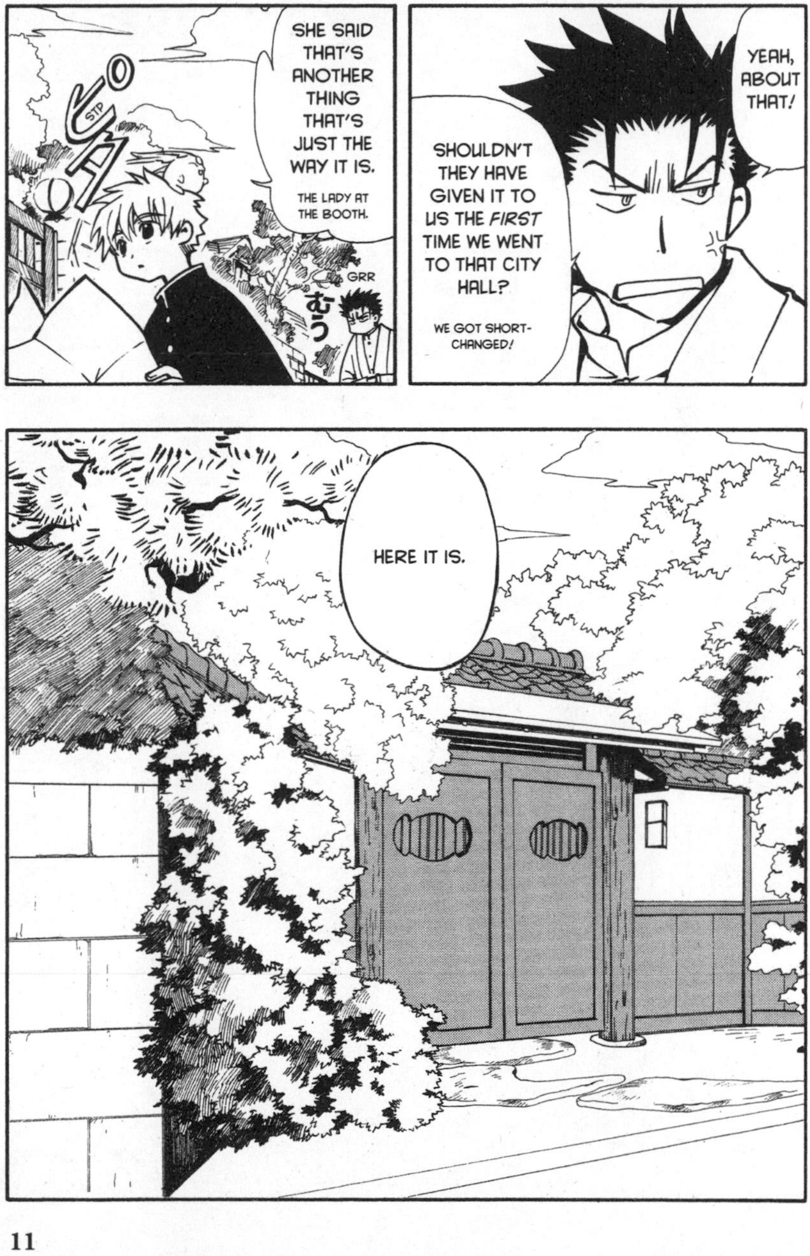
YEAH, ABOUT THAT!
SHOULDN'T THEY HAVE GIVEN IT TO US THE *FIRST* TIME WE WENT TO THAT CITY HALL?
WE GOT SHORT-CHANGED!
SHE SAID THAT'S ANOTHER THING THAT'S JUST THE WAY IT IS.
THE LADY AT THE BOOTH.
STP
GRR
HERE IT IS.

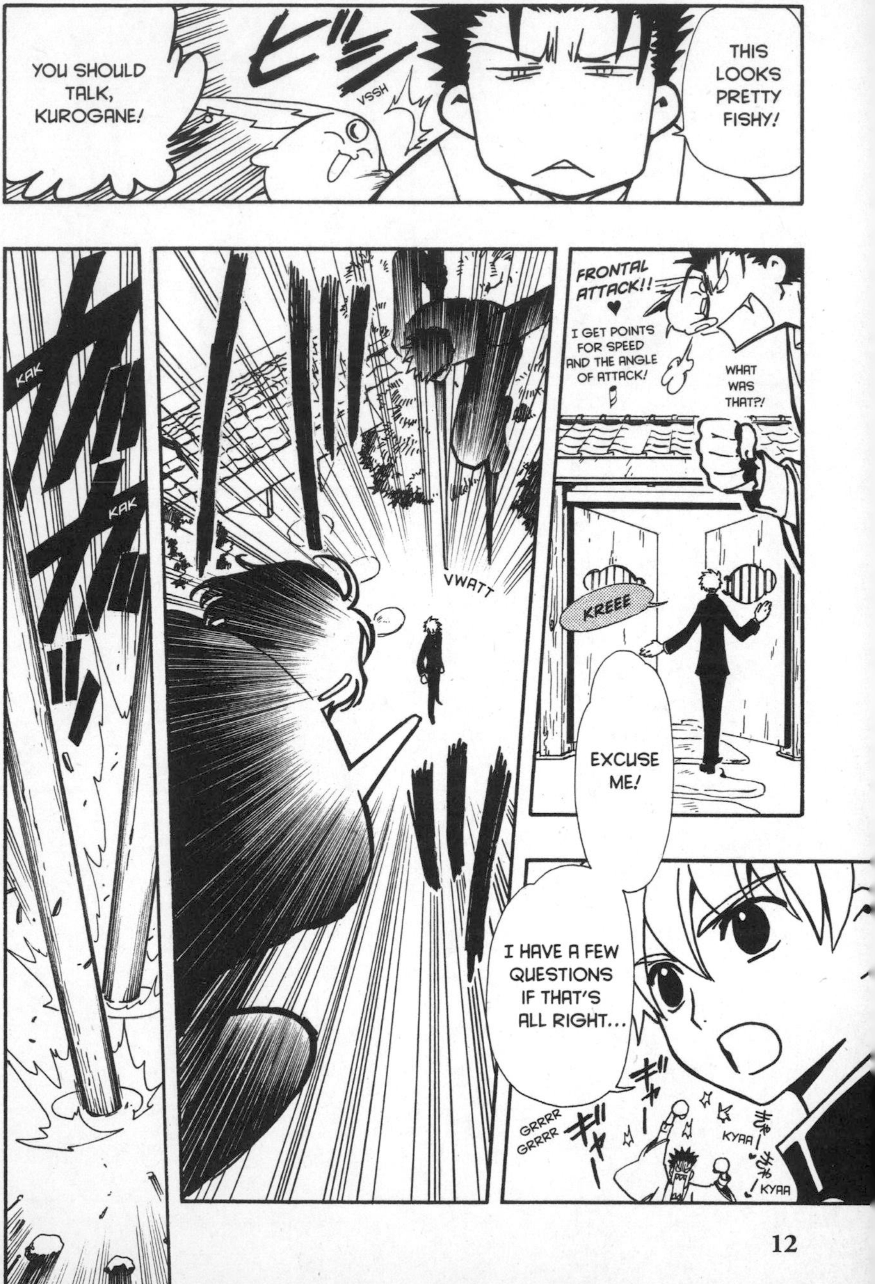
THIS LOOKS PRETTY FISHY!
VSSH
YOU SHOULD TALK, KUROGANE!
FRONTAL ATTACK!! ♥
I GET POINTS FOR SPEED AND THE ANGLE OF ATTACK!
WHAT WAS THAT?!
KREEE
EXCUSE ME!
I HAVE A FEW QUESTIONS IF THAT'S ALL RIGHT...
GRRRR GRRRR
KYAA
KYAA
VWATT
KAK
KAK

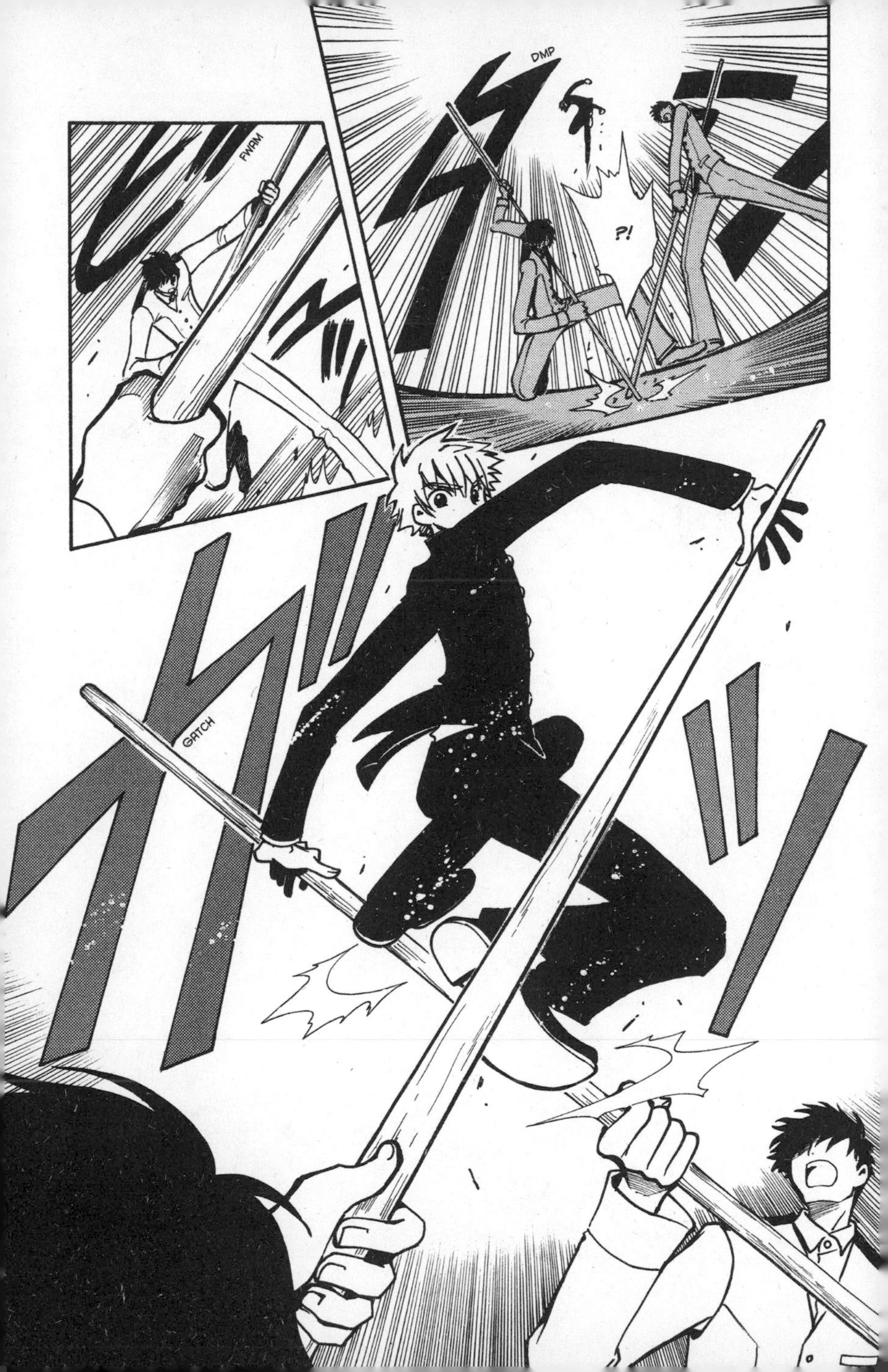
DMP
?!
FWAM
GATCH

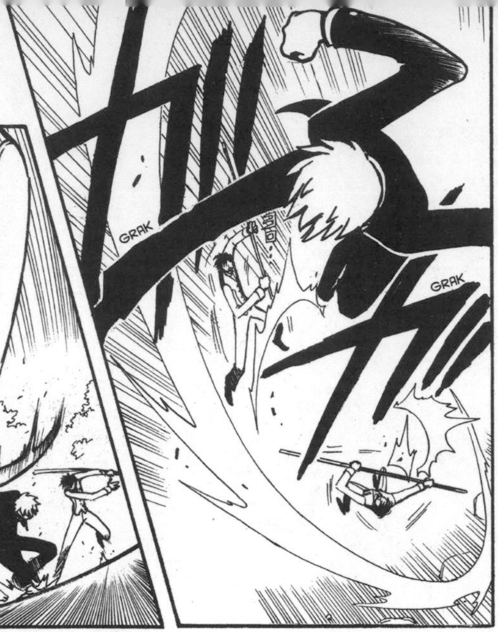
GRAK
GRAK

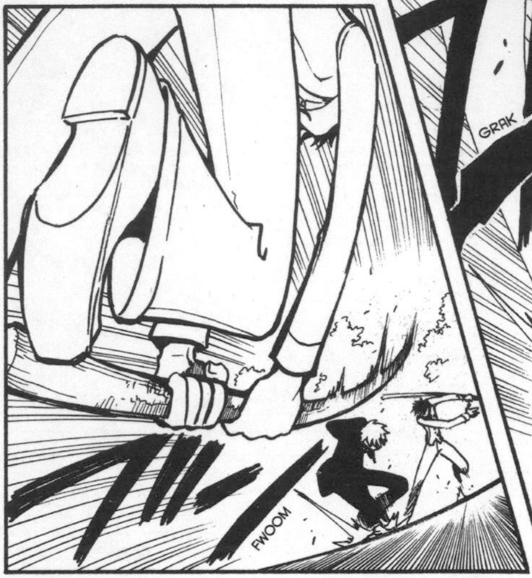
FWOOM

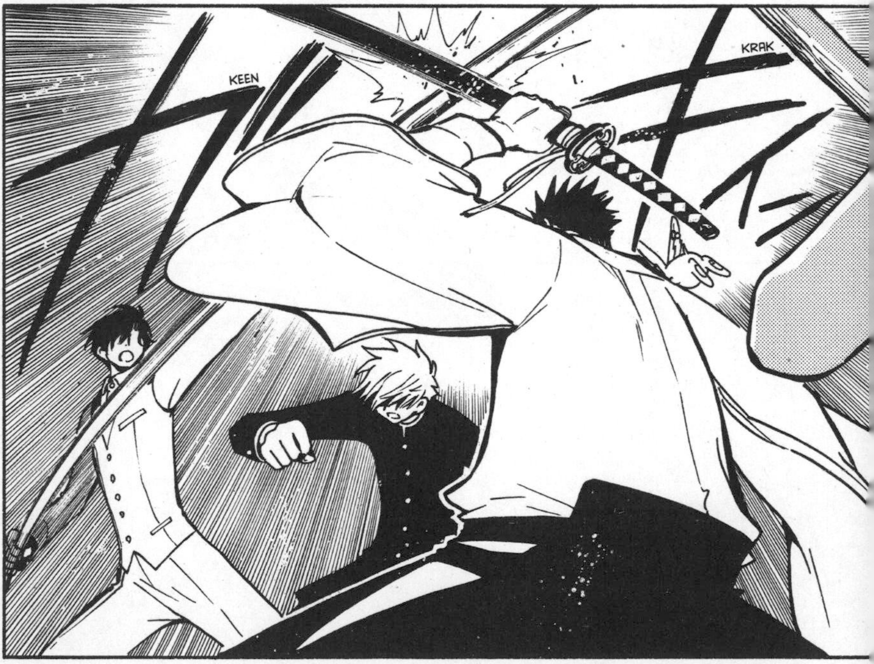
KRAK
KEEN

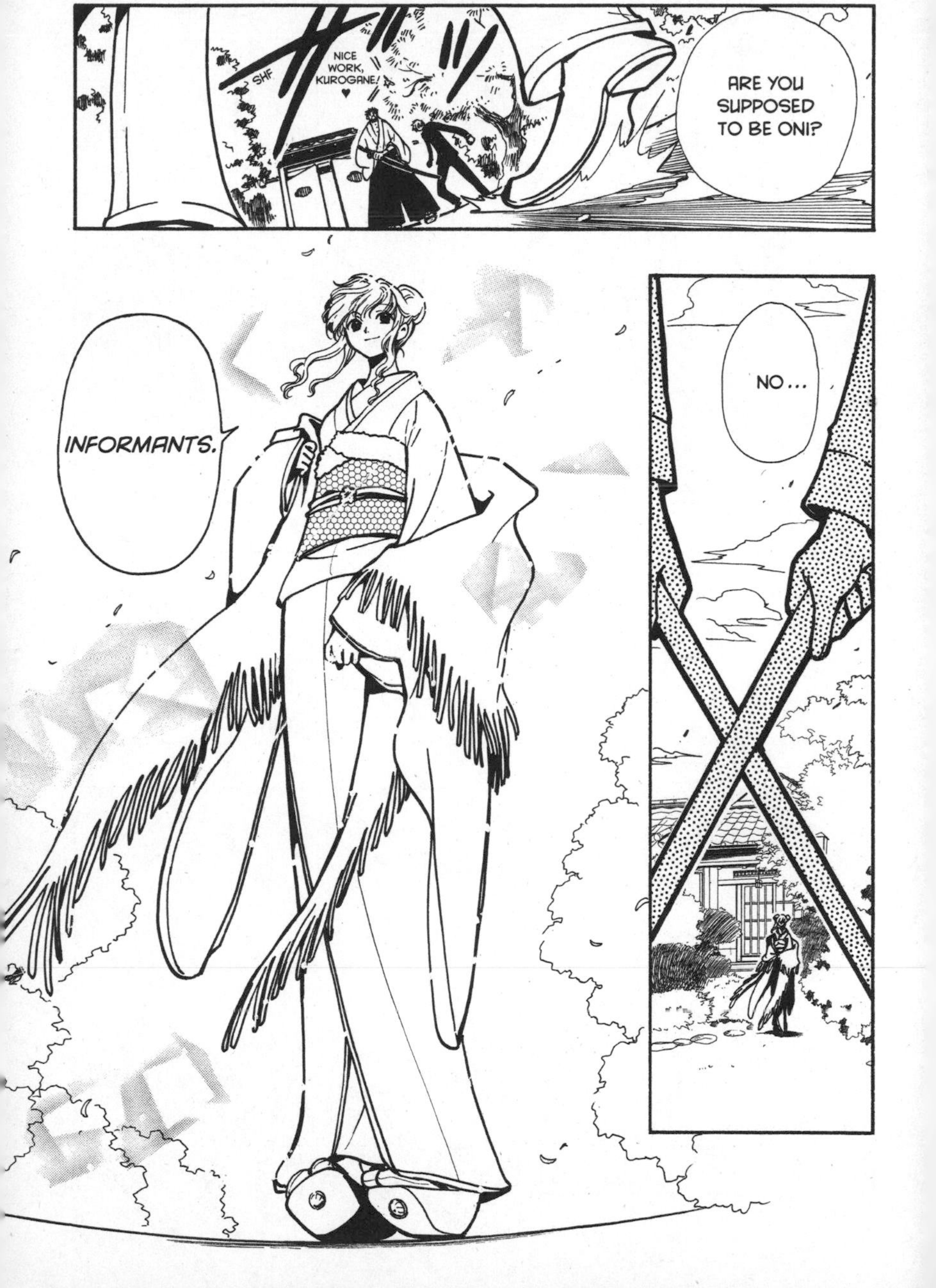
ARE YOU SUPPOSED TO BE ONI?
NICE WORK, KUROGANE! ♥
SHF
NO ...
INFORMANTS.

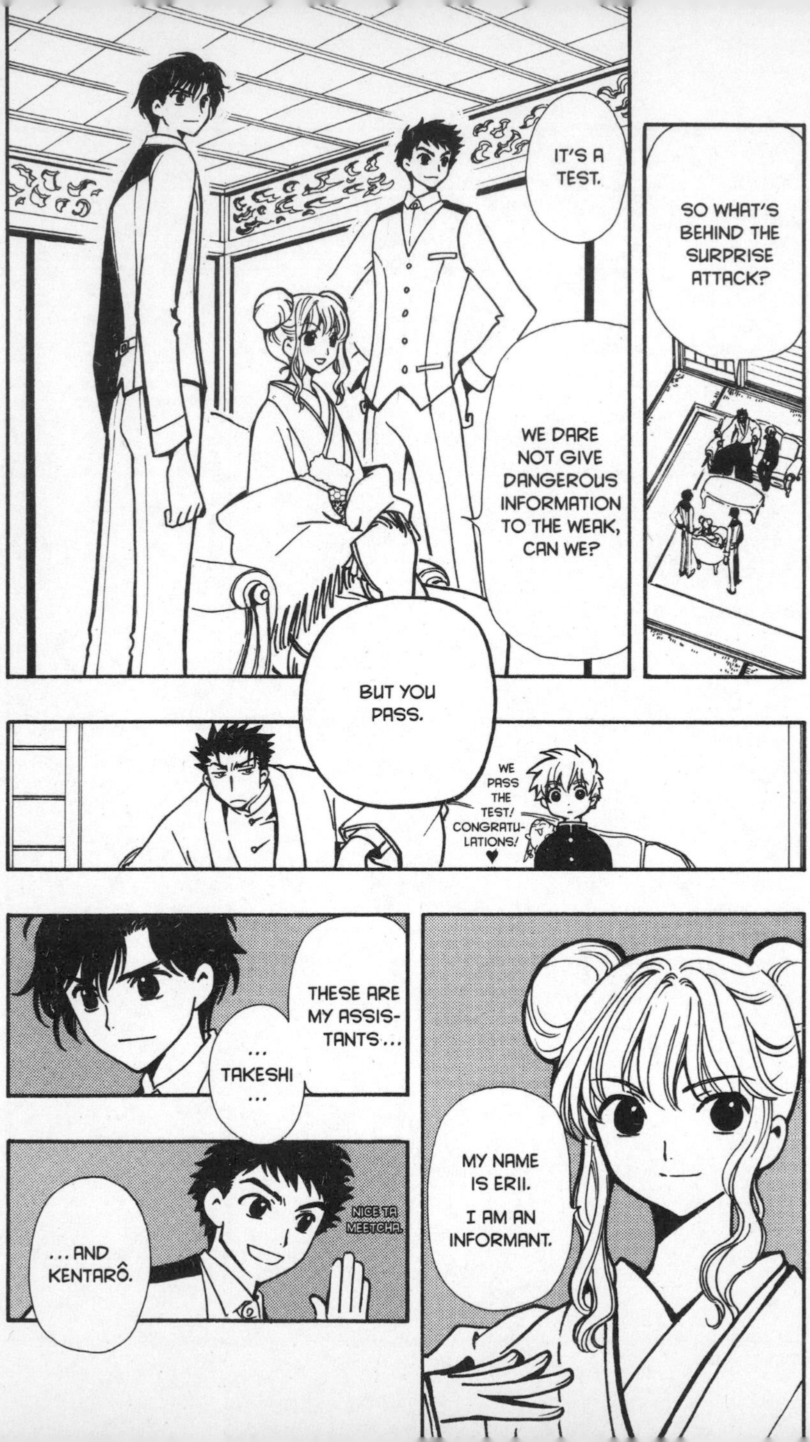
SO WHAT'S BEHIND THE SURPRISE ATTACK?
IT'S A TEST.
WE DARE NOT GIVE DANGEROUS INFORMATION TO THE WEAK, CAN WE?
BUT YOU PASS.
WE PASS THE TEST! CONGRATULATIONS! ♥
MY NAME IS ERII.
I AM AN INFORMANT.
THESE ARE MY ASSISTANTS...
...TAKESHI...
...AND KENTARÔ.
NICE TA MEETCHA.

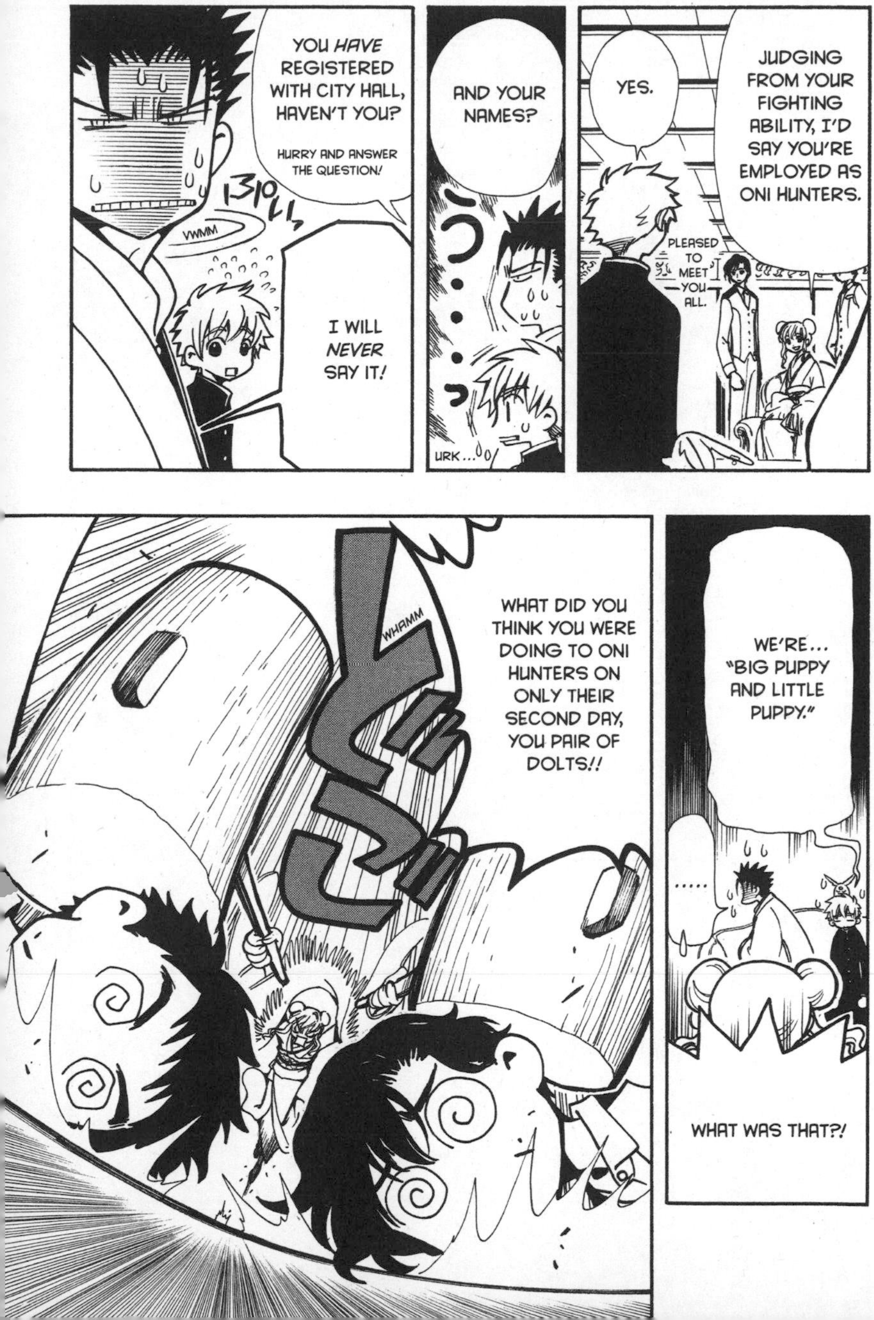
JUDGING FROM YOUR FIGHTING ABILITY, I'D SAY YOU'RE EMPLOYED AS ONI HUNTERS.
YES.
PLEASED TO MEET YOU ALL.
AND YOUR NAMES?
URK...
YOU *HAVE* REGISTERED WITH CITY HALL, HAVEN'T YOU?
HURRY AND ANSWER THE QUESTION!
VWMM
I WILL *NEVER* SAY IT!
WE'RE... "BIG PUPPY AND LITTLE PUPPY."
.....
WHAT WAS THAT?!
WHAT DID YOU THINK YOU WERE DOING TO ONI HUNTERS ON ONLY THEIR SECOND DAY, YOU PAIR OF DOLTS!!
WHAMM

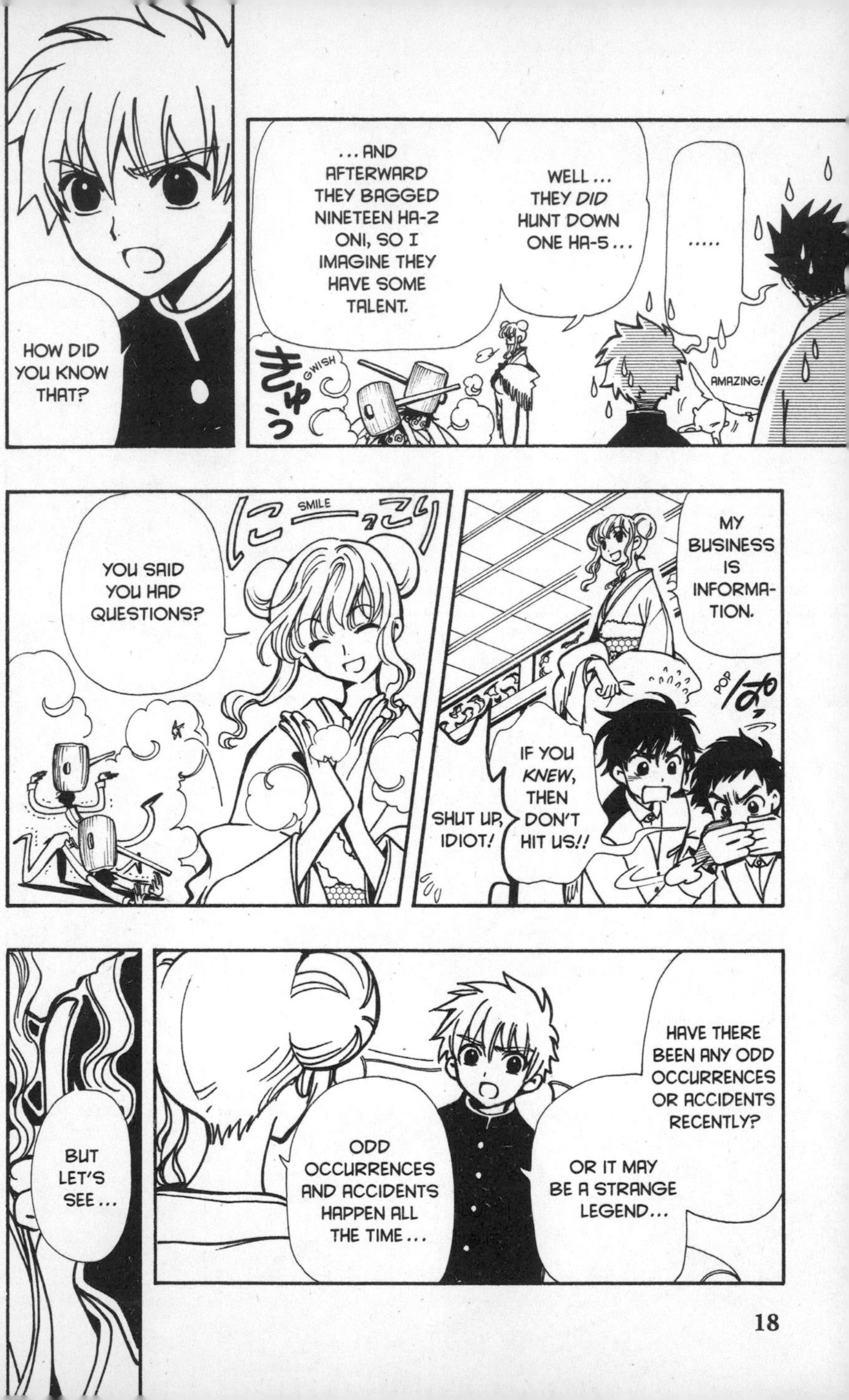
.....
WELL... THEY *DID* HUNT DOWN ONE HA-5...
...AND AFTERWARD THEY BAGGED NINETEEN HA-2 ONI, SO I IMAGINE THEY HAVE SOME TALENT.
AMAZING!
きゅう GWISH
HOW DID YOU KNOW THAT?
MY BUSINESS IS INFORMATION.
ぽっ POP
IF YOU *KNEW*, THEN DON'T HIT US!!
SHUT UP, IDIOT!
にーっこり SMILE
YOU SAID YOU HAD QUESTIONS?
HAVE THERE BEEN ANY ODD OCCURRENCES OR ACCIDENTS RECENTLY?
OR IT MAY BE A STRANGE LEGEND...
ODD OCCURRENCES AND ACCIDENTS HAPPEN ALL THE TIME...
BUT LET'S SEE...

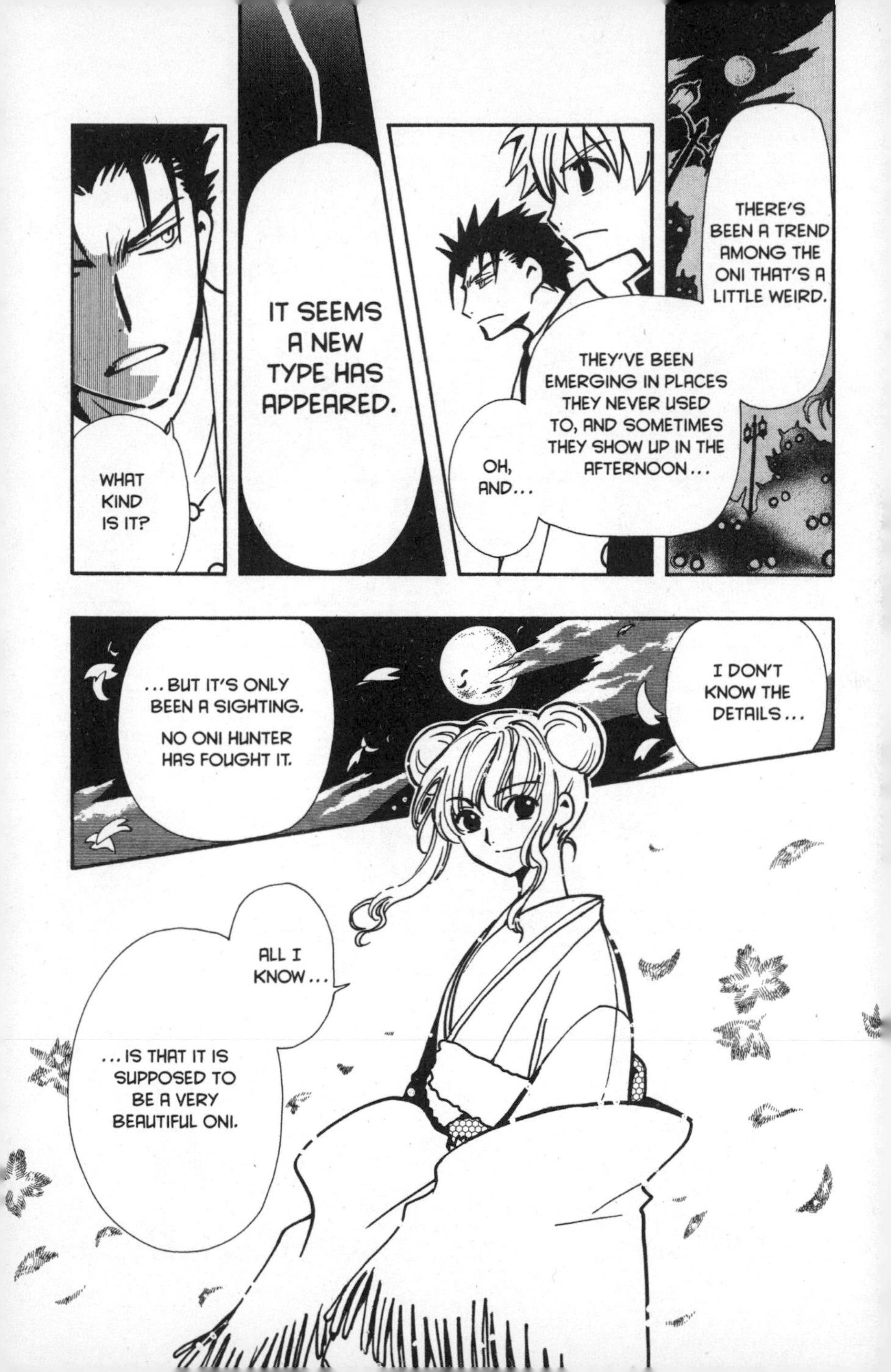
THERE'S BEEN A TREND AMONG THE ONI THAT'S A LITTLE WEIRD.
THEY'VE BEEN EMERGING IN PLACES THEY NEVER USED TO, AND SOMETIMES THEY SHOW UP IN THE AFTERNOON...
OH, AND...
IT SEEMS A NEW TYPE HAS APPEARED.
WHAT KIND IS IT?
I DON'T KNOW THE DETAILS...
...BUT IT'S ONLY BEEN A SIGHTING.
NO ONI HUNTER HAS FOUGHT IT.
ALL I KNOW...
...IS THAT IT IS SUPPOSED TO BE A VERY BEAUTIFUL ONI.

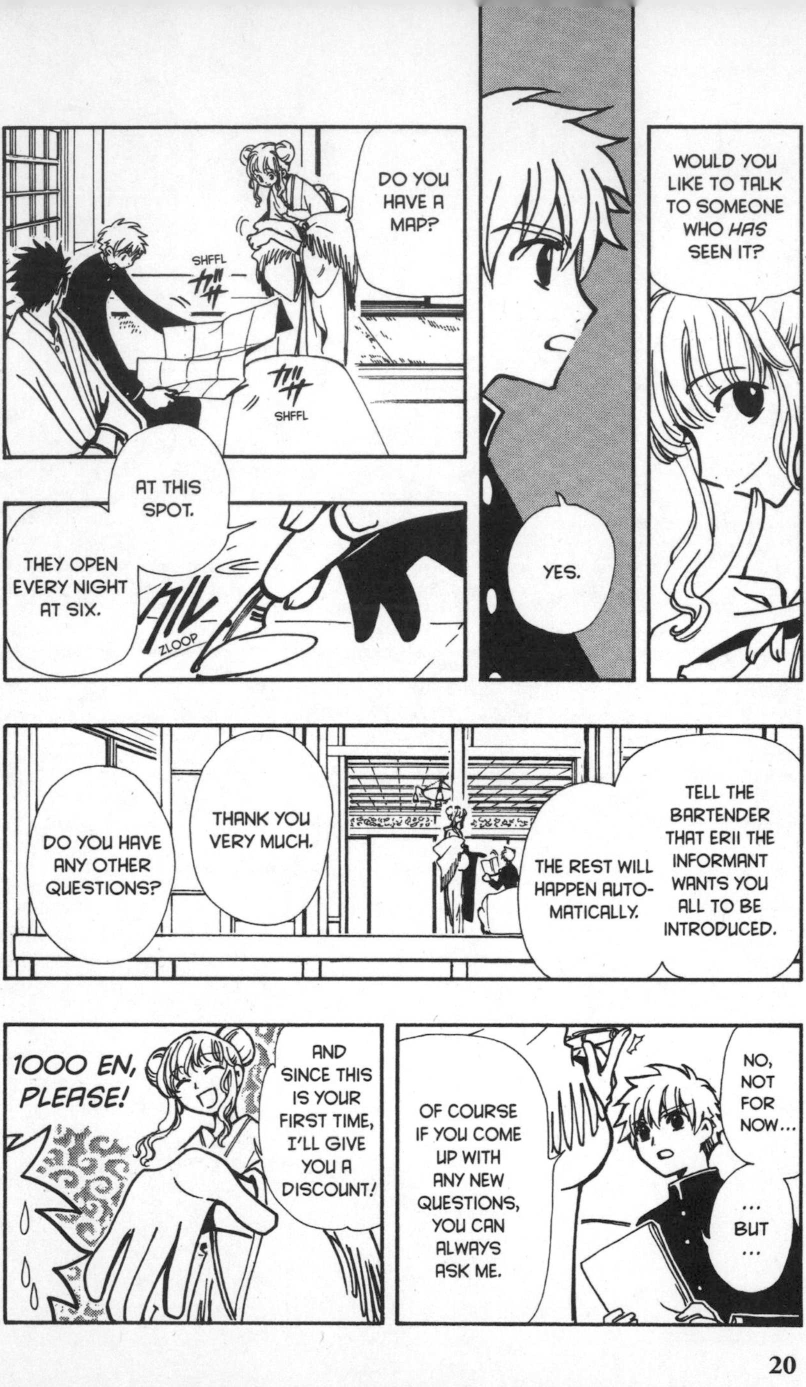
WOULD YOU LIKE TO TALK TO SOMEONE WHO *HAS* SEEN IT?
YES.
DO YOU HAVE A MAP?
SHFFL
SHFFL
AT THIS SPOT.
THEY OPEN EVERY NIGHT AT SIX.
ZLOOP
TELL THE BARTENDER THAT ERII THE INFORMANT WANTS YOU ALL TO BE INTRODUCED.
THE REST WILL HAPPEN AUTO-MATICALLY.
THANK YOU VERY MUCH.
DO YOU HAVE ANY OTHER QUESTIONS?
NO, NOT FOR NOW...
...BUT...
OF COURSE IF YOU COME UP WITH ANY NEW QUESTIONS, YOU CAN ALWAYS ASK ME.
AND SINCE THIS IS YOUR FIRST TIME, I'LL GIVE YOU A DISCOUNT!
1000 EN, PLEASE!

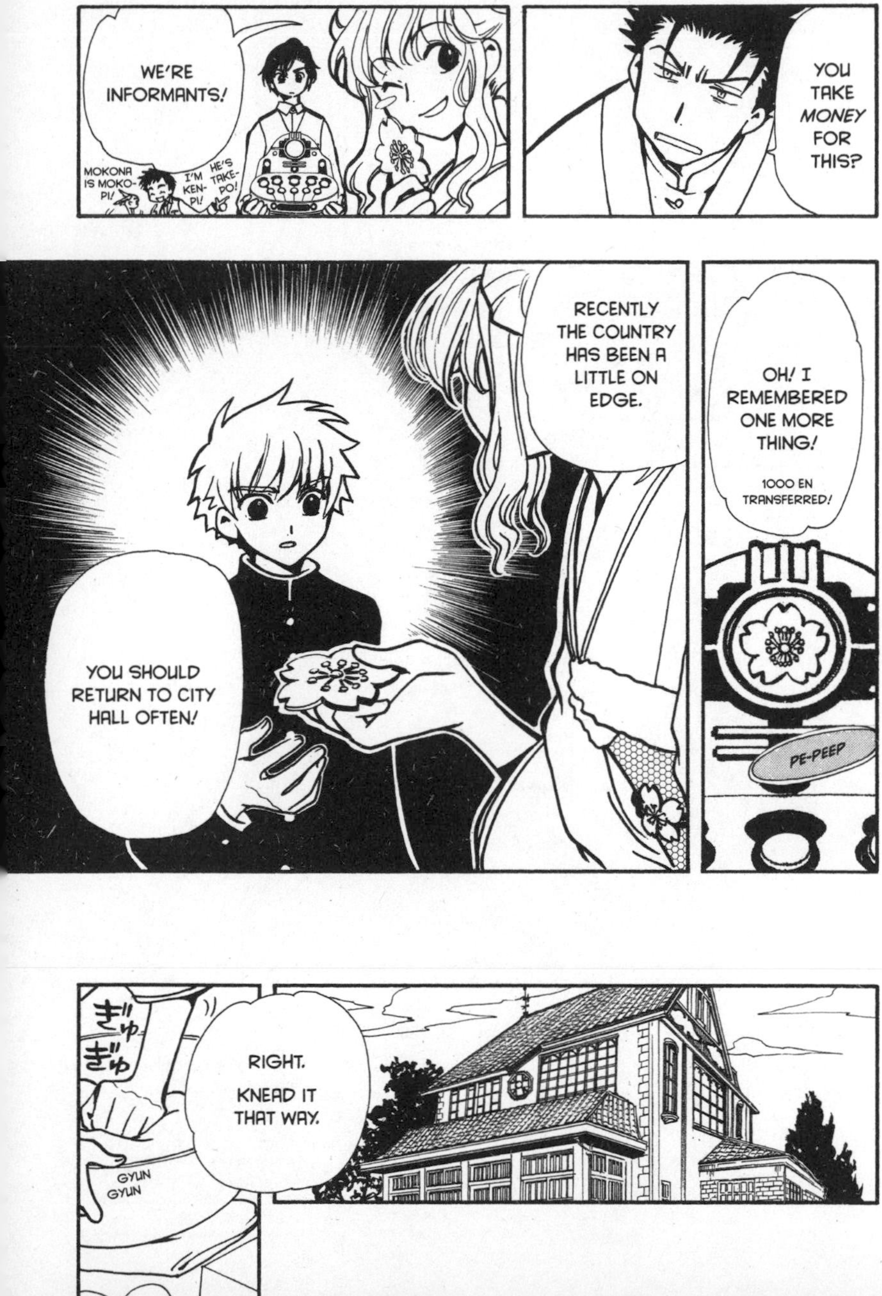

YOU TAKE MONEY FOR THIS?
WE'RE INFORMANTS!
HE'S TAKE-PO!
I'M KEN-PI!
MOKONA IS MOKO-PI!
OH! I REMEMBERED ONE MORE THING!
1000 EN TRANSFERRED!
PE-PEEP
RECENTLY THE COUNTRY HAS BEEN A LITTLE ON EDGE.
YOU SHOULD RETURN TO CITY HALL OFTEN!
RIGHT.
KNEAD IT THAT WAY.
ぎゅぎゅ
GYUN GYUN

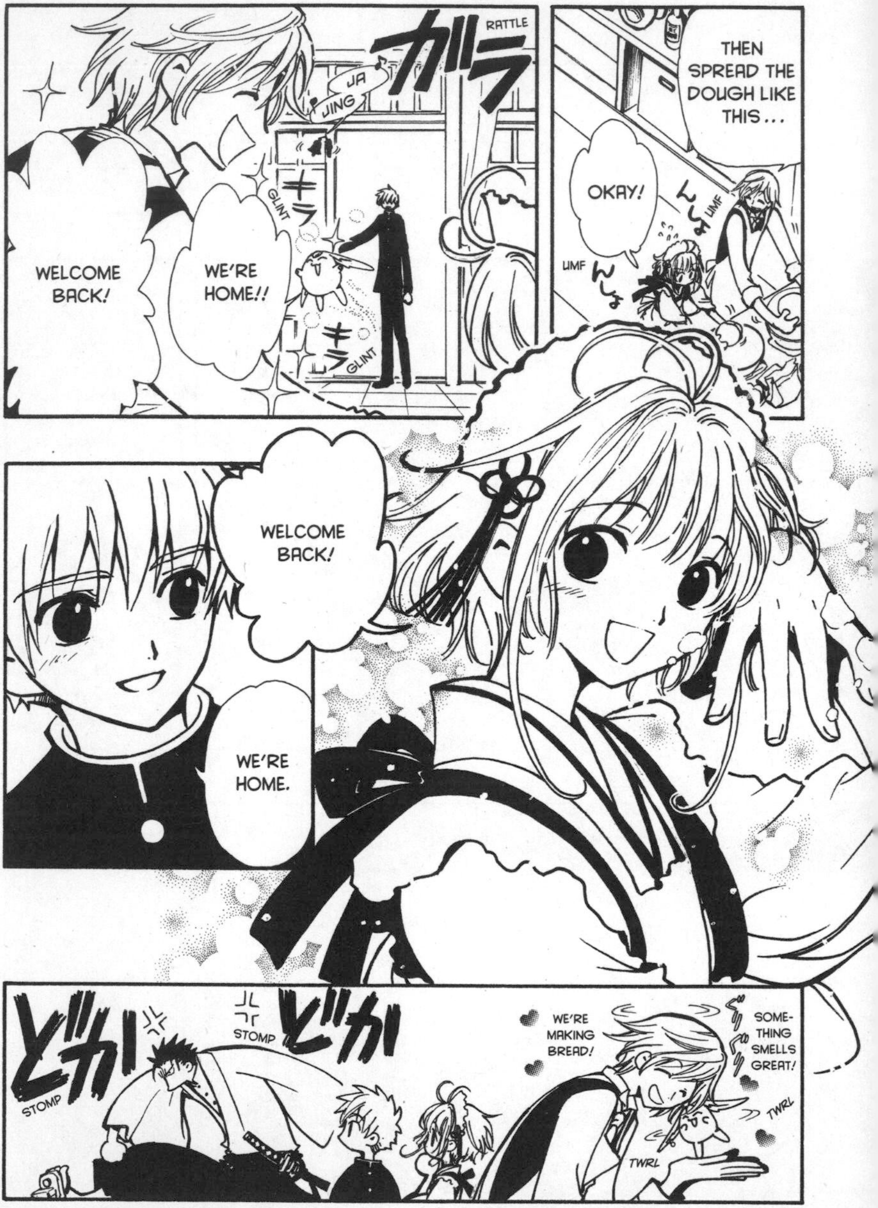
THEN SPREAD THE DOUGH LIKE THIS...
OKAY!
んしょ
UMF
んしょ
UMF
ガラ
RATTLE
JA JING
キラ
GLINT
WE'RE HOME!!
WELCOME BACK!
キラ
GLINT
WELCOME BACK!
WE'RE HOME.
SOME-THING SMELLS GREAT!
TWRL
WE'RE MAKING BREAD!
TWRL
どかどか
STOMP
STOMP

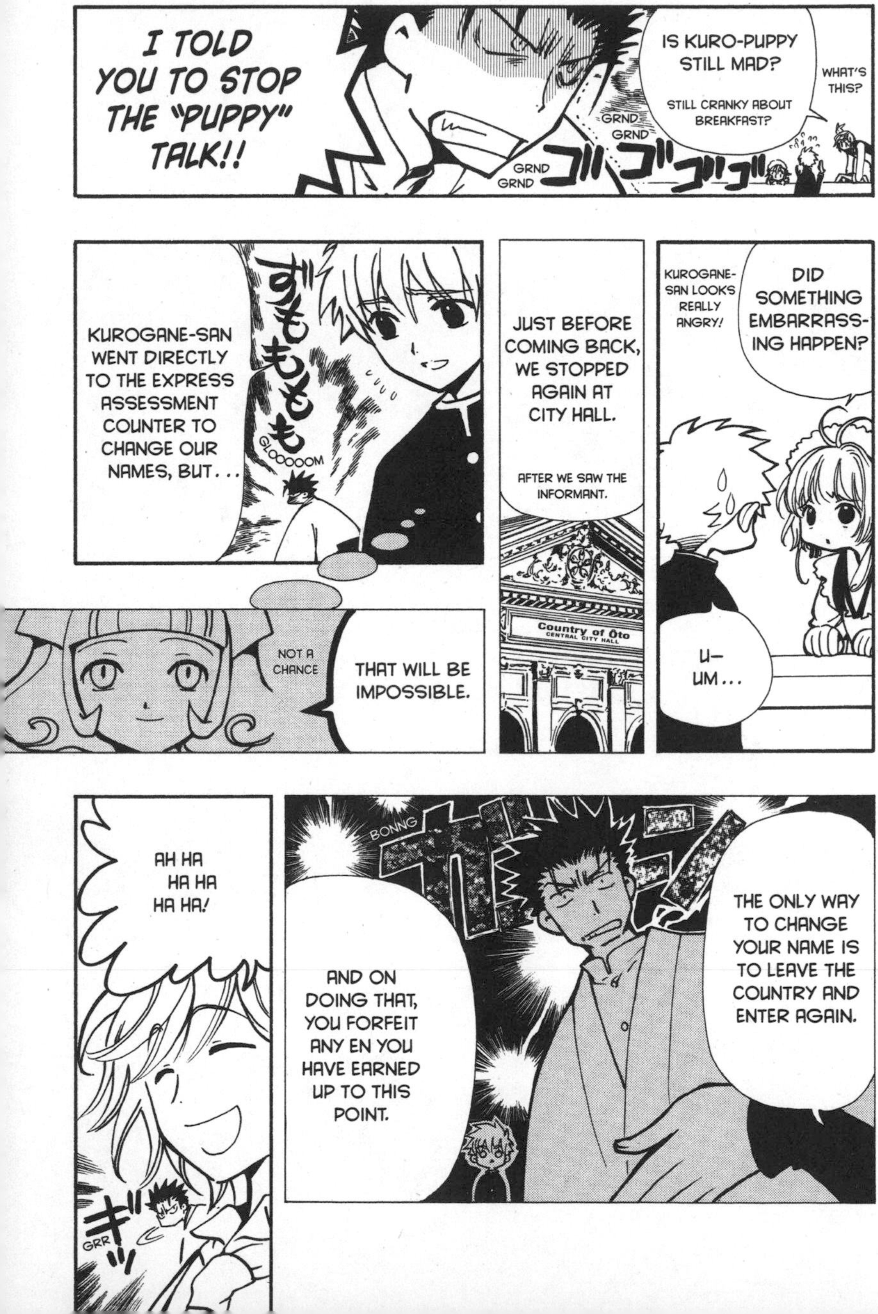
IS KURO-PUPPY STILL MAD?
STILL CRANKY ABOUT BREAKFAST?
WHAT'S THIS?
GRND GRND
GRND GRND
I TOLD YOU TO STOP THE "PUPPY" TALK!!
DID SOMETHING EMBARRASSING HAPPEN?
KUROGANE-SAN LOOKS REALLY ANGRY!
U-UM...
JUST BEFORE COMING BACK, WE STOPPED AGAIN AT CITY HALL.
AFTER WE SAW THE INFORMANT.
Country of Ôto
CENTRAL CITY HALL
KUROGANE-SAN WENT DIRECTLY TO THE EXPRESS ASSESSMENT COUNTER TO CHANGE OUR NAMES, BUT...
GLOOOOOM
THAT WILL BE IMPOSSIBLE.
NOT A CHANCE
THE ONLY WAY TO CHANGE YOUR NAME IS TO LEAVE THE COUNTRY AND ENTER AGAIN.
AND ON DOING THAT, YOU FORFEIT ANY EN YOU HAVE EARNED UP TO THIS POINT.
BONNG
AH HA HA HA HA HA!
GRR

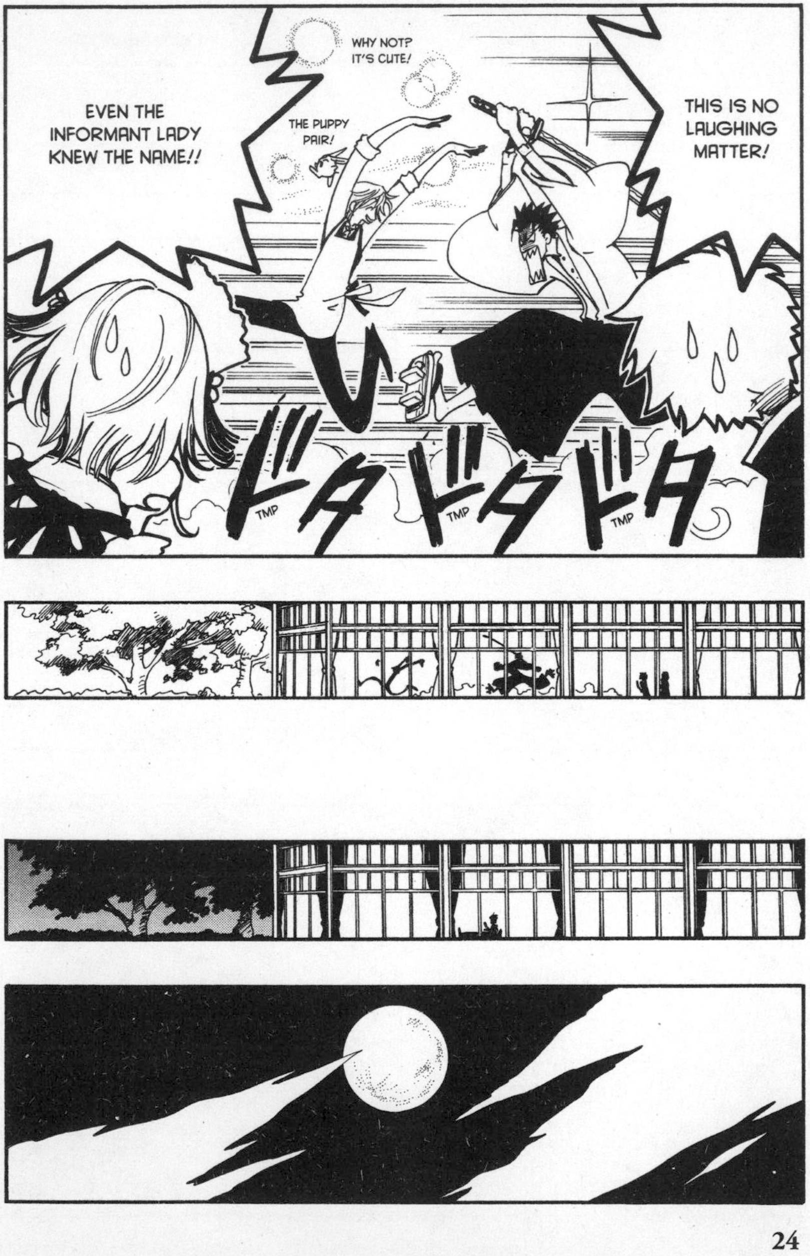
THIS IS NO LAUGHING MATTER!
WHY NOT? IT'S CUTE!
THE PUPPY PAIR!
EVEN THE INFORMANT LADY KNEW THE NAME!!
ドタドタドタ
TMP TMP TMP

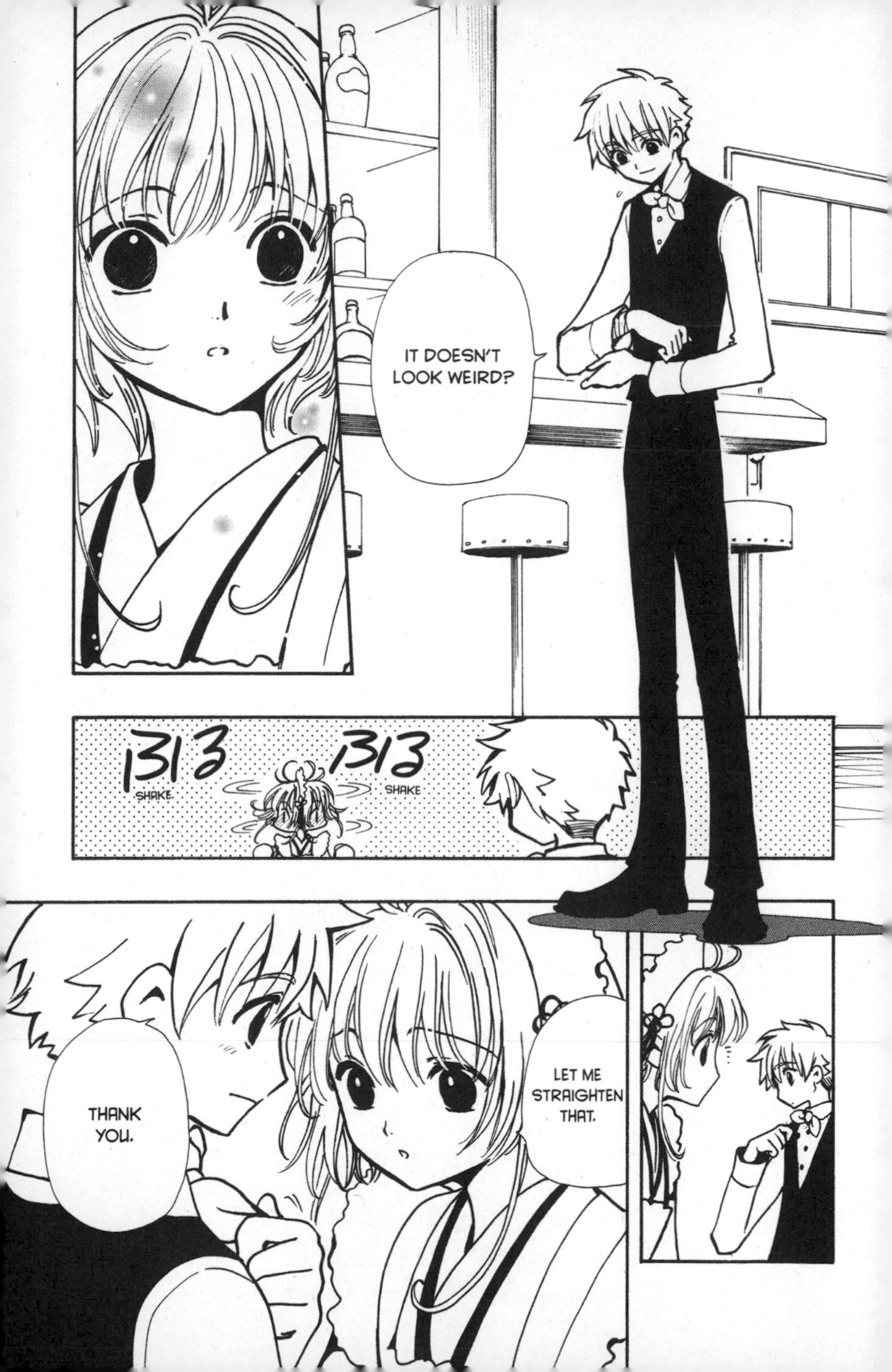
IT DOESN'T LOOK WEIRD?
ふるふる
SHAKE
ふるふる
SHAKE
LET ME STRAIGHTEN THAT.
THANK YOU.

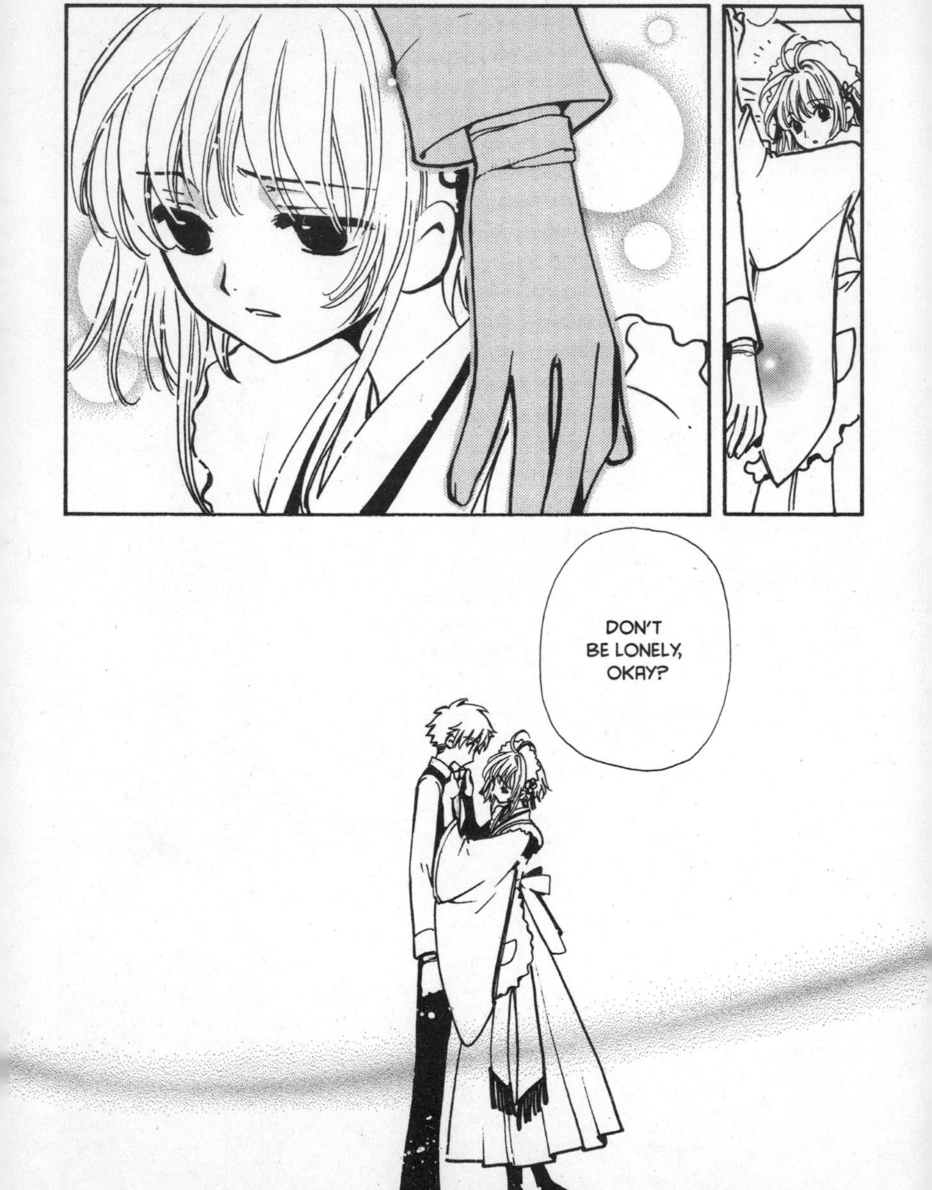
DON'T BE LONELY, OKAY?

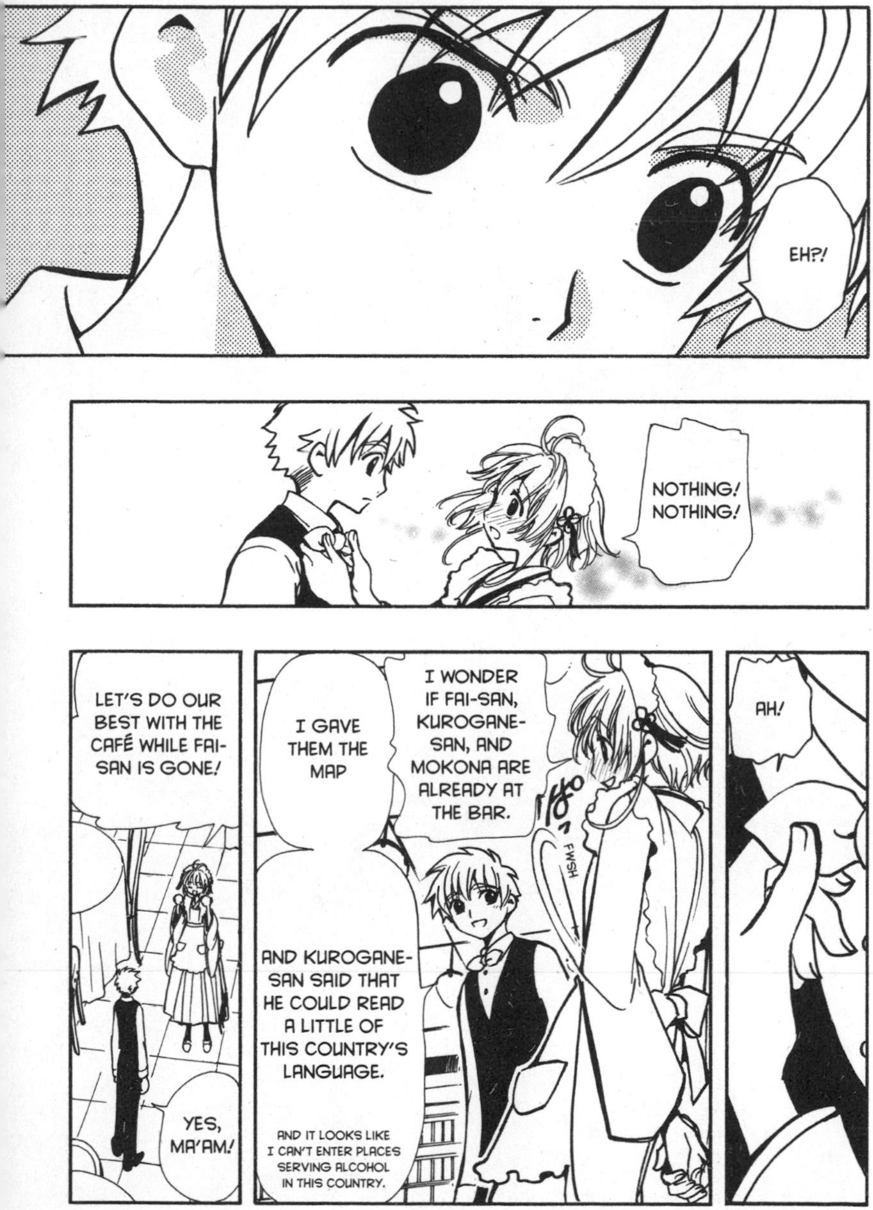

EH?!
NOTHING! NOTHING!
AH!
I WONDER IF FAI-SAN, KUROGANE-SAN, AND MOKONA ARE ALREADY AT THE BAR.
FWSH
I GAVE THEM THE MAP
AND KUROGANE-SAN SAID THAT HE COULD READ A LITTLE OF THIS COUNTRY'S LANGUAGE.
AND IT LOOKS LIKE I CAN'T ENTER PLACES SERVING ALCOHOL IN THIS COUNTRY.
LET'S DO OUR BEST WITH THE CAFÉ WHILE FAI-SAN IS GONE!
YES, MA'AM!

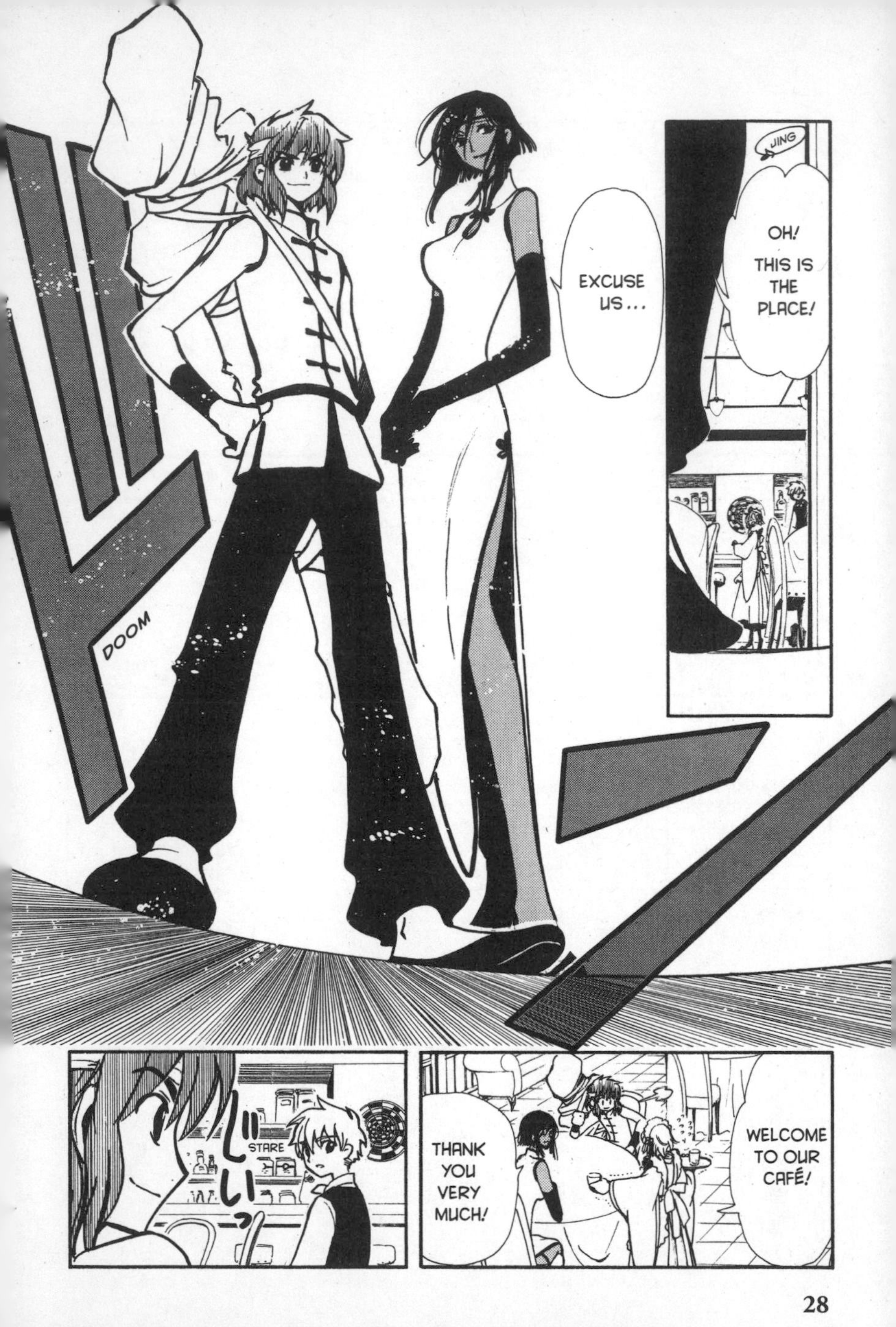
JING
OH!
THIS IS THE PLACE!
EXCUSE US...
DOOM
WELCOME TO OUR CAFÉ!
THANK YOU VERY MUCH!
STARE

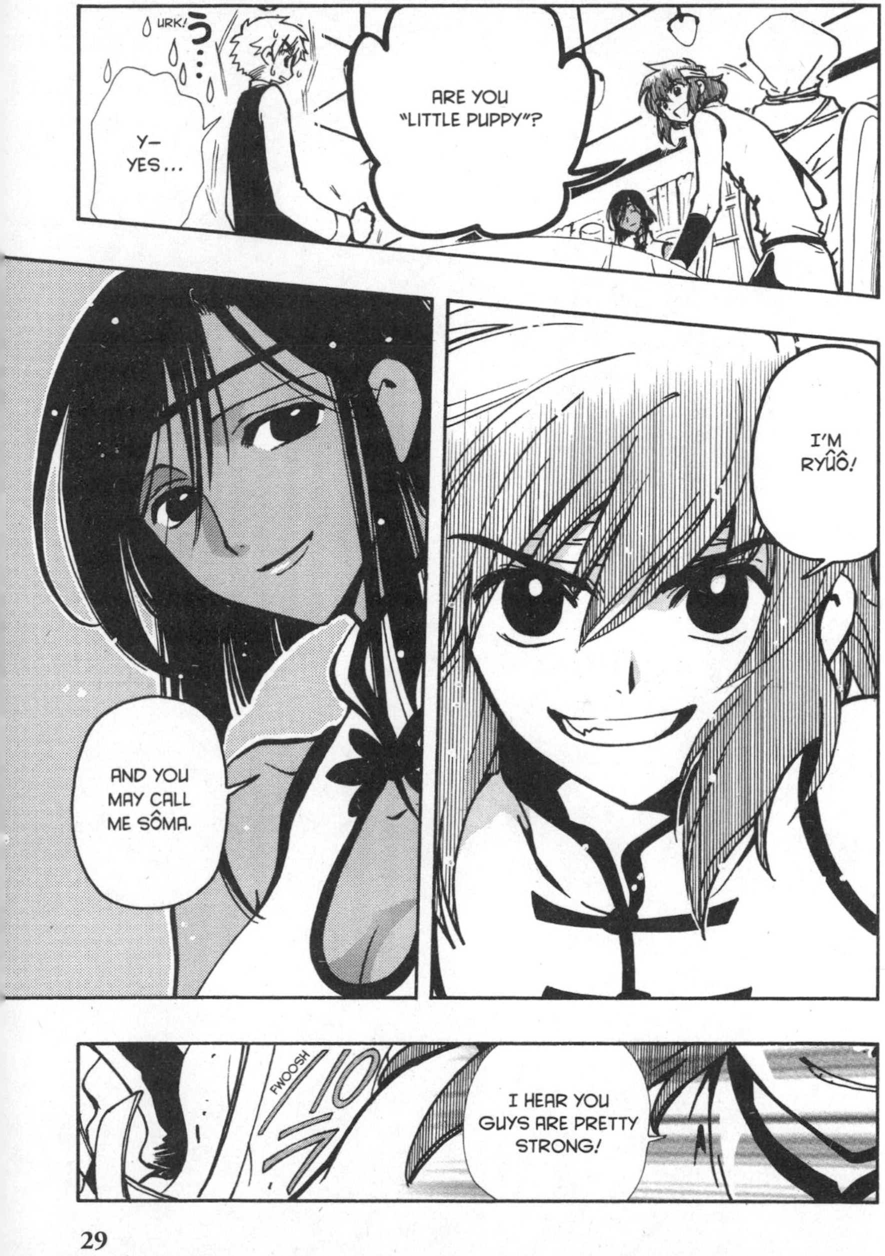
ARE YOU "LITTLE PUPPY"?
URK!
う…
Y— YES…
I'M RYÛÔ!
AND YOU MAY CALL ME SÔMA.
I HEAR YOU GUYS ARE PRETTY STRONG!
FWOOSH

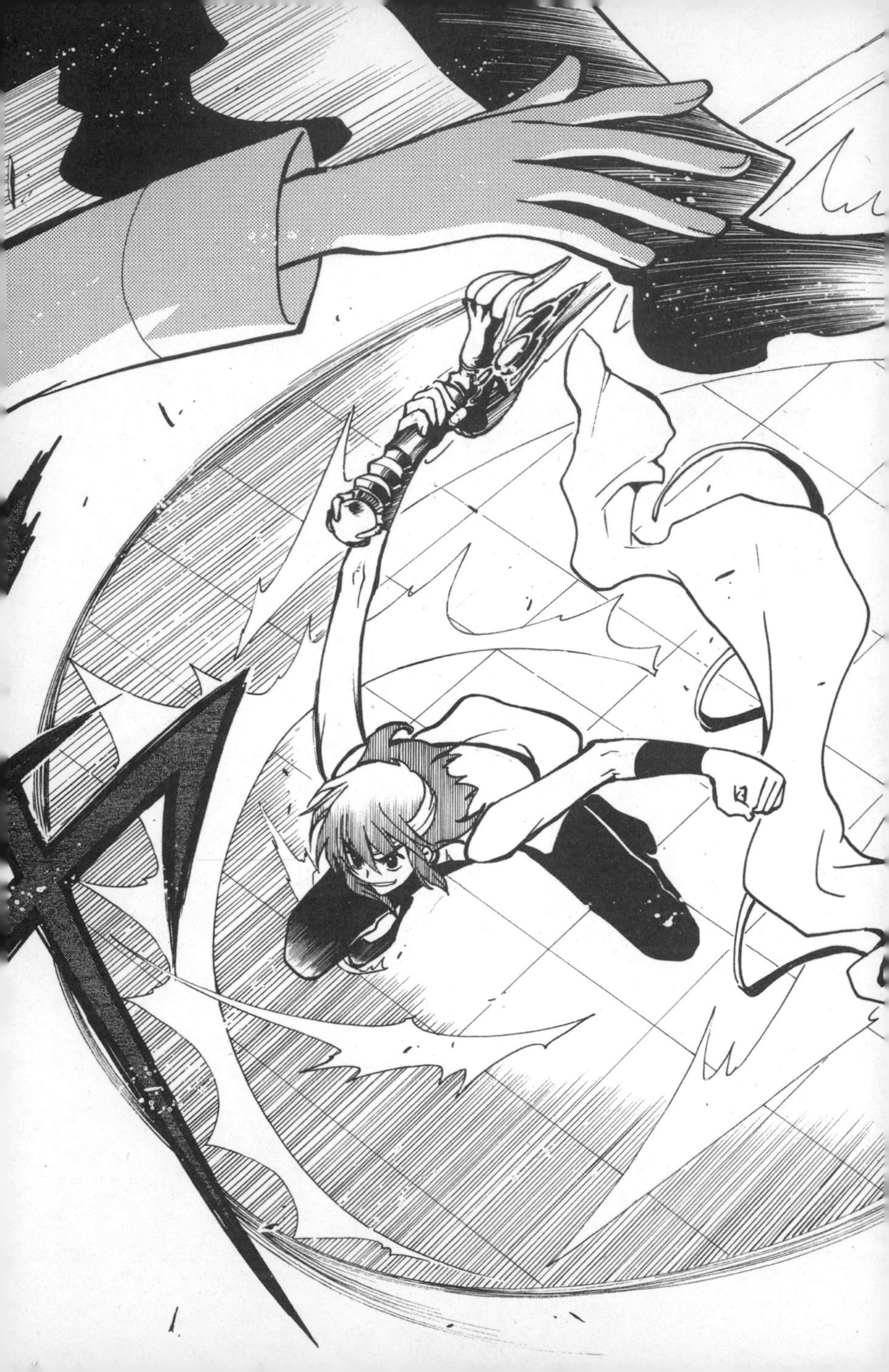

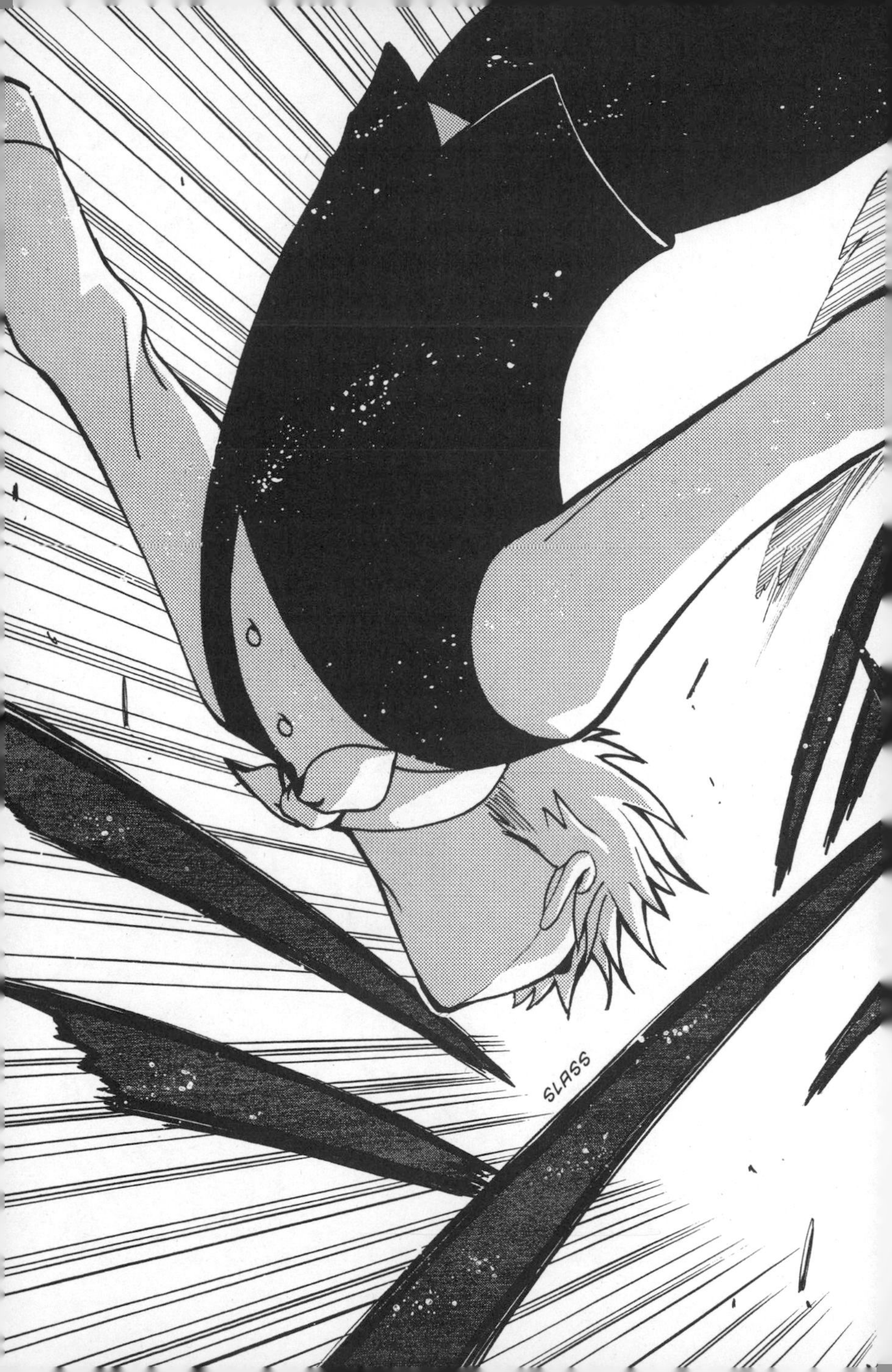
SLASS

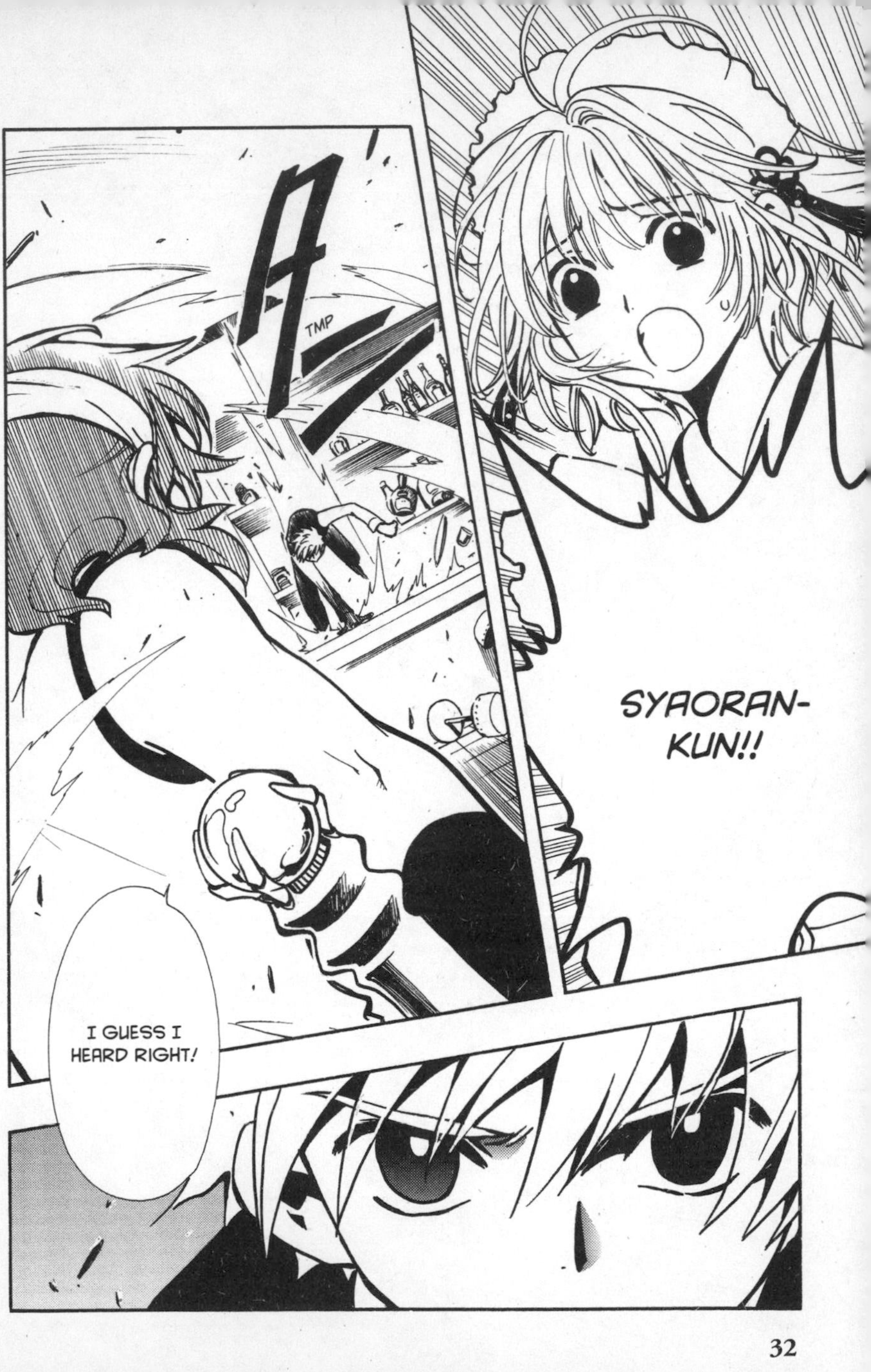
SYAORAN-KUN!!
TMP
I GUESS I HEARD RIGHT!

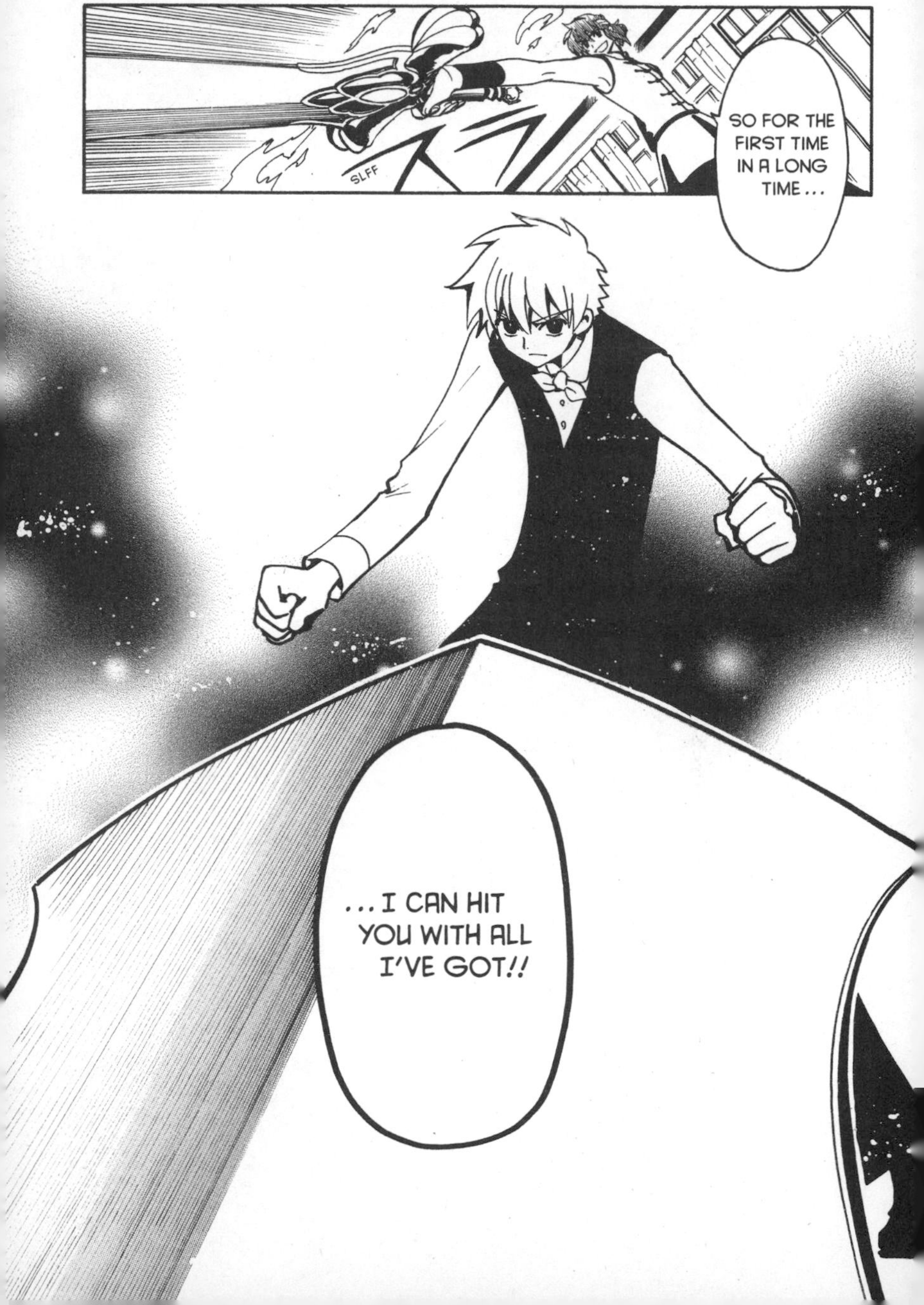
SO FOR THE FIRST TIME IN A LONG TIME...
SLFF
...I CAN HIT YOU WITH ALL I'VE GOT!!

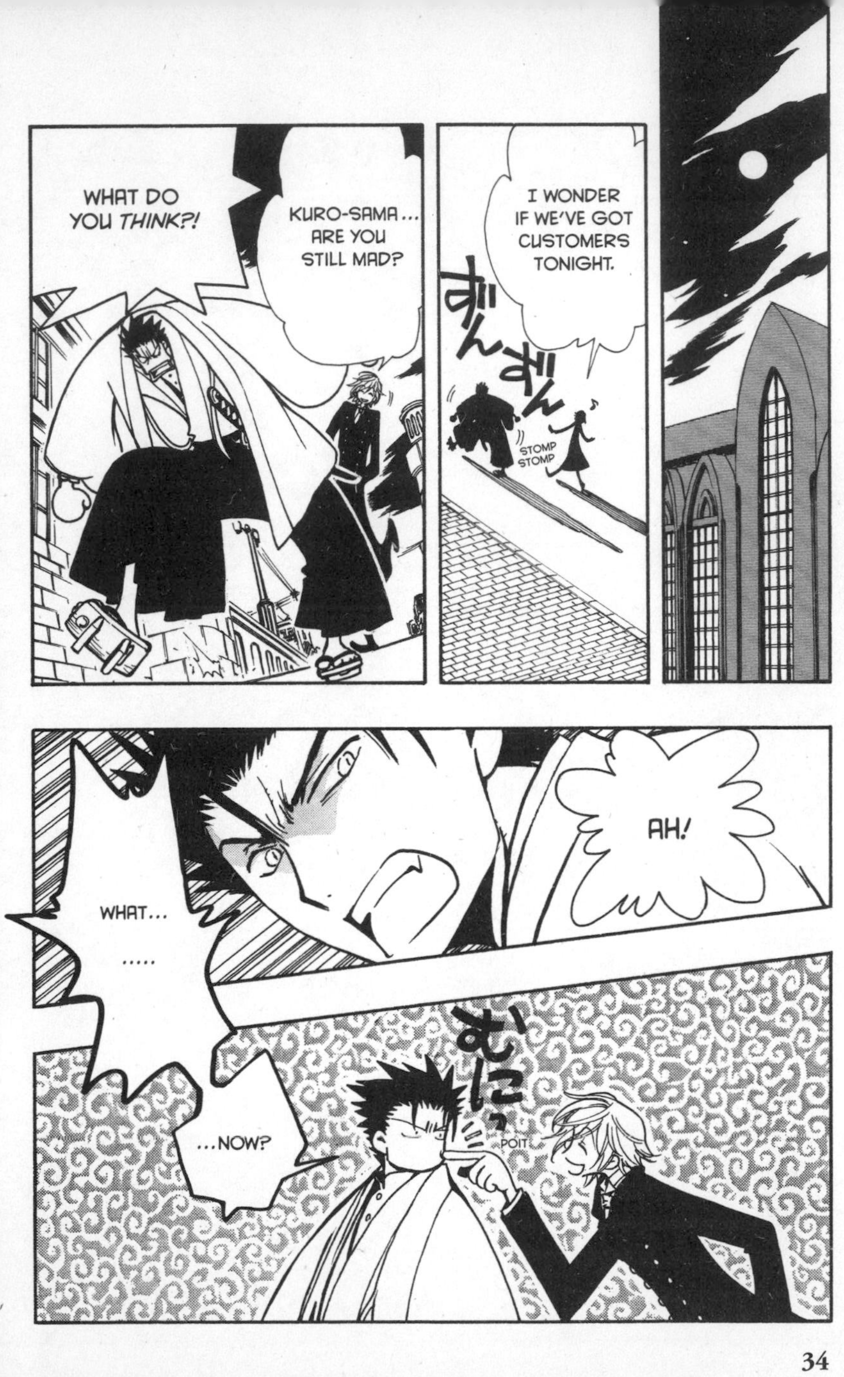
I WONDER IF WE'VE GOT CUSTOMERS TONIGHT.
ずんずん
STOMP STOMP
KURO-SAMA... ARE YOU STILL MAD?
WHAT DO YOU *THINK?!*
AH!
WHAT...
.....
むにっ
POIT
...NOW?

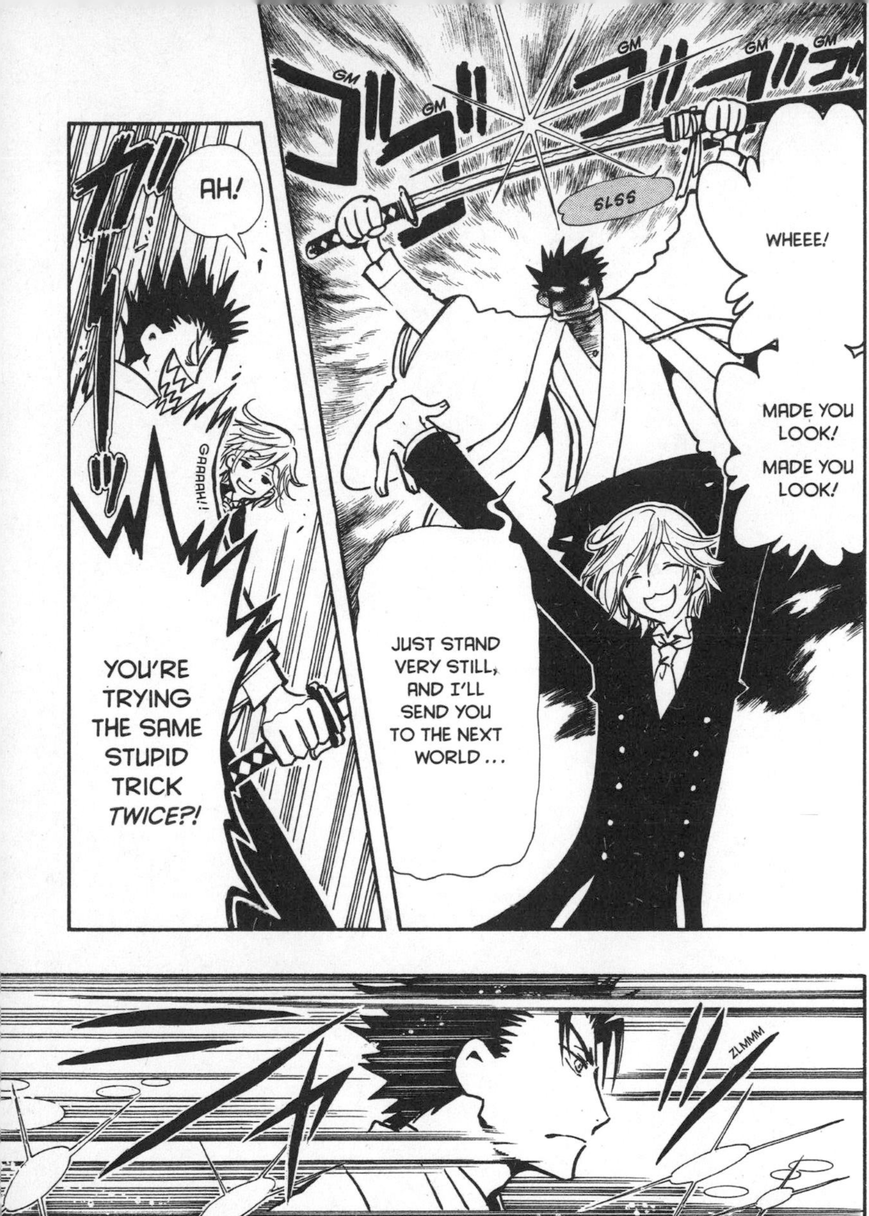
GM GM GM GM GM
WHEEE!
MADE YOU LOOK! MADE YOU LOOK!
JUST STAND VERY STILL, AND I'LL SEND YOU TO THE NEXT WORLD...
AH!
GRAAAAH!!
YOU'RE TRYING THE SAME STUPID TRICK TWICE?!
ZLMMM

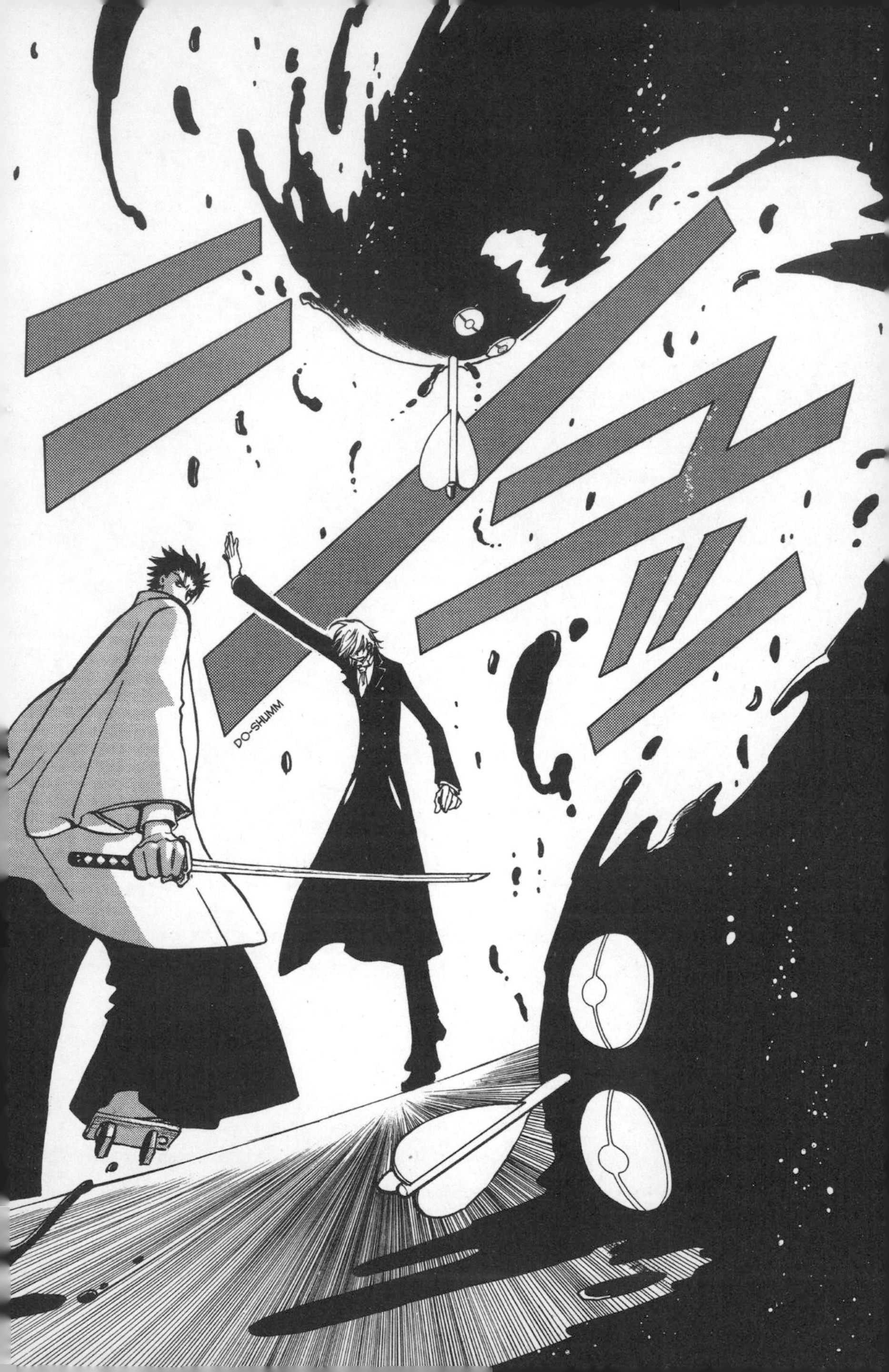
DO-SHUMM

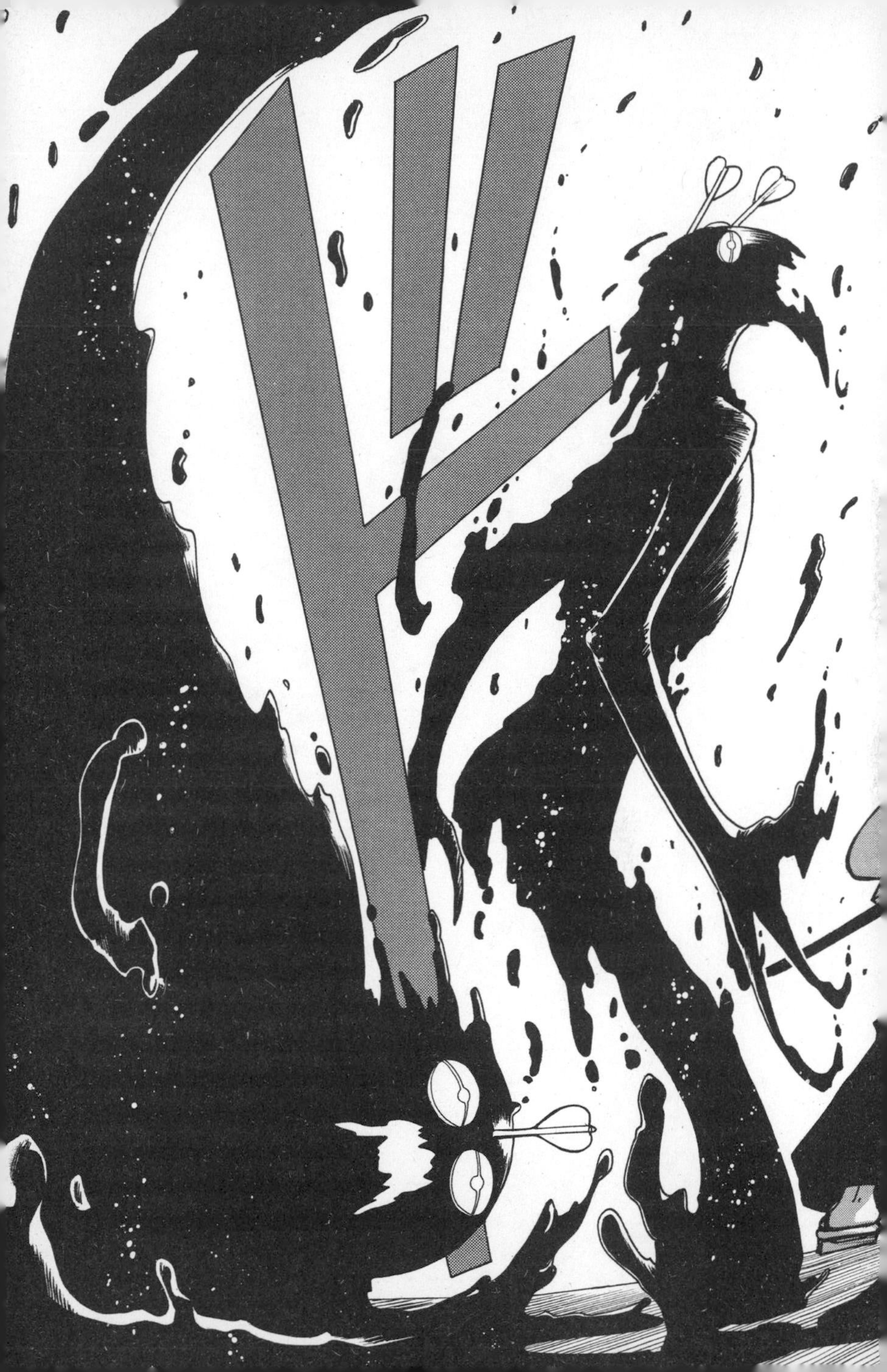

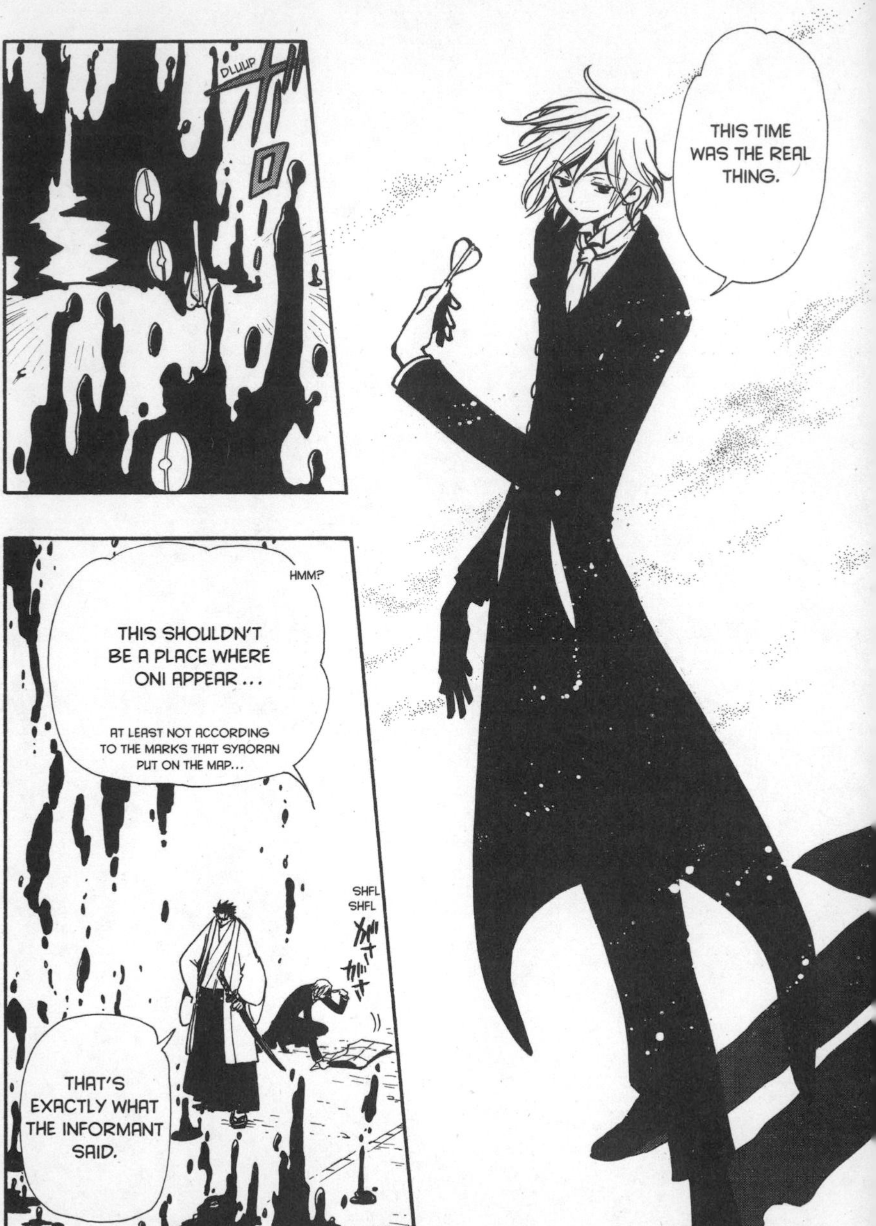
THIS TIME WAS THE REAL THING.
DLUUP
HMM?
THIS SHOULDN'T BE A PLACE WHERE ONI APPEAR...
AT LEAST NOT ACCORDING TO THE MARKS THAT SYAORAN PUT ON THE MAP...
SHFL SHFL
THAT'S EXACTLY WHAT THE INFORMANT SAID.

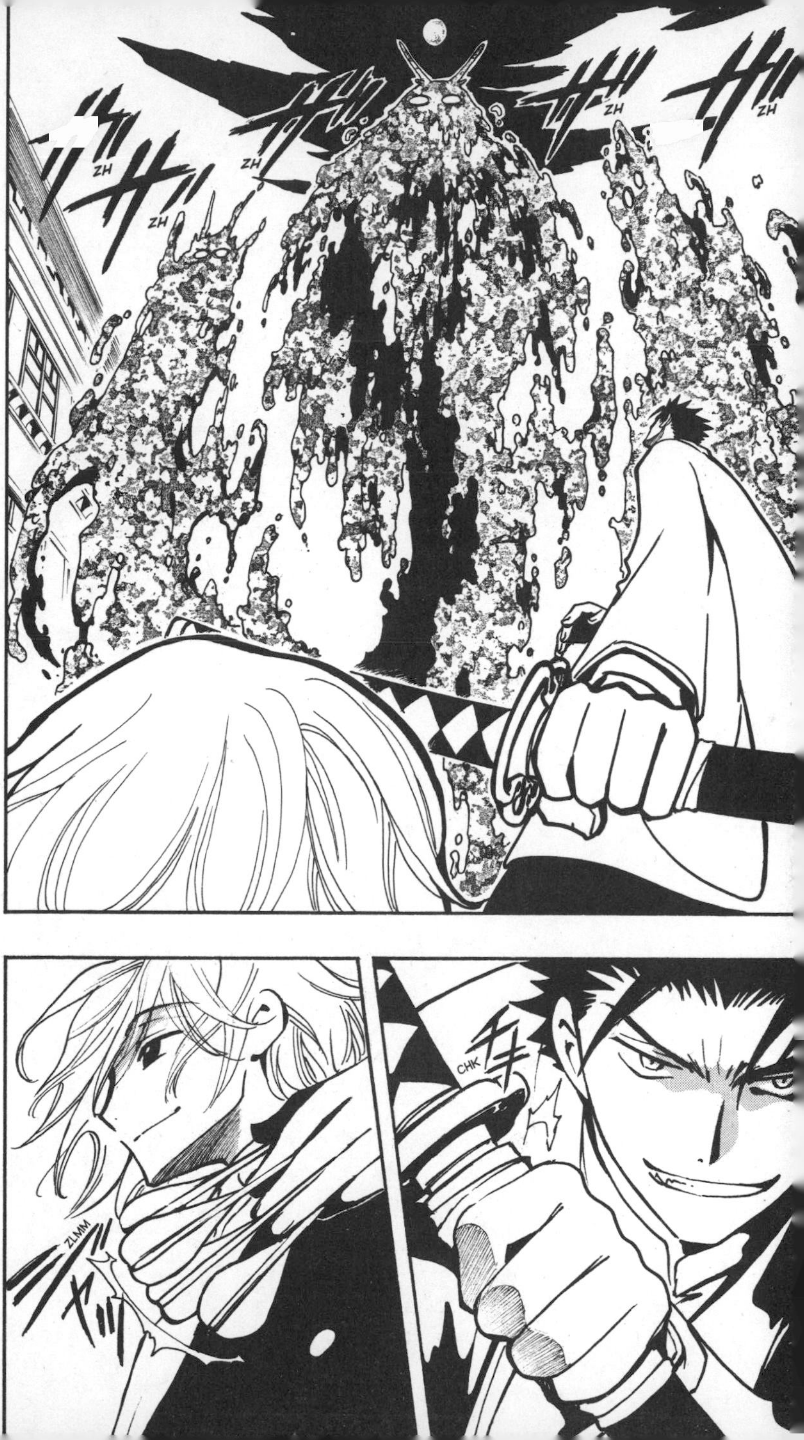
ZH
ZH
ZH
ZH
ZH
CHK
ZLMM

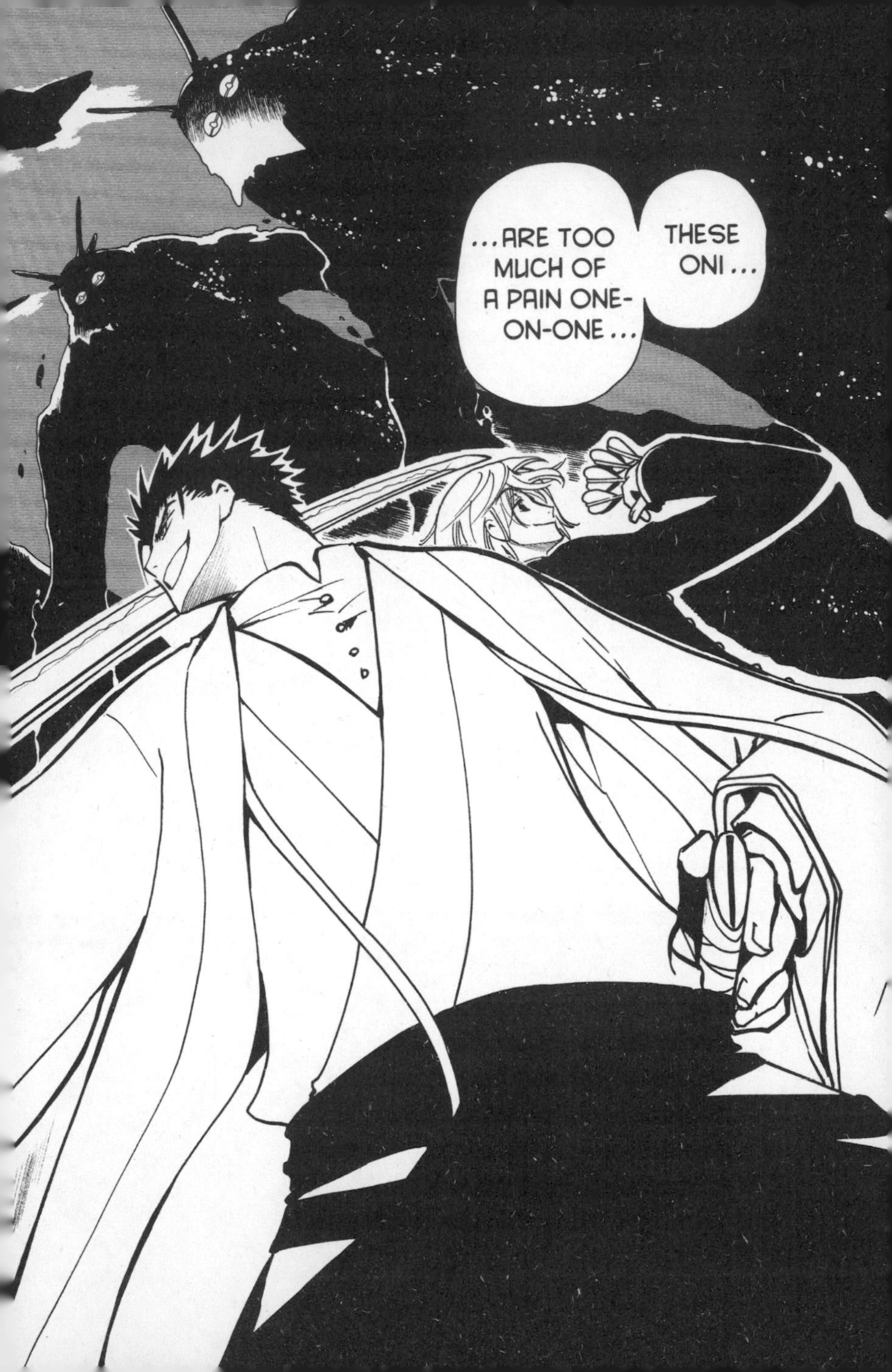
THESE ONI ...
... ARE TOO MUCH OF A PAIN ONE-ON-ONE ...

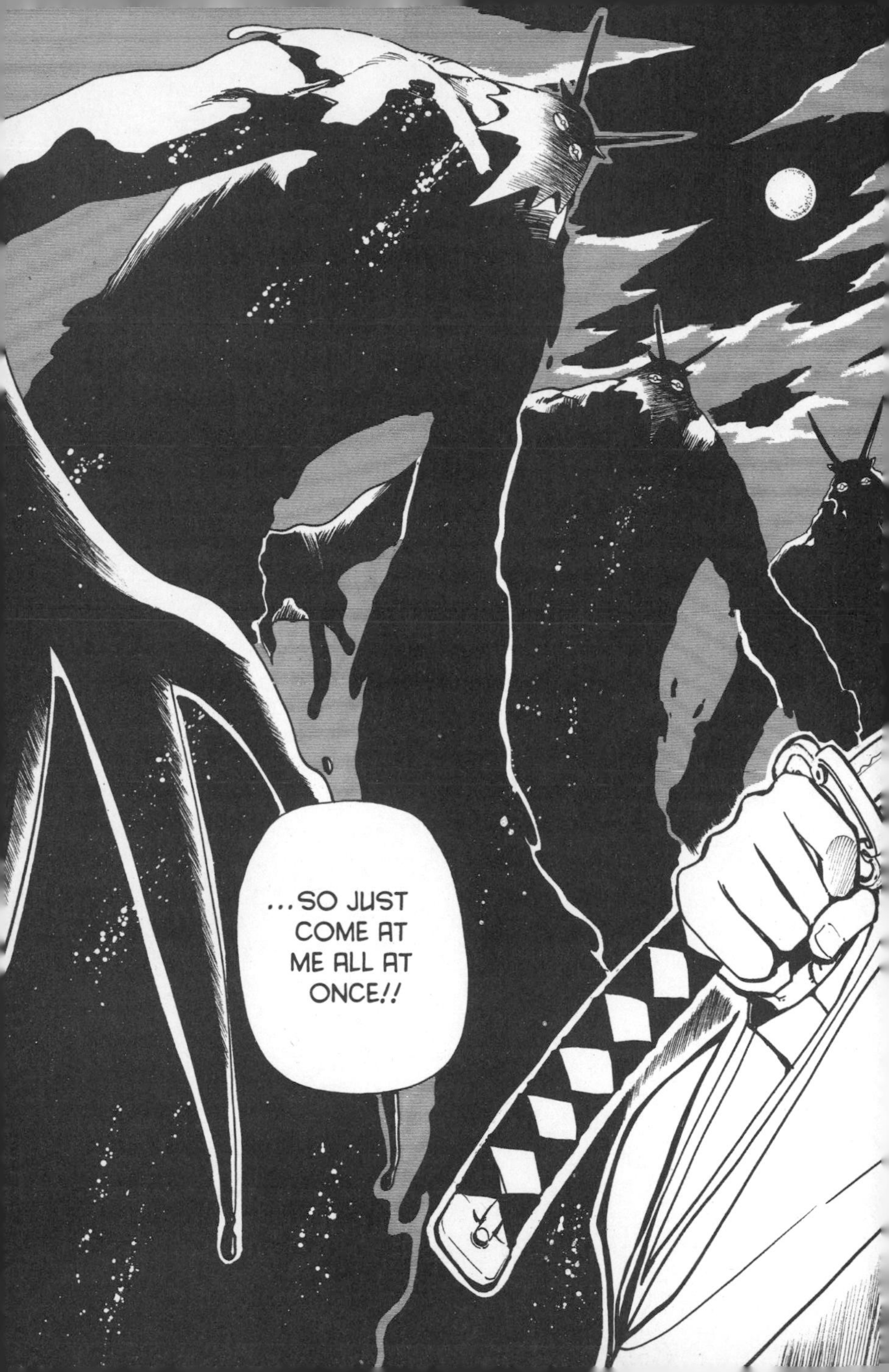
...SO JUST COME AT ME ALL AT ONCE!!

ツバサ
RESERVoir CHRoNiCLE

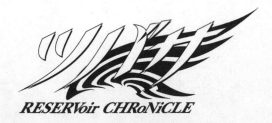

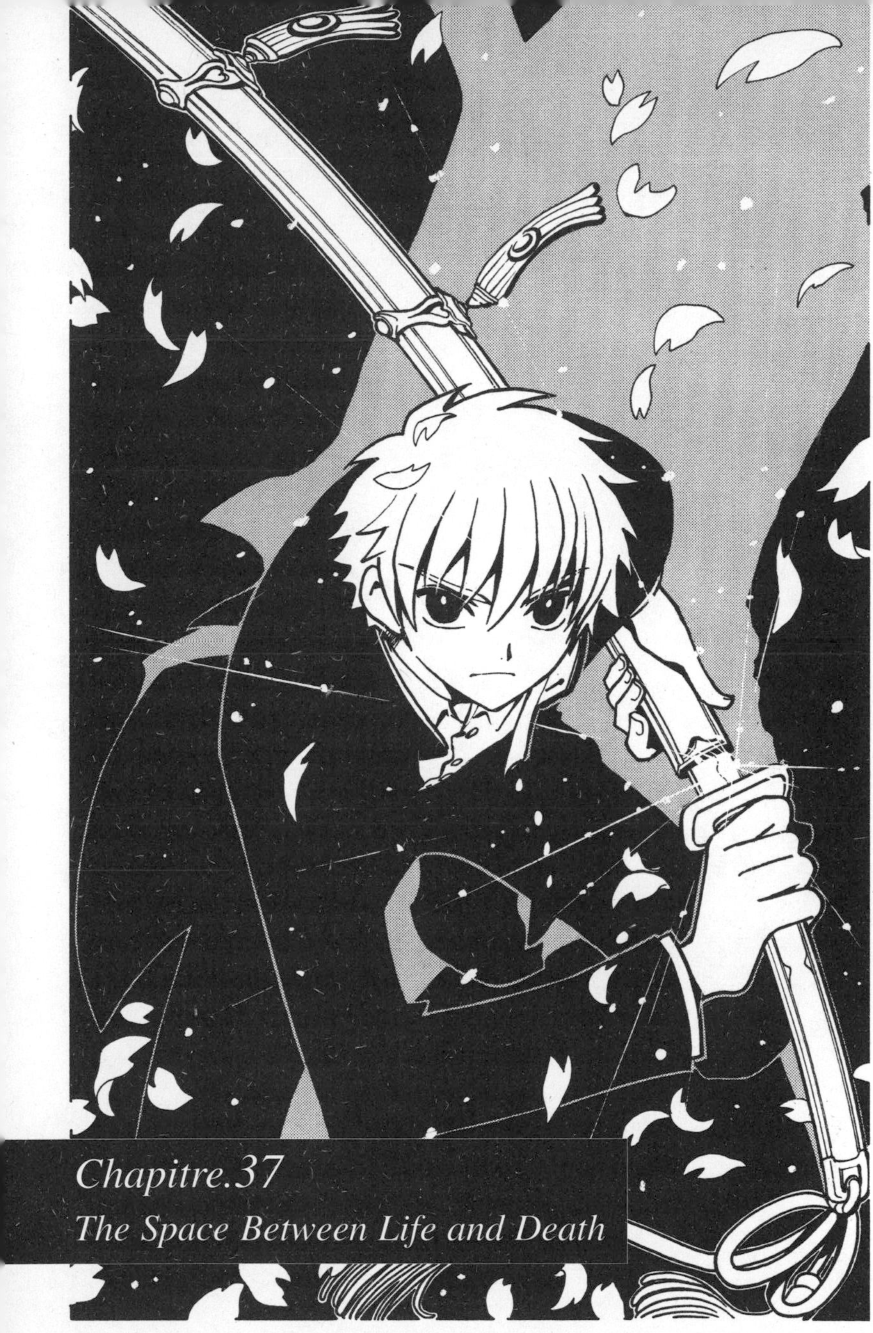

Chapitre.37
The Space Between Life and Death

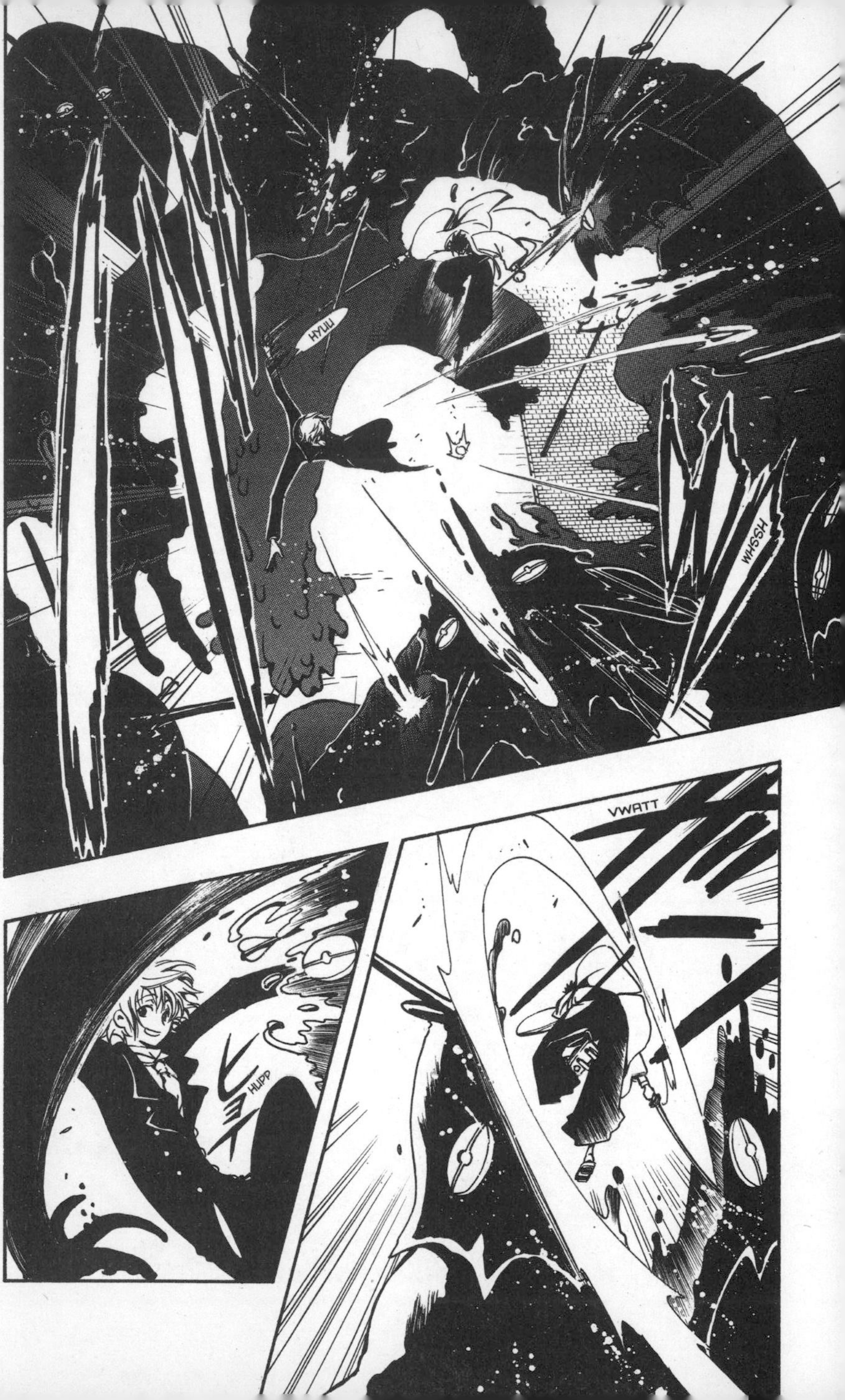
HYUU
WHSSH
VWATT
HUPP

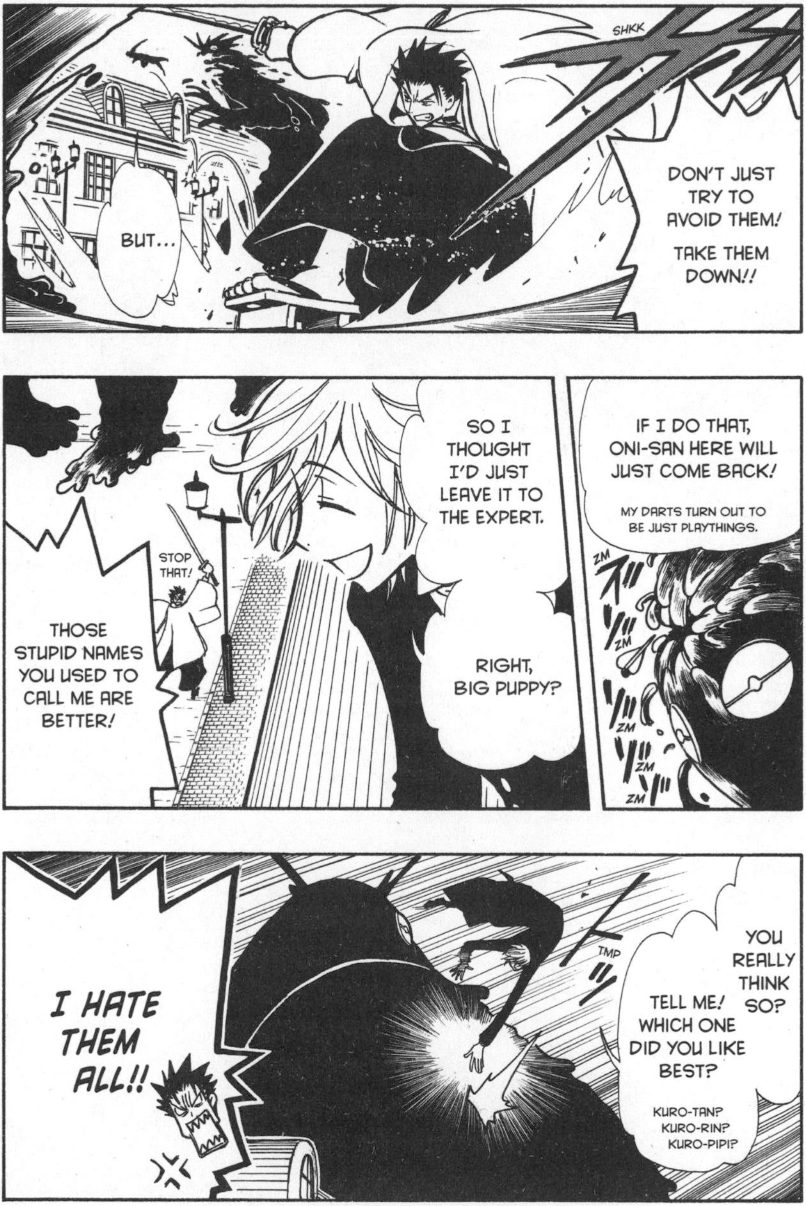
SHKK
DON'T JUST TRY TO AVOID THEM!
TAKE THEM DOWN!!
BUT...
IF I DO THAT, ONI-SAN HERE WILL JUST COME BACK!
MY DARTS TURN OUT TO BE JUST PLAYTHINGS.
ZM ZM ZM ZM ZM
SO I THOUGHT I'D JUST LEAVE IT TO THE EXPERT.
RIGHT, BIG PUPPY?
STOP THAT!
THOSE STUPID NAMES YOU USED TO CALL ME ARE BETTER!
YOU REALLY THINK SO?
TELL ME! WHICH ONE DID YOU LIKE BEST?
KURO-TAN? KURO-RIN? KURO-PIPI?
TMP
I HATE THEM ALL!!

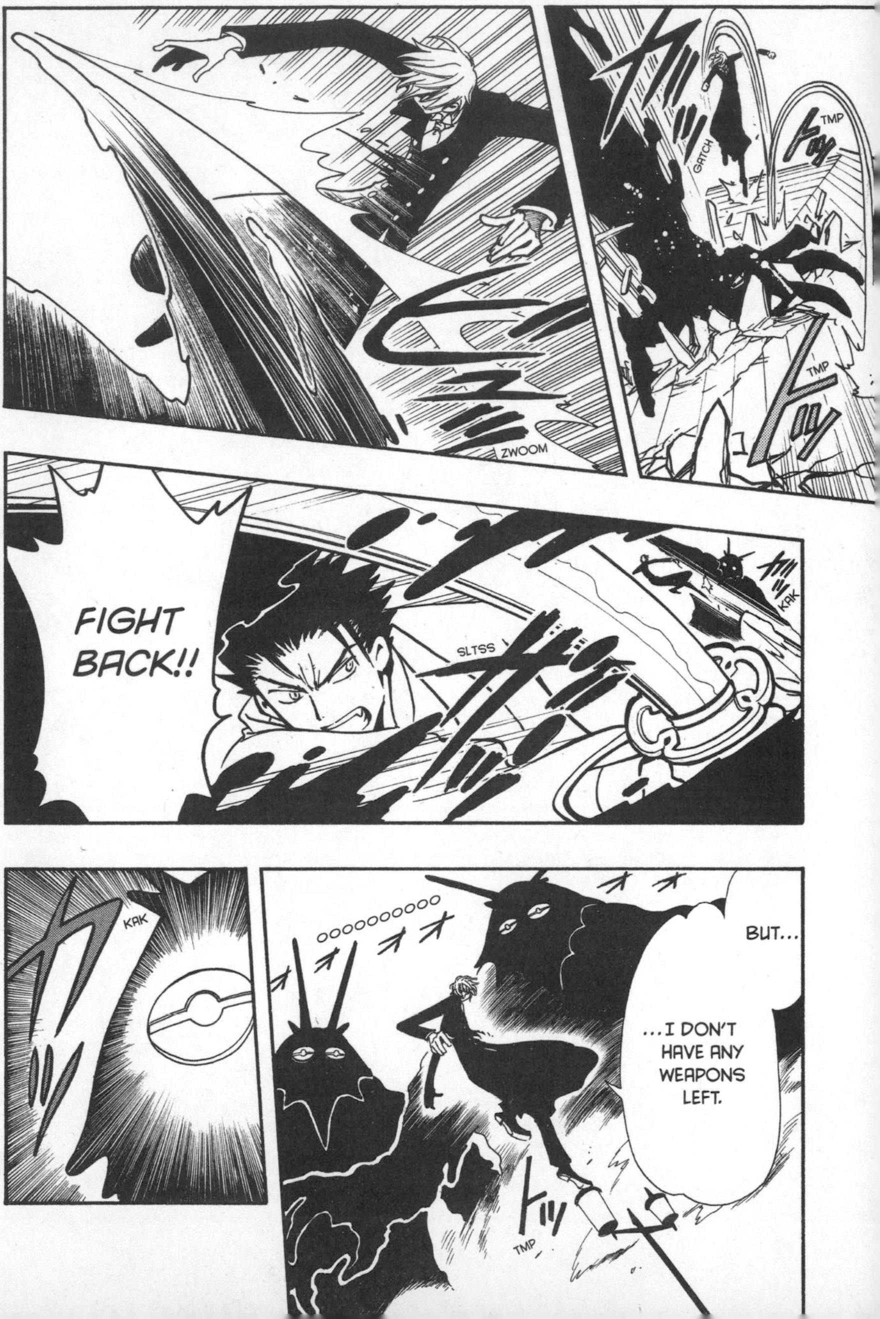
GATCH
TMP
TMP
ZWOOM
KAK
SLTSS
FIGHT BACK!!
BUT...
...I DON'T HAVE ANY WEAPONS LEFT.
OOOOOOOOOO
TMP
KAK

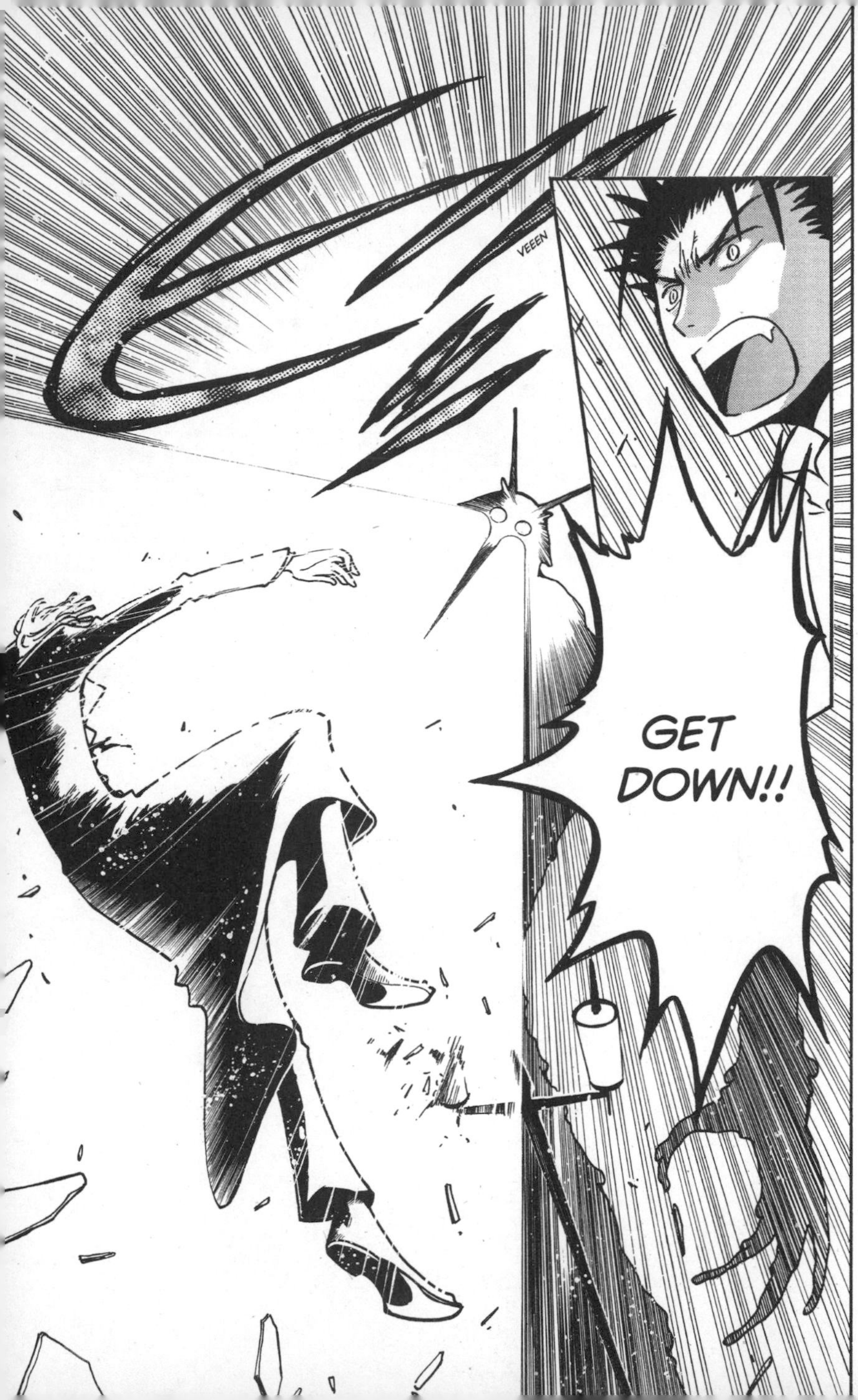
VEEEN
GET DOWN!!

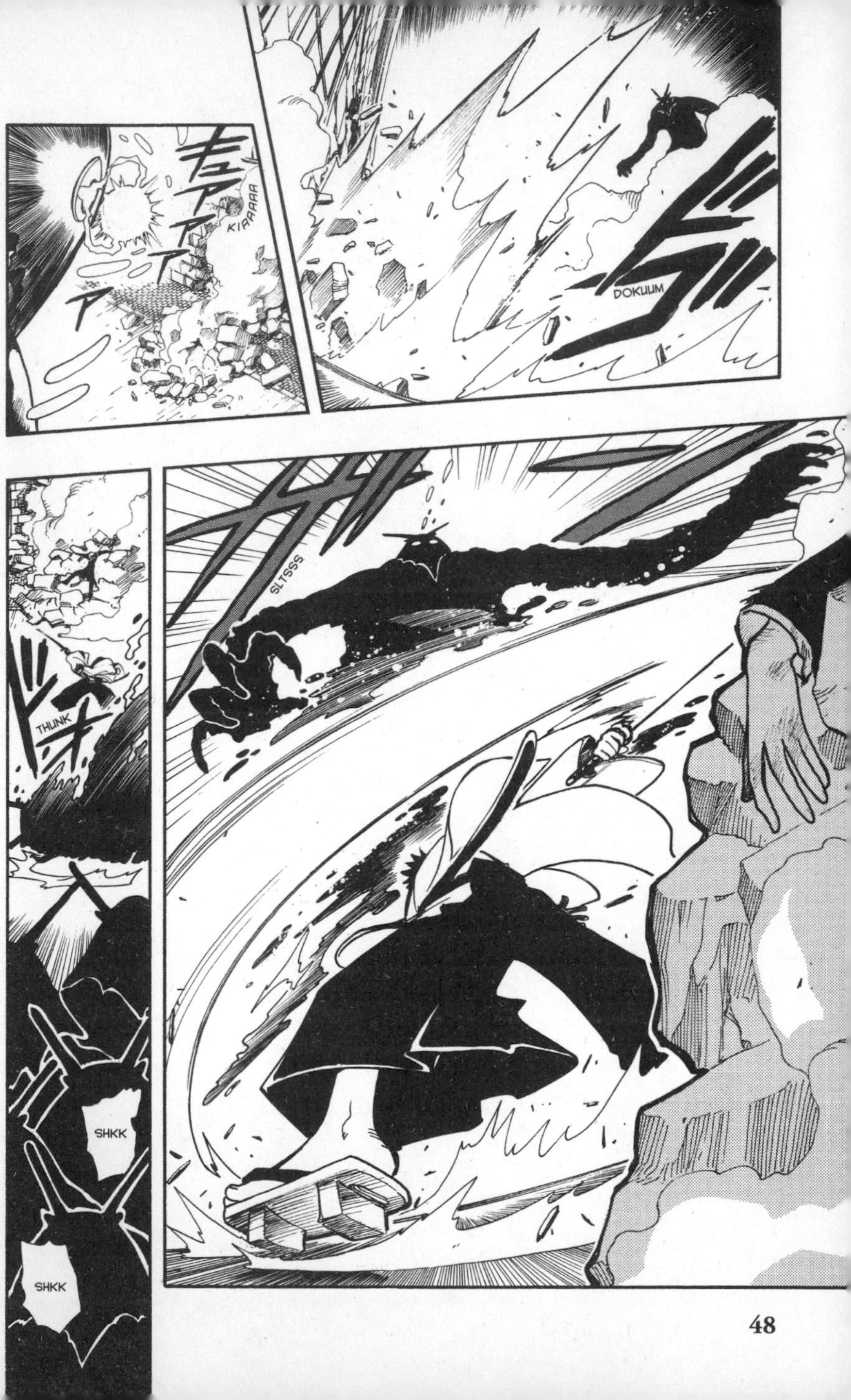
DOKUUM
KIRAAAAA
SLTSSS
THUNK
SHKK
SHKK

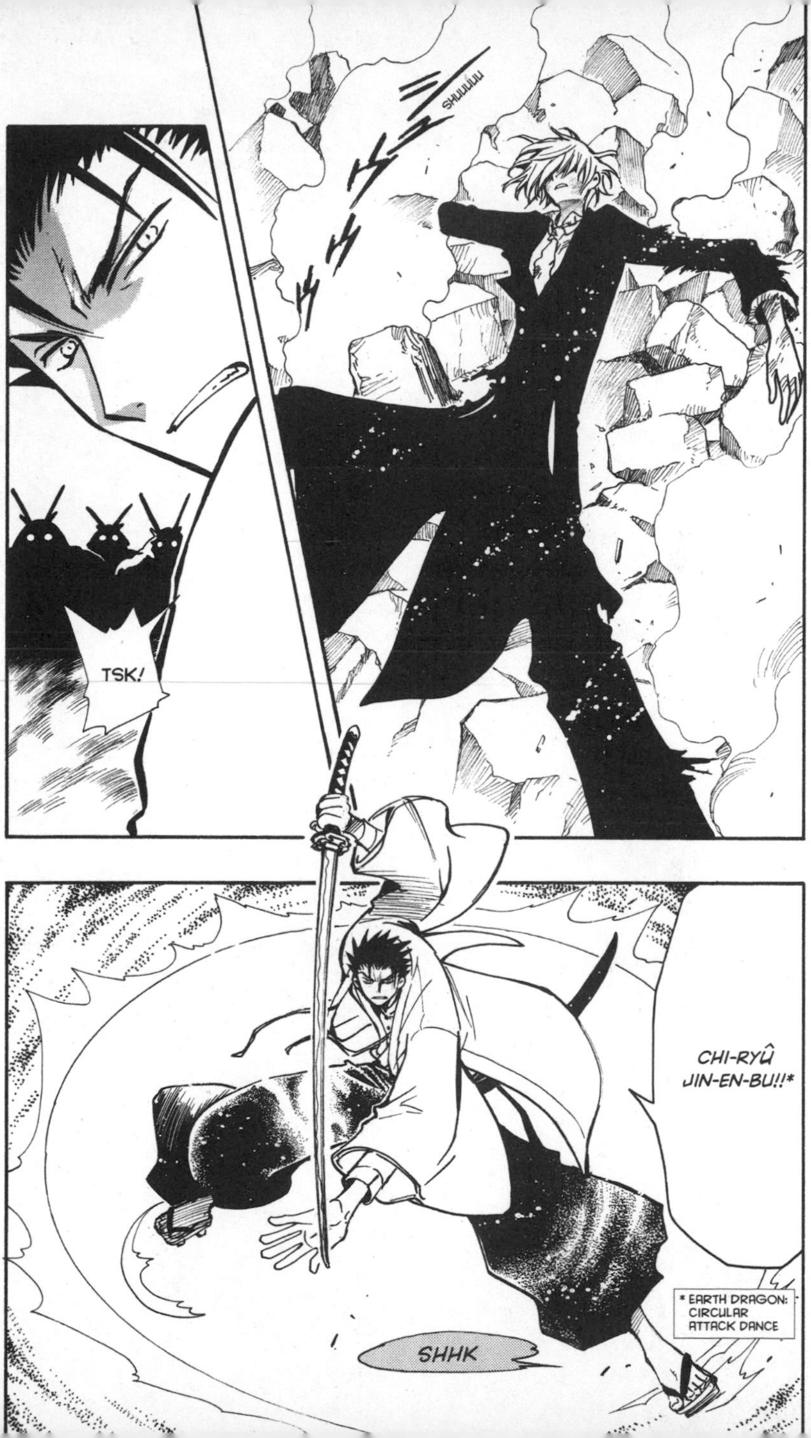
SHUUUUU
TSK!
CHI-RYÛ JIN-EN-BU!!*
SHHK
* EARTH DRAGON: CIRCULAR ATTACK DANCE

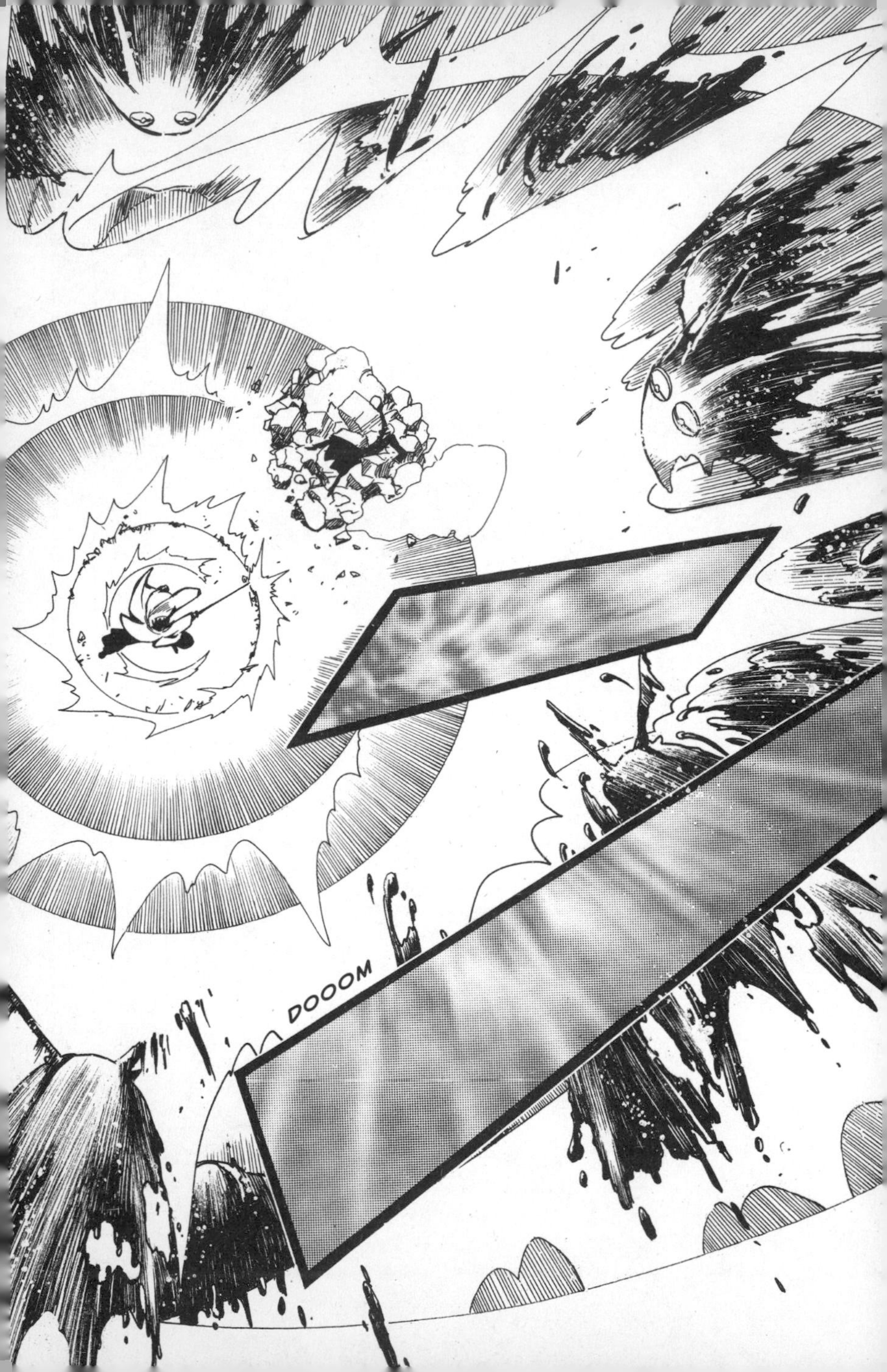
DOOOM

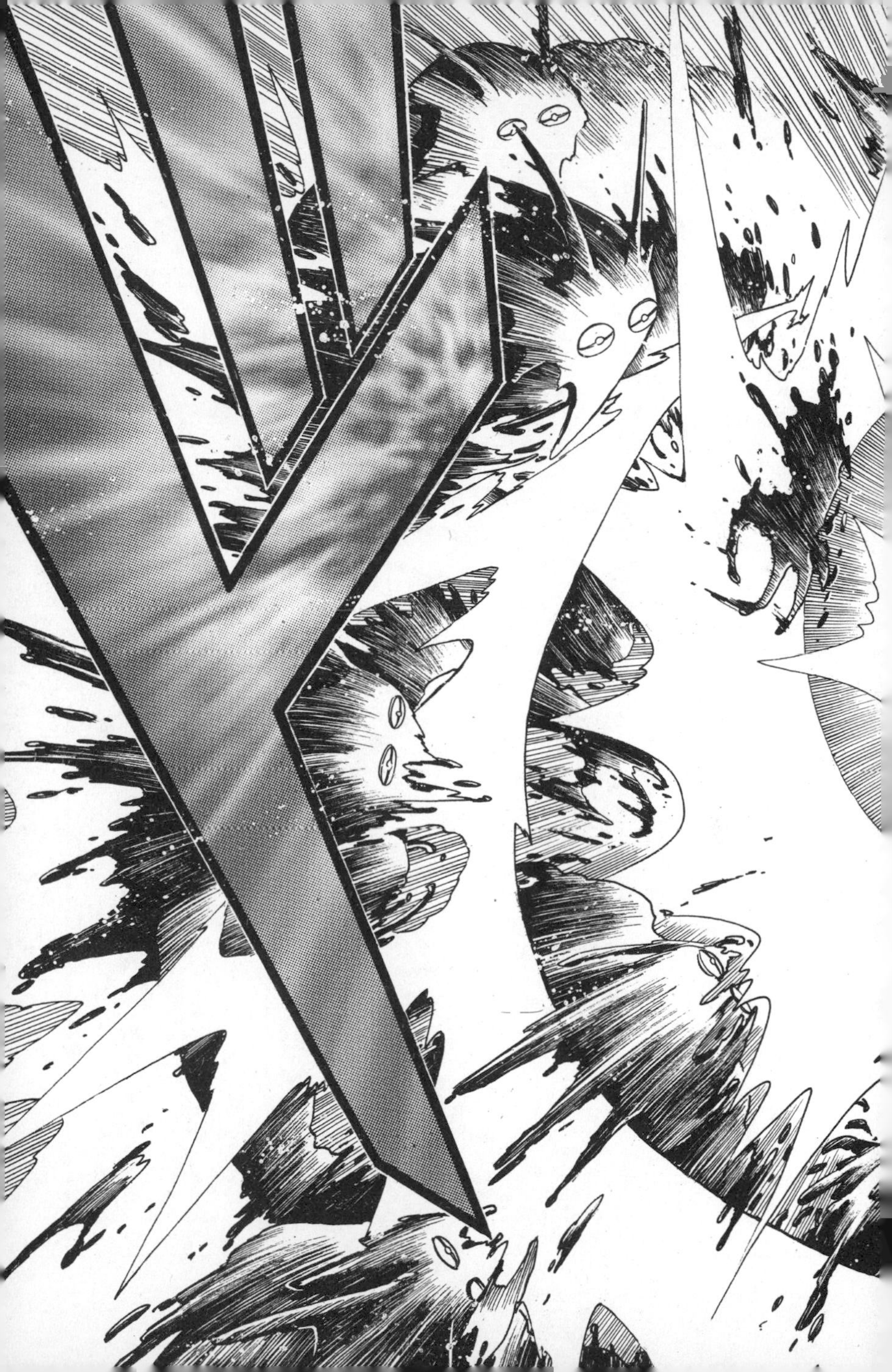

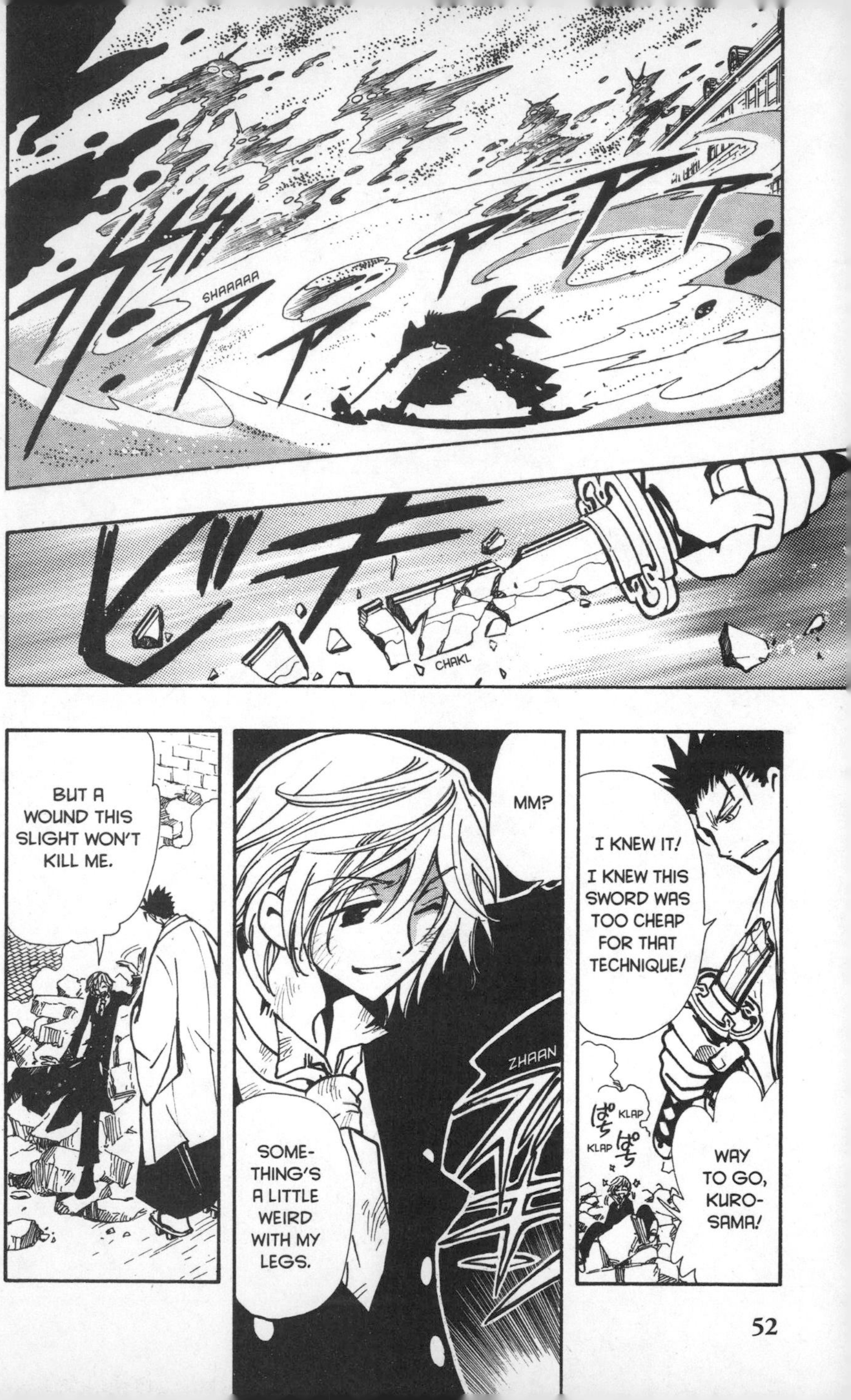
SHAAAAA
CHAKL
I KNEW IT!
I KNEW THIS SWORD WAS TOO CHEAP FOR THAT TECHNIQUE!
KLAP
KLAP
WAY TO GO, KURO-SAMA!
MM?
ZHAAN
SOME-THING'S A LITTLE WEIRD WITH MY LEGS.
BUT A WOUND THIS SLIGHT WON'T KILL ME.

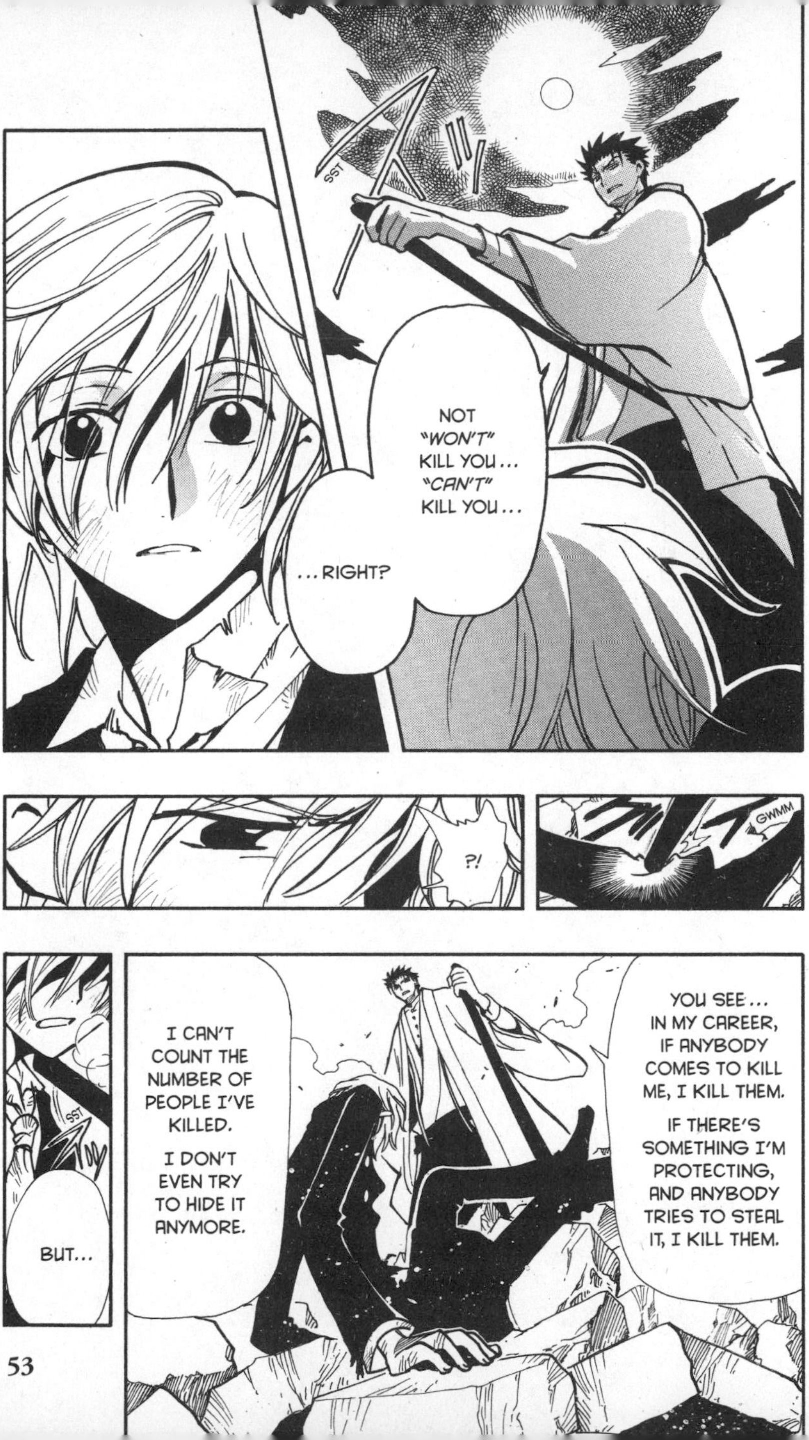
SST
NOT "WON'T" KILL YOU... "CAN'T" KILL YOU...
...RIGHT?
GWMM
?!
YOU SEE... IN MY CAREER, IF ANYBODY COMES TO KILL ME, I KILL THEM.
IF THERE'S SOMETHING I'M PROTECTING, AND ANYBODY TRIES TO STEAL IT, I KILL THEM.
I CAN'T COUNT THE NUMBER OF PEOPLE I'VE KILLED.
I DON'T EVEN TRY TO HIDE IT ANYMORE.
SST
BUT...

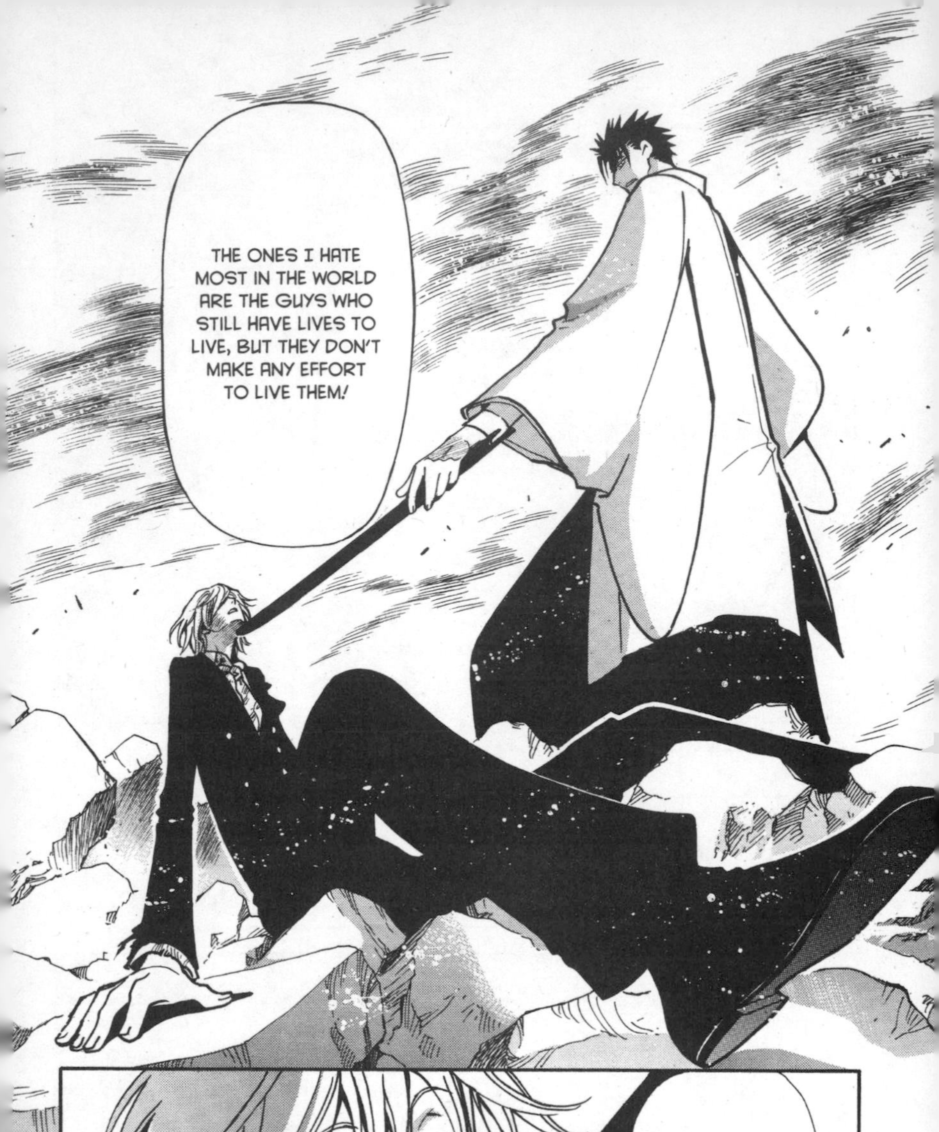
THE ONES I HATE MOST IN THE WORLD ARE THE GUYS WHO STILL HAVE LIVES TO LIVE, BUT THEY DON'T MAKE ANY EFFORT TO LIVE THEM!
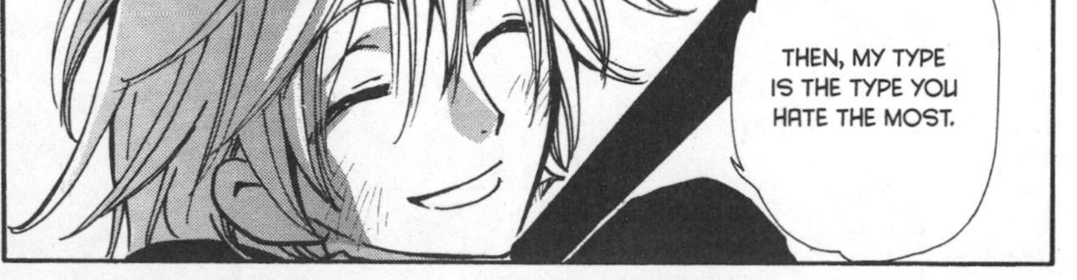
THEN, MY TYPE IS THE TYPE YOU HATE THE MOST.

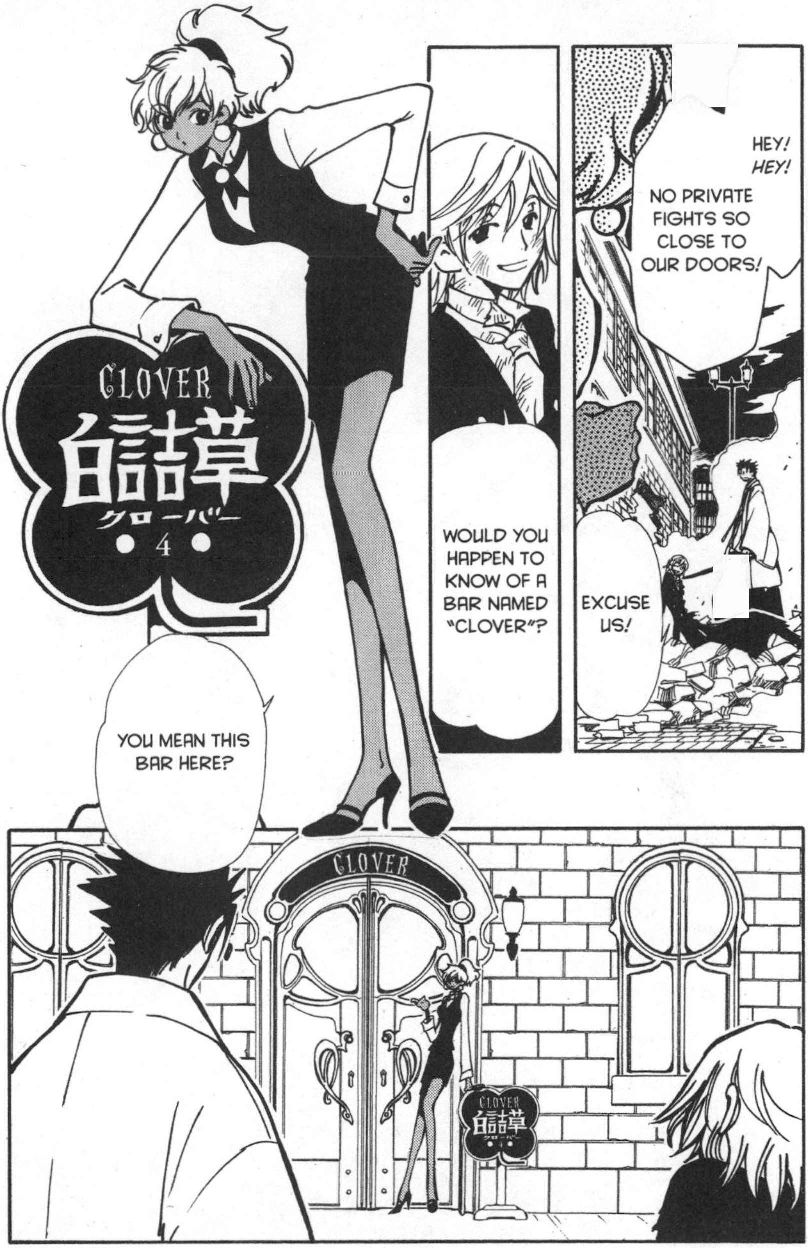
HEY! HEY!
NO PRIVATE FIGHTS SO CLOSE TO OUR DOORS!
EXCUSE US!
WOULD YOU HAPPEN TO KNOW OF A BAR NAMED "CLOVER"?
CLOVER
白詰草
クローバー
4
YOU MEAN THIS BAR HERE?
CLOVER

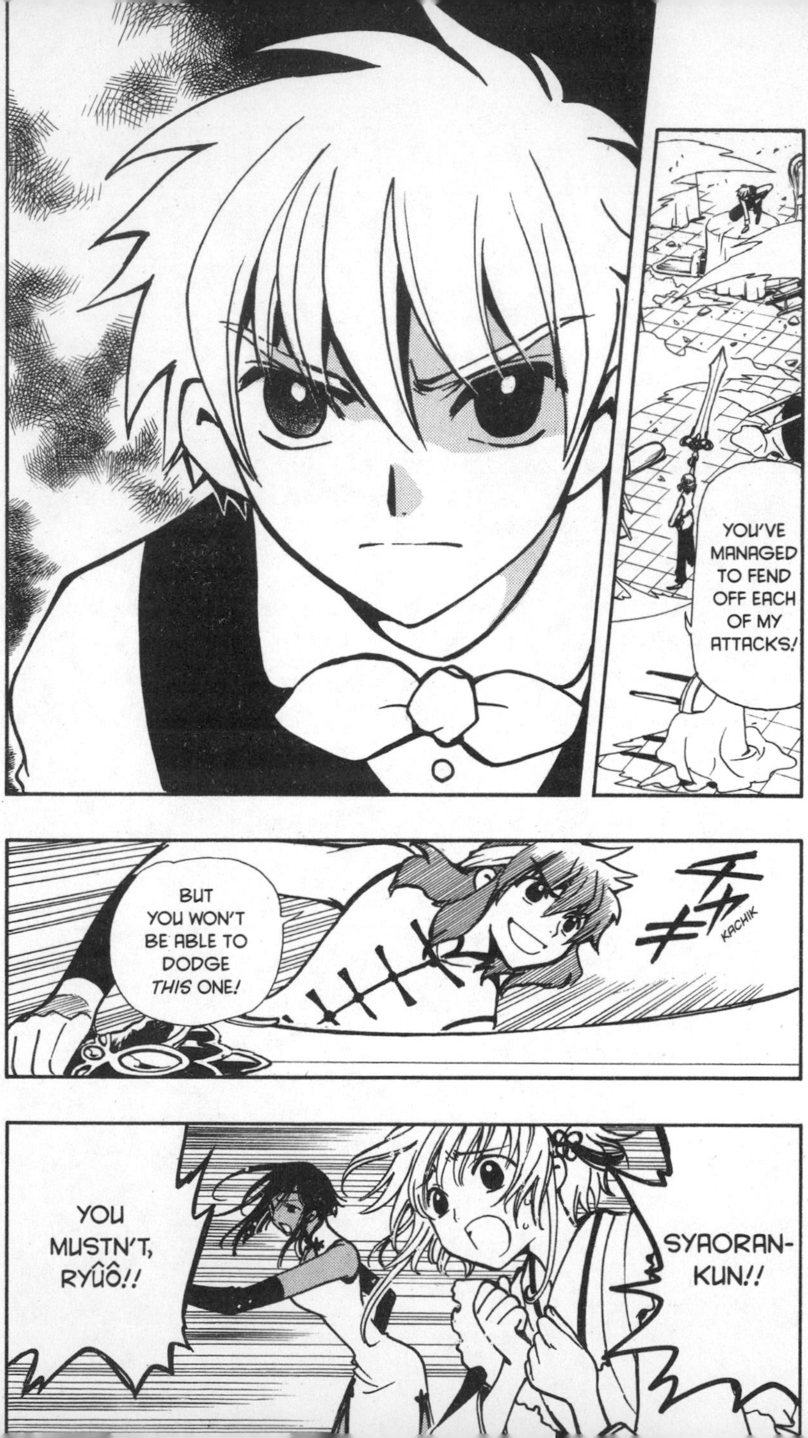
YOU'VE MANAGED TO FEND OFF EACH OF MY ATTACKS!
KACHIK
BUT YOU WON'T BE ABLE TO DODGE *THIS* ONE!
SYAORAN-KUN!!
YOU MUSTN'T, RYÛÔ!!

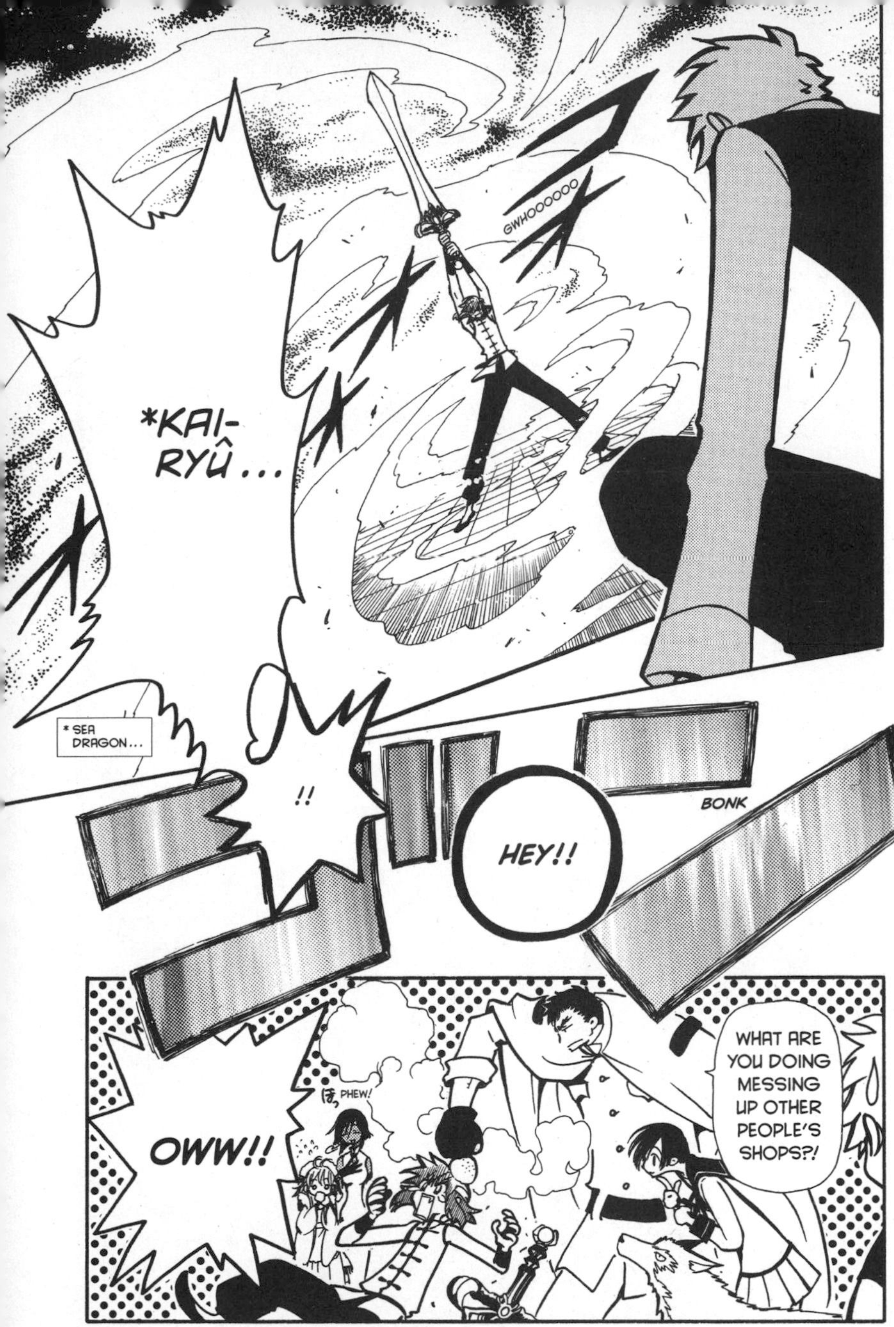
GWHOOOOOO
*KAI-RYÛ...
* SEA DRAGON...
BONK
HEY!!
!!
WHAT ARE YOU DOING MESSING UP OTHER PEOPLE'S SHOPS?!
ほっ PHEW!
OWW!!

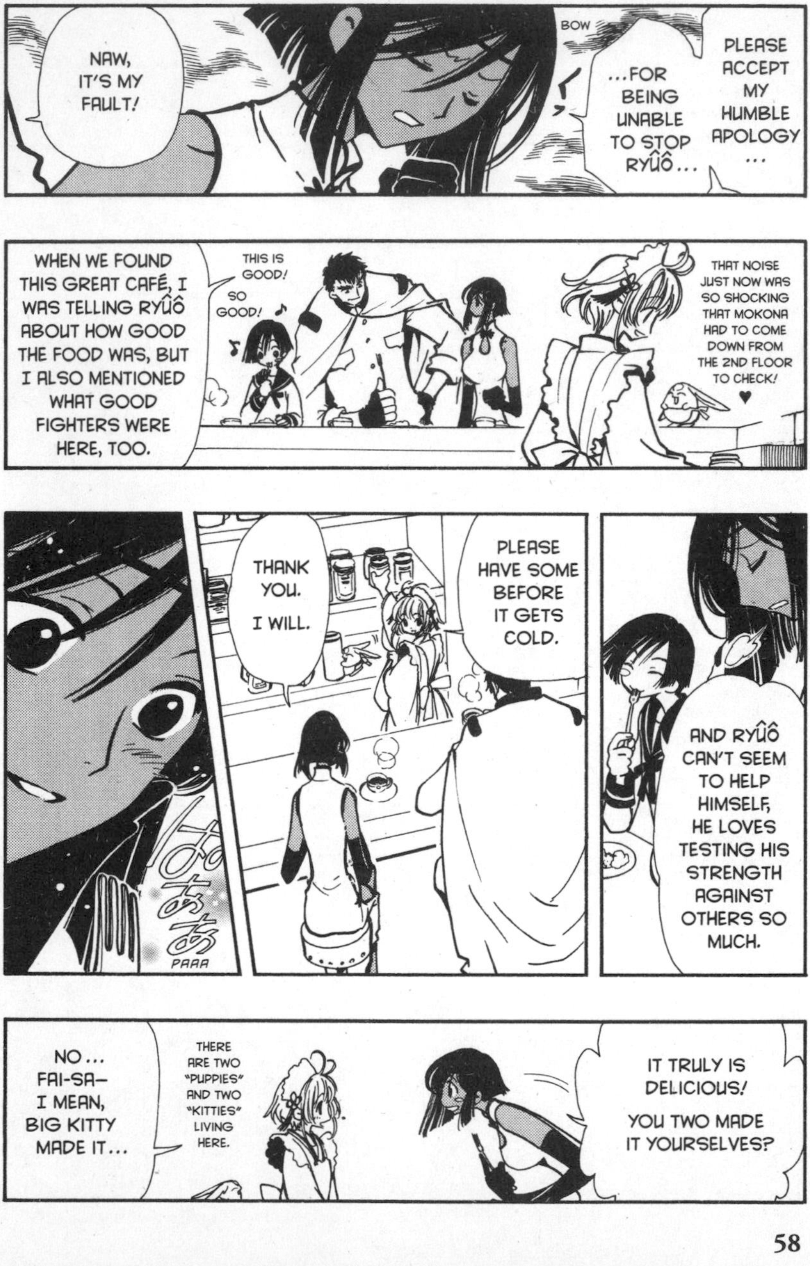
PLEASE ACCEPT MY HUMBLE APOLOGY ...
BOW
...FOR BEING UNABLE TO STOP RYÛÔ...
NAW, IT'S MY FAULT!
THAT NOISE JUST NOW WAS SO SHOCKING THAT MOKONA HAD TO COME DOWN FROM THE 2ND FLOOR TO CHECK! ♥
THIS IS GOOD!
SO GOOD! ♪
WHEN WE FOUND THIS GREAT CAFÉ, I WAS TELLING RYÛÔ ABOUT HOW GOOD THE FOOD WAS, BUT I ALSO MENTIONED WHAT GOOD FIGHTERS WERE HERE, TOO.
AND RYÛÔ CAN'T SEEM TO HELP HIMSELF, HE LOVES TESTING HIS STRENGTH AGAINST OTHERS SO MUCH.
PLEASE HAVE SOME BEFORE IT GETS COLD.
THANK YOU. I WILL.
PAAA
IT TRULY IS DELICIOUS!
YOU TWO MADE IT YOURSELVES?
THERE ARE TWO "PUPPIES" AND TWO "KITTIES" LIVING HERE.
NO... FAI-SA— I MEAN, BIG KITTY MADE IT...

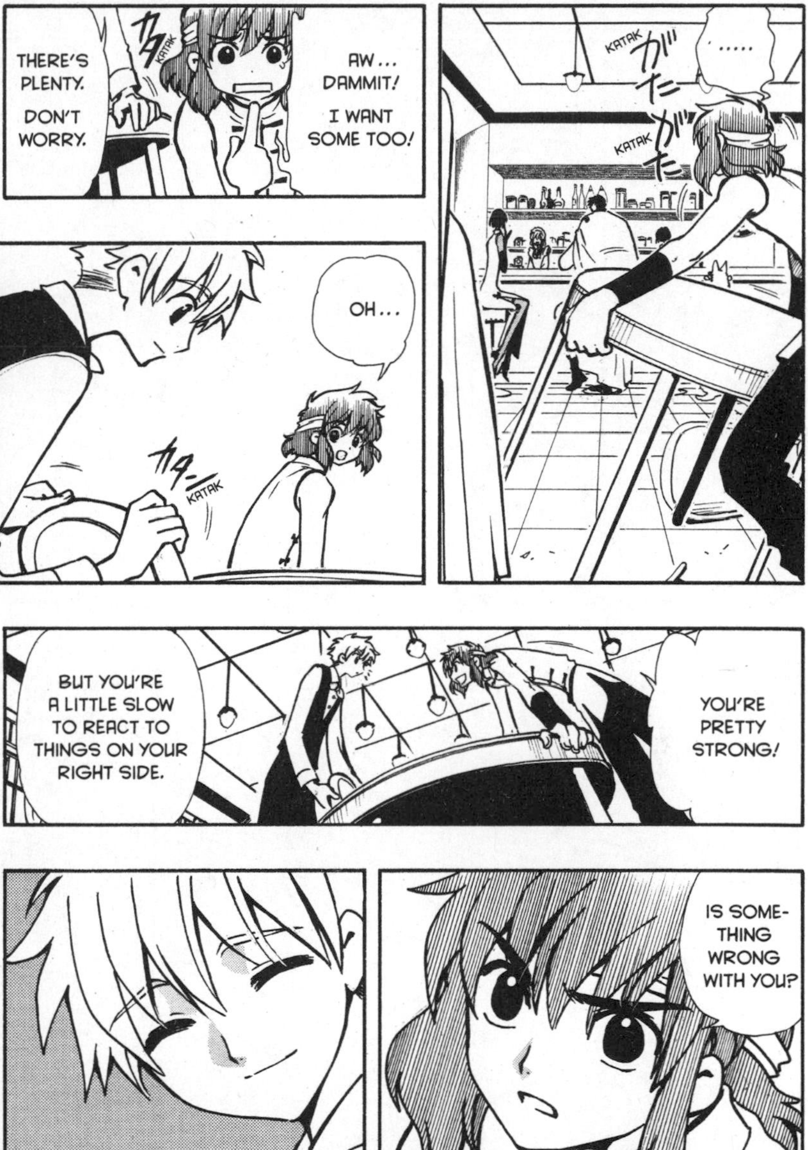
KATAK
KATAK
'.....
AW... DAMMIT! I WANT SOME TOO!
KATAK
THERE'S PLENTY. DON'T WORRY.
OH...
KATAK
YOU'RE PRETTY STRONG!
BUT YOU'RE A LITTLE SLOW TO REACT TO THINGS ON YOUR RIGHT SIDE.
IS SOME-THING WRONG WITH YOU?

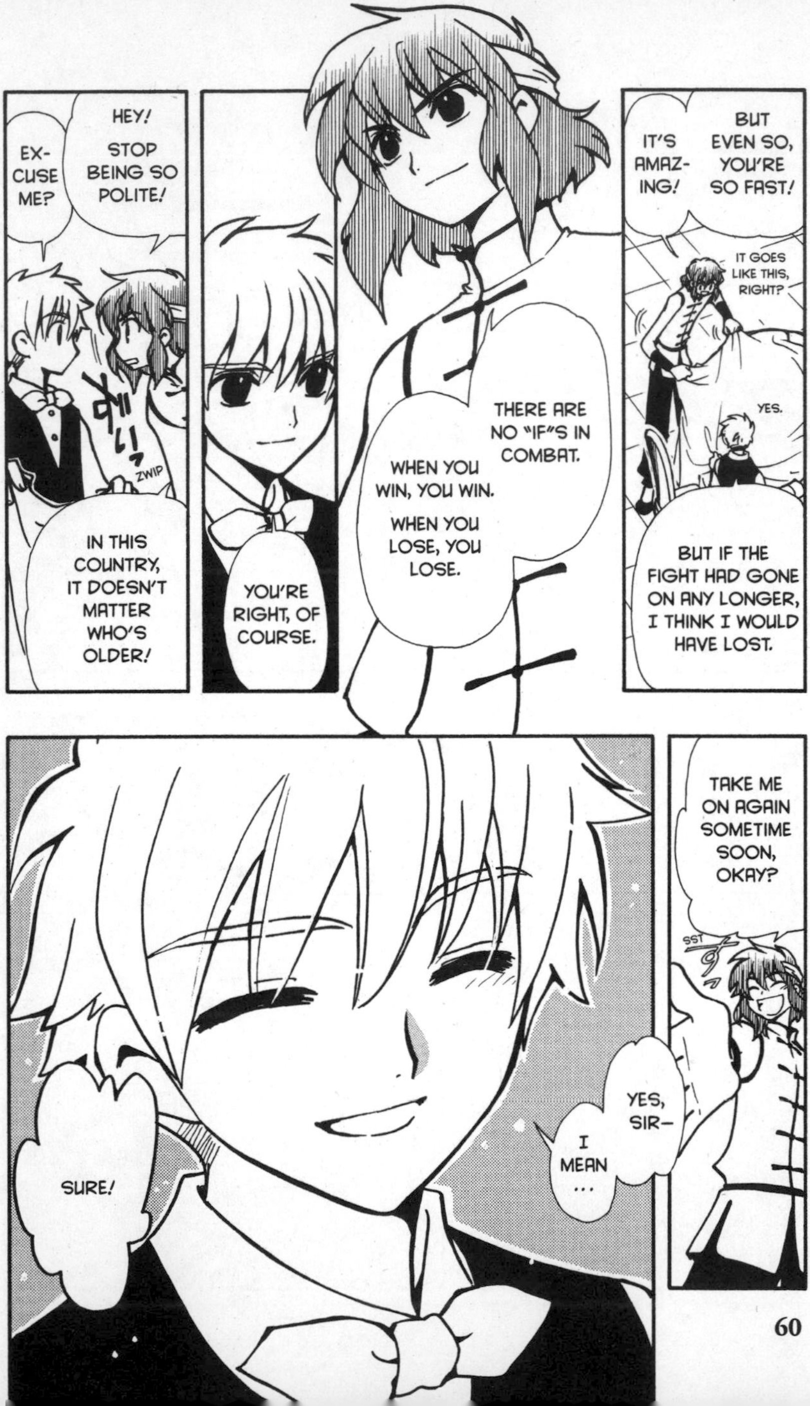
BUT EVEN SO, YOU'RE SO FAST!
IT'S AMAZ-ING!
IT GOES LIKE THIS, RIGHT?
YES.
BUT IF THE FIGHT HAD GONE ON ANY LONGER, I THINK I WOULD HAVE LOST.
THERE ARE NO "IF"S IN COMBAT.
WHEN YOU WIN, YOU WIN.
WHEN YOU LOSE, YOU LOSE.
YOU'RE RIGHT, OF COURSE.
HEY!
STOP BEING SO POLITE!
EX-CUSE ME?
ZWIP
IN THIS COUNTRY, IT DOESN'T MATTER WHO'S OLDER!
TAKE ME ON AGAIN SOMETIME SOON, OKAY?
SST
YES, SIR—
I MEAN ...
SURE!

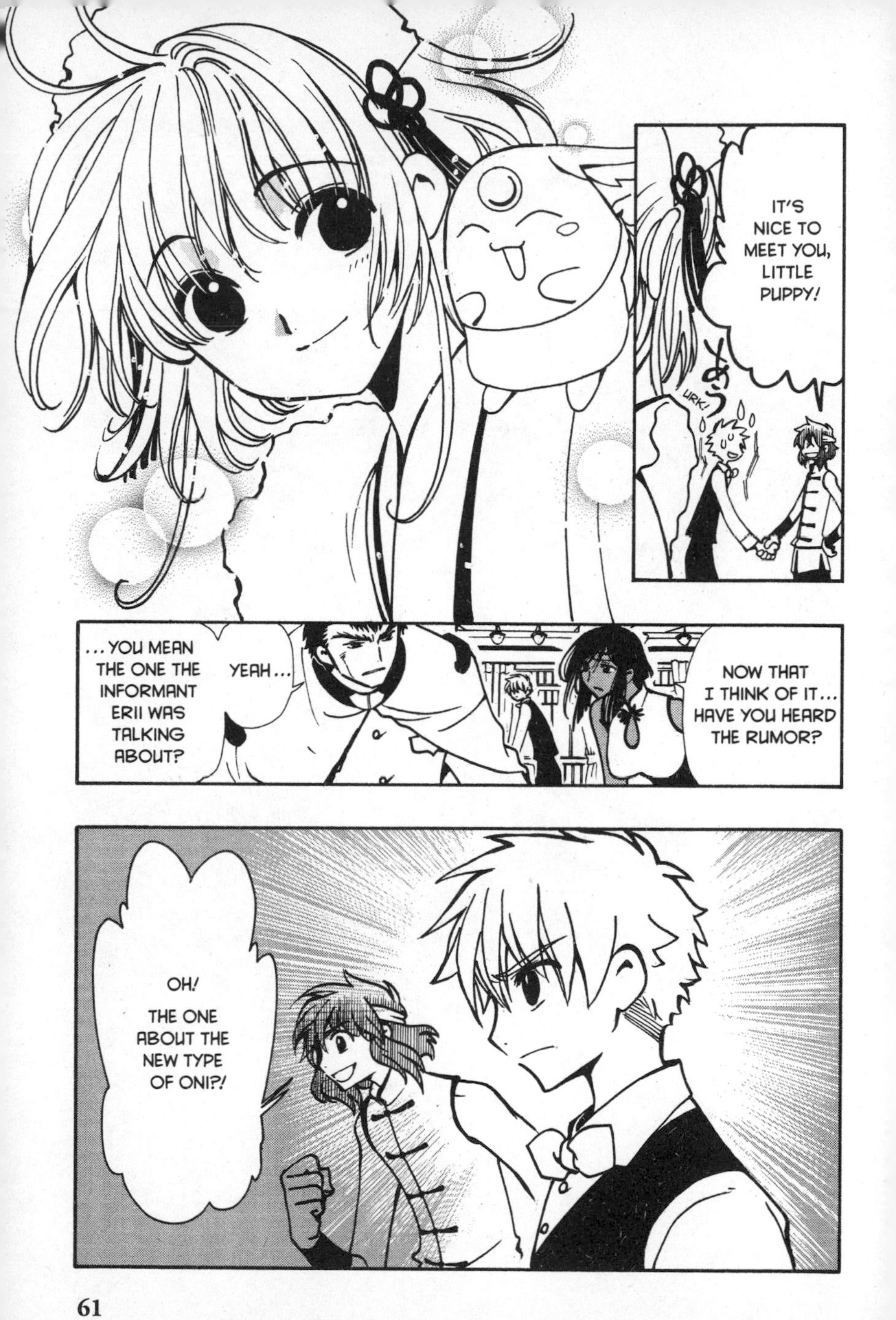
IT'S NICE TO MEET YOU, LITTLE PUPPY!
あう
URK!
NOW THAT I THINK OF IT... HAVE YOU HEARD THE RUMOR?
YEAH...
...YOU MEAN THE ONE THE INFORMANT ERII WAS TALKING ABOUT?
OH! THE ONE ABOUT THE NEW TYPE OF ONI?!

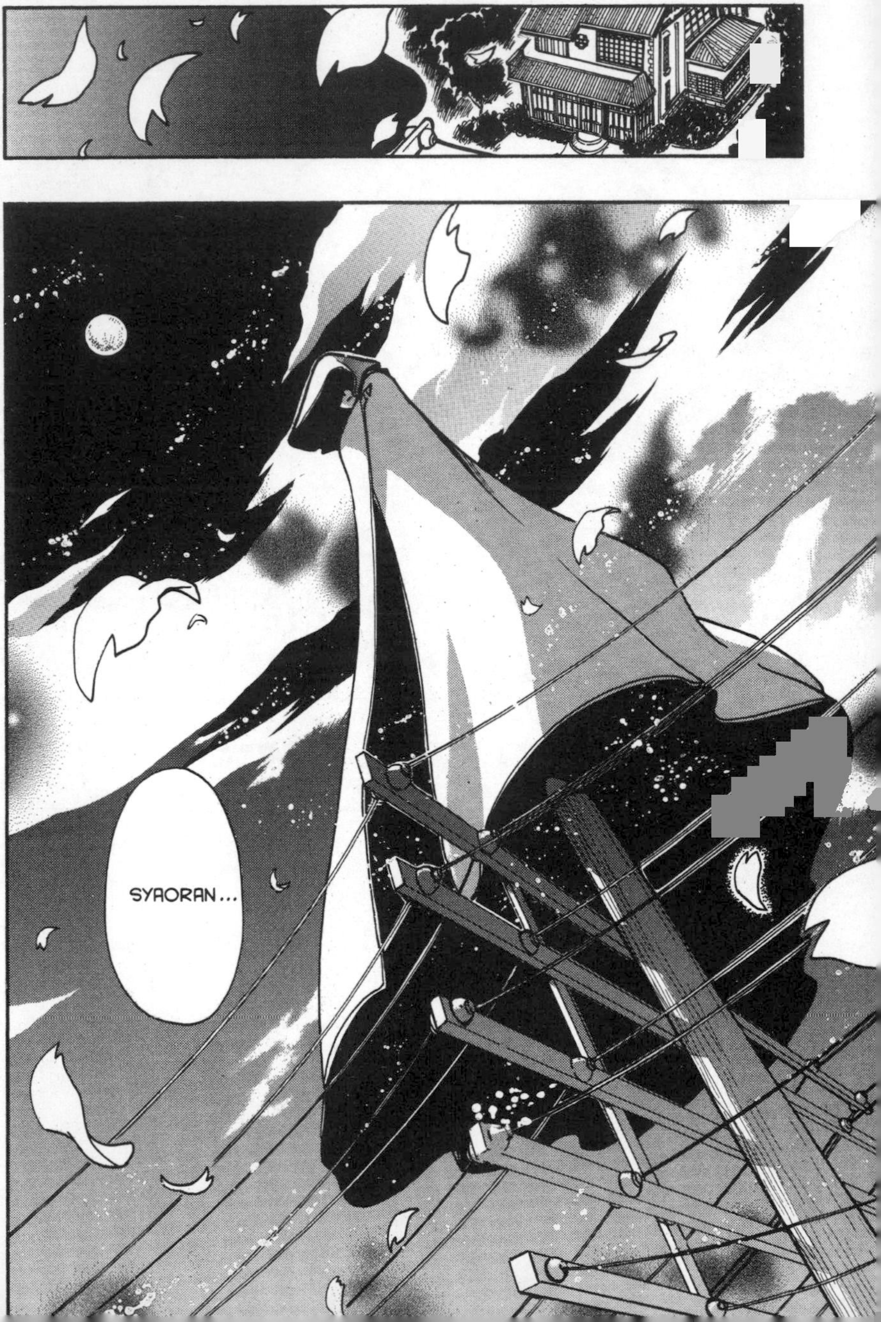
SYAORAN...

Chapitre.38
The Shape of Happiness

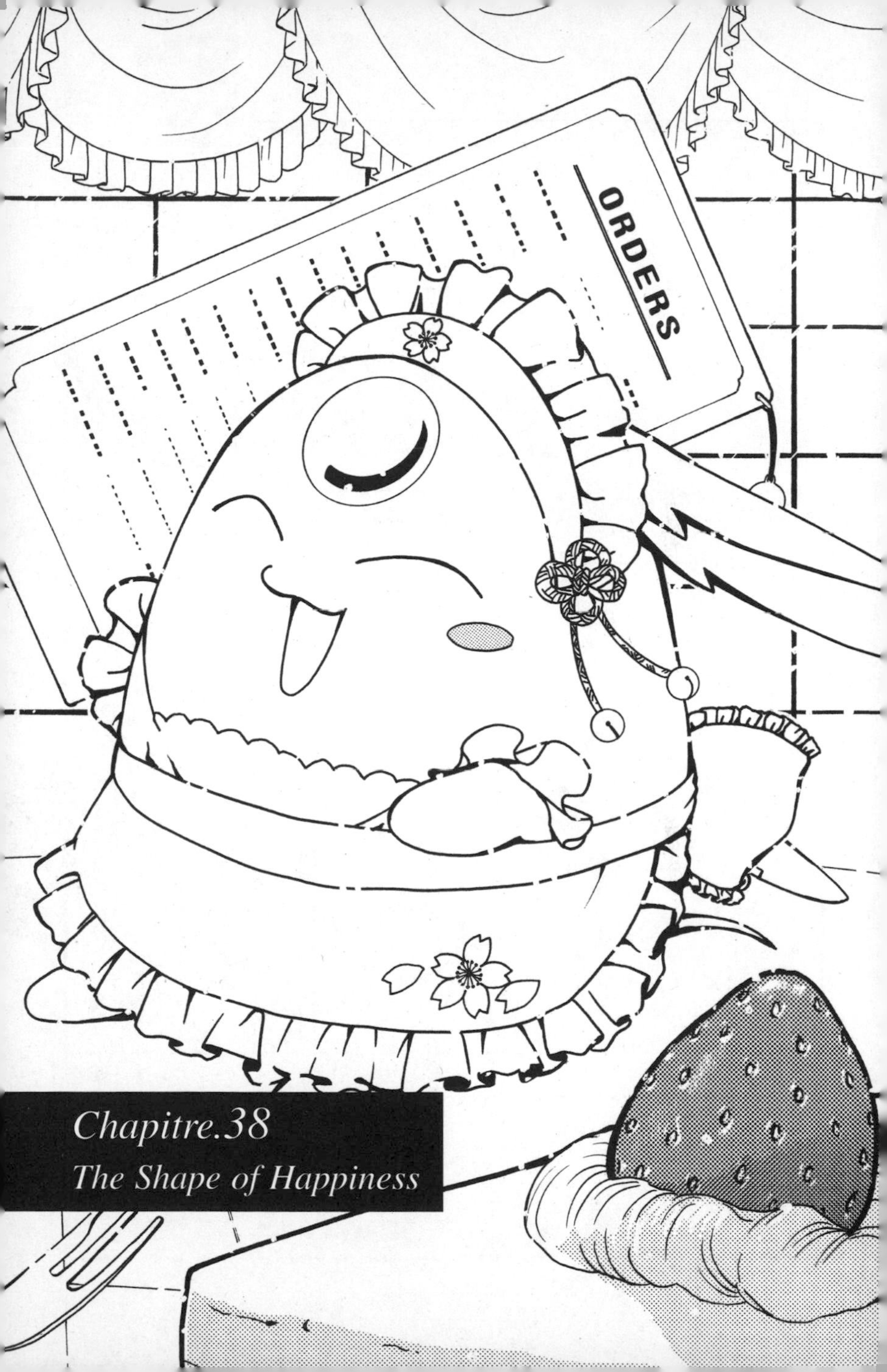
ORDERS

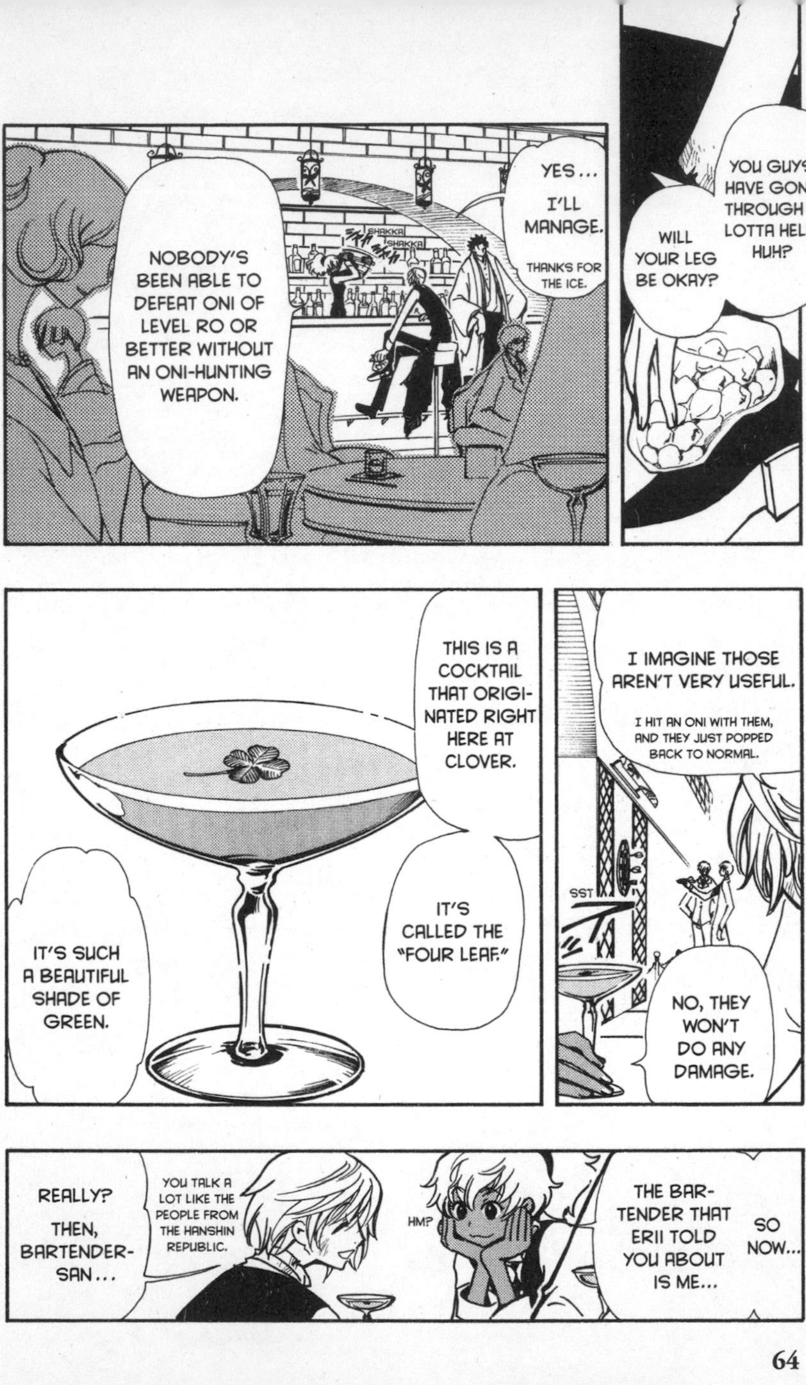
YOU GUYS HAVE GONE THROUGH A LOTTA HELL, HUH?
WILL YOUR LEG BE OKAY?
YES... I'LL MANAGE.
THANKS FOR THE ICE.
SHAKKA
SHAKKA
NOBODY'S BEEN ABLE TO DEFEAT ONI OF LEVEL RO OR BETTER WITHOUT AN ONI-HUNTING WEAPON.
I IMAGINE THOSE AREN'T VERY USEFUL.
I HIT AN ONI WITH THEM, AND THEY JUST POPPED BACK TO NORMAL.
SST
NO, THEY WON'T DO ANY DAMAGE.
THIS IS A COCKTAIL THAT ORIGINATED RIGHT HERE AT CLOVER.
IT'S CALLED THE "FOUR LEAF."
IT'S SUCH A BEAUTIFUL SHADE OF GREEN.
SO NOW...
THE BARTENDER THAT ERII TOLD YOU ABOUT IS ME...
HM?
YOU TALK A LOT LIKE THE PEOPLE FROM THE HANSHIN REPUBLIC.
REALLY? THEN, BARTENDER-SAN...

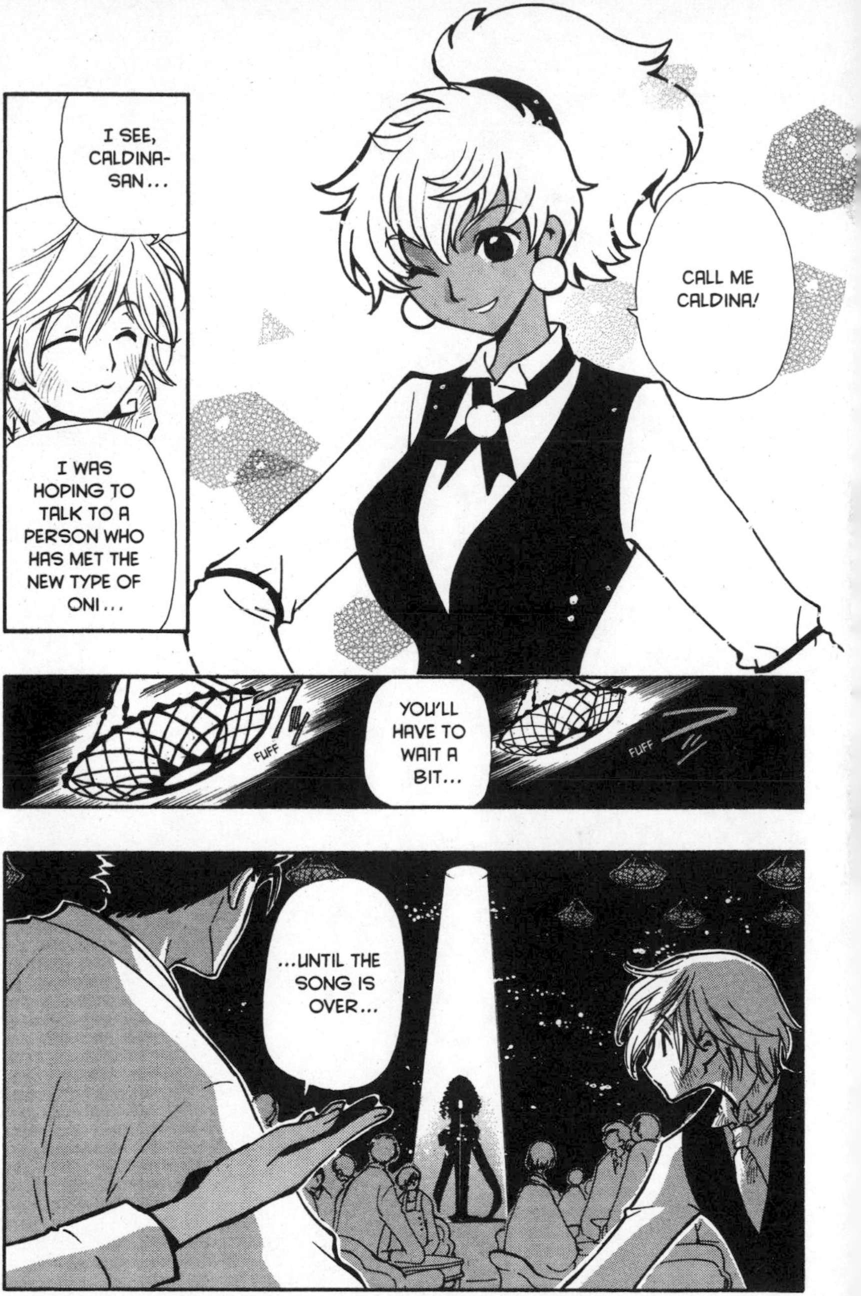
CALL ME CALDINA!
I SEE, CALDINA-SAN...
I WAS HOPING TO TALK TO A PERSON WHO HAS MET THE NEW TYPE OF ONI...
FUFF
YOU'LL HAVE TO WAIT A BIT...
FUFF
...UNTIL THE SONG IS OVER...

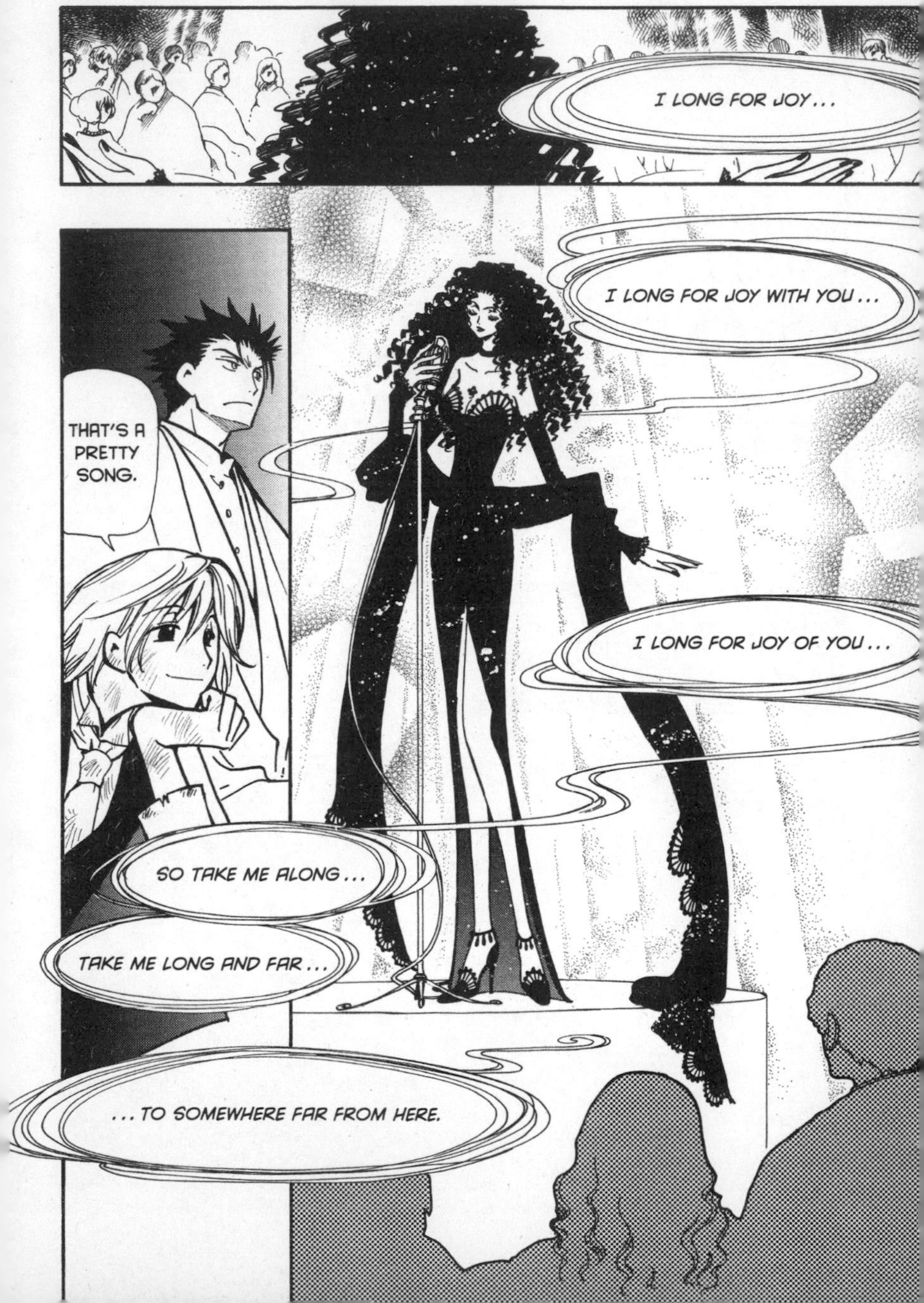
I LONG FOR JOY...
I LONG FOR JOY WITH YOU...
I LONG FOR JOY OF YOU...
SO TAKE ME ALONG...
TAKE ME LONG AND FAR...
...TO SOMEWHERE FAR FROM HERE.
THAT'S A PRETTY SONG.

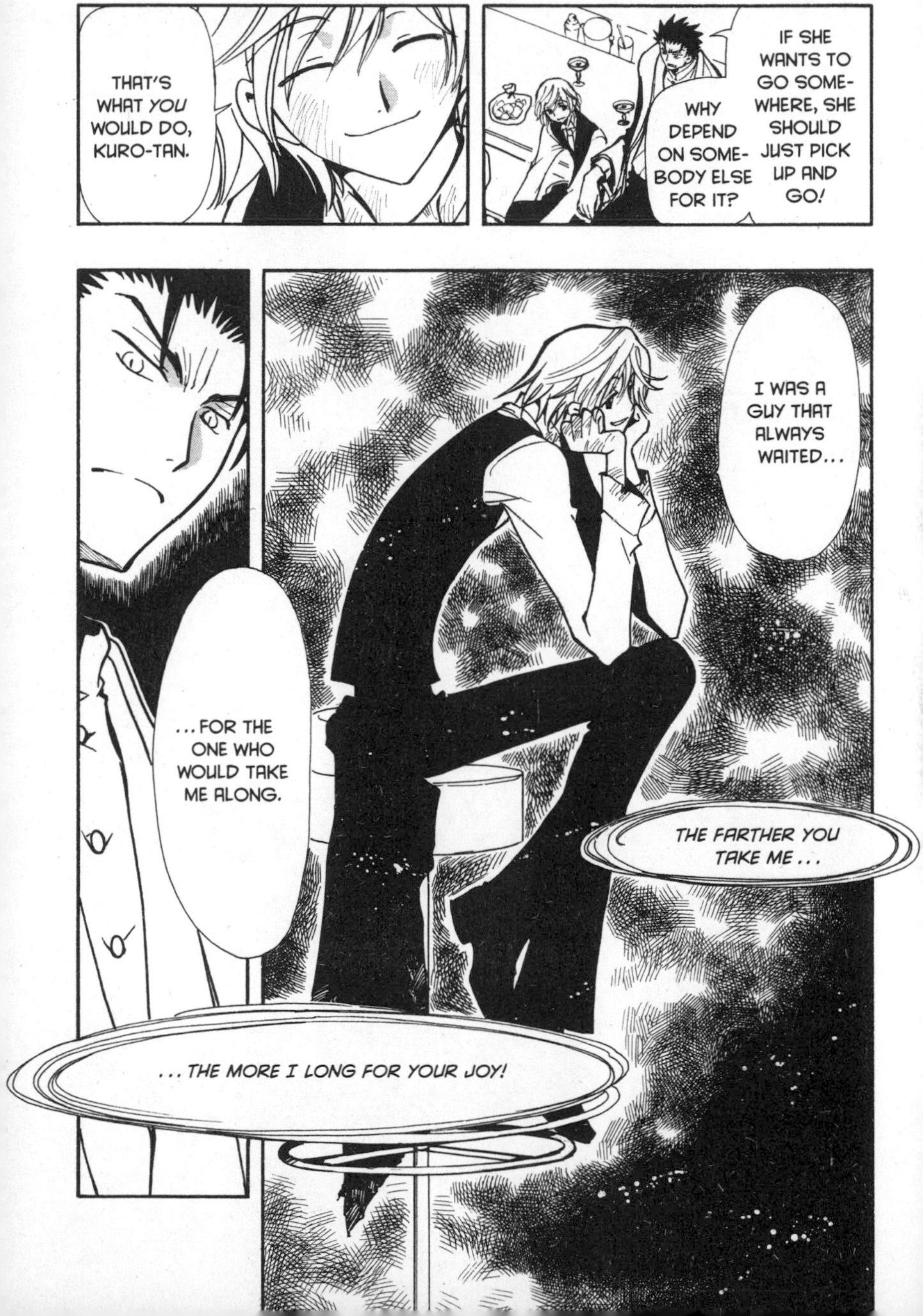
IF SHE WANTS TO GO SOME-WHERE, SHE SHOULD JUST PICK UP AND GO!
WHY DEPEND ON SOME-BODY ELSE FOR IT?
THAT'S WHAT *YOU* WOULD DO, KURO-TAN.
I WAS A GUY THAT ALWAYS WAITED...
...FOR THE ONE WHO WOULD TAKE ME ALONG.
THE FARTHER YOU TAKE ME...
...THE MORE I LONG FOR YOUR JOY!

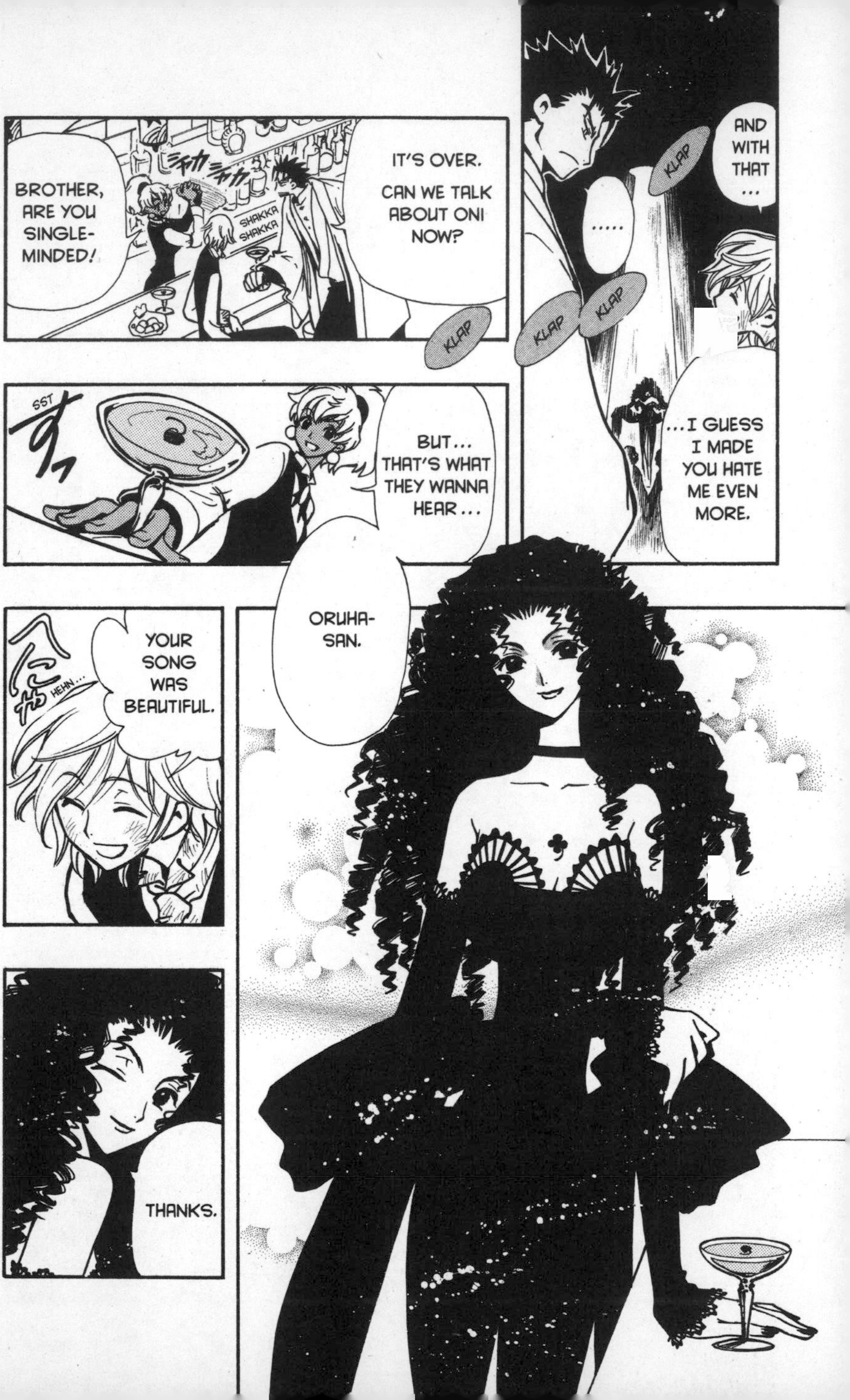
AND WITH THAT ...
.....
KLAP
KLAP
KLAP
KLAP
...I GUESS I MADE YOU HATE ME EVEN MORE.
IT'S OVER.
CAN WE TALK ABOUT ONI NOW?
SHAKKA SHAKKA
BROTHER, ARE YOU SINGLE-MINDED!
BUT... THAT'S WHAT THEY WANNA HEAR...
SST
ORUHA-SAN.
YOUR SONG WAS BEAUTIFUL.
HEHN...
THANKS.

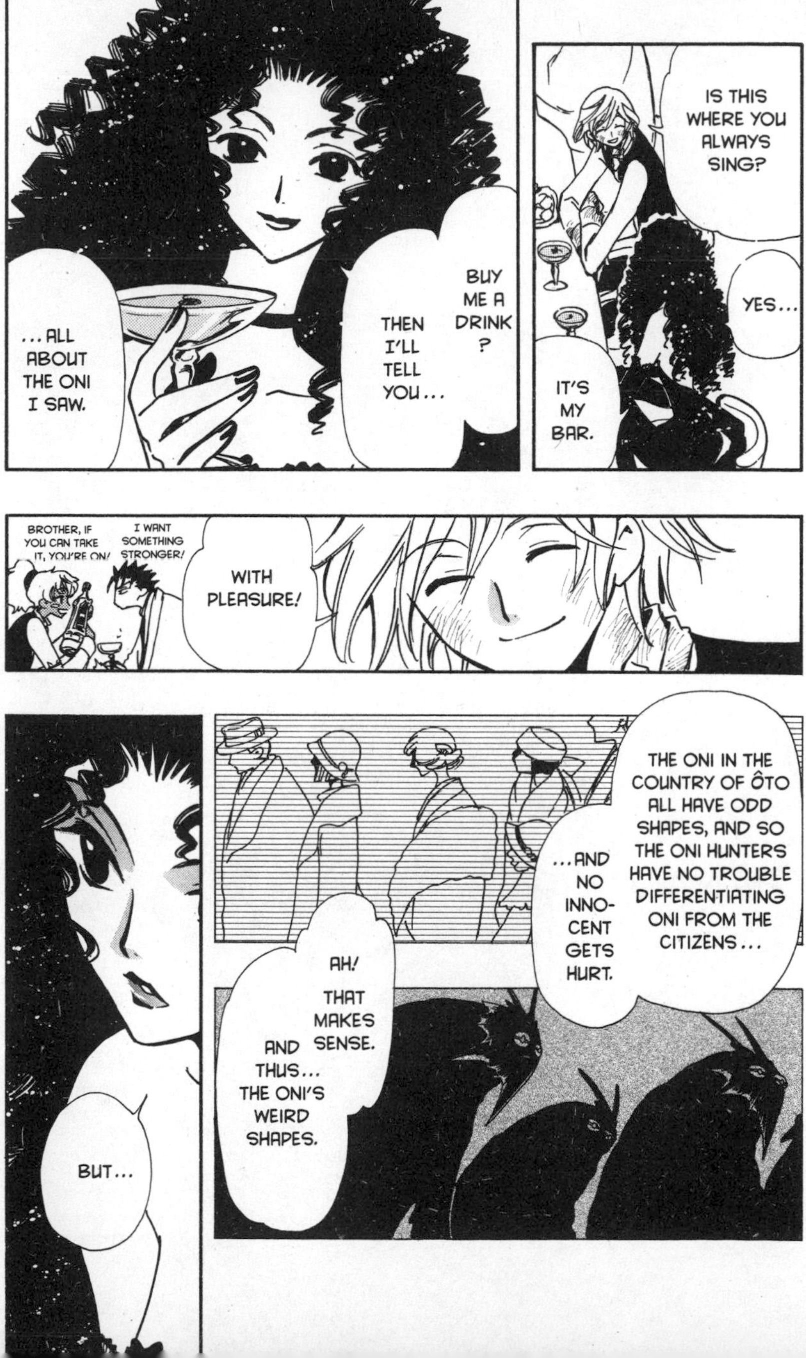
IS THIS WHERE YOU ALWAYS SING?
YES...
IT'S MY BAR.
BUY ME A DRINK?
THEN I'LL TELL YOU...
...ALL ABOUT THE ONI I SAW.
WITH PLEASURE!
I WANT SOMETHING STRONGER!
BROTHER, IF YOU CAN TAKE IT, YOU'RE ON!
THE ONI IN THE COUNTRY OF ÔTO ALL HAVE ODD SHAPES, AND SO THE ONI HUNTERS HAVE NO TROUBLE DIFFERENTIATING ONI FROM THE CITIZENS...
...AND NO INNO-CENT GETS HURT.
AH! THAT MAKES SENSE.
AND THUS... THE ONI'S WEIRD SHAPES.
BUT...

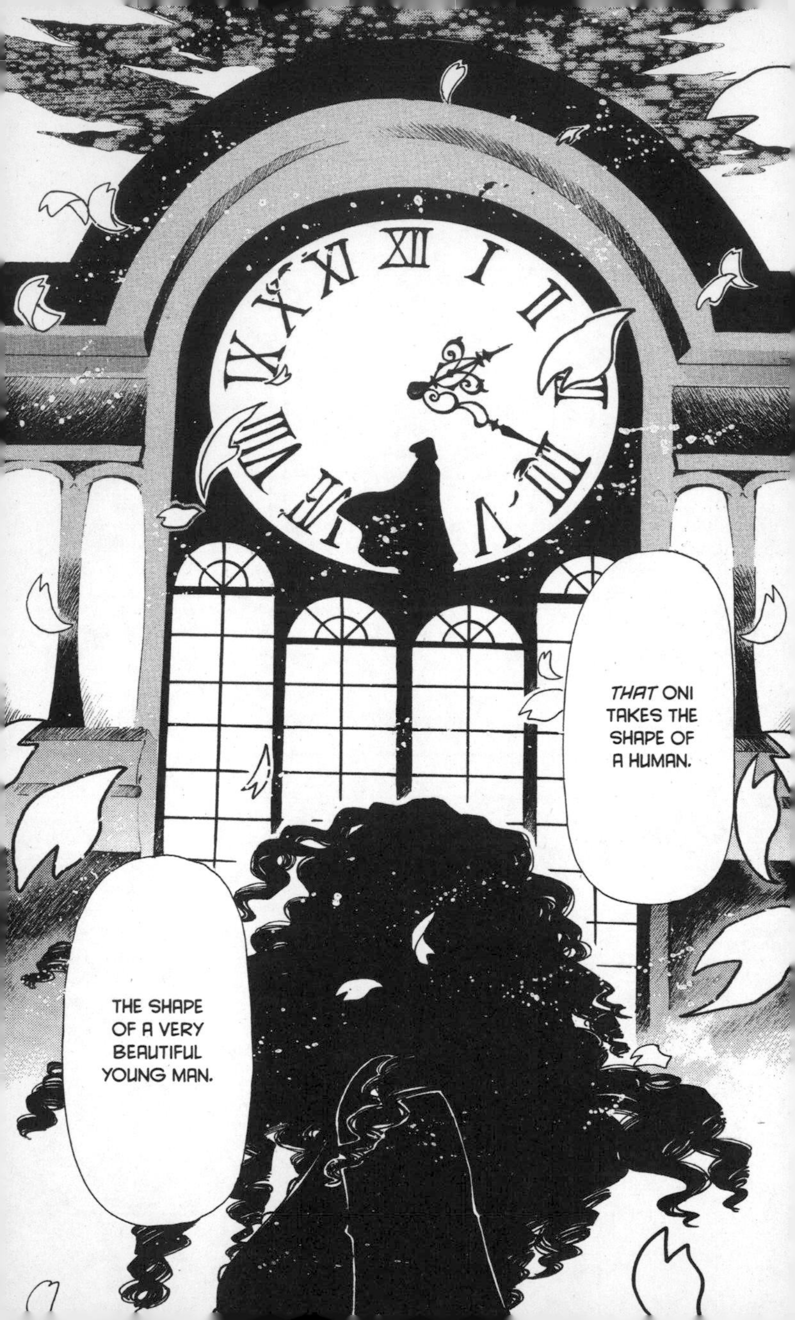
THAT ONI TAKES THE SHAPE OF A HUMAN.
THE SHAPE OF A VERY BEAUTIFUL YOUNG MAN.

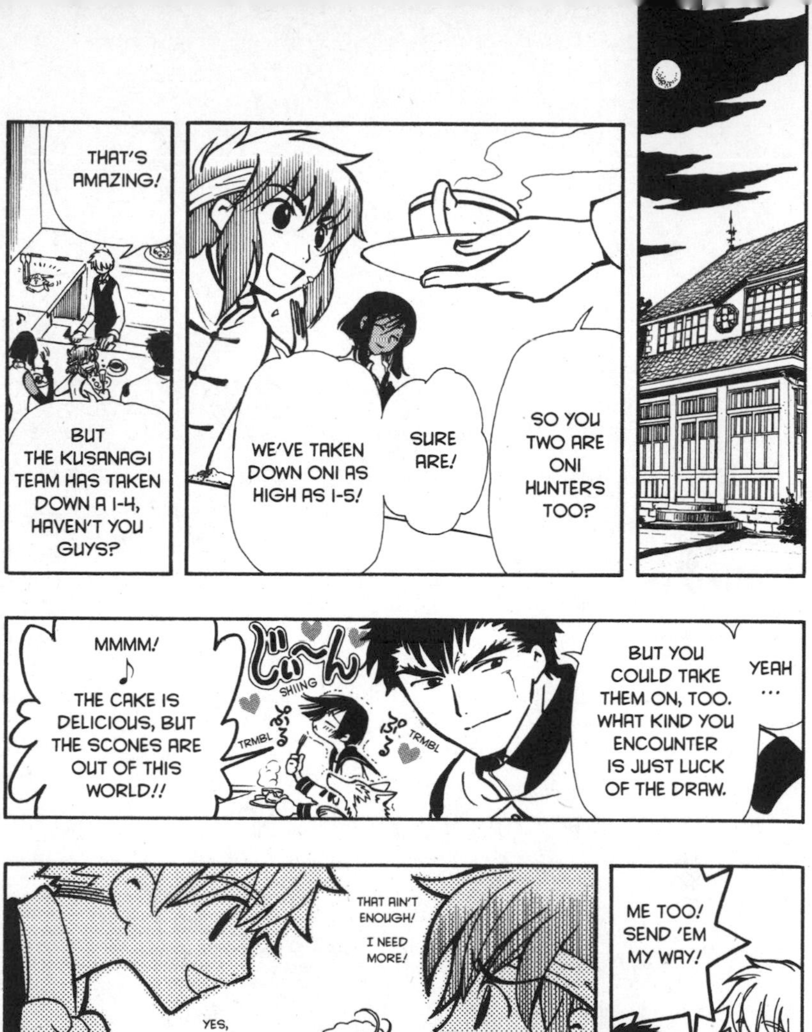
SO YOU TWO ARE ONI HUNTERS TOO?
SURE ARE!
WE'VE TAKEN DOWN ONI AS HIGH AS 1-5!
THAT'S AMAZING!
BUT THE KUSANAGI TEAM HAS TAKEN DOWN A 1-4, HAVEN'T YOU GUYS?
YEAH ...
BUT YOU COULD TAKE THEM ON, TOO. WHAT KIND YOU ENCOUNTER IS JUST LUCK OF THE DRAW.
じぃ~ん
SHIING
TRMBL
TRMBL
MMMM! ♪ THE CAKE IS DELICIOUS, BUT THE SCONES ARE OUT OF THIS WORLD!!
ME TOO! SEND 'EM MY WAY!
OKAY.
THAT AIN'T ENOUGH!
I NEED MORE!
YES, SIR.
MOKONA HELPED MAKE THEM TOO! ♥

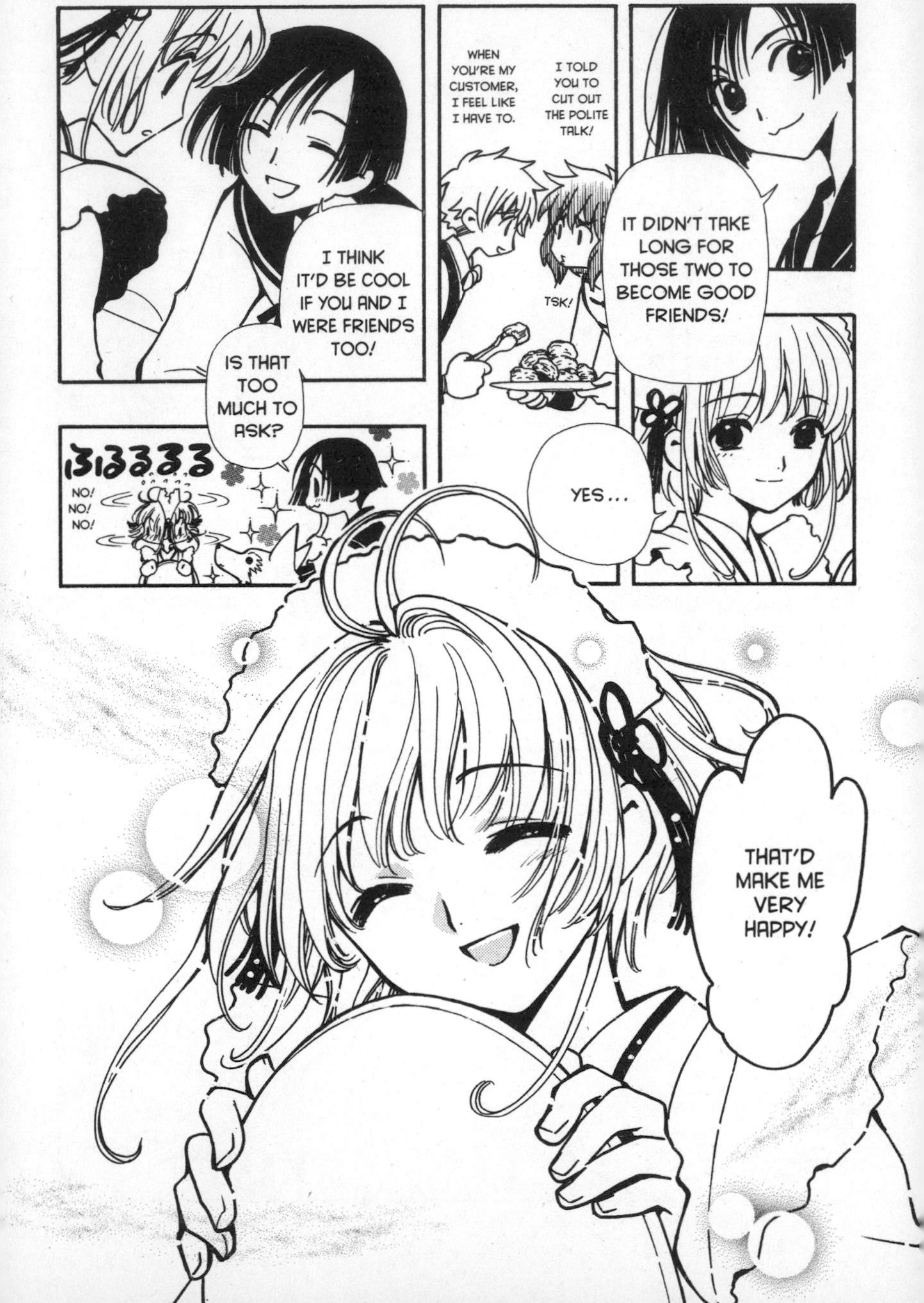
IT DIDN'T TAKE LONG FOR THOSE TWO TO BECOME GOOD FRIENDS!
I TOLD YOU TO CUT OUT THE POLITE TALK!
WHEN YOU'RE MY CUSTOMER, I FEEL LIKE I HAVE TO.
TSK!
I THINK IT'D BE COOL IF YOU AND I WERE FRIENDS TOO!
IS THAT TOO MUCH TO ASK?
ふるるるる
NO! NO! NO!
YES...
THAT'D MAKE ME VERY HAPPY!

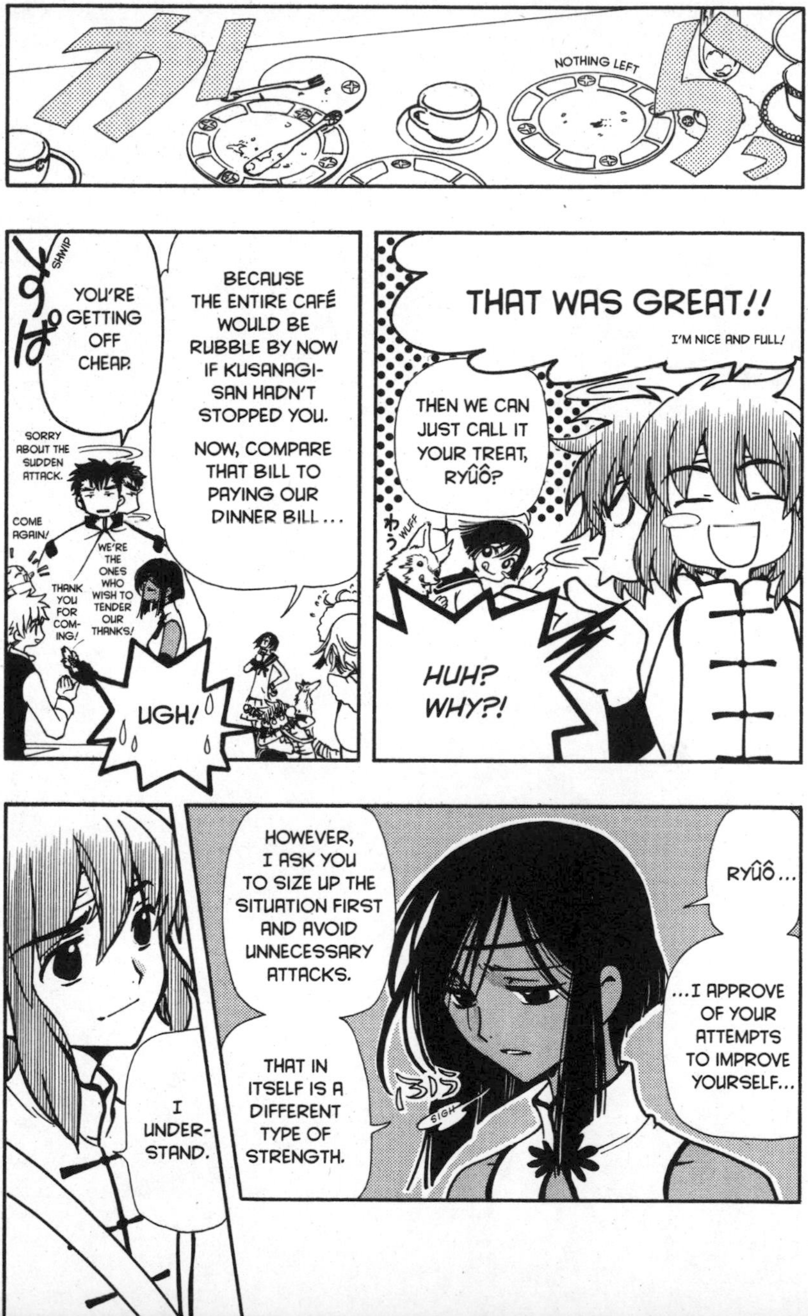
NOTHING LEFT
THAT WAS GREAT!!
I'M NICE AND FULL!
THEN WE CAN JUST CALL IT YOUR TREAT, RYÛÔ?
WUFF
HUH? WHY?!
SHWIP
YOU'RE GETTING OFF CHEAP.
BECAUSE THE ENTIRE CAFÉ WOULD BE RUBBLE BY NOW IF KUSANAGI-SAN HADN'T STOPPED YOU.
NOW, COMPARE THAT BILL TO PAYING OUR DINNER BILL...
SORRY ABOUT THE SUDDEN ATTACK.
COME AGAIN!
WE'RE THE ONES WHO WISH TO TENDER OUR THANKS!
THANK YOU FOR COMING!
UGH!
RYÛÔ...
...I APPROVE OF YOUR ATTEMPTS TO IMPROVE YOURSELF...
HOWEVER, I ASK YOU TO SIZE UP THE SITUATION FIRST AND AVOID UNNECESSARY ATTACKS.
THAT IN ITSELF IS A DIFFERENT TYPE OF STRENGTH.
SIGH
I UNDERSTAND.

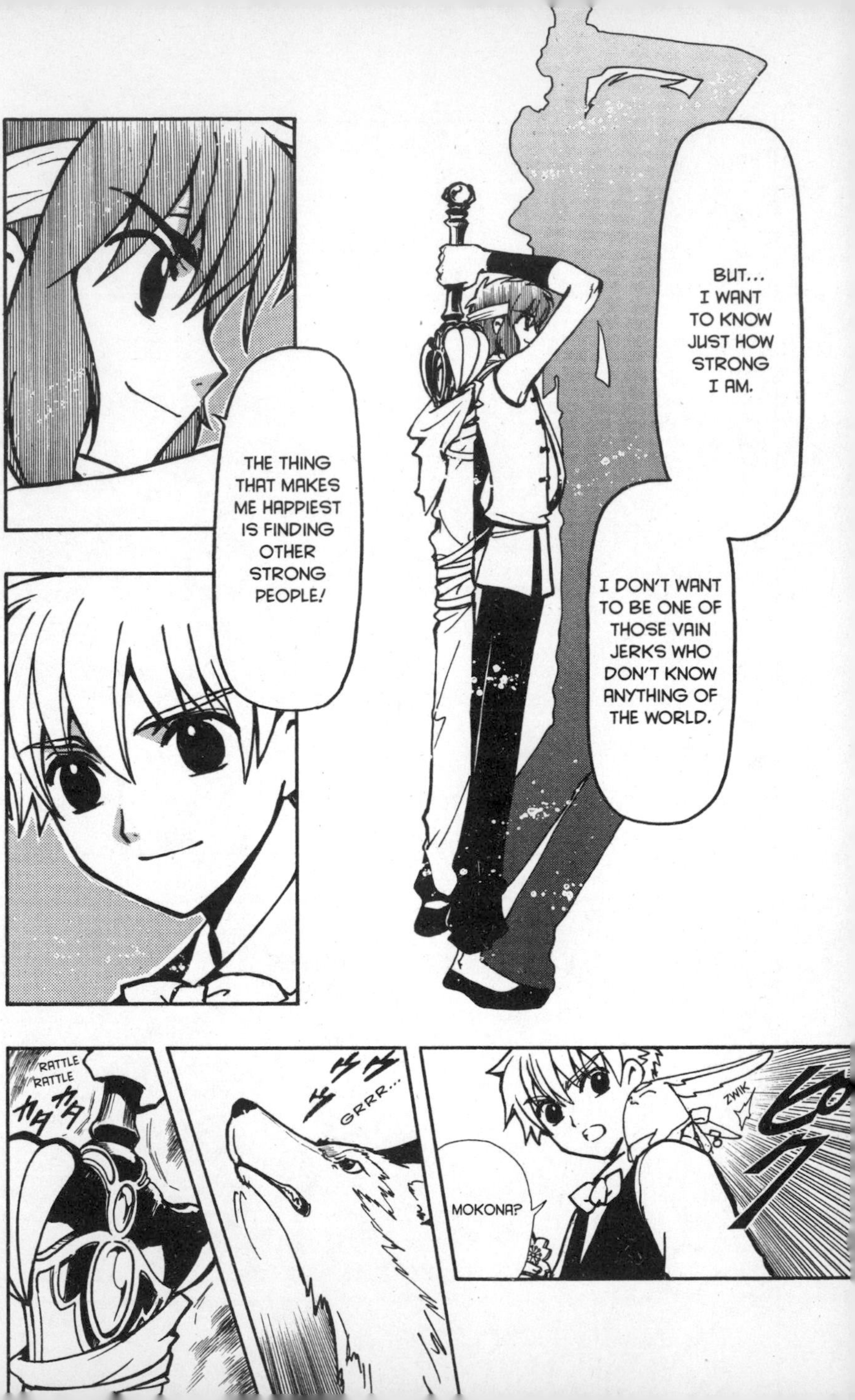
BUT... I WANT TO KNOW JUST HOW STRONG I AM.
I DON'T WANT TO BE ONE OF THOSE VAIN JERKS WHO DON'T KNOW ANYTHING OF THE WORLD.
THE THING THAT MAKES ME HAPPIEST IS FINDING OTHER STRONG PEOPLE!
ZWIK
MOKONA?
GRRR...
RATTLE RATTLE

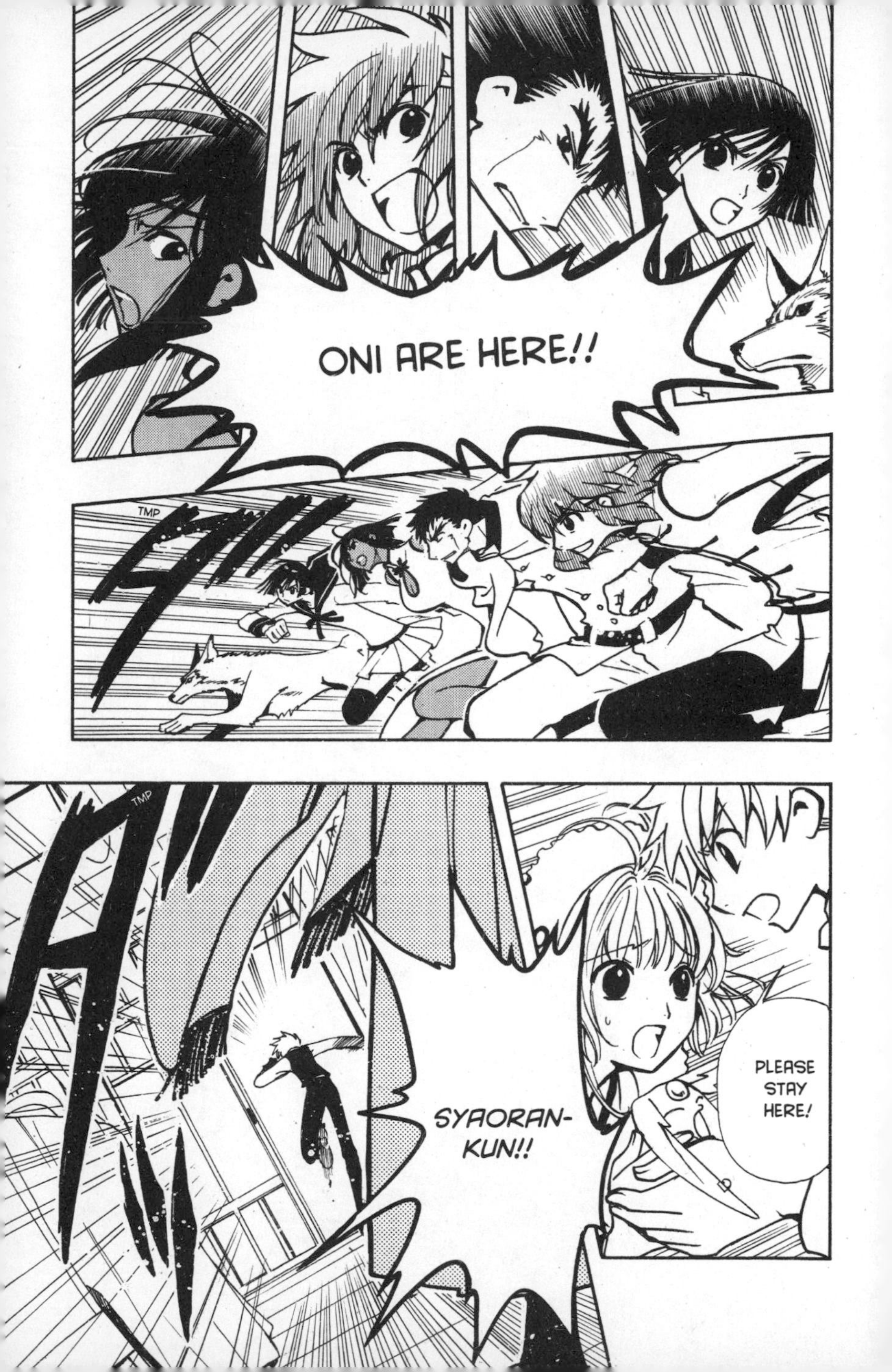
ONI ARE HERE!!
TMP
PLEASE STAY HERE!
SYAORAN-KUN!!
TMP

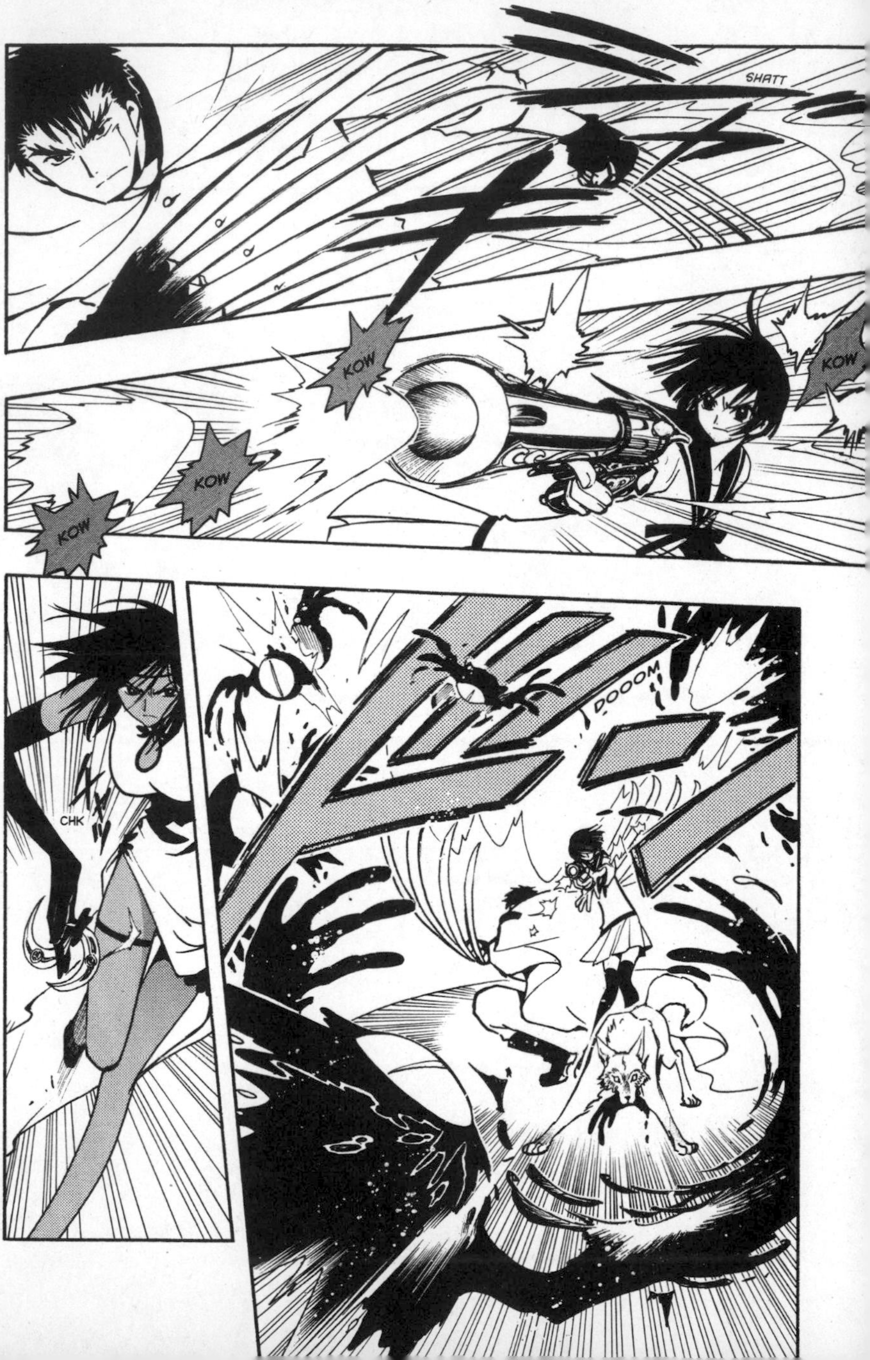
SHATT
KOW
KOW
KOW
KOW
DOOOM
CHK

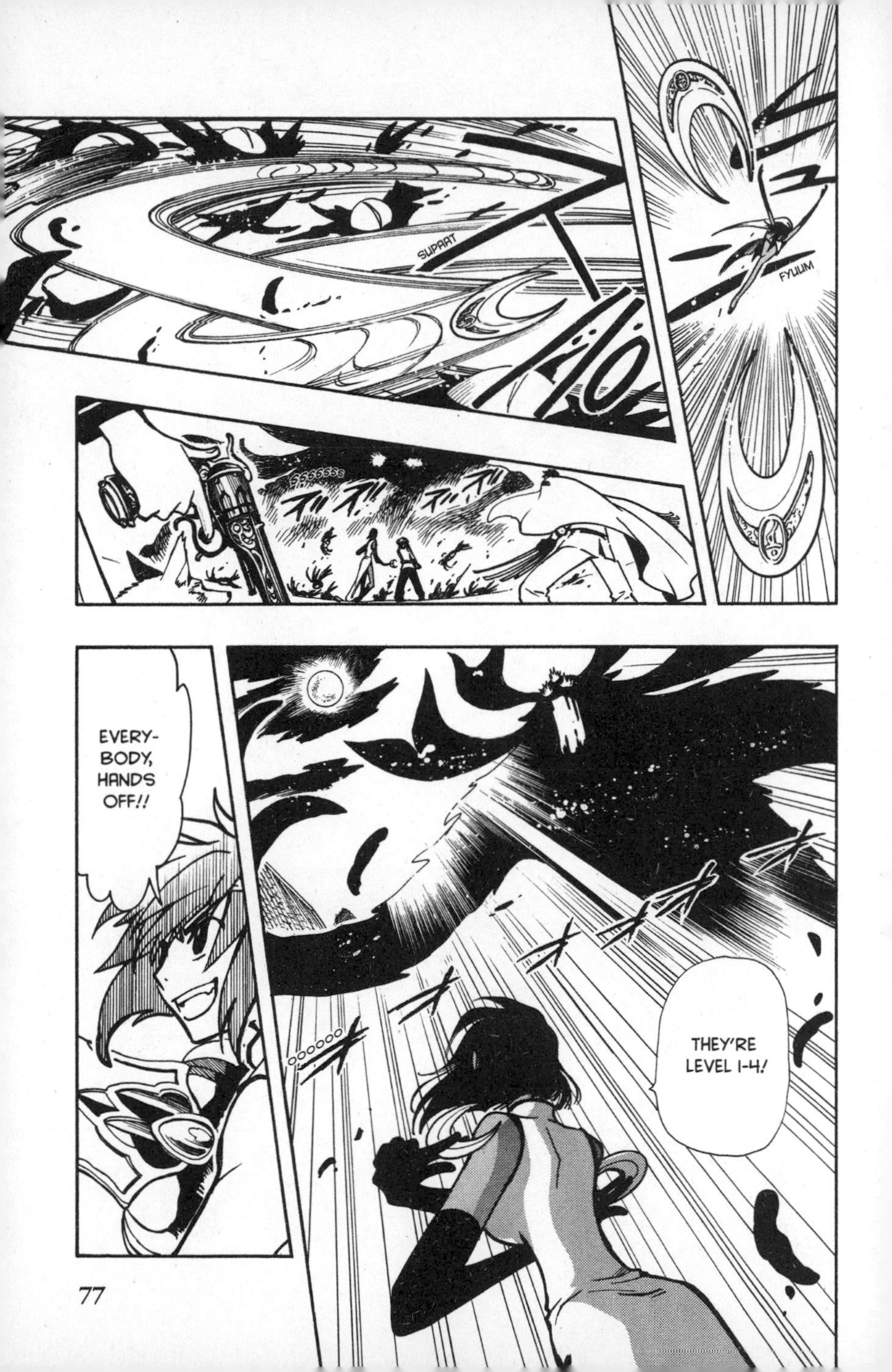
FYUUM
SUPAAT
SSSSSSS
THEY'RE LEVEL 1-4!
OOOOOO
EVERY-BODY, HANDS OFF!!

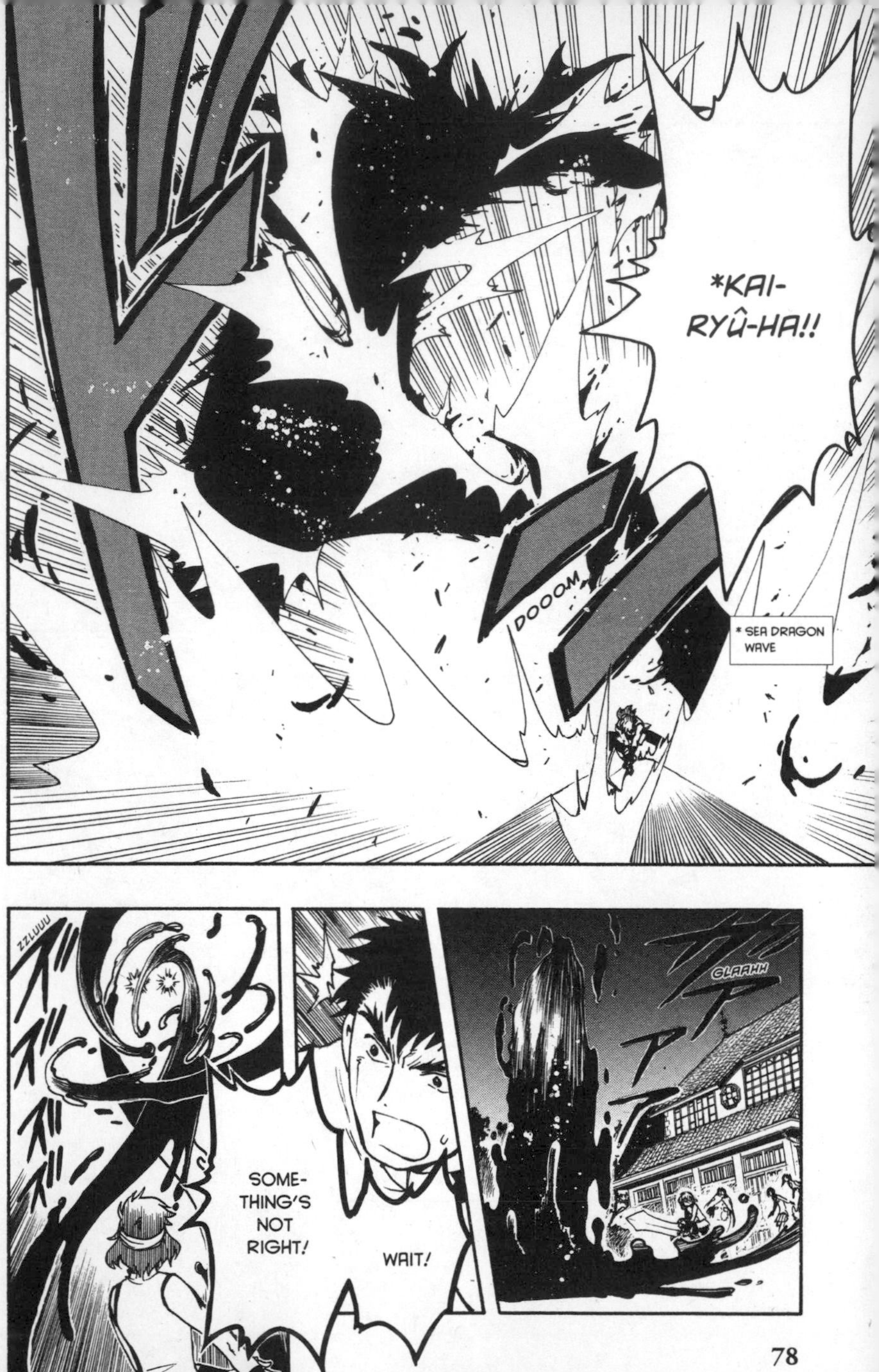
*KAI-RYÛ-HA!!
DOOOM
* SEA DRAGON WAVE
GLAAHH
WAIT!
SOME-THING'S NOT RIGHT!
ZZLUUU

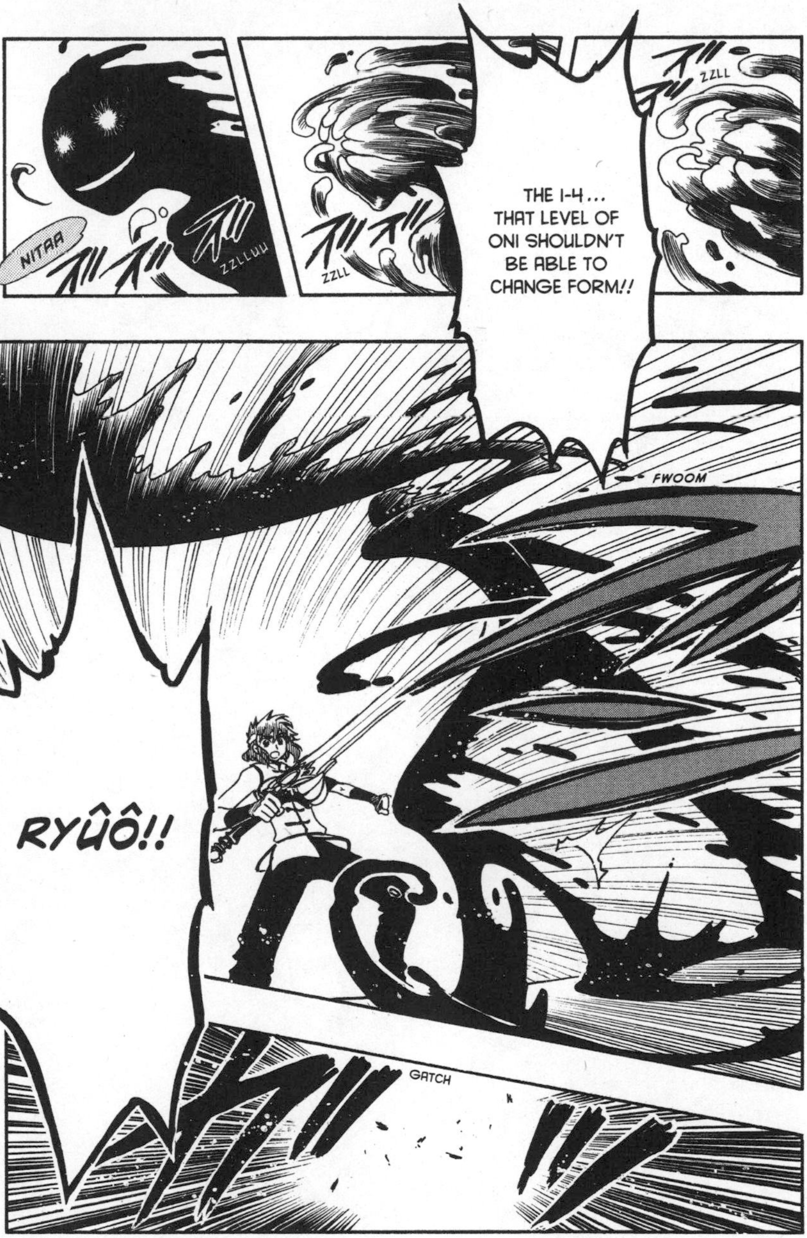
ZZLL
THE 1-4...
THAT LEVEL OF
ONI SHOULDN'T
BE ABLE TO
CHANGE FORM!!
ZZLL
NITAA
ZZLLUU
FWOOM
RYÛÔ!!
GATCH

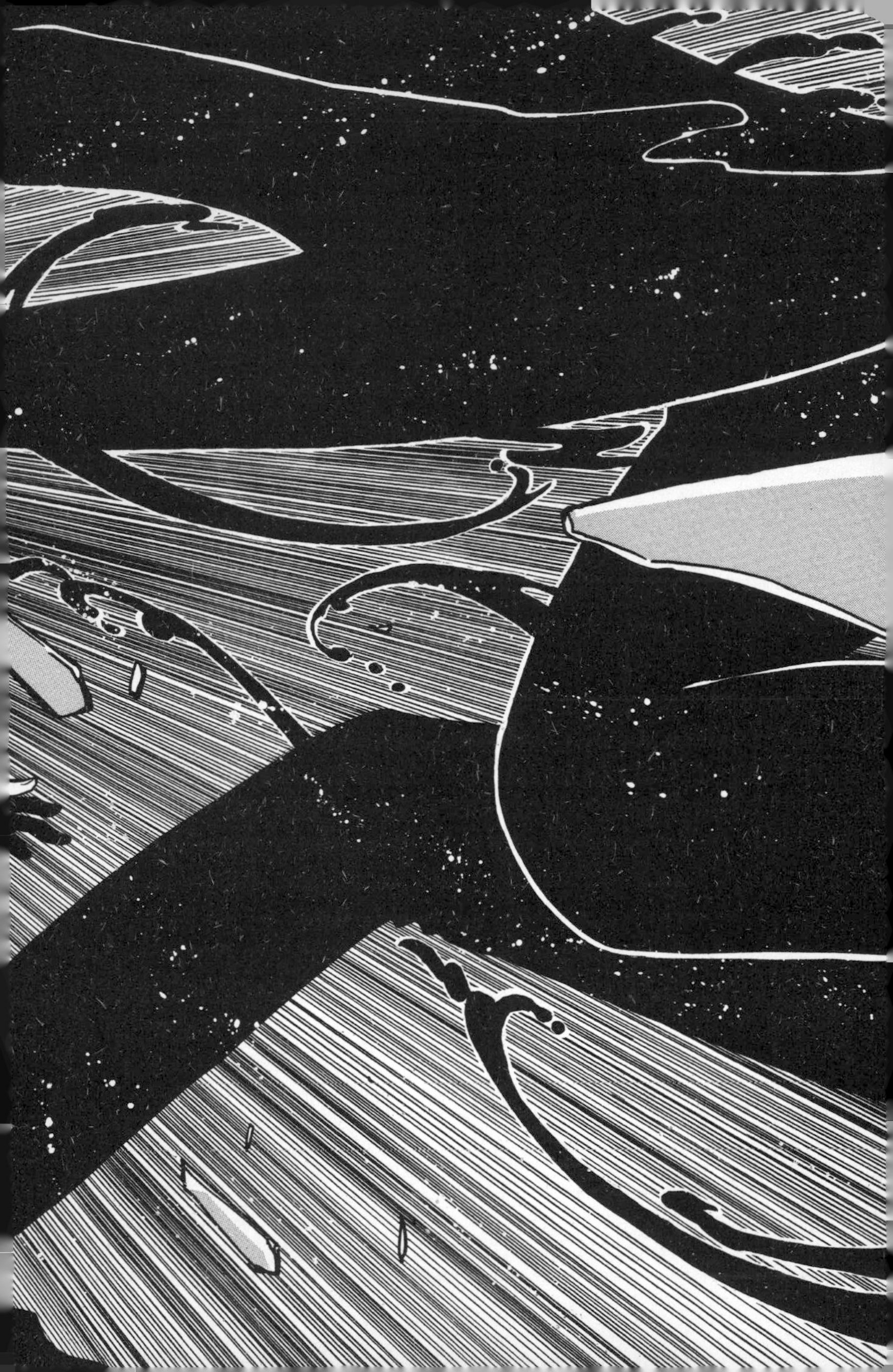

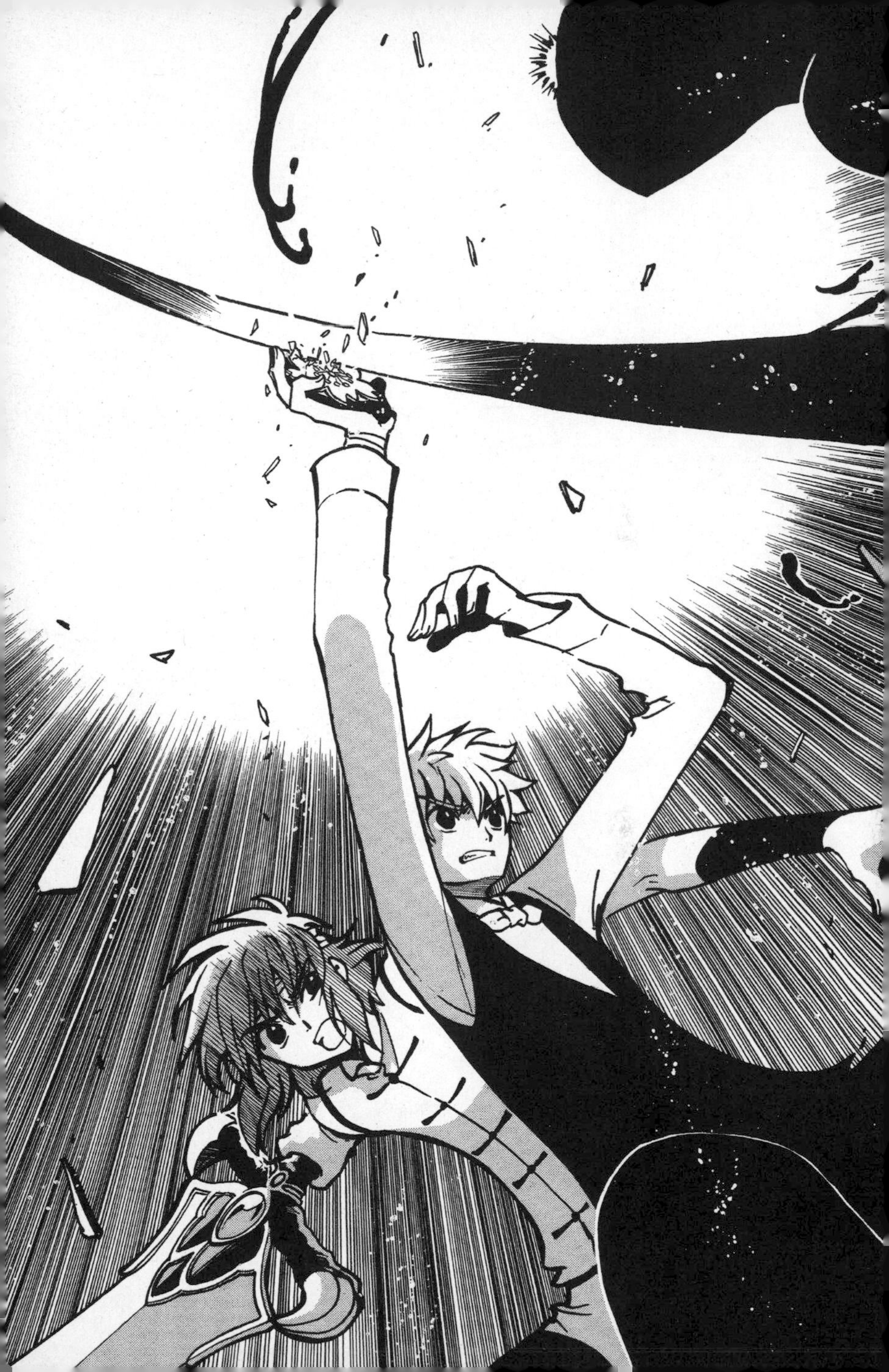

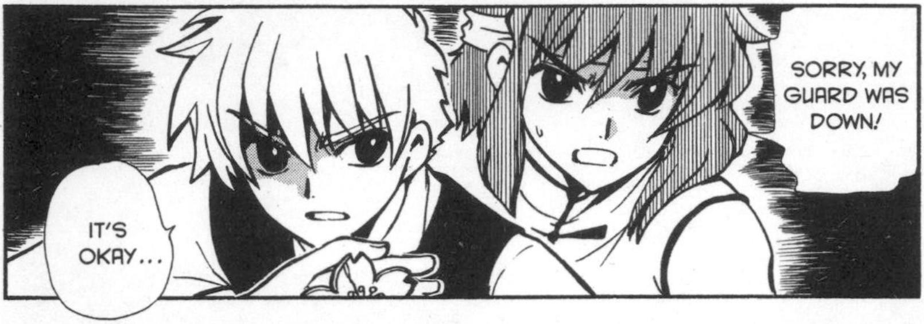
SORRY, MY GUARD WAS DOWN!
IT'S OKAY...

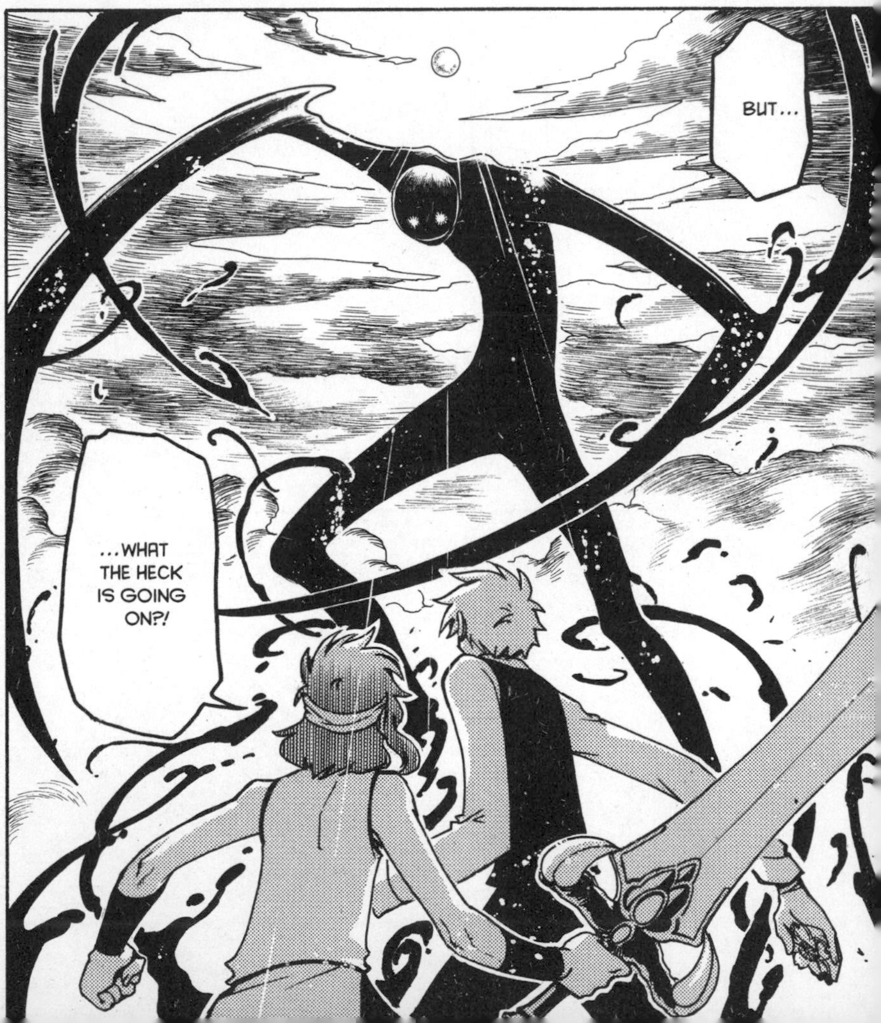
BUT...
...WHAT THE HECK IS GOING ON?!

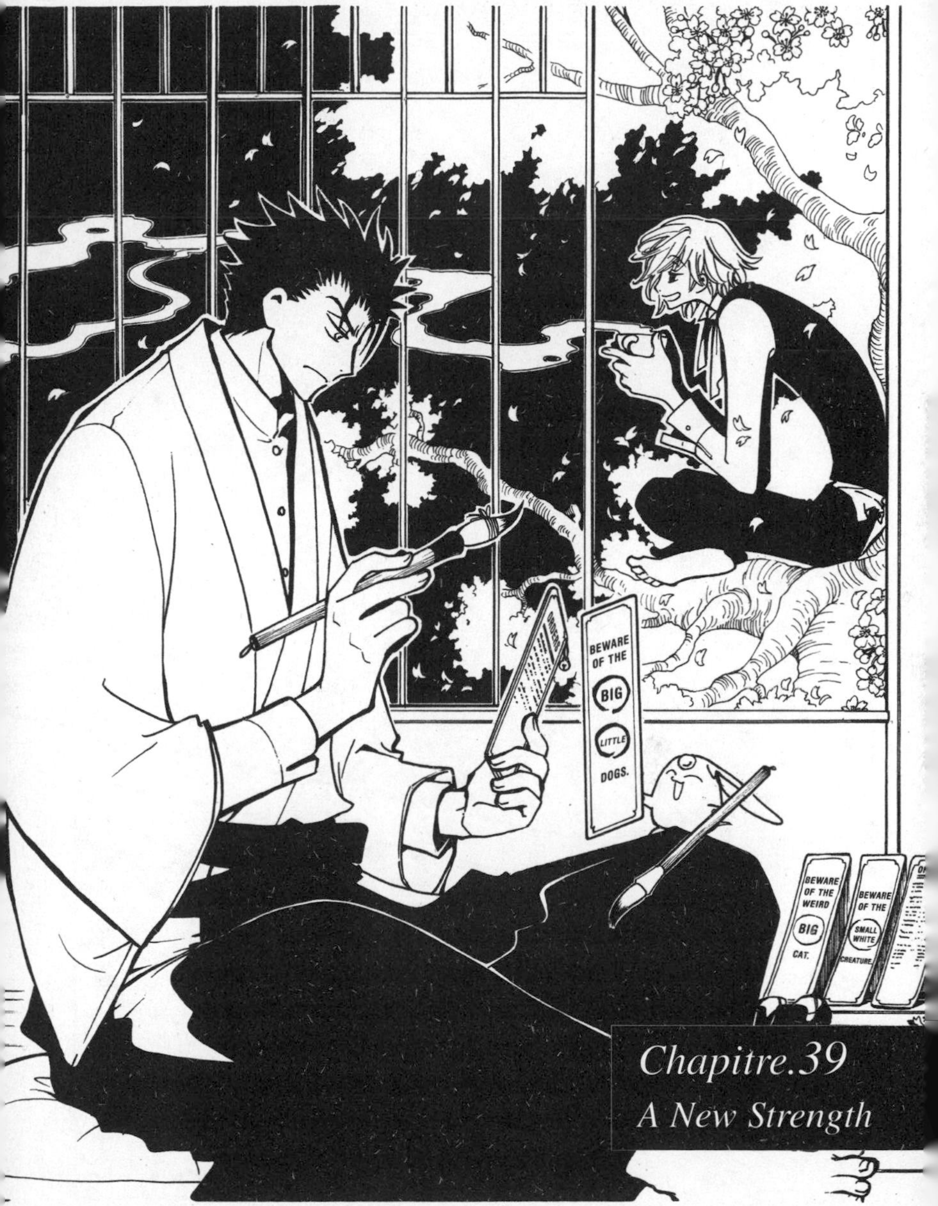
BEWARE OF THE BIG LITTLE DOGS.
BEWARE OF THE WEIRD BIG CAT.
BEWARE OF THE SMALL WHITE CREATURE.
Chapitre.39
A New Strength

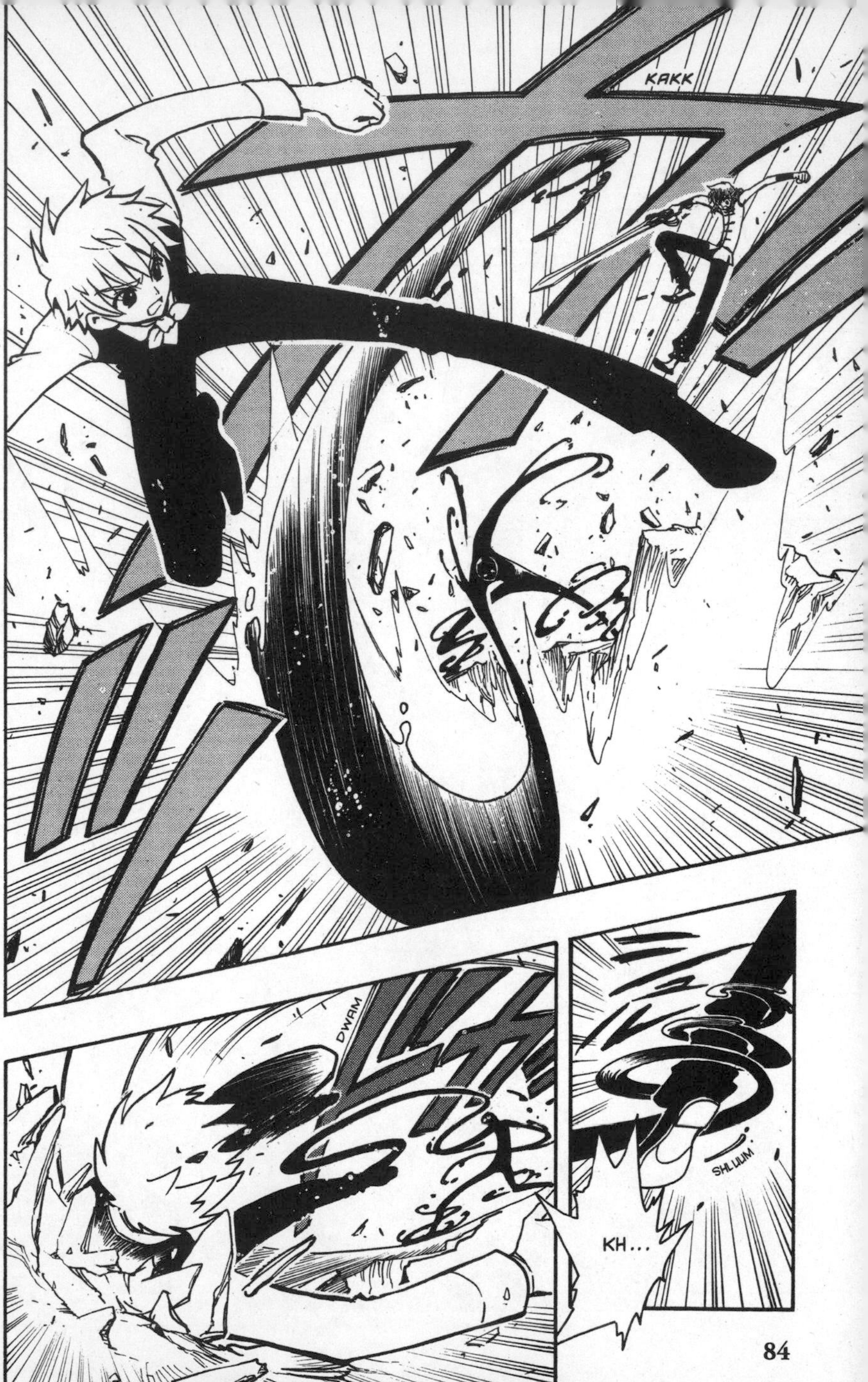
KAKK
SHLUUM
KH...
DWAM

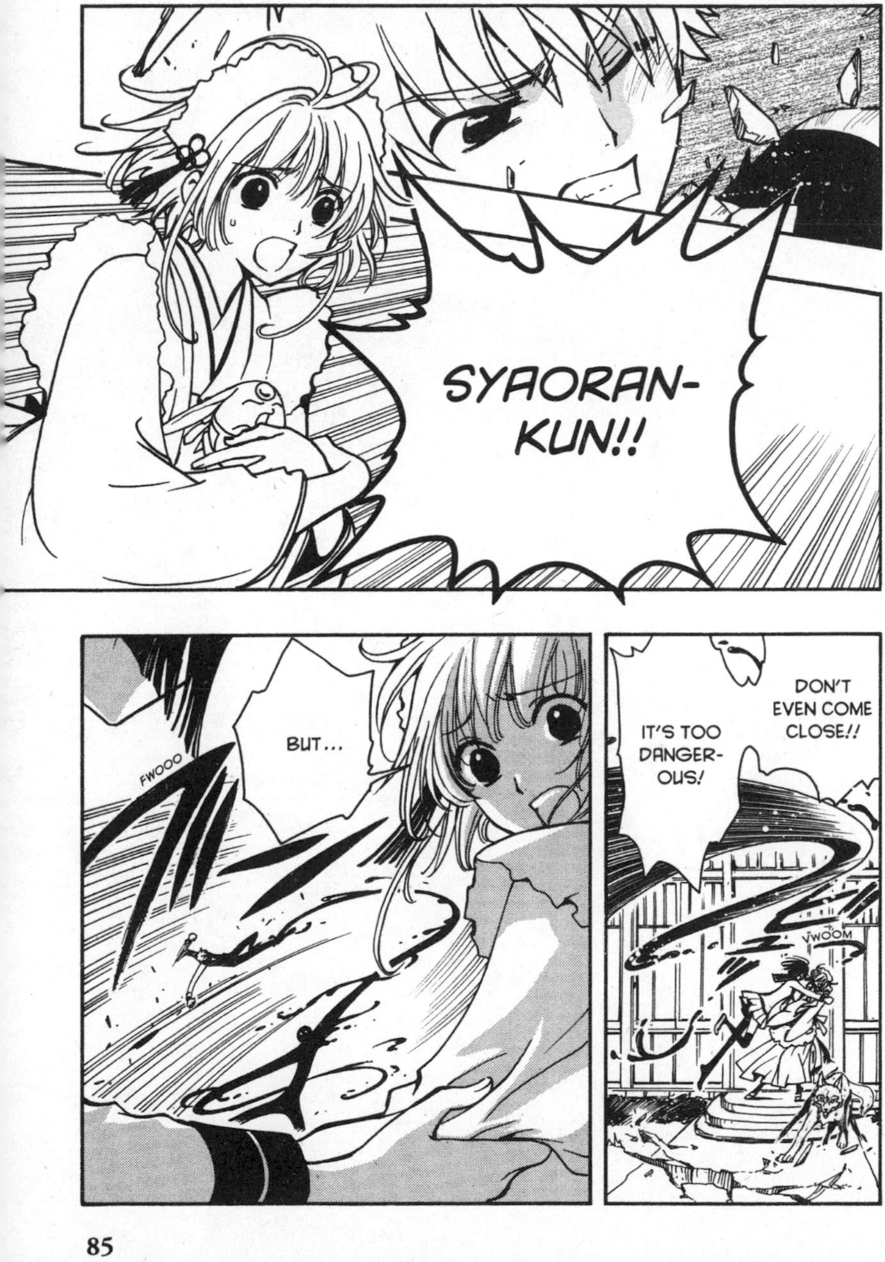
SYAORAN-KUN!!
DON'T EVEN COME CLOSE!!
IT'S TOO DANGER-OUS!
VWOOM
BUT...
FWOOO

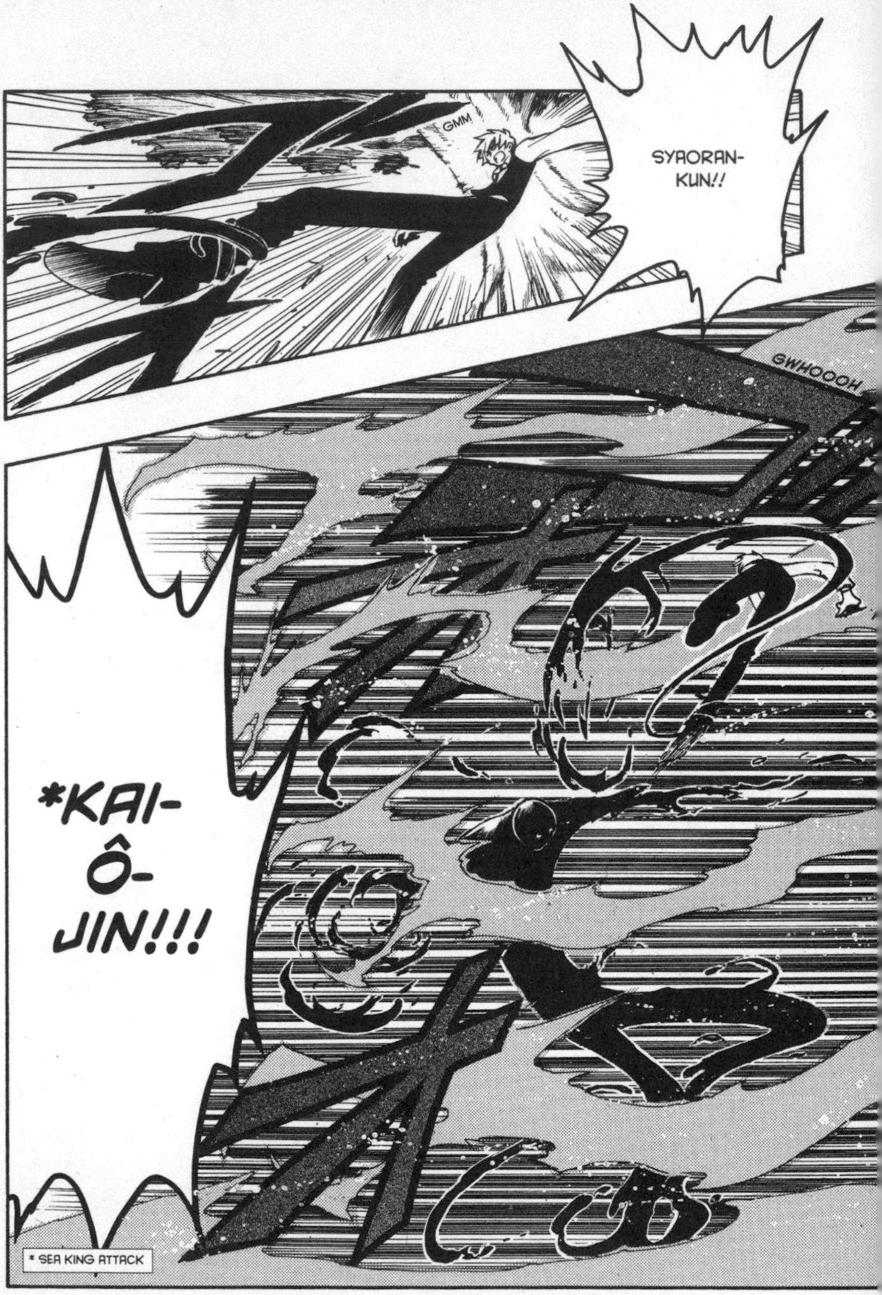
SYAORAN-KUN!!
GMM
GWHOOOH
*KAI-Ô-JIN!!!
* SEA KING ATTACK

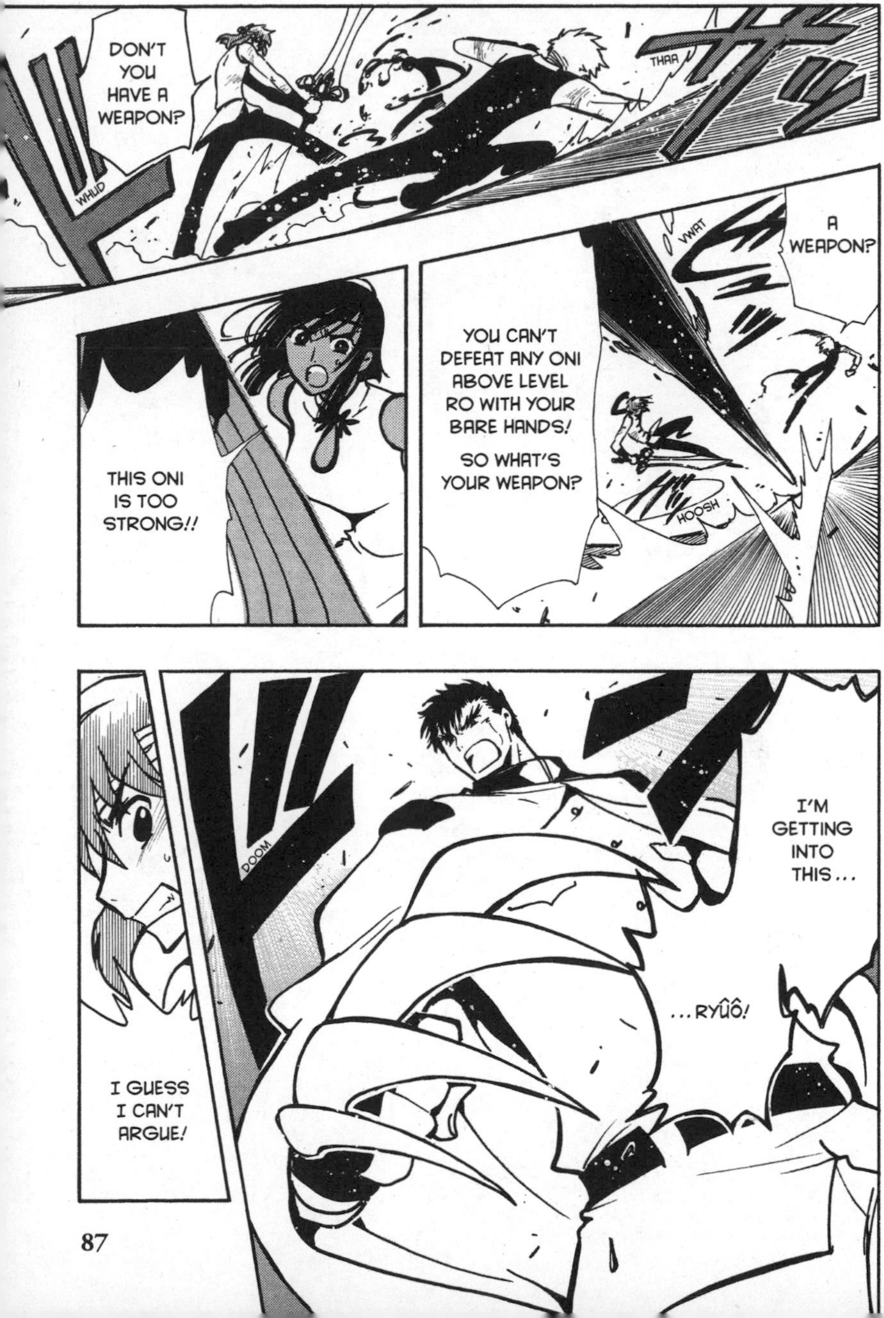
THAA
DON'T YOU HAVE A WEAPON?
WHUD
A WEAPON?
VWAT
YOU CAN'T DEFEAT ANY ONI ABOVE LEVEL RO WITH YOUR BARE HANDS!
SO WHAT'S YOUR WEAPON?
HOOSH
THIS ONI IS TOO STRONG!!
I'M GETTING INTO THIS...
...RYÛÔ!
DOOM
I GUESS I CAN'T ARGUE!

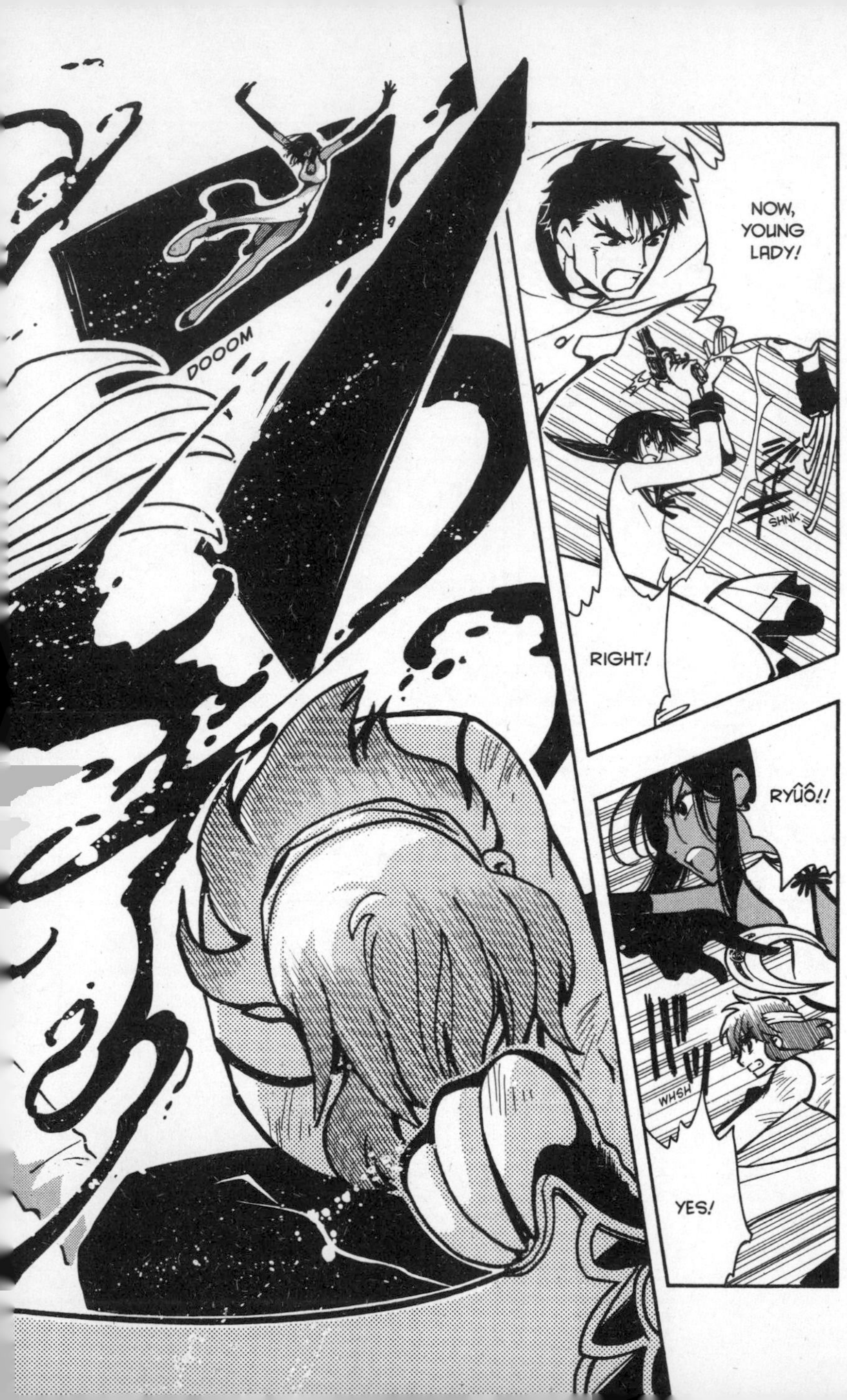
NOW, YOUNG LADY!
SHNK
RIGHT!
RYÛÔ!!
WHSH
YES!
DOOOM

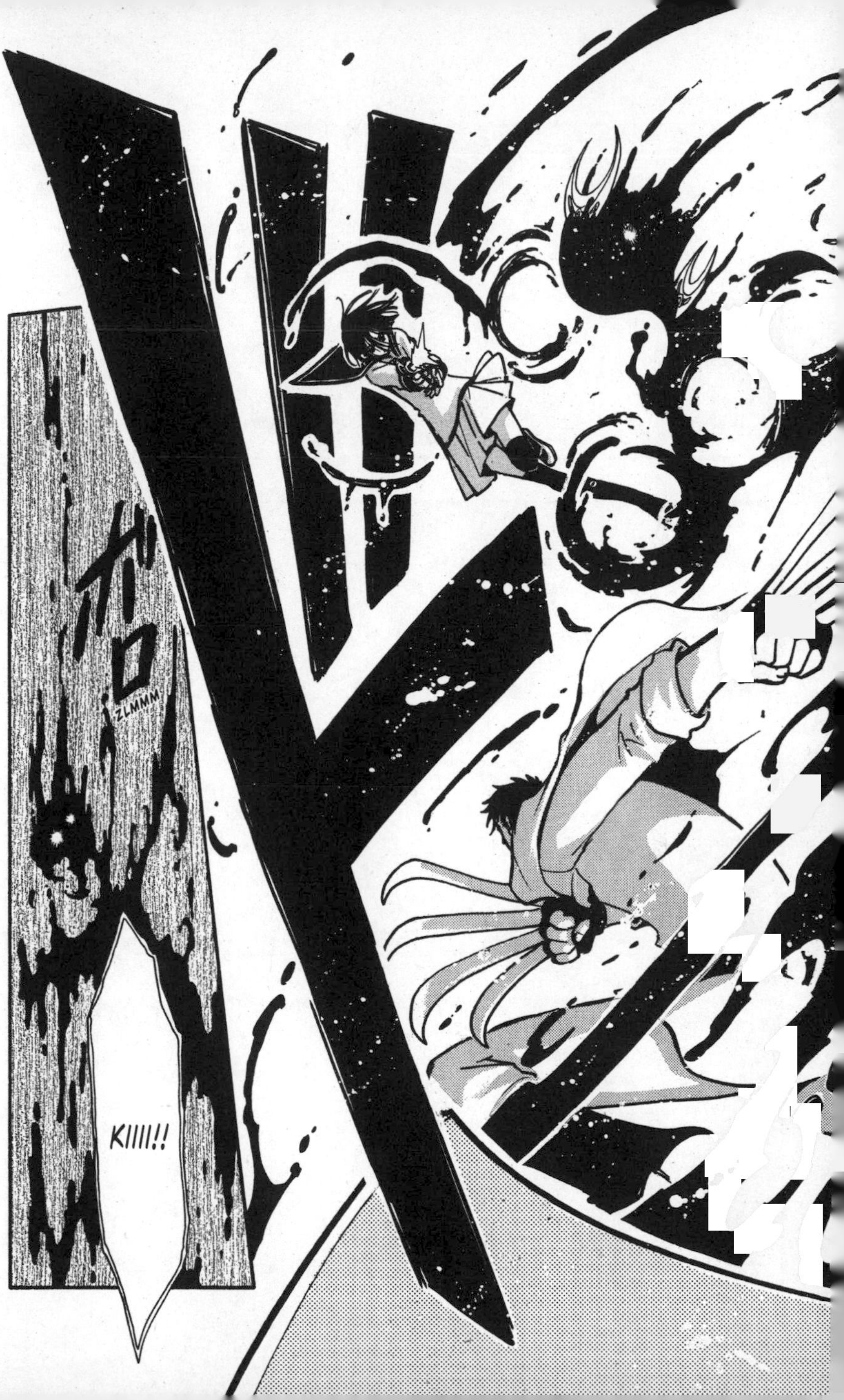
ZLMMM
KIIII!!

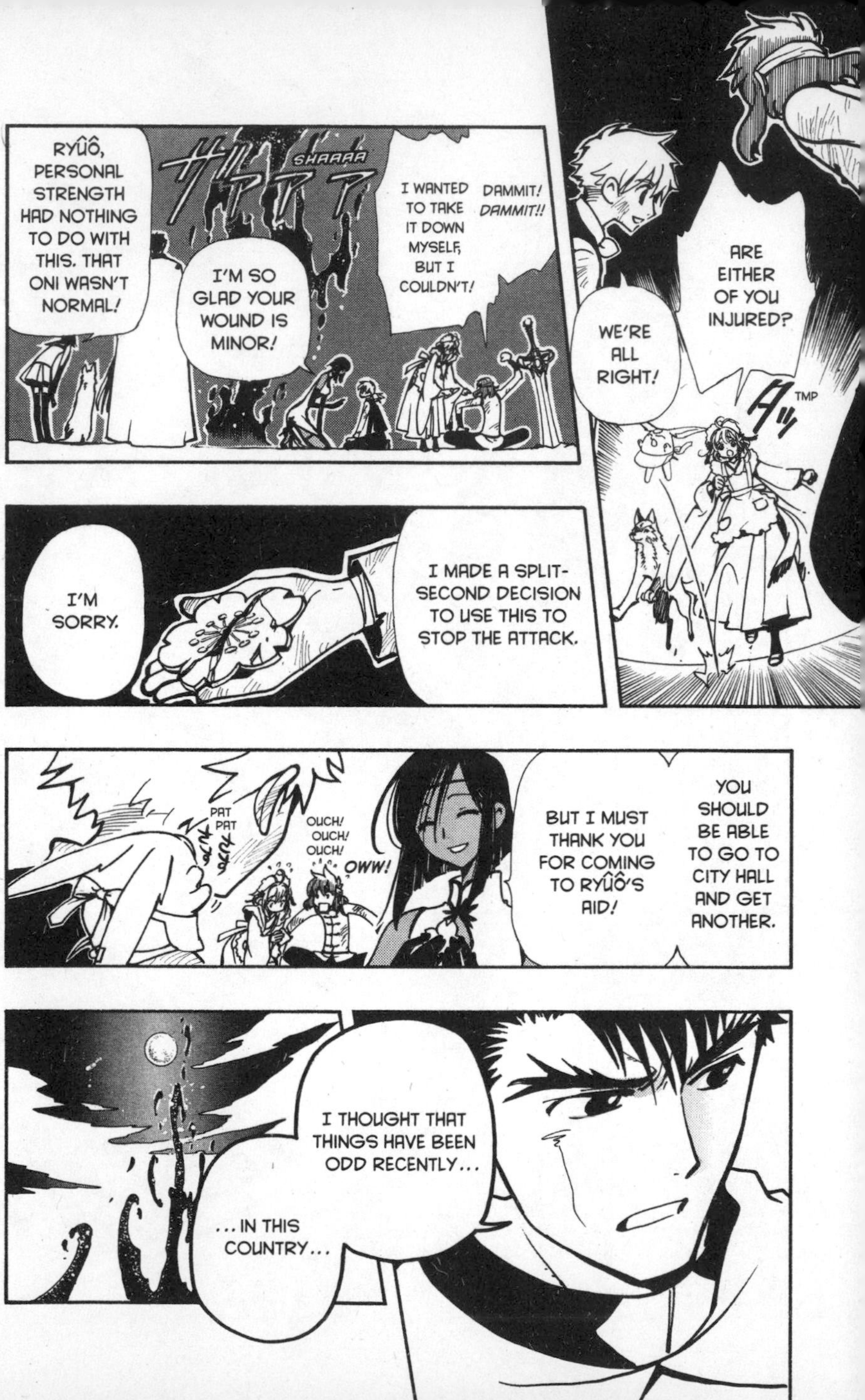
ARE EITHER OF YOU INJURED?
WE'RE ALL RIGHT!
TMP
DAMMIT! DAMMIT!!
I WANTED TO TAKE IT DOWN MYSELF, BUT I COULDN'T!
SHAAAA
I'M SO GLAD YOUR WOUND IS MINOR!
RYÛÔ, PERSONAL STRENGTH HAD NOTHING TO DO WITH THIS. THAT ONI WASN'T NORMAL!
I MADE A SPLIT-SECOND DECISION TO USE THIS TO STOP THE ATTACK.
I'M SORRY.
YOU SHOULD BE ABLE TO GO TO CITY HALL AND GET ANOTHER.
BUT I MUST THANK YOU FOR COMING TO RYÛÔ'S AID!
OWW!
OUCH! OUCH! OUCH!
PAT PAT
I THOUGHT THAT THINGS HAVE BEEN ODD RECENTLY...
...IN THIS COUNTRY...

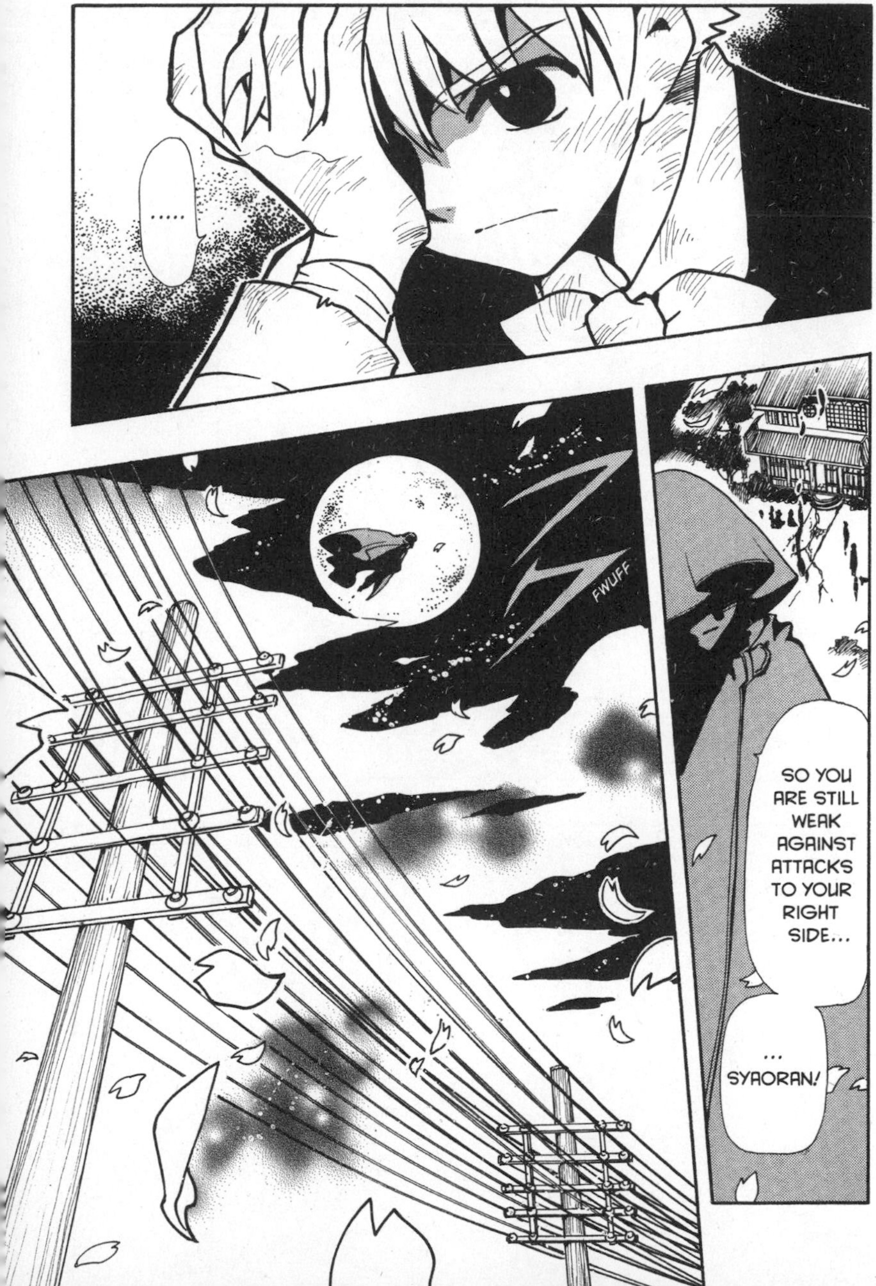
.....
SO YOU ARE STILL WEAK AGAINST ATTACKS TO YOUR RIGHT SIDE...
...SYAORAN!
FWUFF

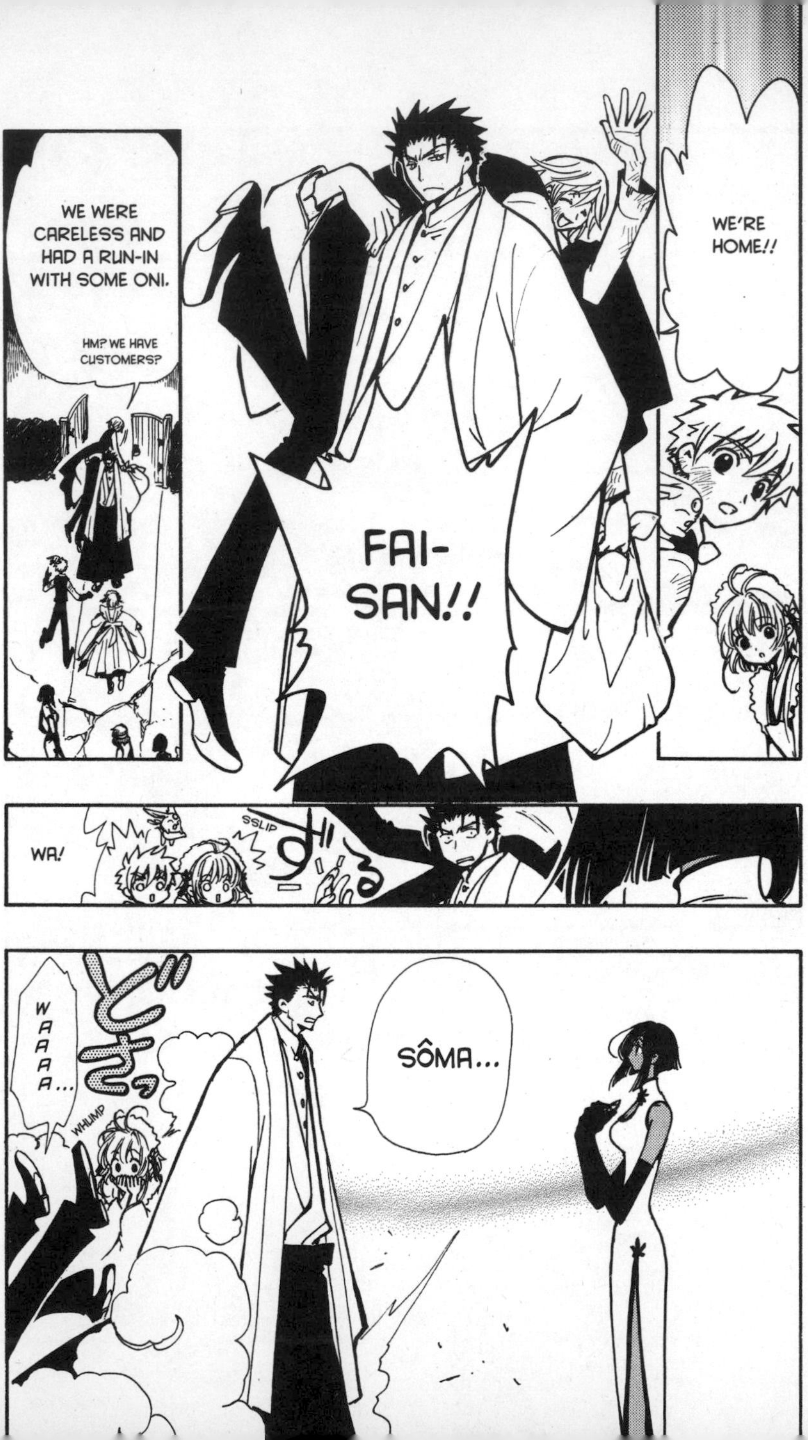

WE'RE HOME!!
FAI-SAN!!
WE WERE CARELESS AND HAD A RUN-IN WITH SOME ONI.
HM? WE HAVE CUSTOMERS?
SSLIP
WA!
SÔMA...
WAAAA...
WHUMP

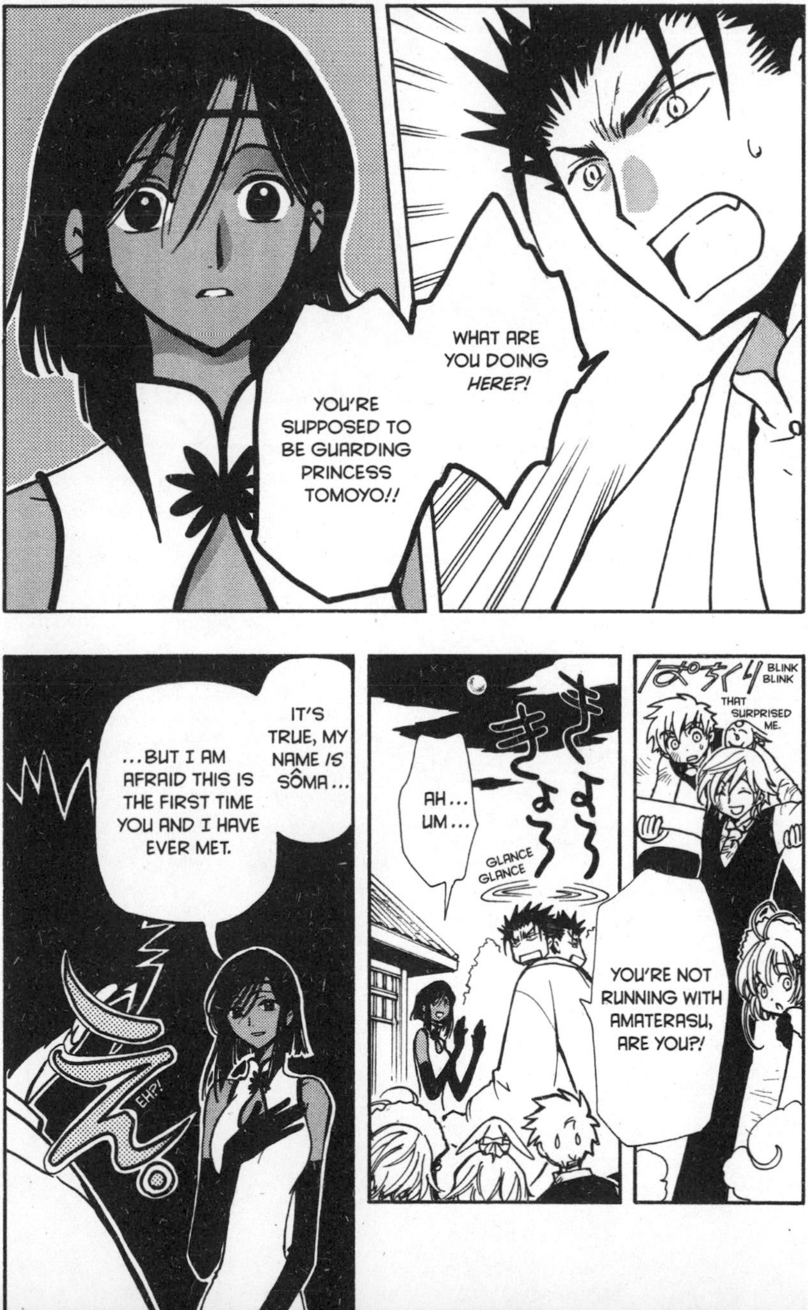
WHAT ARE YOU DOING *HERE?!*
YOU'RE SUPPOSED TO BE GUARDING PRINCESS TOMOYO!!
ぱちくり
BLINK BLINK
THAT SURPRISED ME.
YOU'RE NOT RUNNING WITH AMATERASU, ARE YOU?!
きょろきょろ
GLANCE GLANCE
AH... UM...
IT'S TRUE, MY NAME *IS* SÔMA...
...BUT I AM AFRAID THIS IS THE FIRST TIME YOU AND I HAVE EVER MET.
EH?!

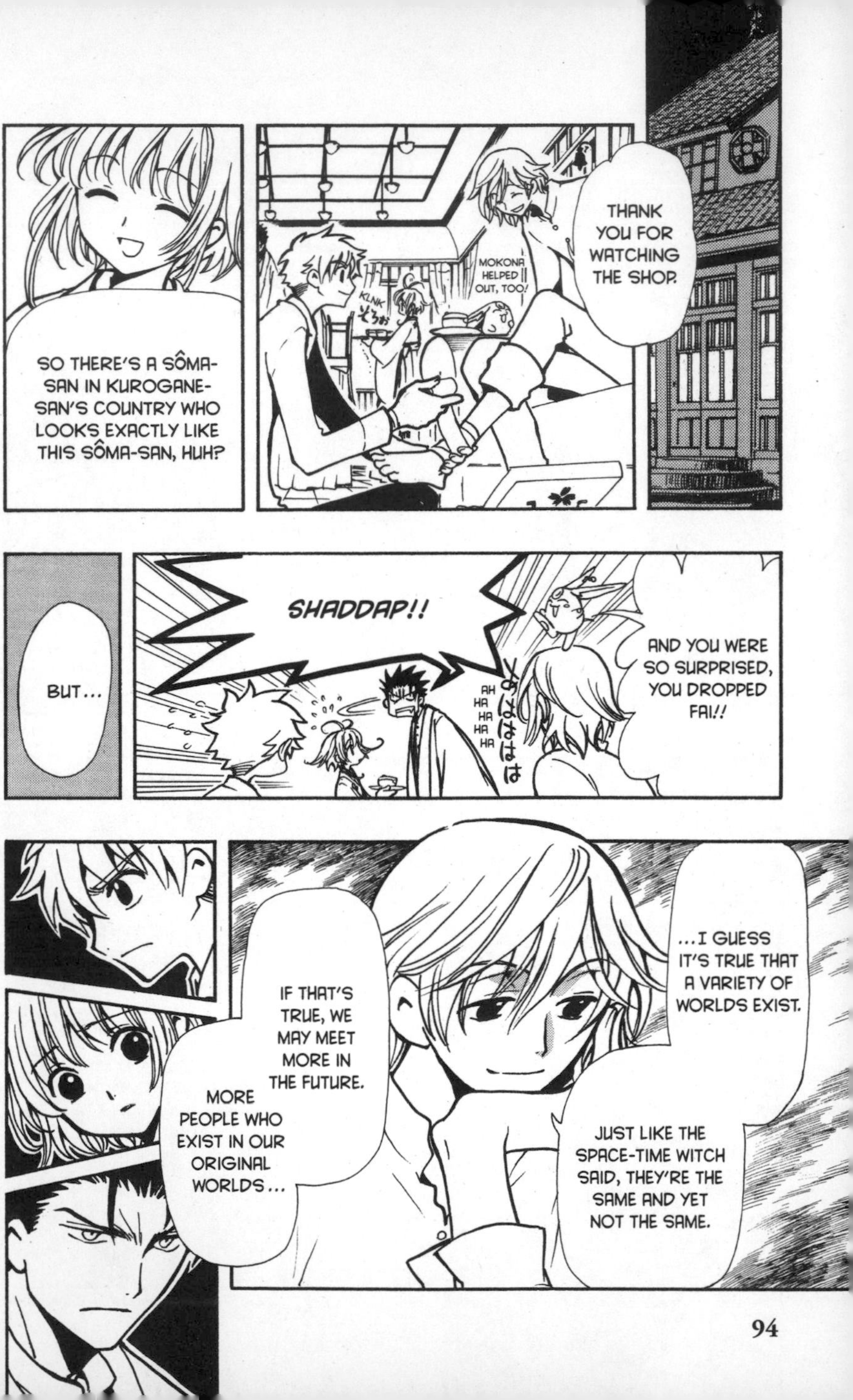
THANK YOU FOR WATCHING THE SHOP.
MOKONA HELPED OUT, TOO!
KLNK
SO THERE'S A SÔMA-SAN IN KUROGANE-SAN'S COUNTRY WHO LOOKS EXACTLY LIKE THIS SÔMA-SAN, HUH?
AND YOU WERE SO SURPRISED, YOU DROPPED FAI!!
AH HA HA HA HA
SHADDAP!!
BUT...
...I GUESS IT'S TRUE THAT A VARIETY OF WORLDS EXIST.
JUST LIKE THE SPACE-TIME WITCH SAID, THEY'RE THE SAME AND YET NOT THE SAME.
IF THAT'S TRUE, WE MAY MEET MORE IN THE FUTURE.
MORE PEOPLE WHO EXIST IN OUR ORIGINAL WORLDS...

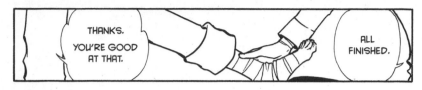

ALL FINISHED.
THANKS. YOU'RE GOOD AT THAT.
WHAT HAPPENED AT THE BAR?
THAT'S RIGHT! I BROUGHT BACK PRESENTS!
ごそごそ
RUSTLE RUSTLE
I'M GLAD THEY DIDN'T BREAK!
I BOUGHT THEM AT THE BAR!
CALDINA-SAN RECOMMENDED THEM!
LET'S ALL HAVE A DRINK AND TALK IT OVER.
FWOOOM
EH?!
はにゃん
HA-MEOWW
EH HEH HEH!
UH HU HU!
ほにょん
HO-MEOWN
ふにゃん
HU-MEOWW
AH HA HA!

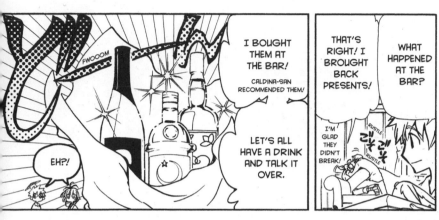

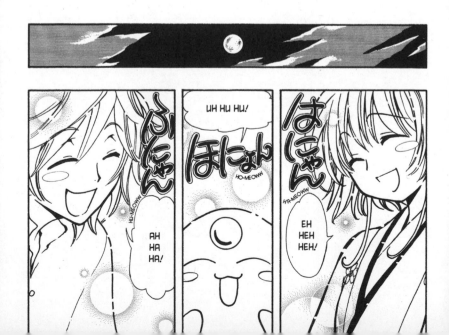

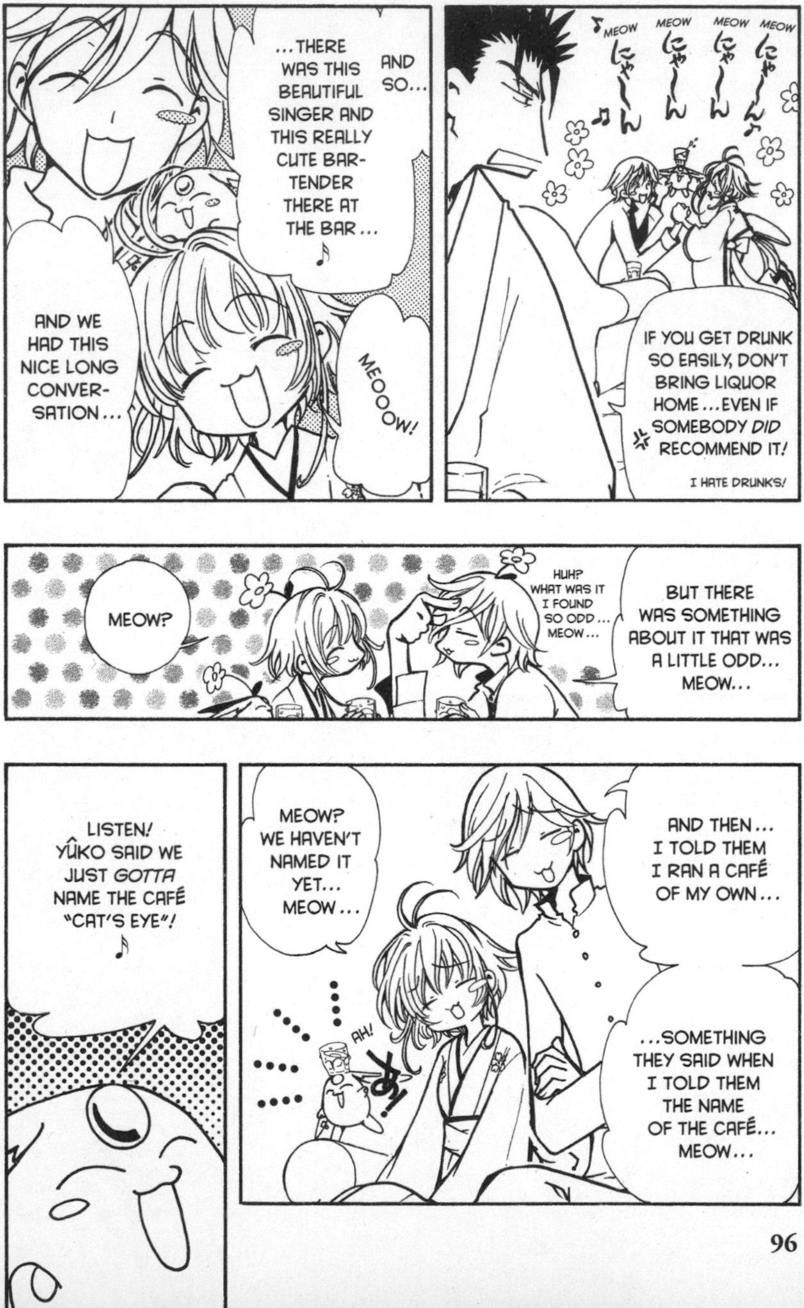
MEOW MEOW MEOW MEOW
にゃ〜ん♪ にゃ〜ん にゃ〜ん にゃ〜ん♪
IF YOU GET DRUNK SO EASILY, DON'T BRING LIQUOR HOME... EVEN IF SOMEBODY *DID* RECOMMEND IT!
I HATE DRUNKS!
AND SO...
...THERE WAS THIS BEAUTIFUL SINGER AND THIS REALLY CUTE BAR-TENDER THERE AT THE BAR... ♪
MEOOOW!
AND WE HAD THIS NICE LONG CONVER-SATION...
BUT THERE WAS SOMETHING ABOUT IT THAT WAS A LITTLE ODD... MEOW...
HUH? WHAT WAS IT I FOUND SO ODD... MEOW...
MEOW?
AND THEN... I TOLD THEM I RAN A CAFÉ OF MY OWN...
...SOMETHING THEY SAID WHEN I TOLD THEM THE NAME OF THE CAFÉ... MEOW...
MEOW? WE HAVEN'T NAMED IT YET... MEOW...
AH!
あ!
LISTEN! YÛKO SAID WE JUST *GOTTA* NAME THE CAFÉ "CAT'S EYE"! ♪

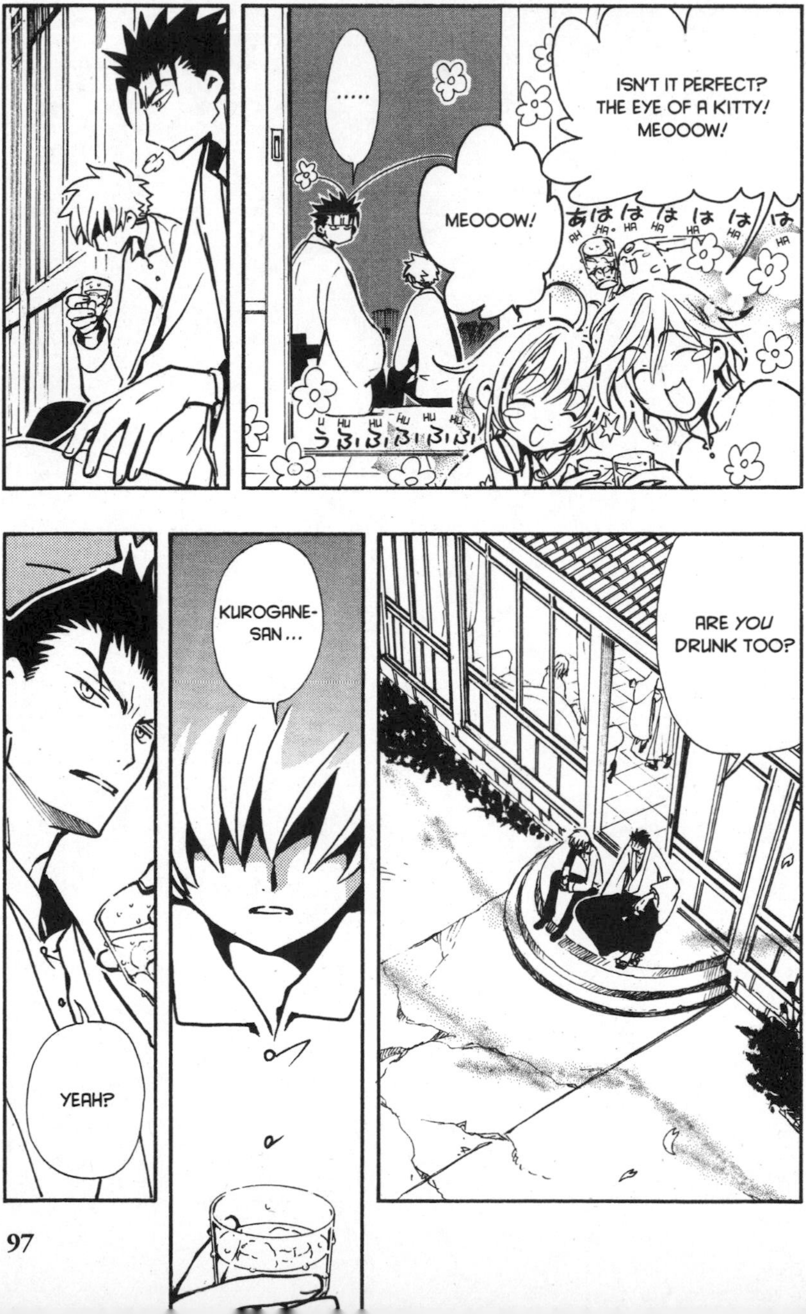
ISN'T IT PERFECT? THE EYE OF A KITTY! MEOOOW!
MEOOOW!
あはははははは
AH HA HA HA HA HA HA
うふふふふふ
U HU HU HU HU HU
......
ARE YOU DRUNK TOO?
KUROGANE-SAN...
YEAH?

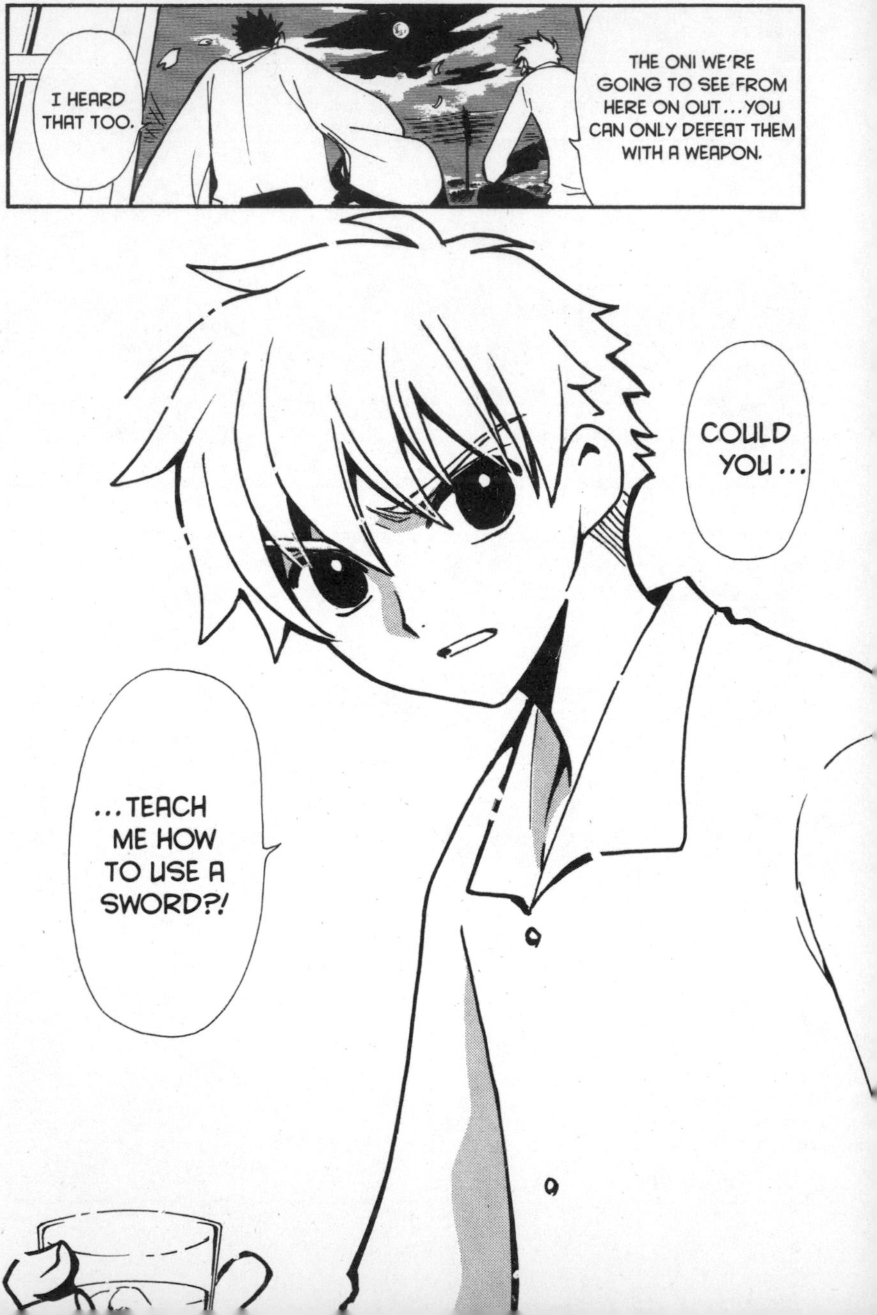
THE ONI WE'RE GOING TO SEE FROM HERE ON OUT...YOU CAN ONLY DEFEAT THEM WITH A WEAPON.
I HEARD THAT TOO.
COULD YOU...
...TEACH ME HOW TO USE A SWORD?!

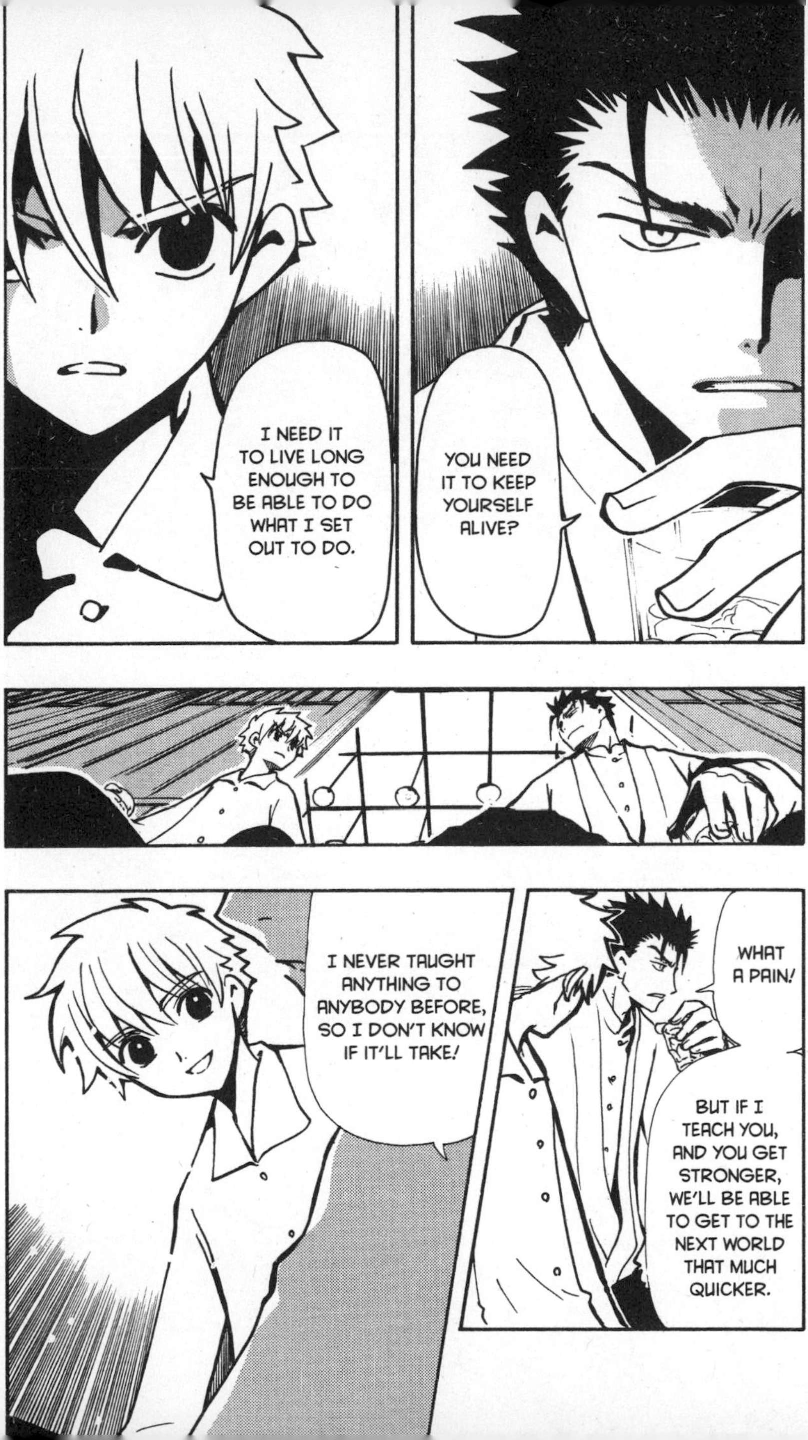
YOU NEED IT TO KEEP YOURSELF ALIVE?
I NEED IT TO LIVE LONG ENOUGH TO BE ABLE TO DO WHAT I SET OUT TO DO.
WHAT A PAIN!
BUT IF I TEACH YOU, AND YOU GET STRONGER, WE'LL BE ABLE TO GET TO THE NEXT WORLD THAT MUCH QUICKER.
I NEVER TAUGHT ANYTHING TO ANYBODY BEFORE, SO I DON'T KNOW IF IT'LL TAKE!

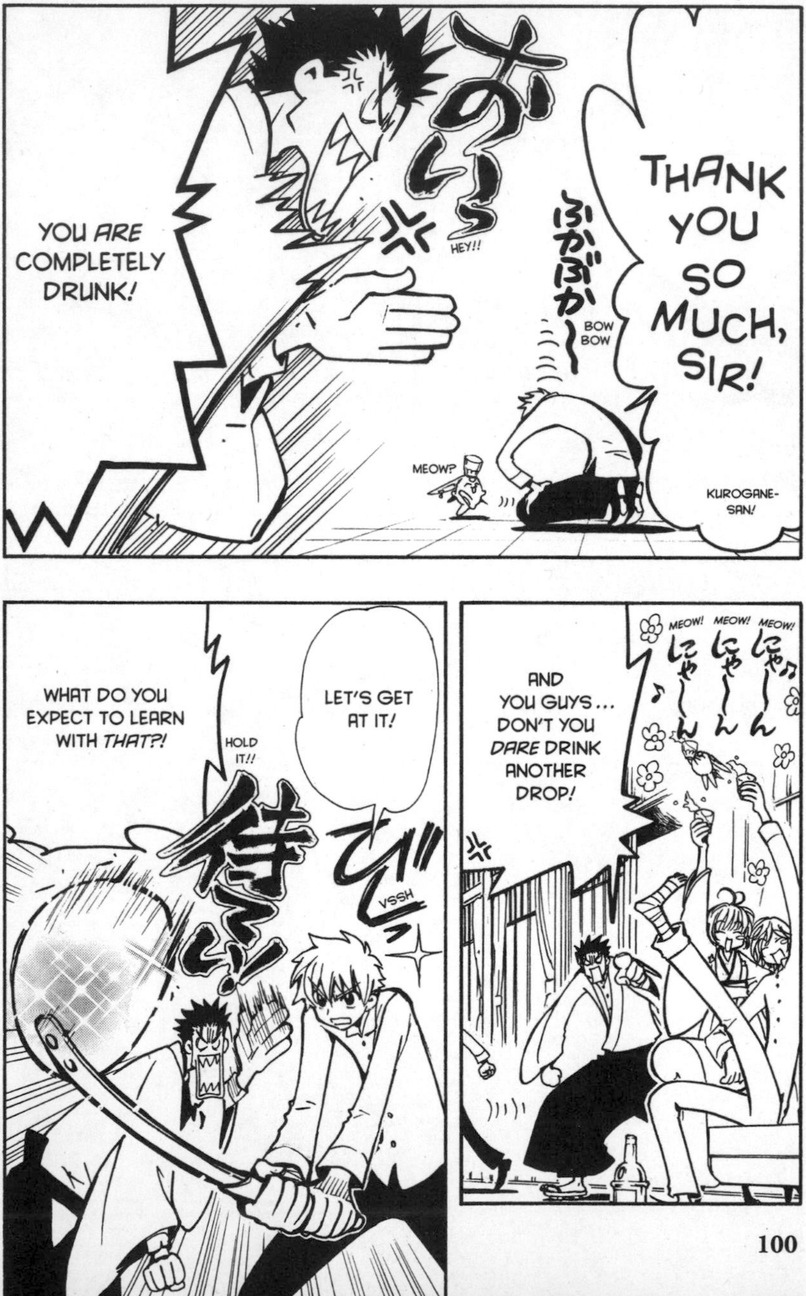
THANK YOU SO MUCH, SIR!
KUROGANE-SAN!
ふかぶか～
BOW BOW
おいっ
HEY!!
MEOW?
YOU ARE COMPLETELY DRUNK!
にゃーん
MEOW!
にゃーん
MEOW!
にゃーん
MEOW!
AND YOU GUYS... DON'T YOU DARE DRINK ANOTHER DROP!
LET'S GET AT IT!
びゅ
VSSH
待てい!
HOLD IT!!
WHAT DO YOU EXPECT TO LEARN WITH THAT?!

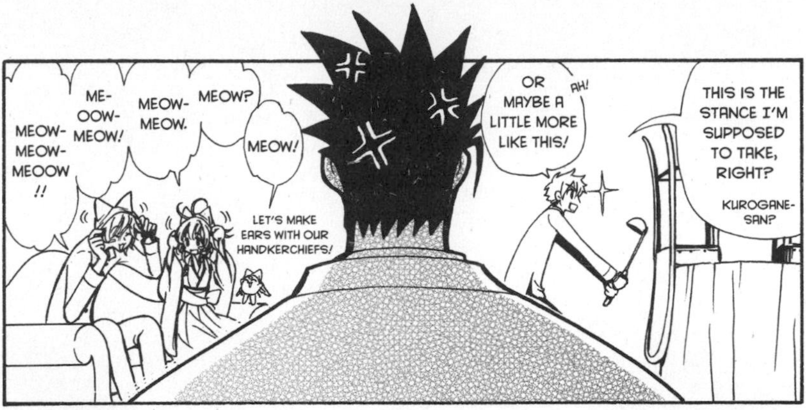
THIS IS THE STANCE I'M SUPPOSED TO TAKE, RIGHT?
KUROGANE-SAN?
AH!
OR MAYBE A LITTLE MORE LIKE THIS!
MEOW!
LET'S MAKE EARS WITH OUR HANDKERCHIEFS!
MEOW?
MEOW-MEOW.
ME-OOW-MEOW!
MEOW-MEOW-MEOOW!!

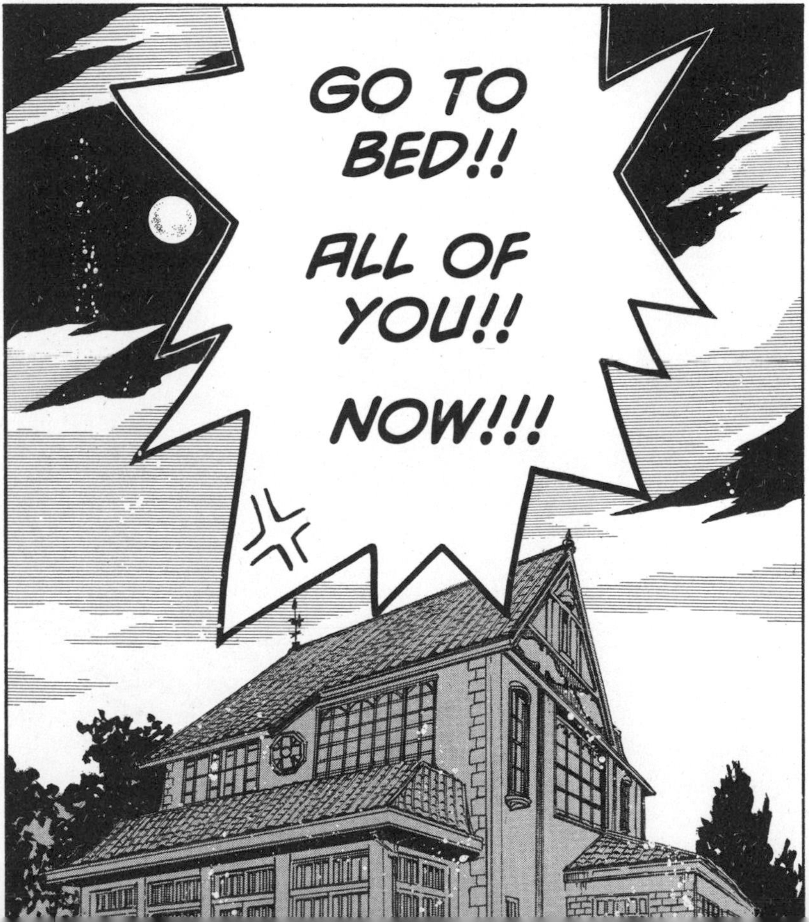
GO TO BED!! ALL OF YOU!! NOW!!!

ツバサ
RESERVoir CHRoNiCLE

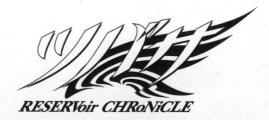

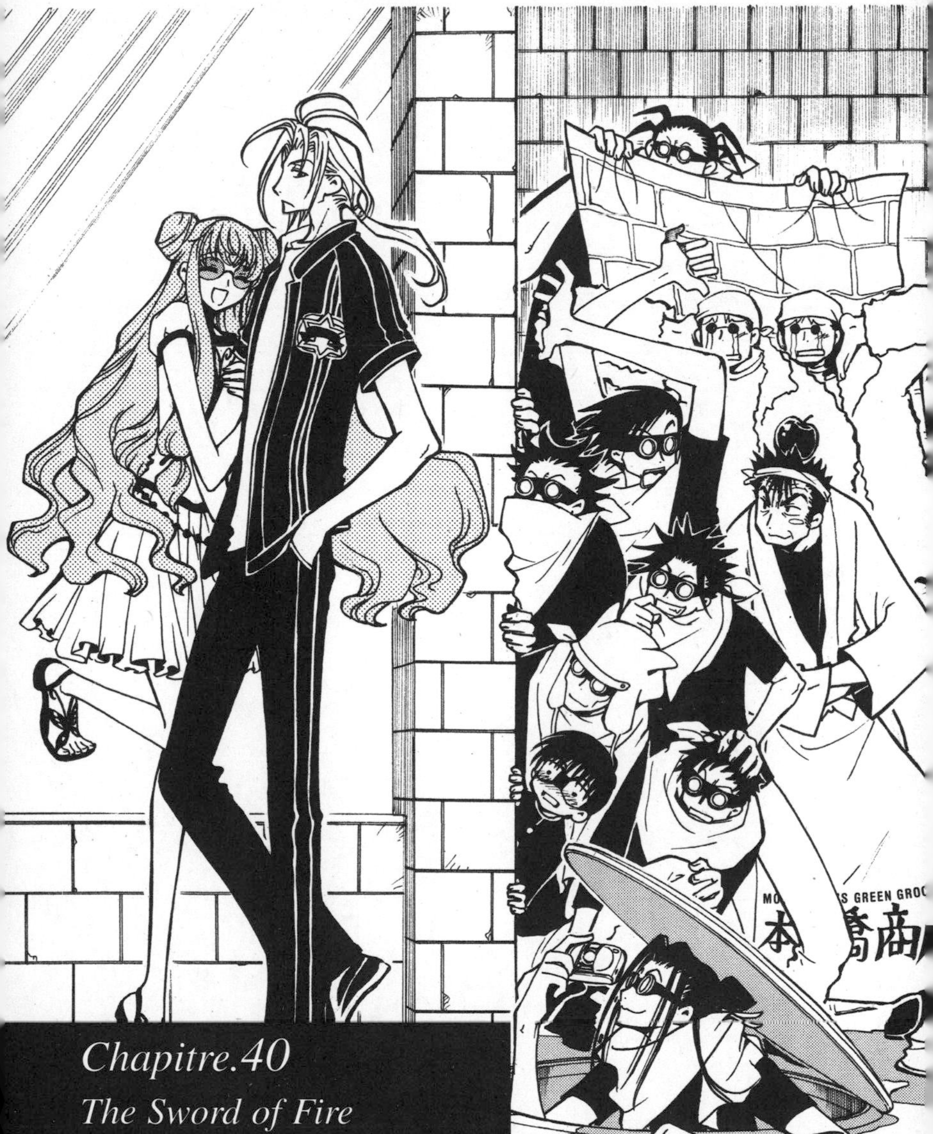

Chapitre.40

The Sword of Fire

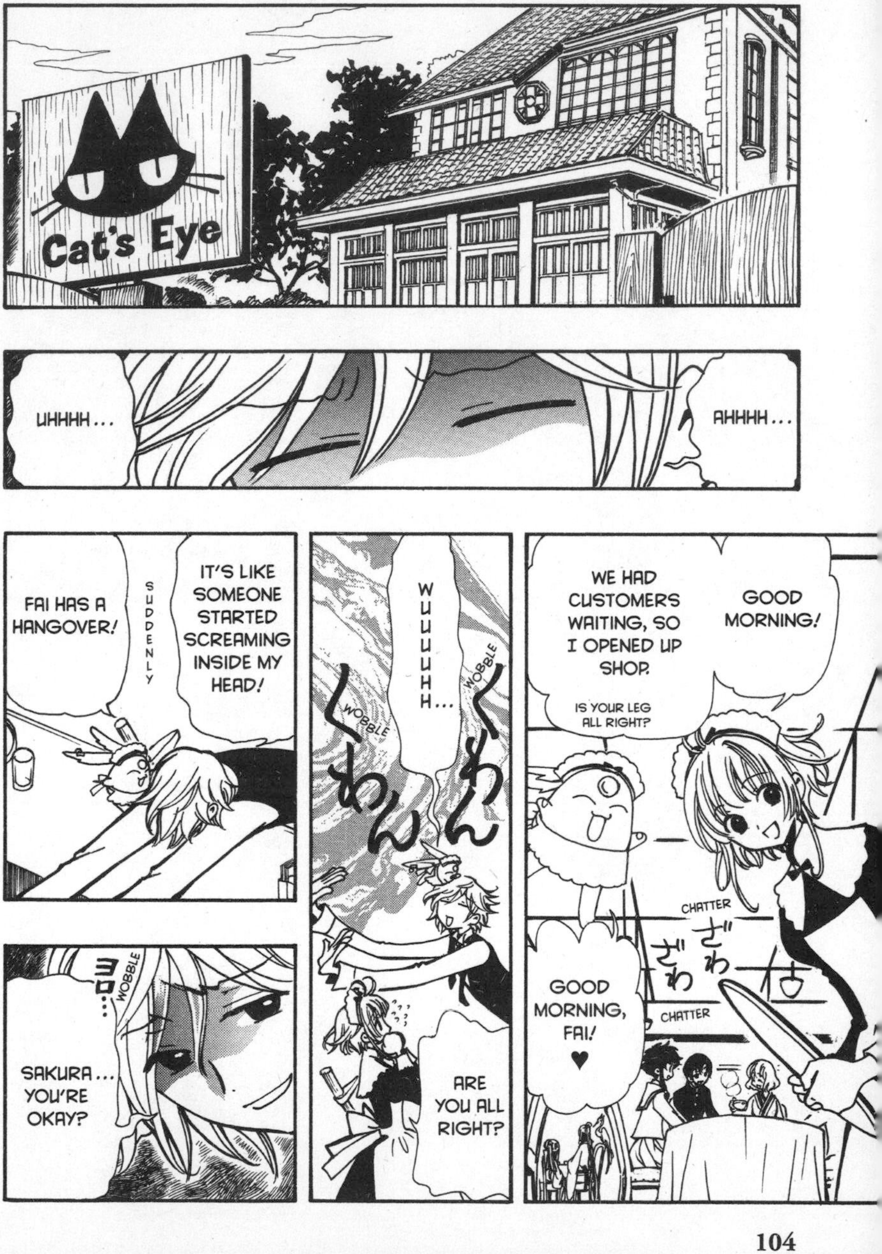

Cat's Eye
AHHHH...
UHHHH...
GOOD MORNING!
WE HAD CUSTOMERS WAITING, SO I OPENED UP SHOP.
IS YOUR LEG ALL RIGHT?
ざわ
CHATTER
ざわ
CHATTER
GOOD MORNING, FAI! ♥
WUUUUHH...
くわん
WOBBLE
くわん
WOBBLE
ARE YOU ALL RIGHT?
IT'S LIKE SOMEONE STARTED SCREAMING INSIDE MY HEAD!
SUDDENLY
FAI HAS A HANGOVER!
ヨロ…
WOBBLE
SAKURA... YOU'RE OKAY?

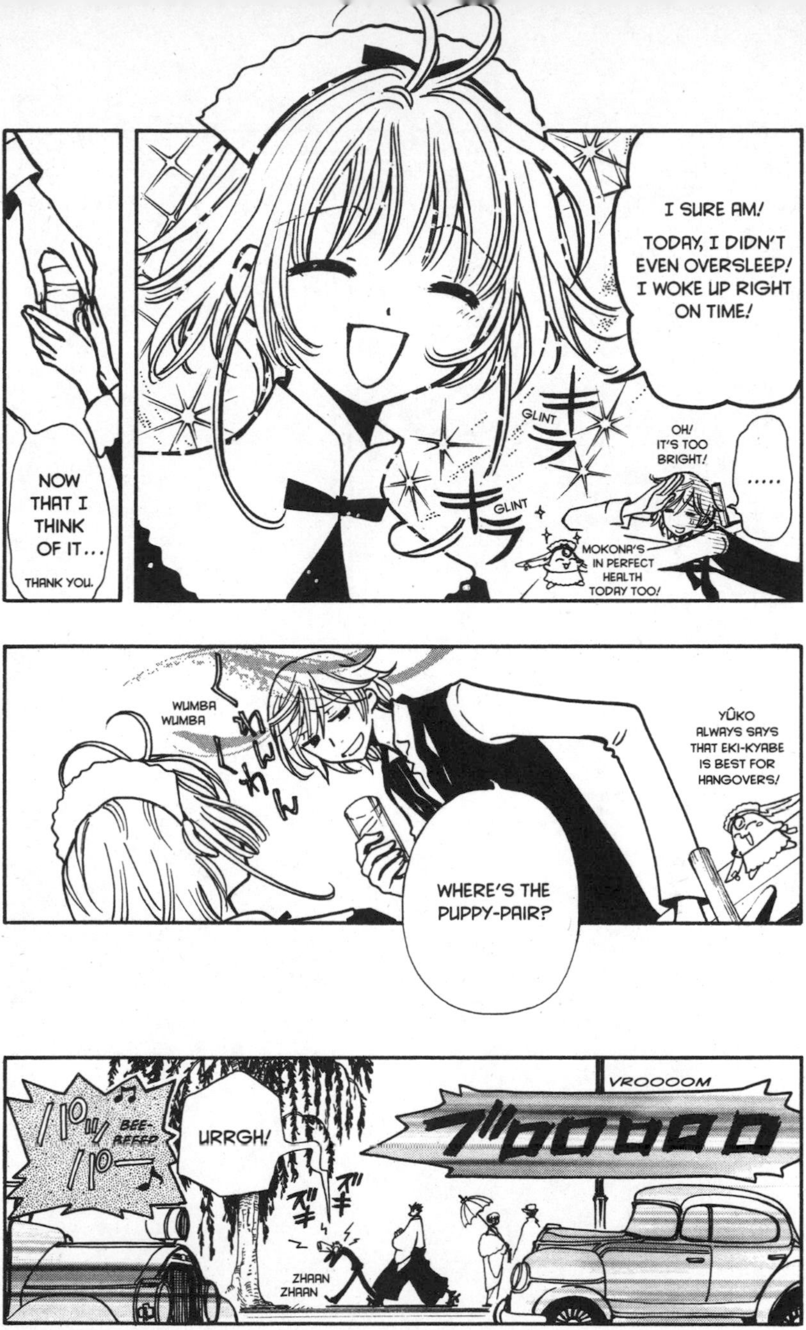
I SURE AM!
TODAY, I DIDN'T EVEN OVERSLEEP! I WOKE UP RIGHT ON TIME!
GLINT
GLINT
.....
OH! IT'S TOO BRIGHT!
MOKONA'S IN PERFECT HEALTH TODAY TOO!
NOW THAT I THINK OF IT...
THANK YOU.
YÛKO ALWAYS SAYS THAT EKI-KYABE IS BEST FOR HANGOVERS!
WHERE'S THE PUPPY-PAIR?
WUMBA WUMBA
VROOOOM
URRGH!
ZHAAN ZHAAN
BEE-REEEP

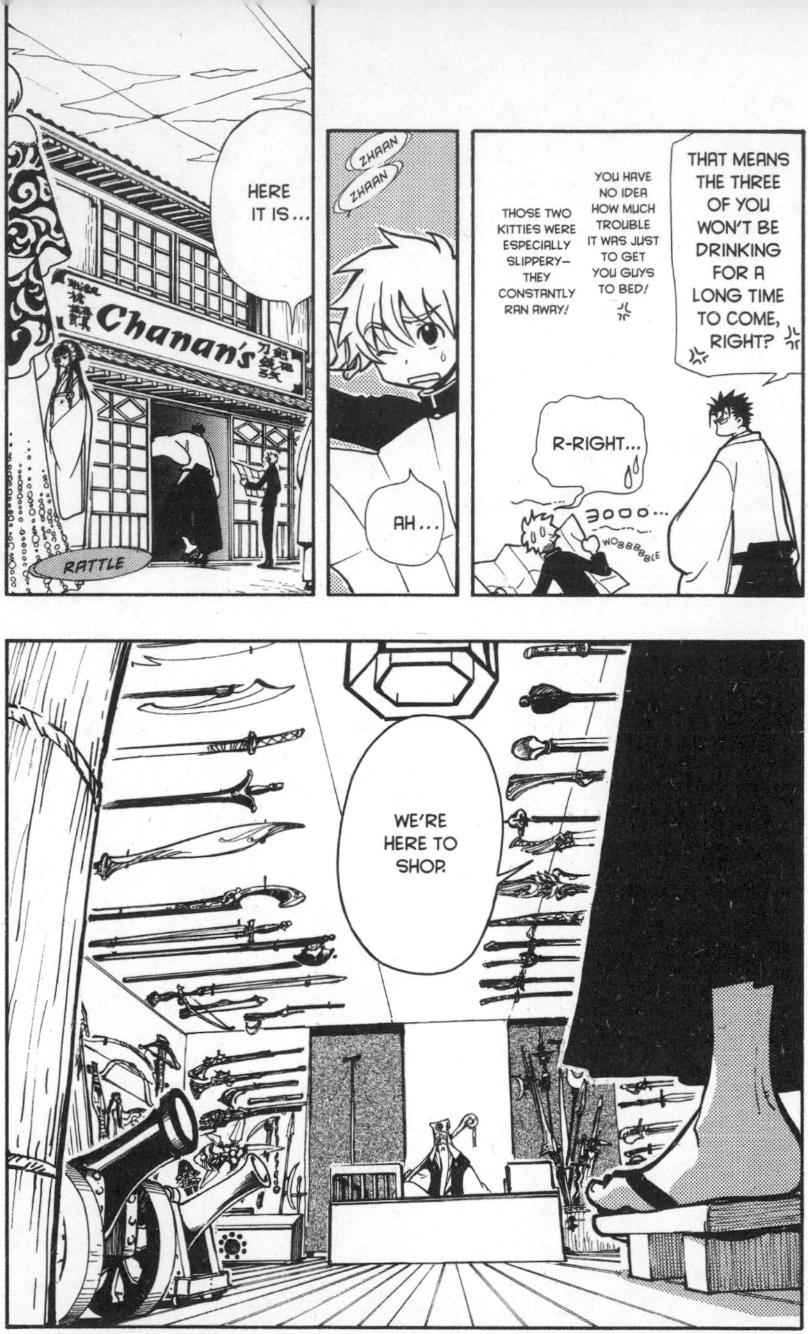
THAT MEANS THE THREE OF YOU WON'T BE DRINKING FOR A LONG TIME TO COME, RIGHT?
YOU HAVE NO IDEA HOW MUCH TROUBLE IT WAS JUST TO GET YOU GUYS TO BED!
THOSE TWO KITTIES WERE ESPECIALLY SLIPPERY— THEY CONSTANTLY RAN AWAY!
R-RIGHT...
WOBBBBBLE
ZHAAN
ZHAAN
AH...
HERE IT IS...
Chanan's
RATTLE
WE'RE HERE TO SHOP.

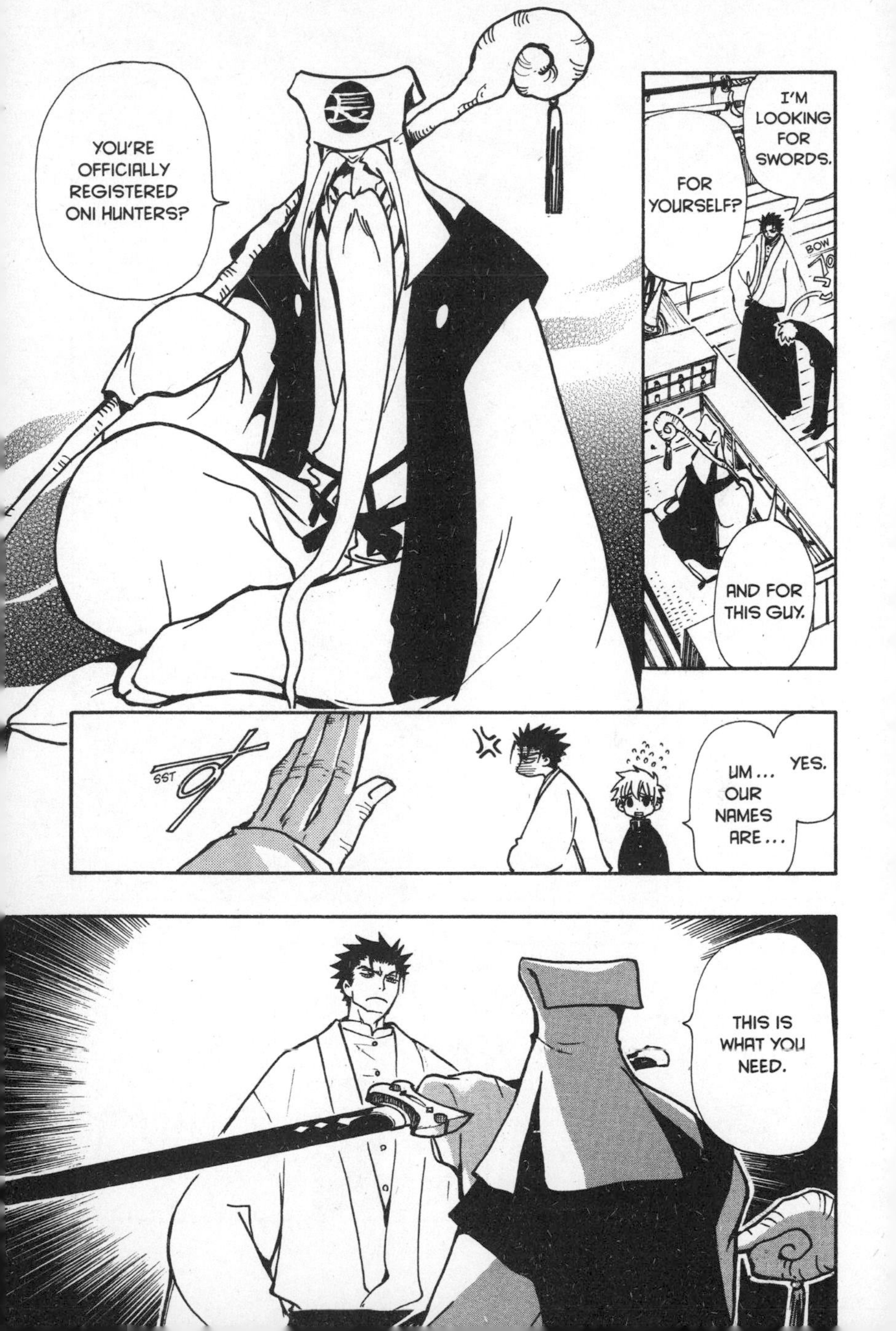
I'M LOOKING FOR SWORDS.
FOR YOURSELF?
BOW
AND FOR THIS GUY.
YOU'RE OFFICIALLY REGISTERED ONI HUNTERS?
YES.
UM... OUR NAMES ARE...
SST
THIS IS WHAT YOU NEED.

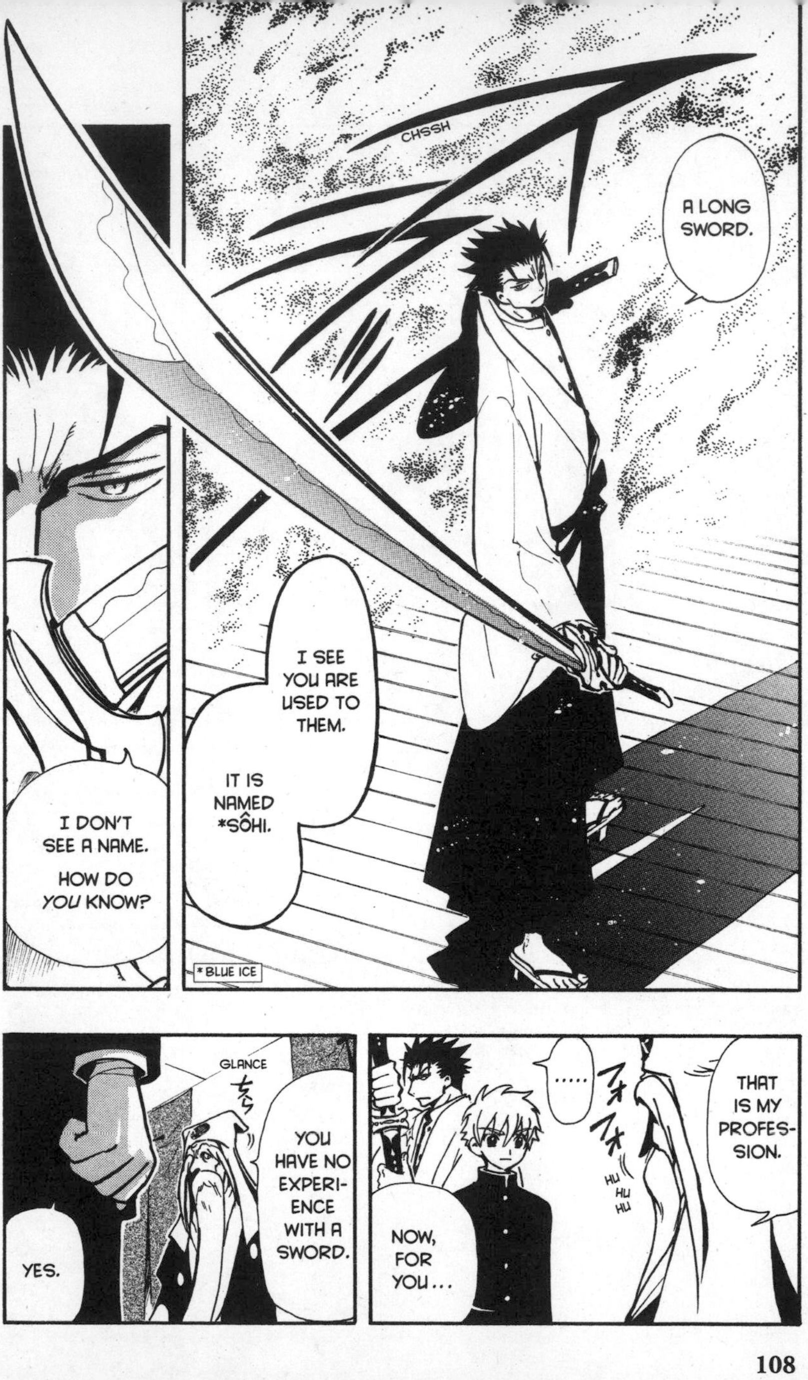
CHSSH
A LONG SWORD.
I SEE YOU ARE USED TO THEM.
IT IS NAMED *SÔHI.
*BLUE ICE
I DON'T SEE A NAME.
HOW DO *YOU* KNOW?
THAT IS MY PROFES-SION.
HU HU HU
.....
NOW, FOR YOU...
GLANCE
YOU HAVE NO EXPERI-ENCE WITH A SWORD.
YES.

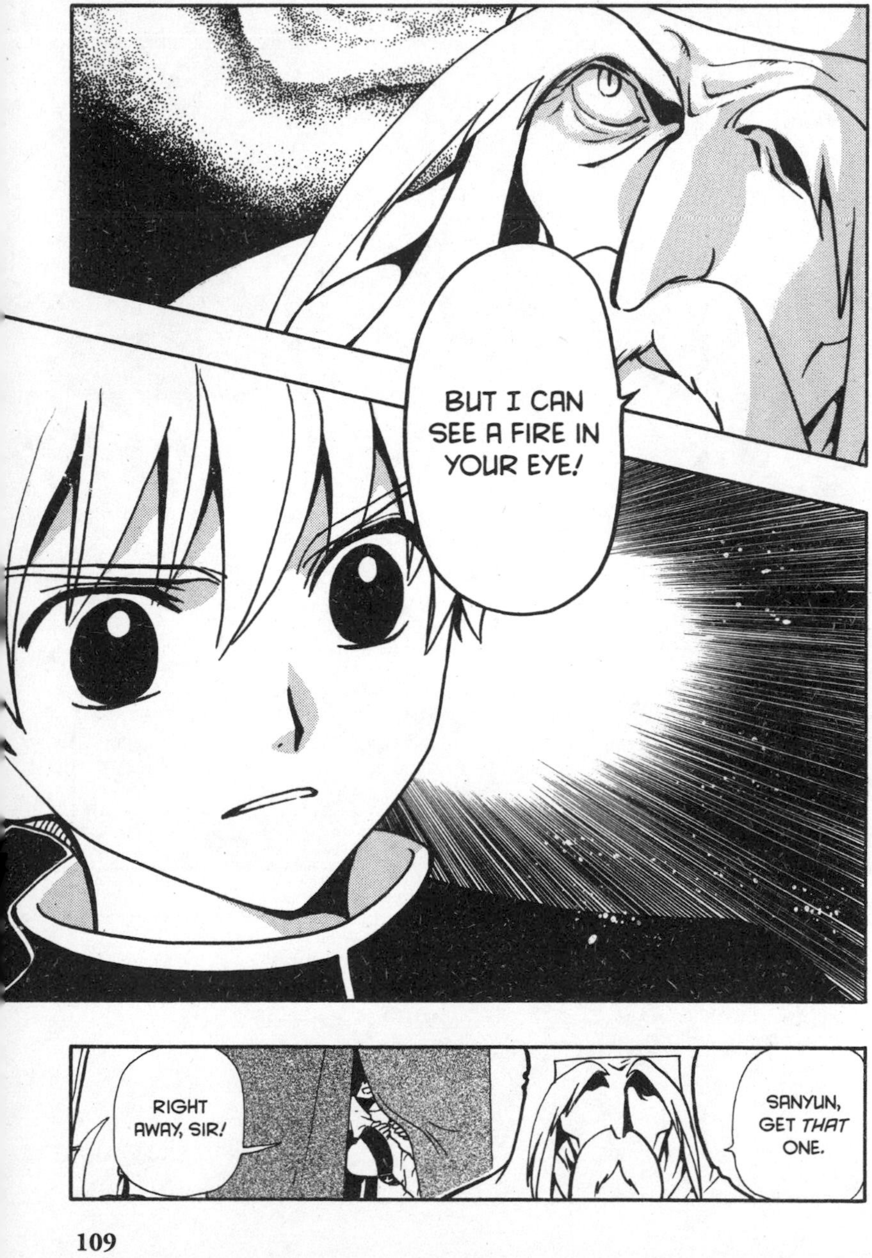
BUT I CAN SEE A FIRE IN YOUR EYE!
SANYUN, GET *THAT* ONE.
RIGHT AWAY, SIR!

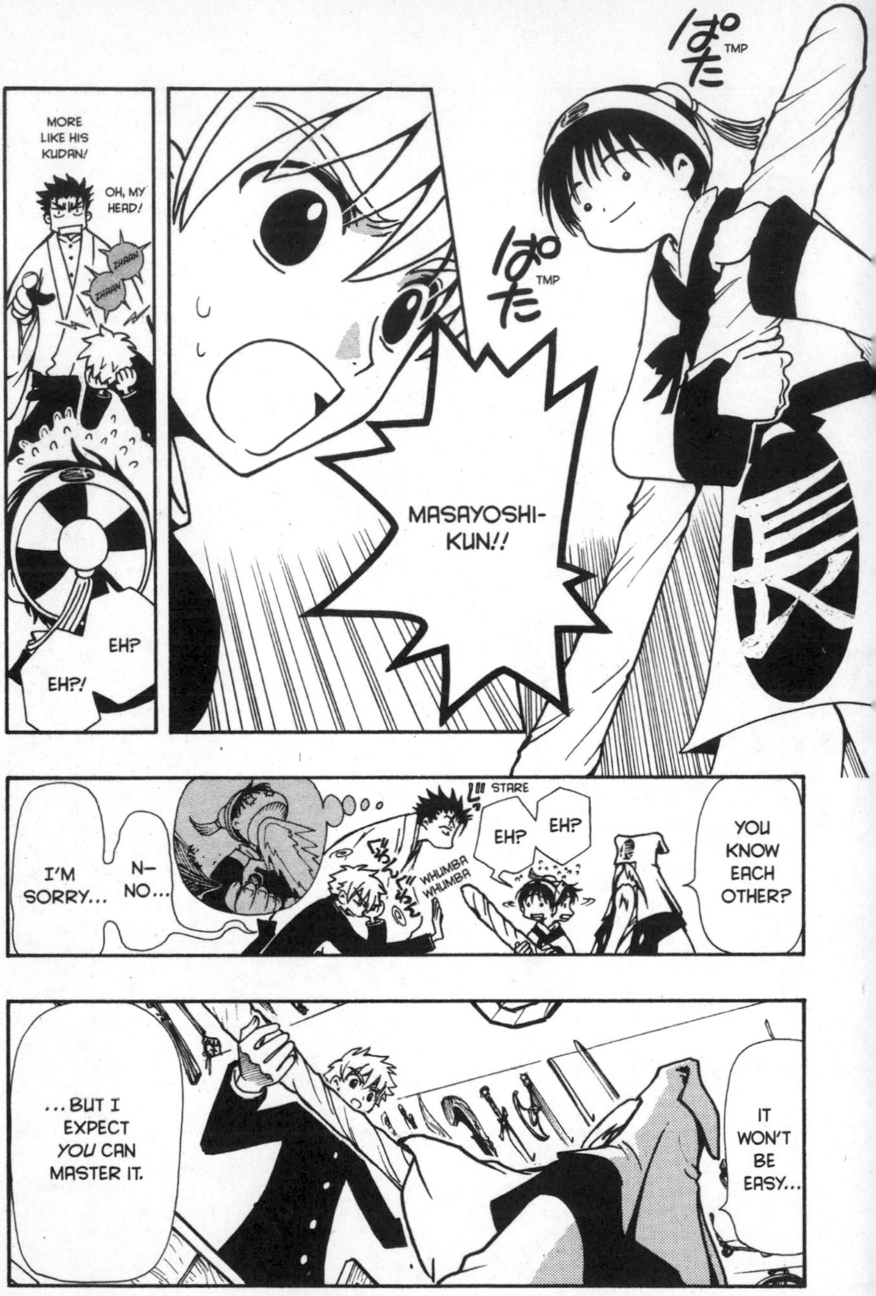

TMP
TMP
MASAYOSHI-KUN!!
MORE LIKE HIS KUDAN!
OH, MY HEAD!
ZHAAN
ZHAAN
EH?
EH?!
YOU KNOW EACH OTHER?
EH?
EH?
STARE
WHUMBA WHUMBA
N— NO...
I'M SORRY...
IT WON'T BE EASY...
...BUT I EXPECT *YOU* CAN MASTER IT.

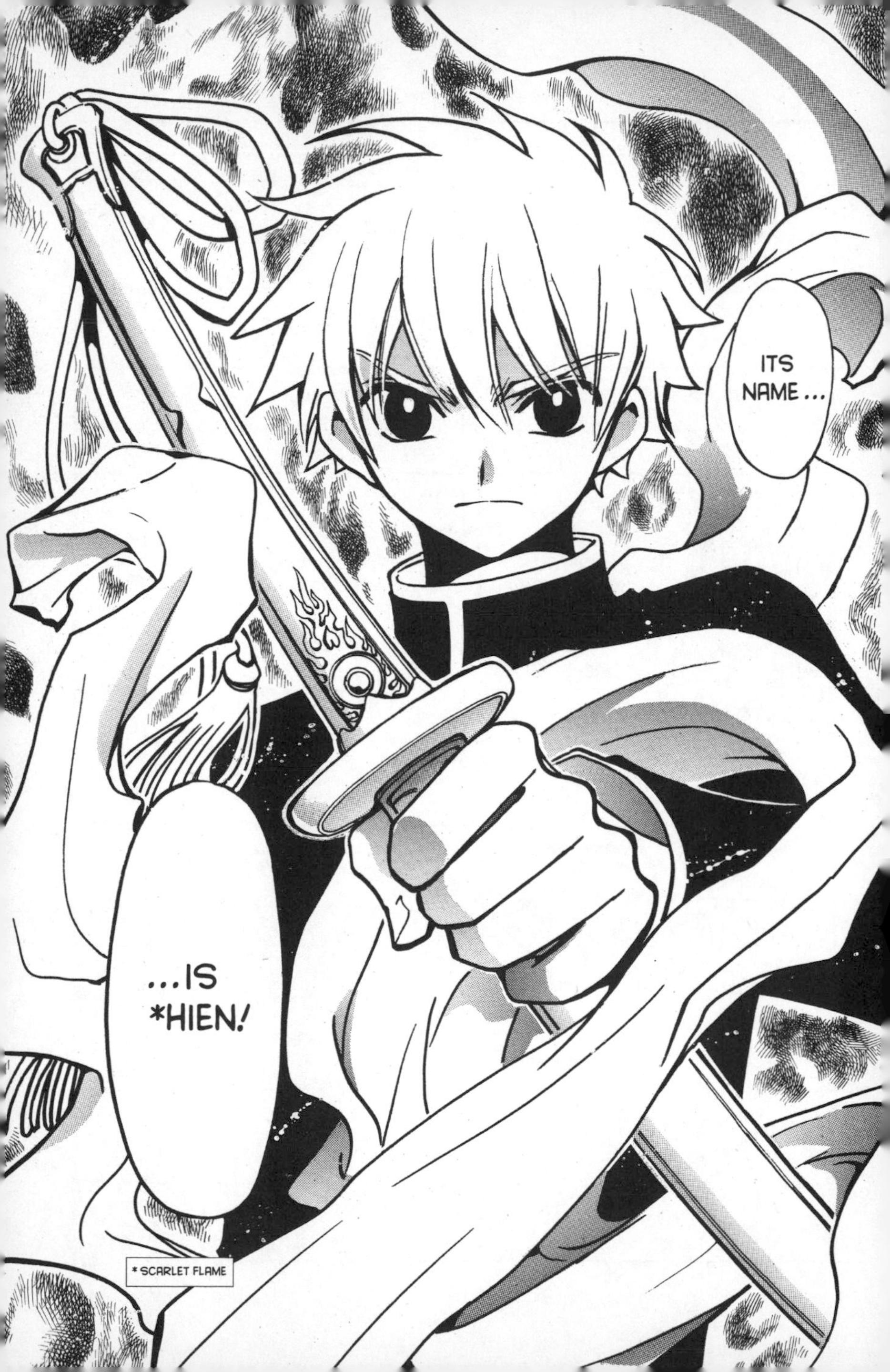
ITS NAME ...
...IS *HIEN!
* SCARLET FLAME

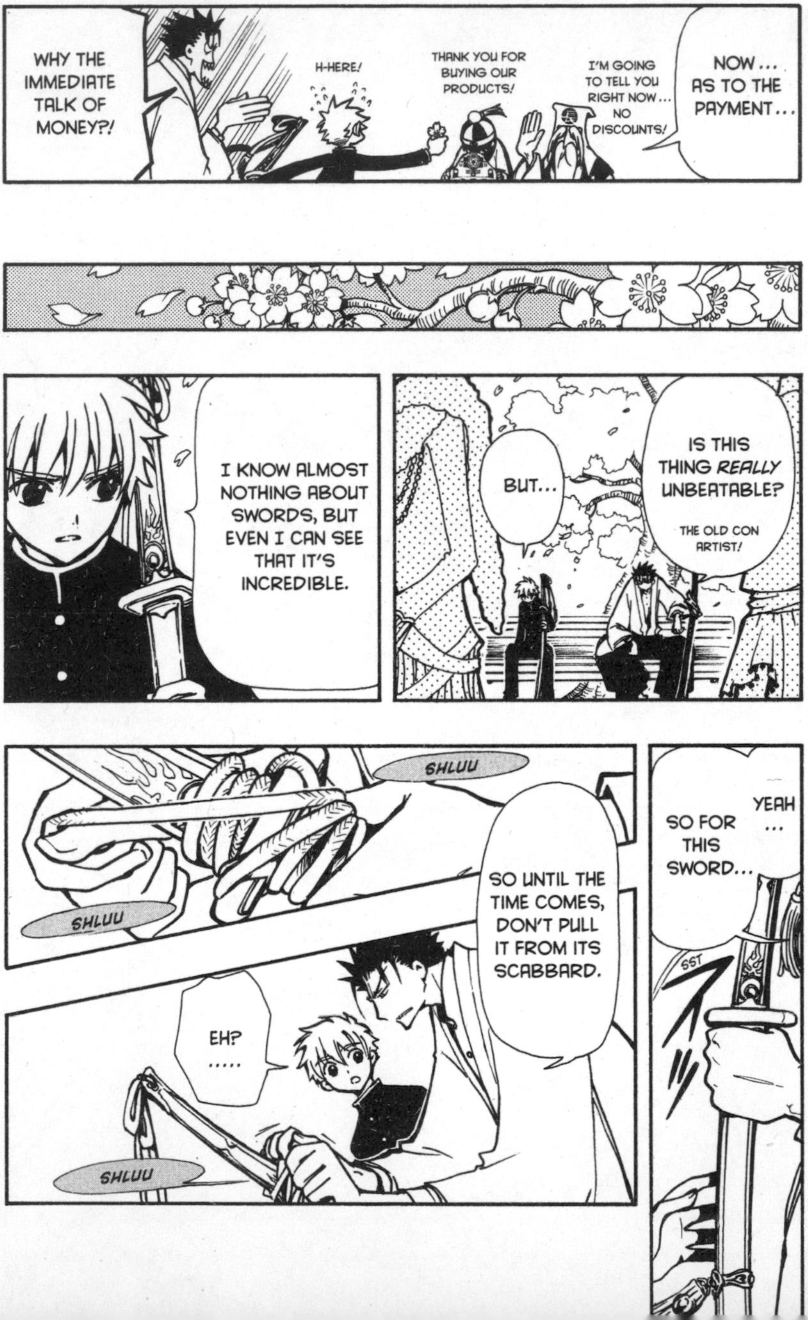
NOW... AS TO THE PAYMENT...
I'M GOING TO TELL YOU RIGHT NOW... NO DISCOUNTS!
THANK YOU FOR BUYING OUR PRODUCTS!
H-HERE!
WHY THE IMMEDIATE TALK OF MONEY?!
IS THIS THING REALLY UNBEATABLE?
THE OLD CON ARTIST!
BUT...
I KNOW ALMOST NOTHING ABOUT SWORDS, BUT EVEN I CAN SEE THAT IT'S INCREDIBLE.
YEAH ...
SO FOR THIS SWORD...
SST
SHLUU
SHLUU
SO UNTIL THE TIME COMES, DON'T PULL IT FROM ITS SCABBARD.
EH? .....
SHLUU

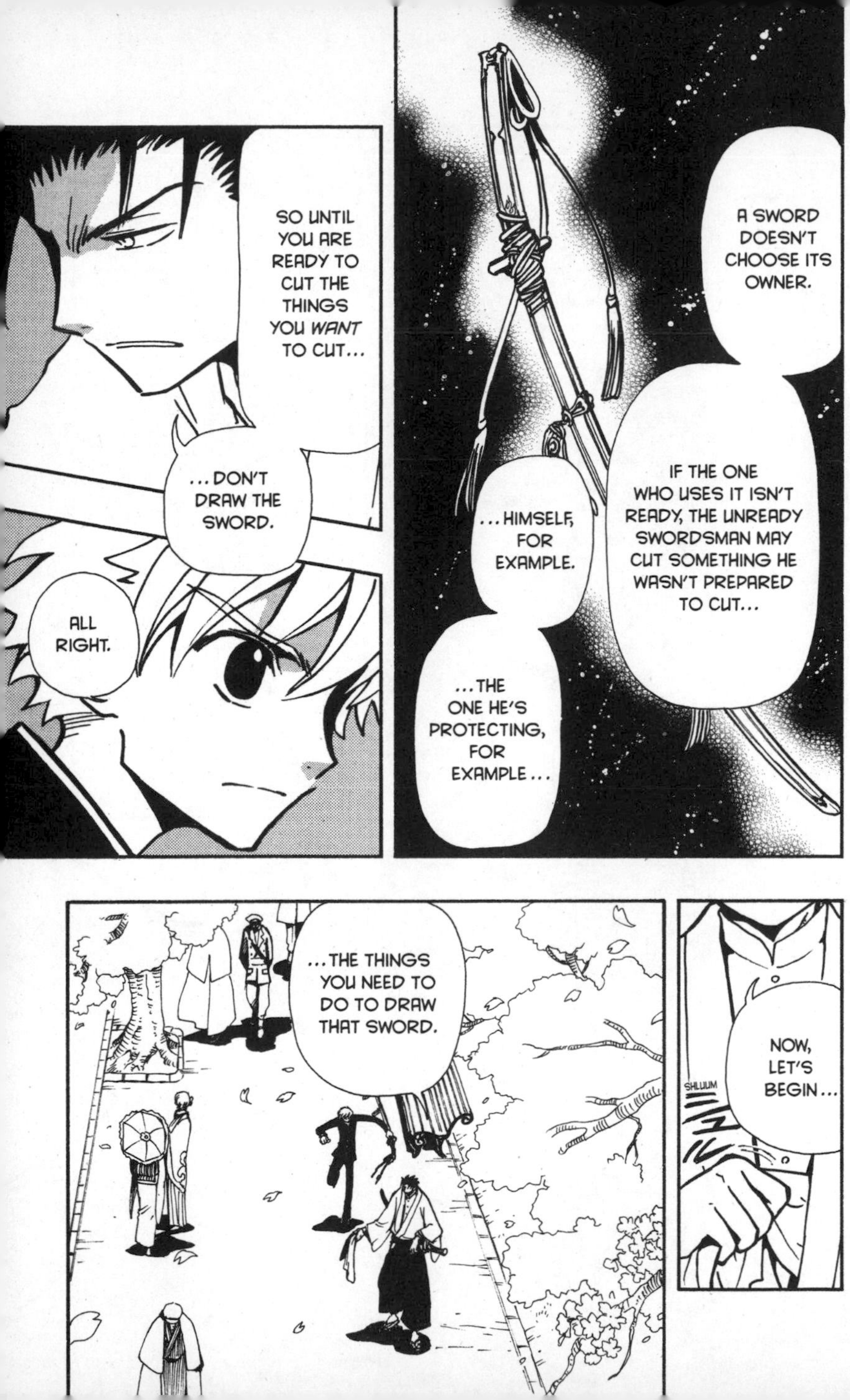
A SWORD DOESN'T CHOOSE ITS OWNER.
IF THE ONE WHO USES IT ISN'T READY, THE UNREADY SWORDSMAN MAY CUT SOMETHING HE WASN'T PREPARED TO CUT...
...HIMSELF, FOR EXAMPLE.
...THE ONE HE'S PROTECTING, FOR EXAMPLE...
SO UNTIL YOU ARE READY TO CUT THE THINGS YOU *WANT* TO CUT...
...DON'T DRAW THE SWORD.
ALL RIGHT.
SHLUUM
NOW, LET'S BEGIN...
...THE THINGS YOU NEED TO DO TO DRAW THAT SWORD.

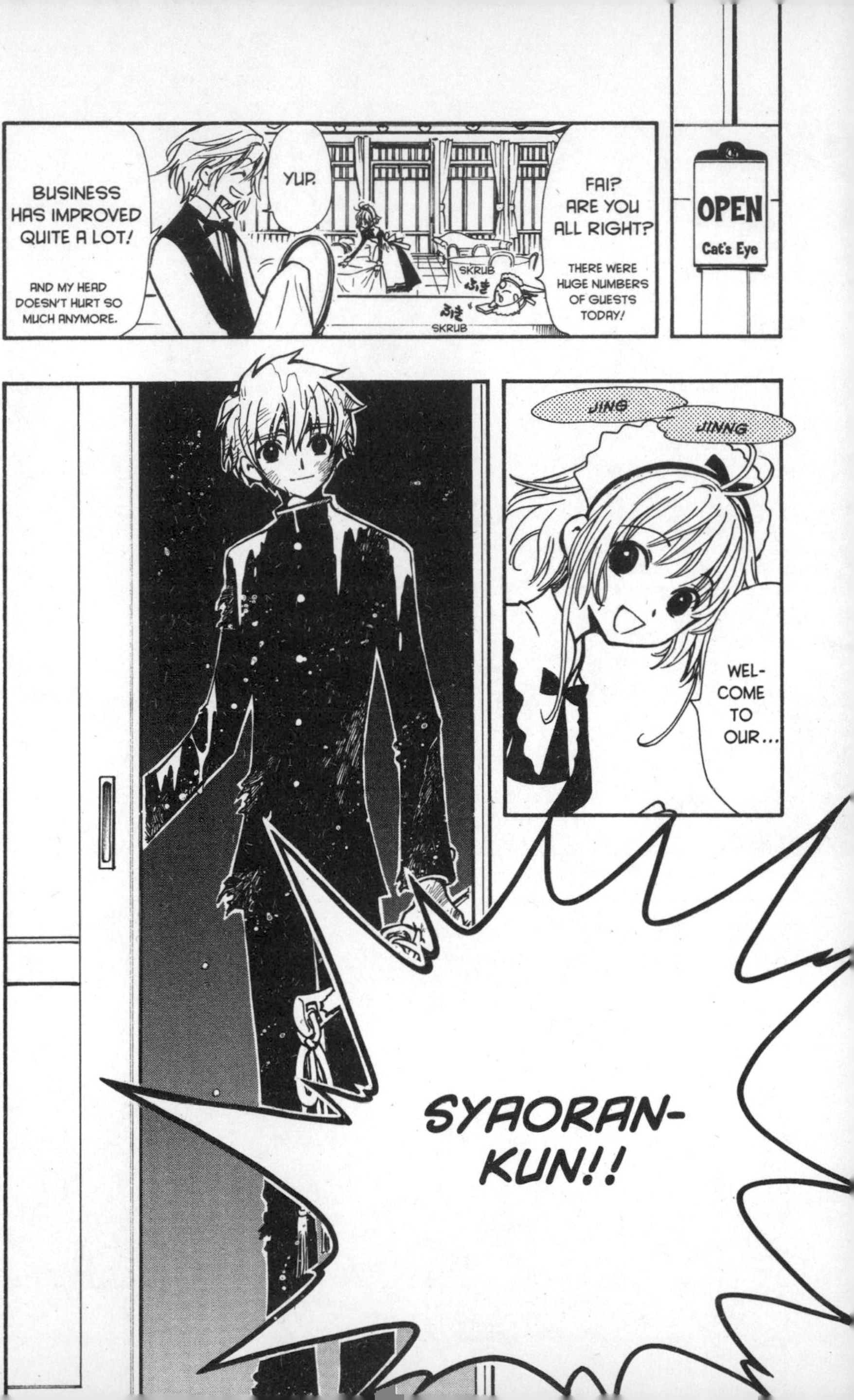
OPEN
Cat's Eye
FAI? ARE YOU ALL RIGHT?
THERE WERE HUGE NUMBERS OF GUESTS TODAY!
SKRUB
ふき
ふき
SKRUB
YUP.
BUSINESS HAS IMPROVED QUITE A LOT!
AND MY HEAD DOESN'T HURT SO MUCH ANYMORE.
JING
JINNG
WEL-COME TO OUR...
SYAORAN-KUN!!

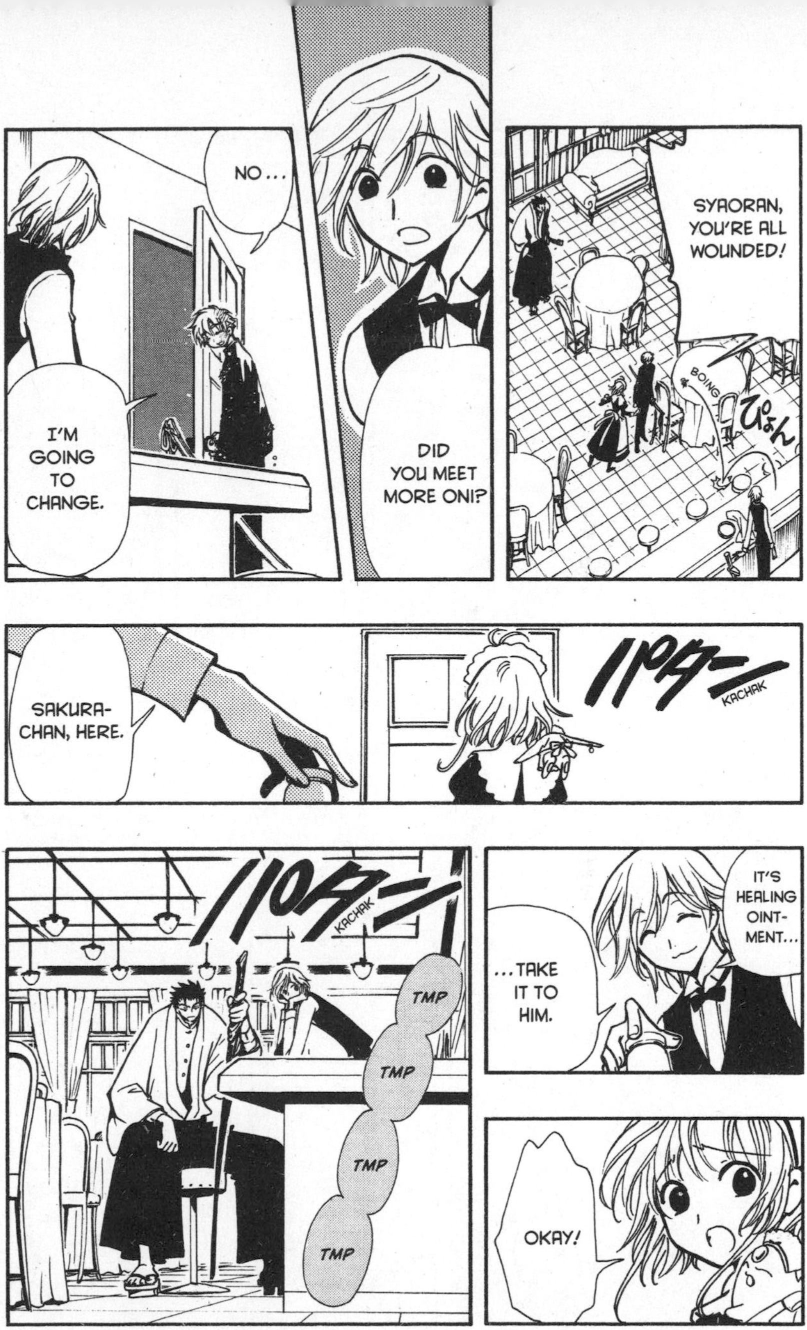
SYAORAN, YOU'RE ALL WOUNDED!
BOING
ぴょん
DID YOU MEET MORE ONI?
NO...
I'M GOING TO CHANGE.
パタン
KACHAK
SAKURA-CHAN, HERE.
IT'S HEALING OINTMENT...
...TAKE IT TO HIM.
OKAY!
パタン
KACHAK
TMP
TMP
TMP
TMP

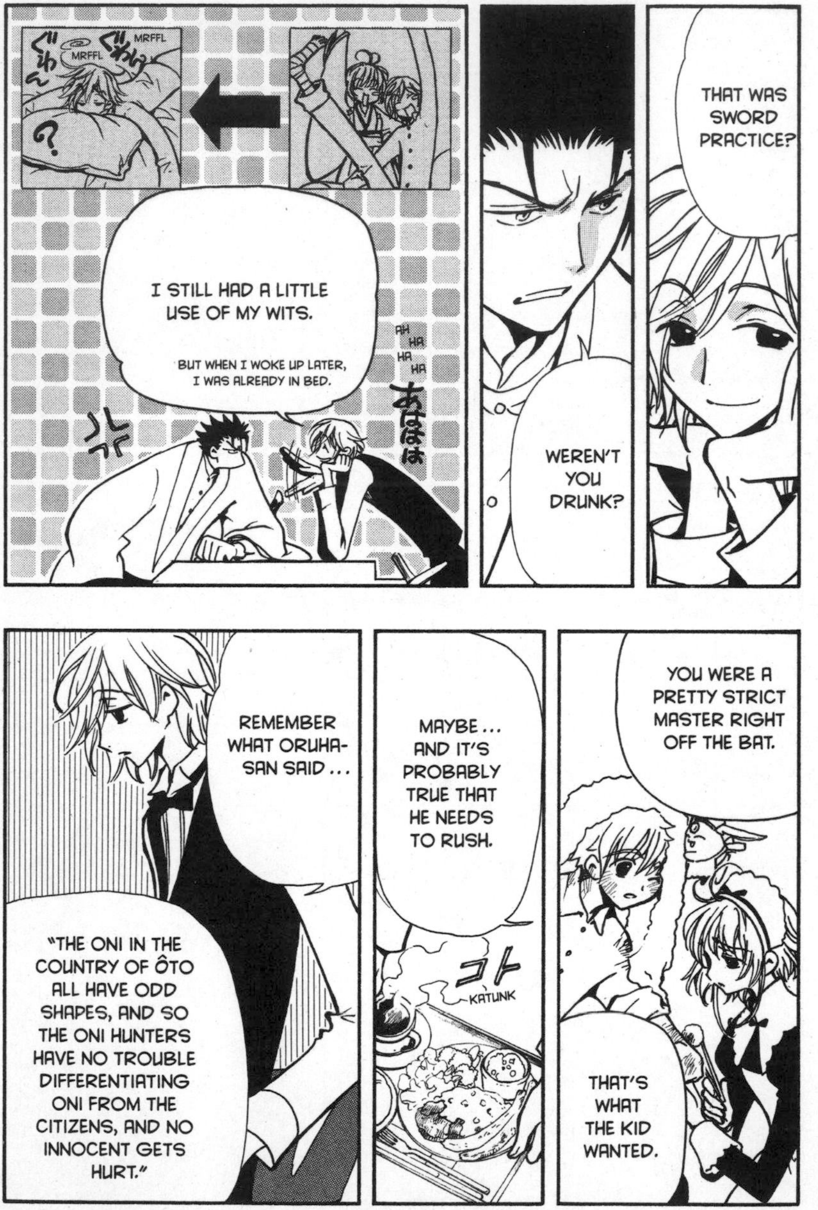
THAT WAS SWORD PRACTICE?
WEREN'T YOU DRUNK?
MRFFL
MRFFL
I STILL HAD A LITTLE USE OF MY WITS.
BUT WHEN I WOKE UP LATER, I WAS ALREADY IN BED.
AH HA HA HA
あははは
YOU WERE A PRETTY STRICT MASTER RIGHT OFF THE BAT.
THAT'S WHAT THE KID WANTED.
MAYBE ... AND IT'S PROBABLY TRUE THAT HE NEEDS TO RUSH.
コト
KATUNK
REMEMBER WHAT ORUHA-SAN SAID ...
"THE ONI IN THE COUNTRY OF ÔTO ALL HAVE ODD SHAPES, AND SO THE ONI HUNTERS HAVE NO TROUBLE DIFFERENTIATING ONI FROM THE CITIZENS, AND NO INNOCENT GETS HURT."

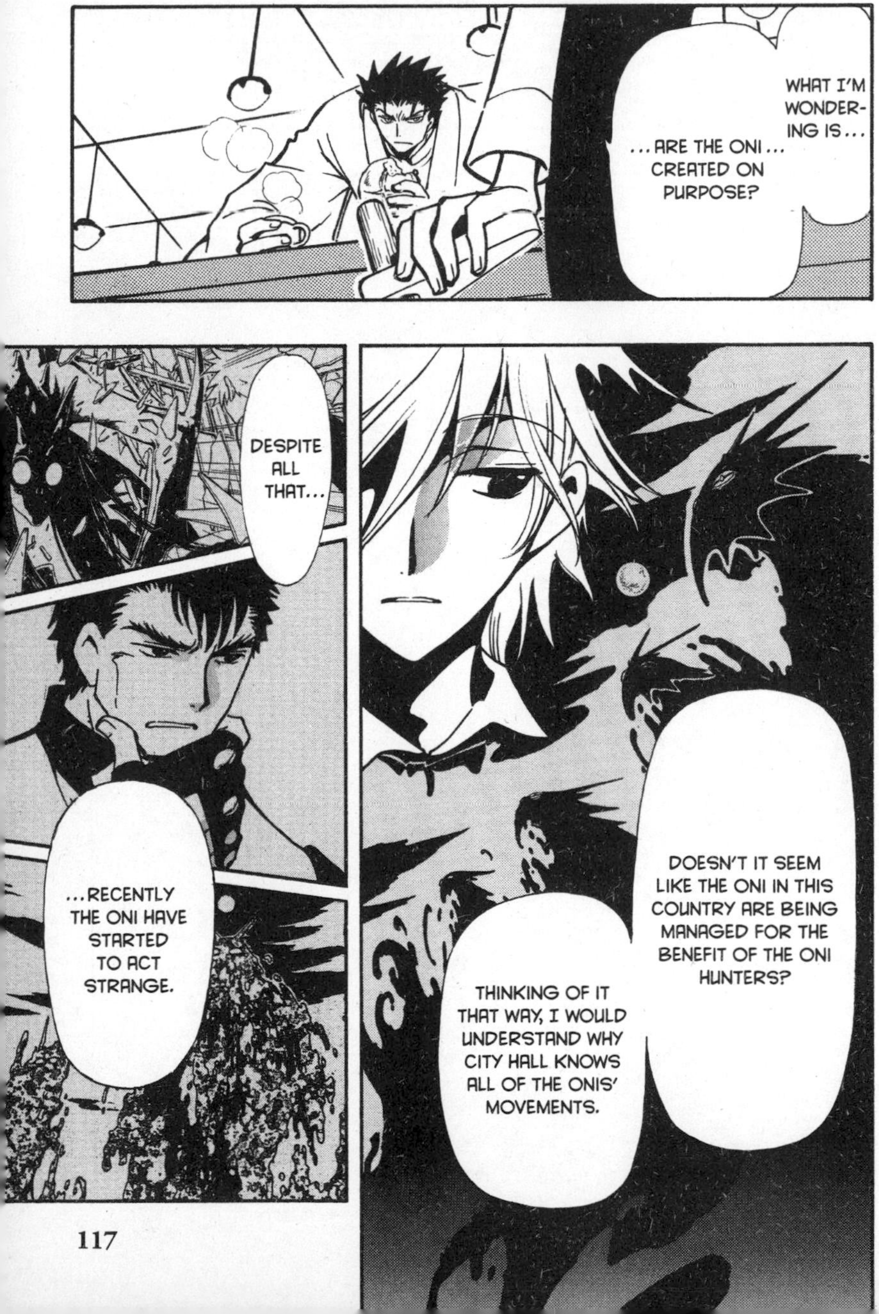
WHAT I'M WONDER-ING IS...
...ARE THE ONI... CREATED ON PURPOSE?
DOESN'T IT SEEM LIKE THE ONI IN THIS COUNTRY ARE BEING MANAGED FOR THE BENEFIT OF THE ONI HUNTERS?
THINKING OF IT THAT WAY, I WOULD UNDERSTAND WHY CITY HALL KNOWS ALL OF THE ONIS' MOVEMENTS.
DESPITE ALL THAT...
...RECENTLY THE ONI HAVE STARTED TO ACT STRANGE.

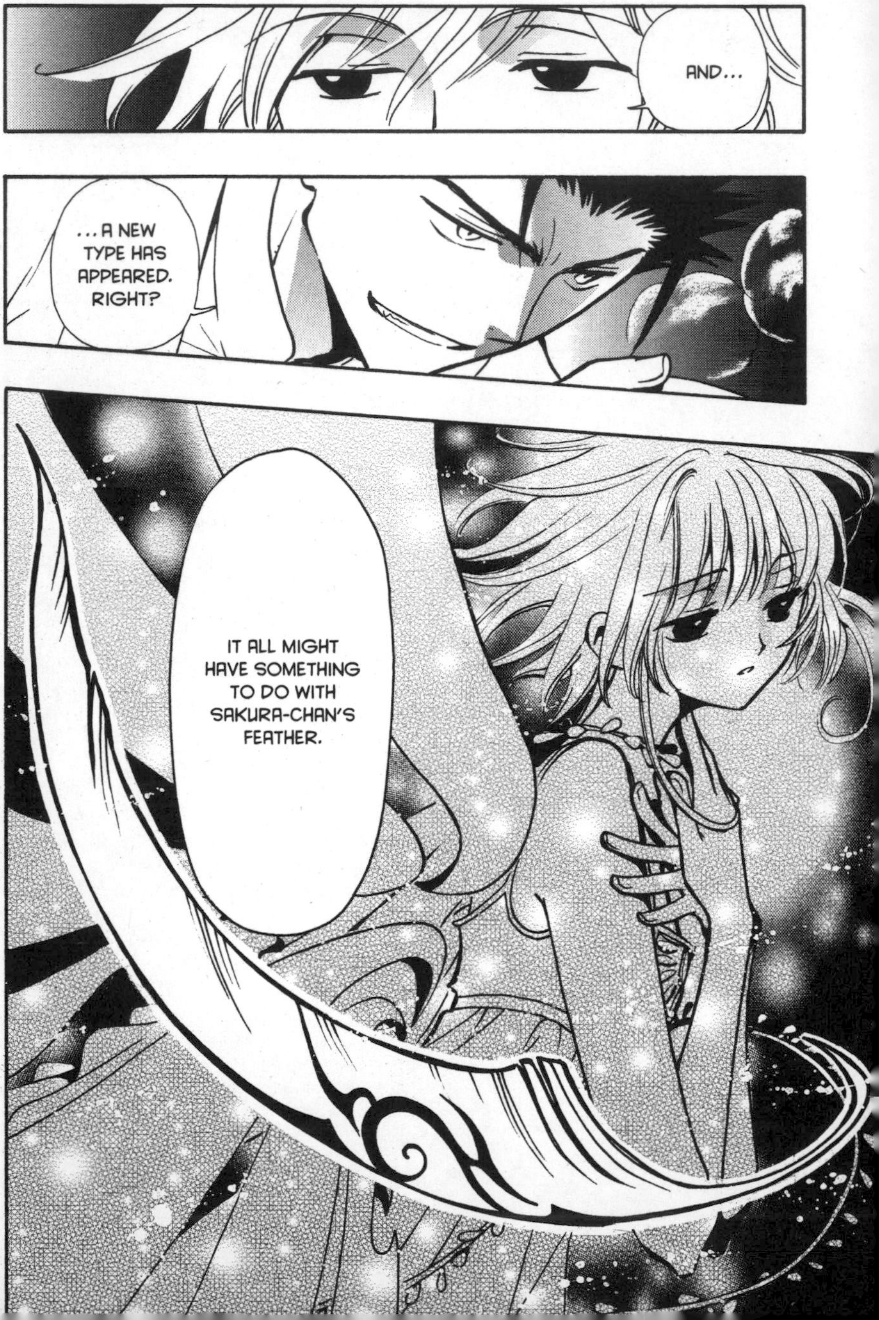
AND...
...A NEW TYPE HAS APPEARED. RIGHT?
IT ALL MIGHT HAVE SOMETHING TO DO WITH SAKURA-CHAN'S FEATHER.

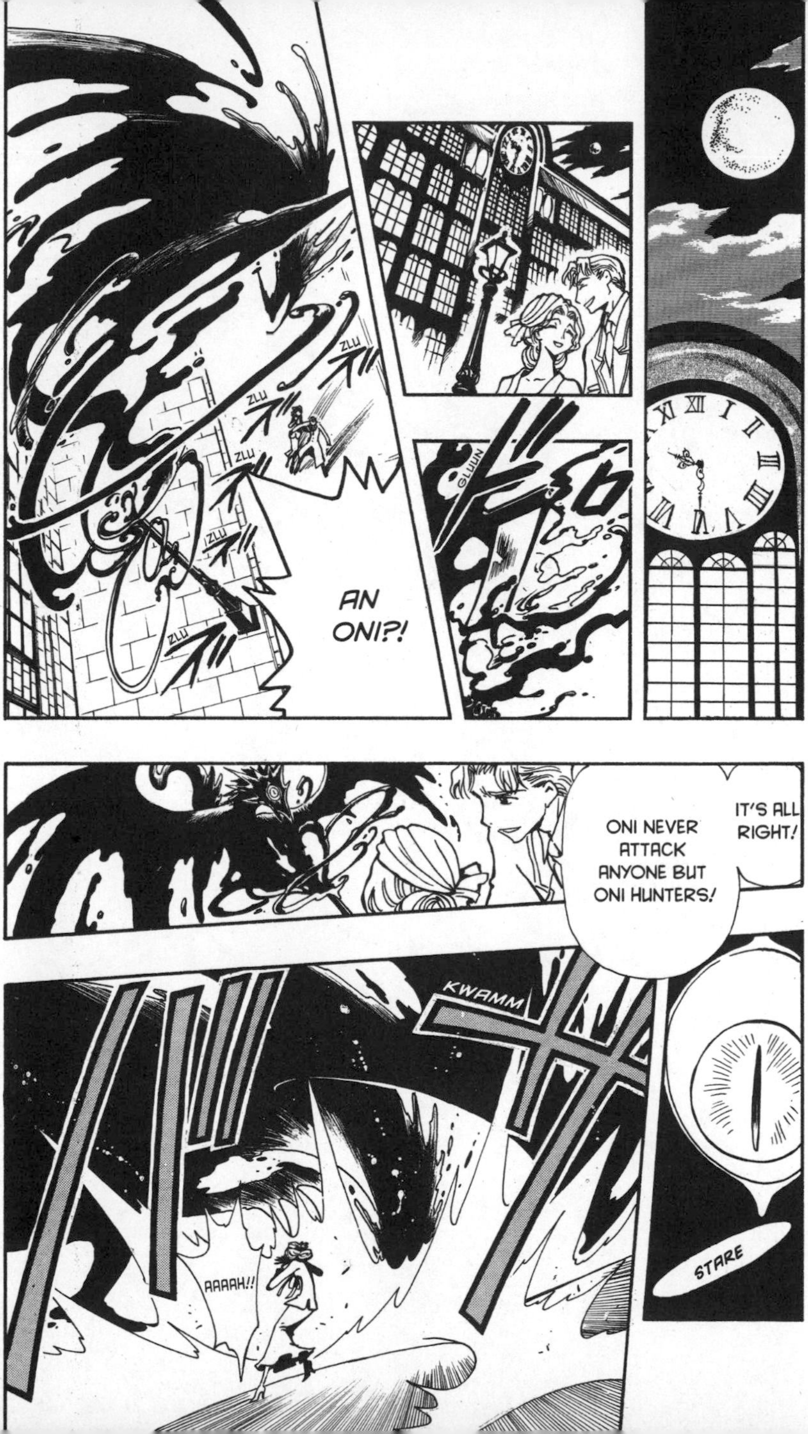
GLUUN
ZLU
ZLU
ZLU
ZLU
ZLU
AN ONI?!
IT'S ALL RIGHT!
ONI NEVER ATTACK ANYONE BUT ONI HUNTERS!
STARE
KWAMM
AAAAH!!

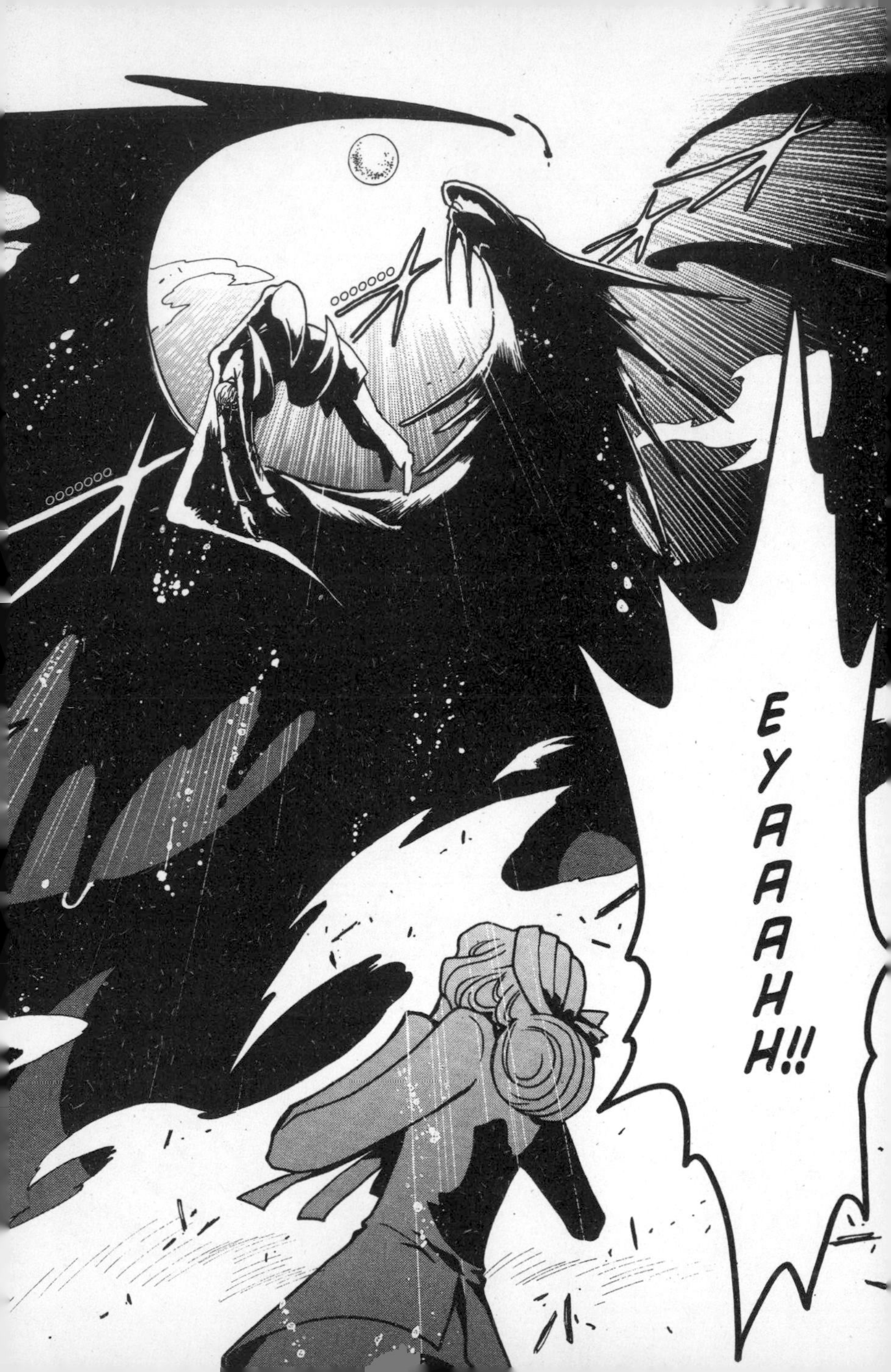
OOOOOOO
OOOOOOOO
EYAAAAHH!!

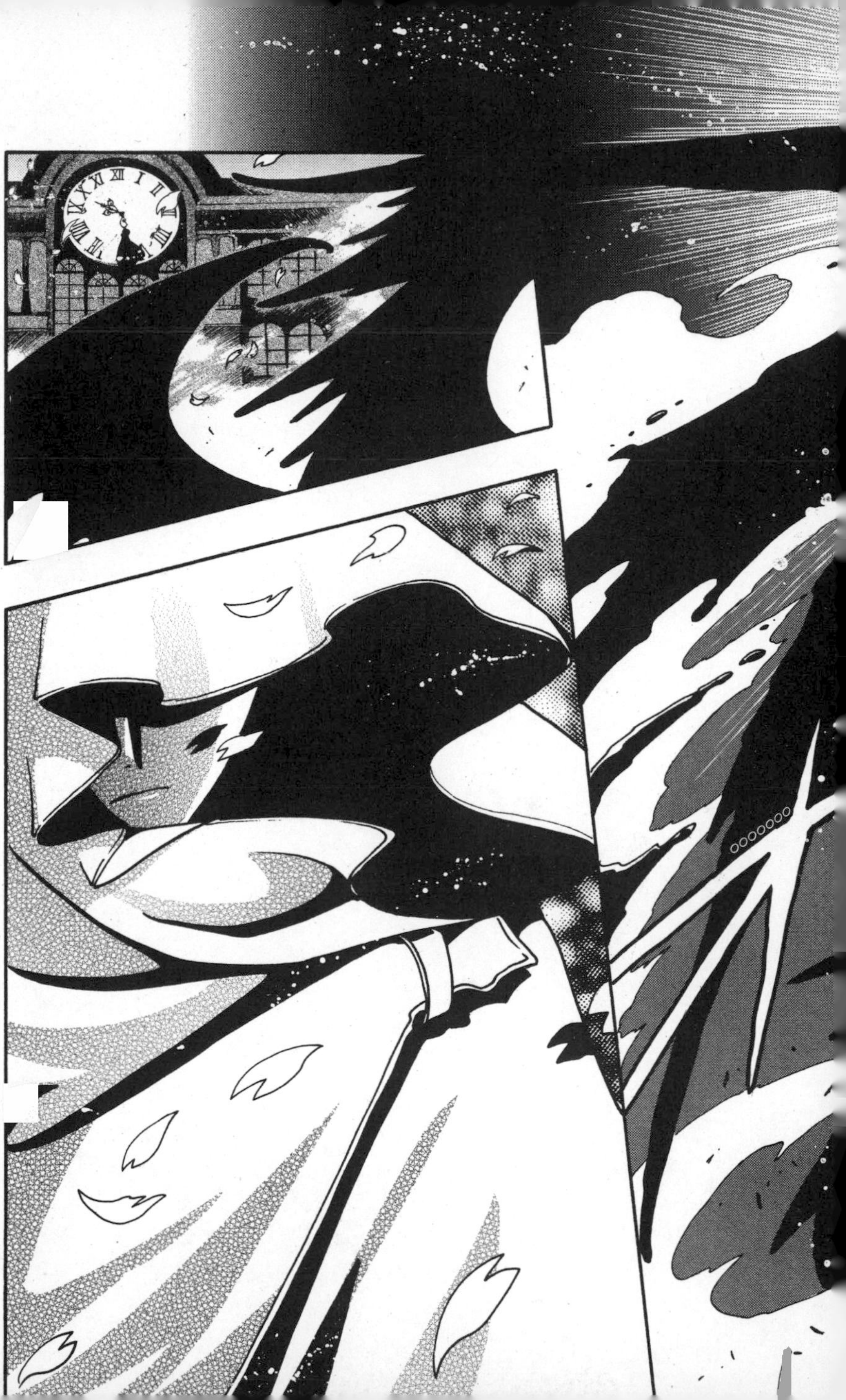

ツバサ

RESERVoir CHRoNiCLE

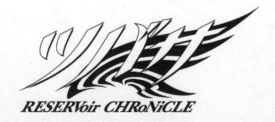

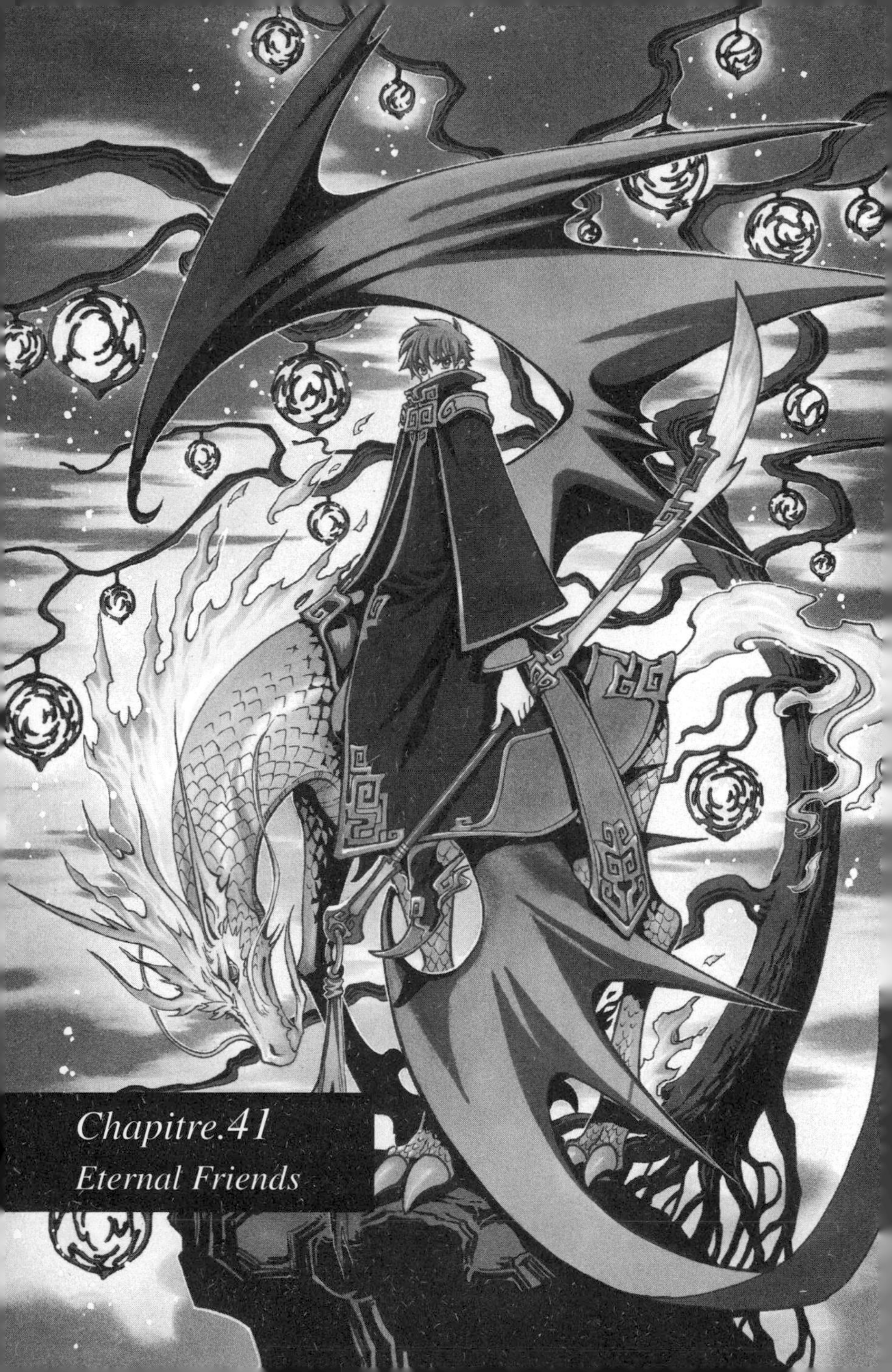

Chapitre.41

Eternal Friends

ツバサ

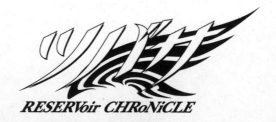

RESERVoir CHRoNiCLE

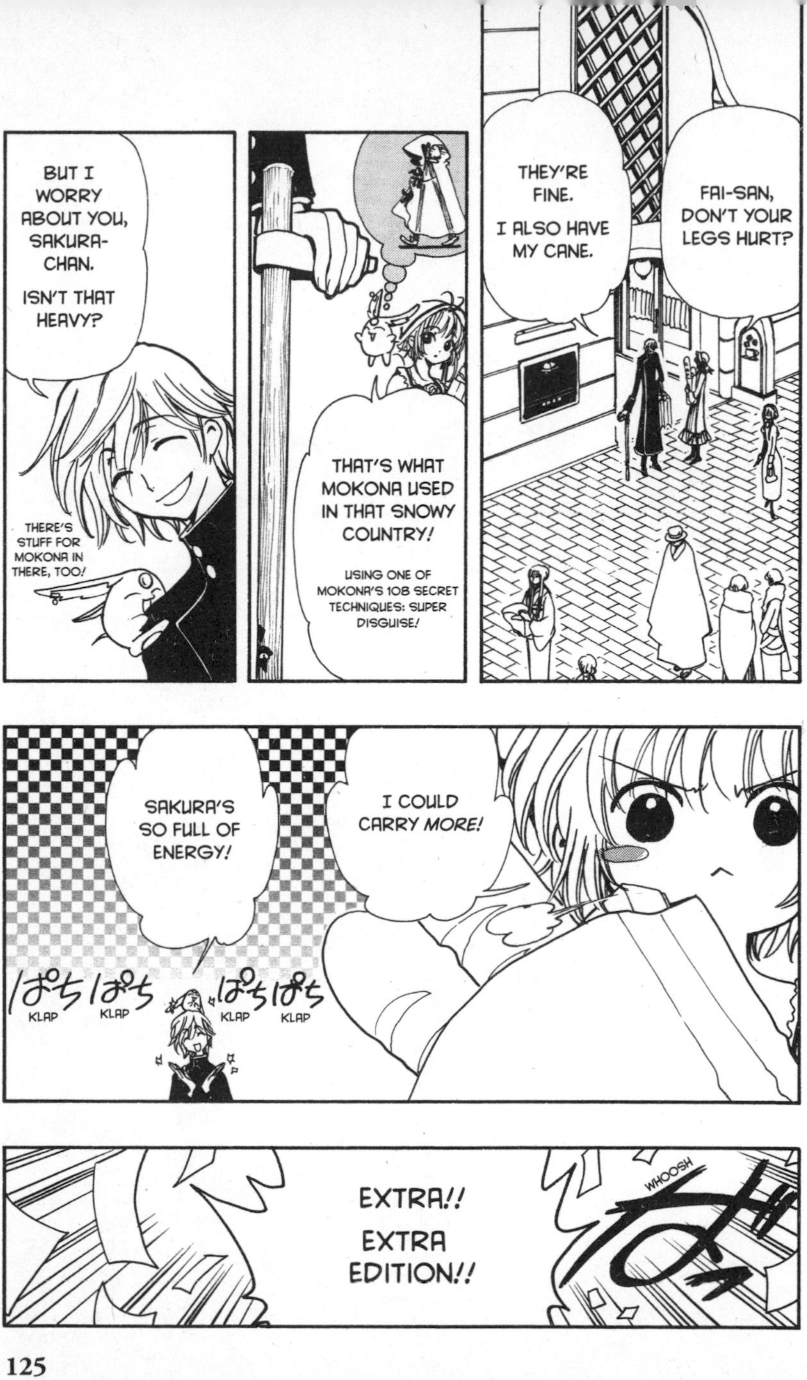
FAI-SAN, DON'T YOUR LEGS HURT?
THEY'RE FINE.
I ALSO HAVE MY CANE.
THAT'S WHAT MOKONA USED IN THAT SNOWY COUNTRY!
USING ONE OF MOKONA'S 108 SECRET TECHNIQUES: SUPER DISGUISE!
BUT I WORRY ABOUT YOU, SAKURA-CHAN.
ISN'T THAT HEAVY?
THERE'S STUFF FOR MOKONA IN THERE, TOO!
I COULD CARRY MORE!
SAKURA'S SO FULL OF ENERGY!
ぱちぱち KLAP KLAP
ぱちぱち KLAP KLAP
WHOOSH
EXTRA!!
EXTRA EDITION!!

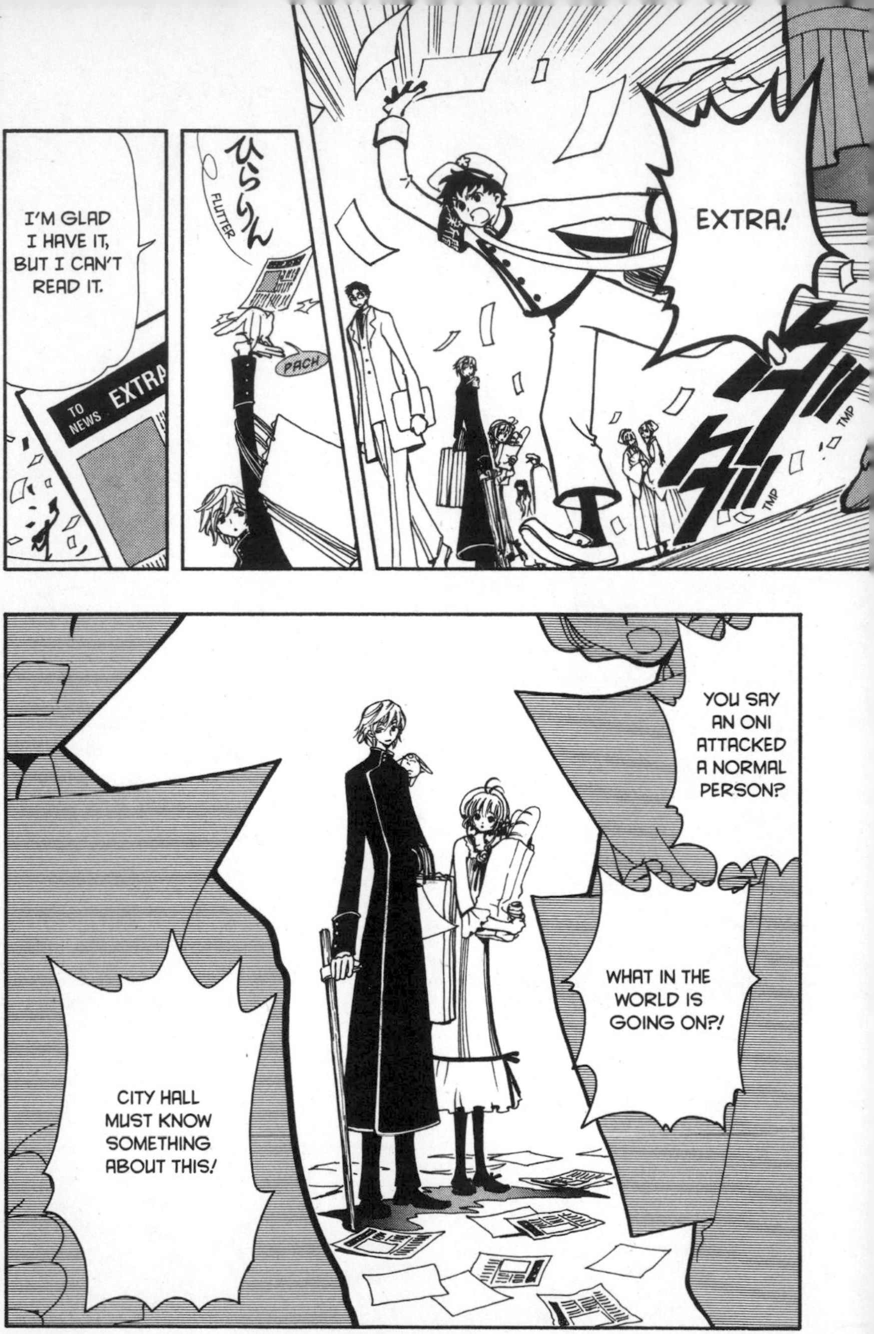
EXTRA!
TMP
TMP
ひらりん
FLUTTER
PACH
I'M GLAD I HAVE IT, BUT I CAN'T READ IT.
TO NEWS
EXTRA
YOU SAY AN ONI ATTACKED A NORMAL PERSON?
WHAT IN THE WORLD IS GOING ON?!
CITY HALL MUST KNOW SOMETHING ABOUT THIS!

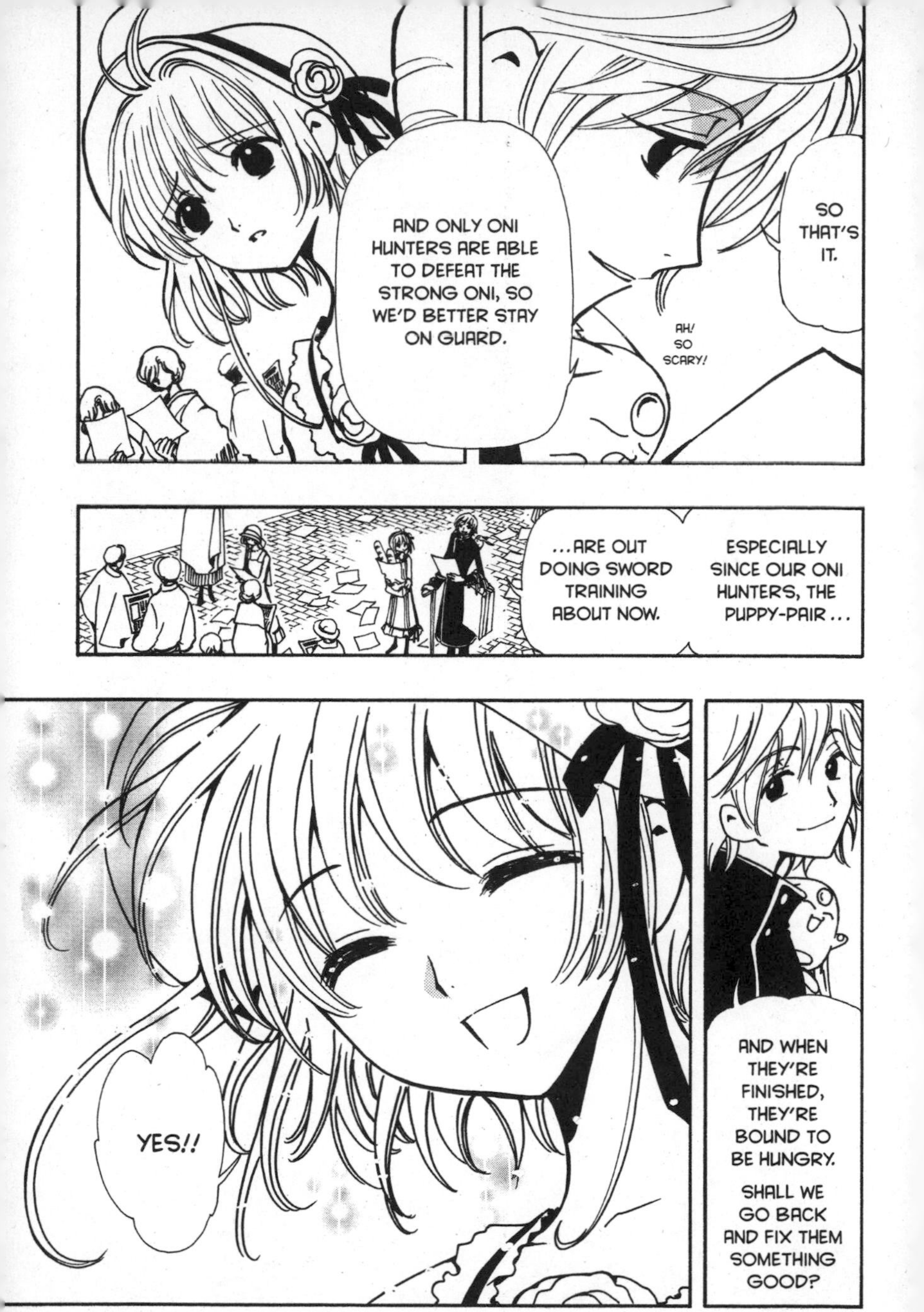
SO THAT'S IT.
AH! SO SCARY!
AND ONLY ONI HUNTERS ARE ABLE TO DEFEAT THE STRONG ONI, SO WE'D BETTER STAY ON GUARD.
ESPECIALLY SINCE OUR ONI HUNTERS, THE PUPPY-PAIR...
...ARE OUT DOING SWORD TRAINING ABOUT NOW.
AND WHEN THEY'RE FINISHED, THEY'RE BOUND TO BE HUNGRY.
SHALL WE GO BACK AND FIX THEM SOMETHING GOOD?
YES!!

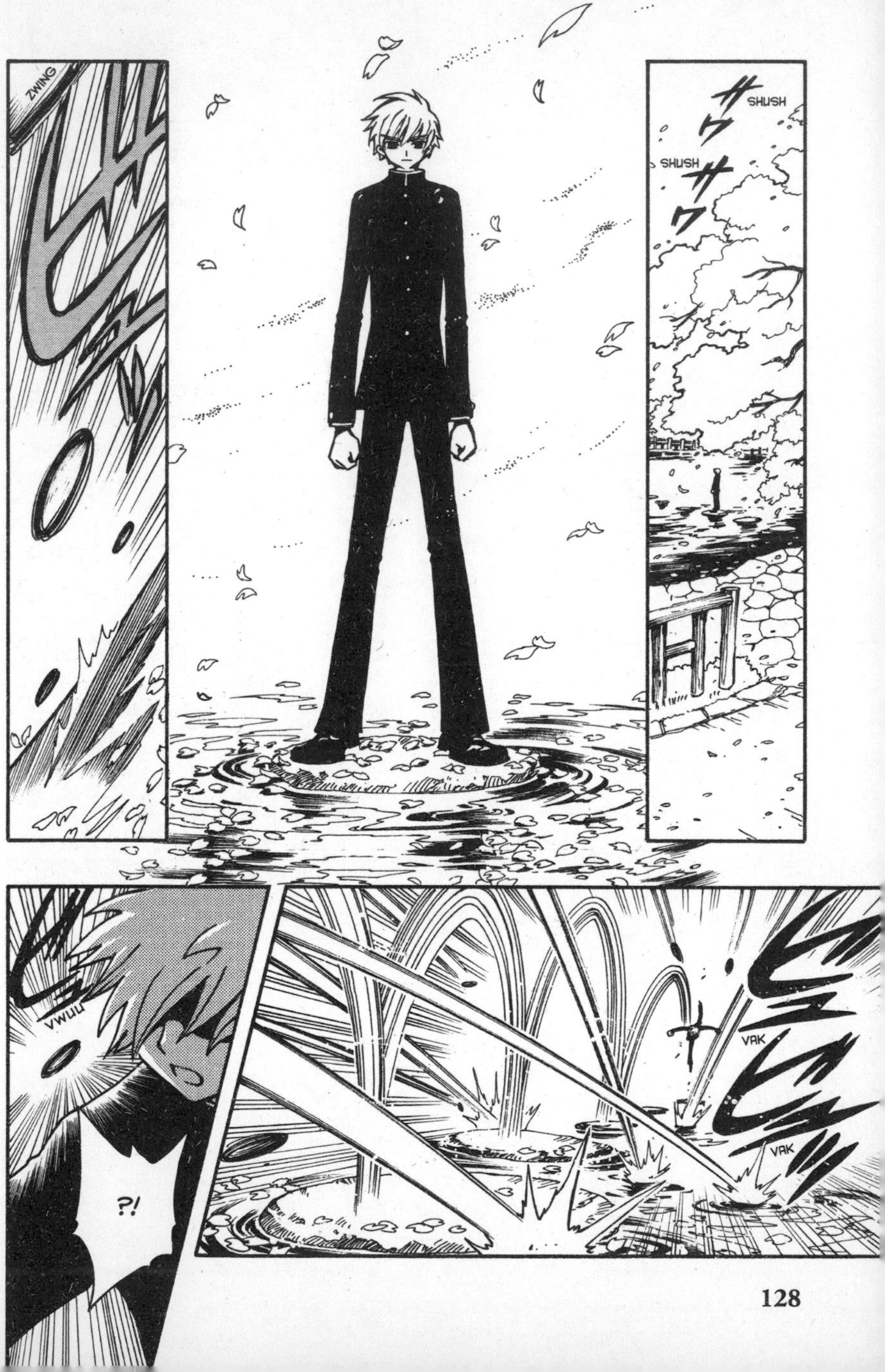
サワ
SHUSH
サワ
SHUSH
ZWING
VAK
VAK
VWUU
?!

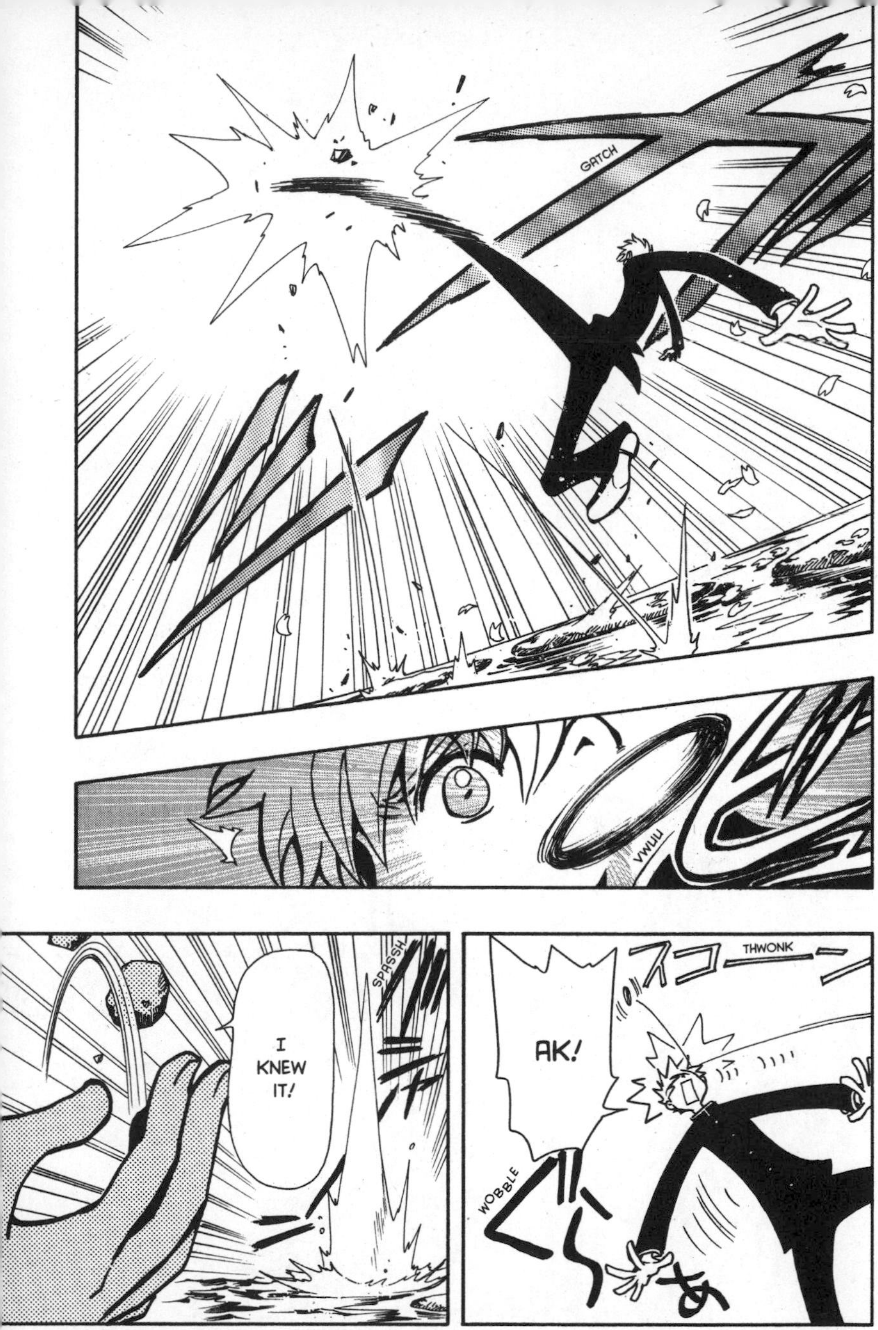
GATCH
VWUU
THWONK
AK!
WOBBLE
SPASSH
I KNEW IT!

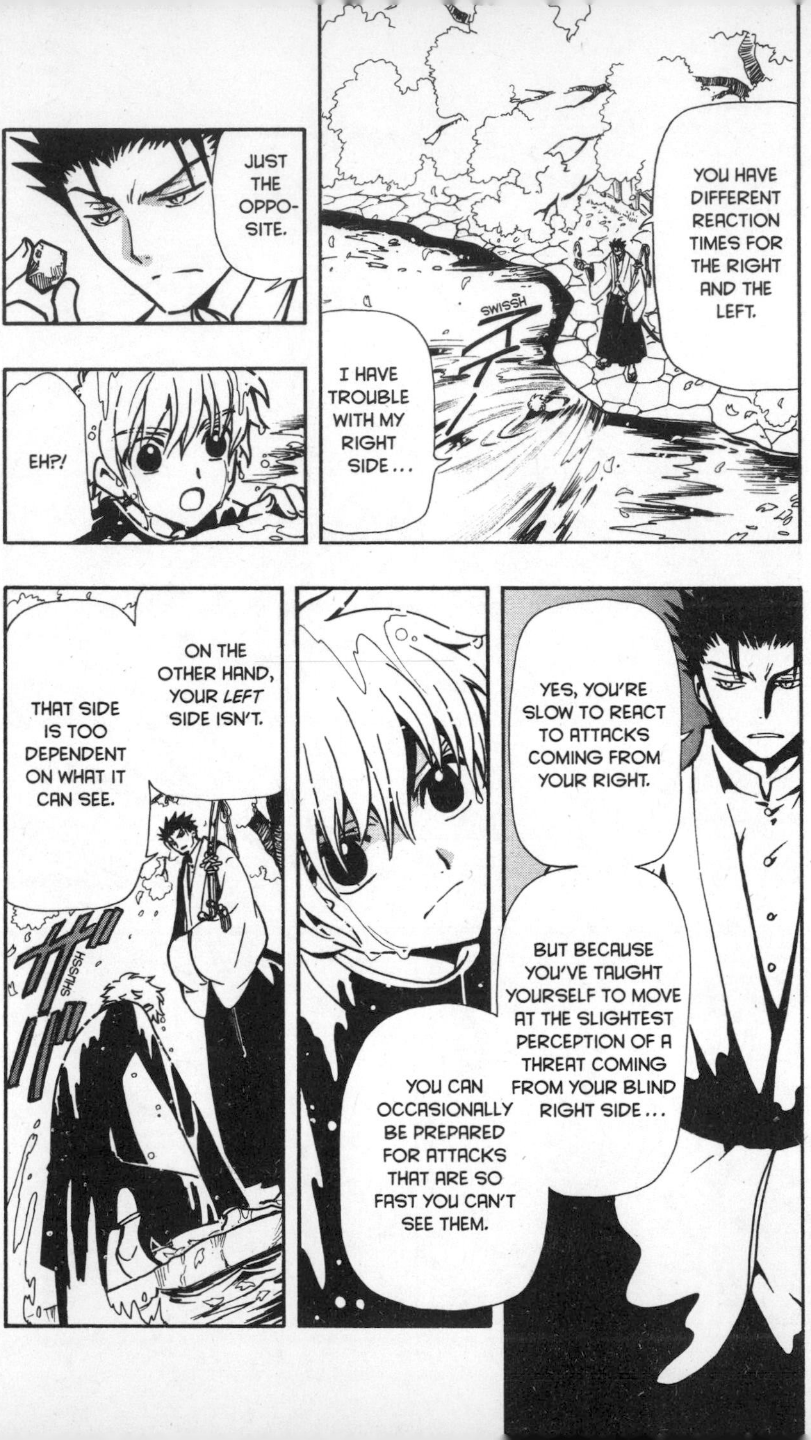
YOU HAVE DIFFERENT REACTION TIMES FOR THE RIGHT AND THE LEFT.
SWISSH
I HAVE TROUBLE WITH MY RIGHT SIDE...
JUST THE OPPO-SITE.
EH?!
YES, YOU'RE SLOW TO REACT TO ATTACKS COMING FROM YOUR RIGHT.
BUT BECAUSE YOU'VE TAUGHT YOURSELF TO MOVE AT THE SLIGHTEST PERCEPTION OF A THREAT COMING FROM YOUR BLIND RIGHT SIDE...
YOU CAN OCCASIONALLY BE PREPARED FOR ATTACKS THAT ARE SO FAST YOU CAN'T SEE THEM.
ON THE OTHER HAND, YOUR *LEFT* SIDE ISN'T.
THAT SIDE IS TOO DEPENDENT ON WHAT IT CAN SEE.
SHUSSH

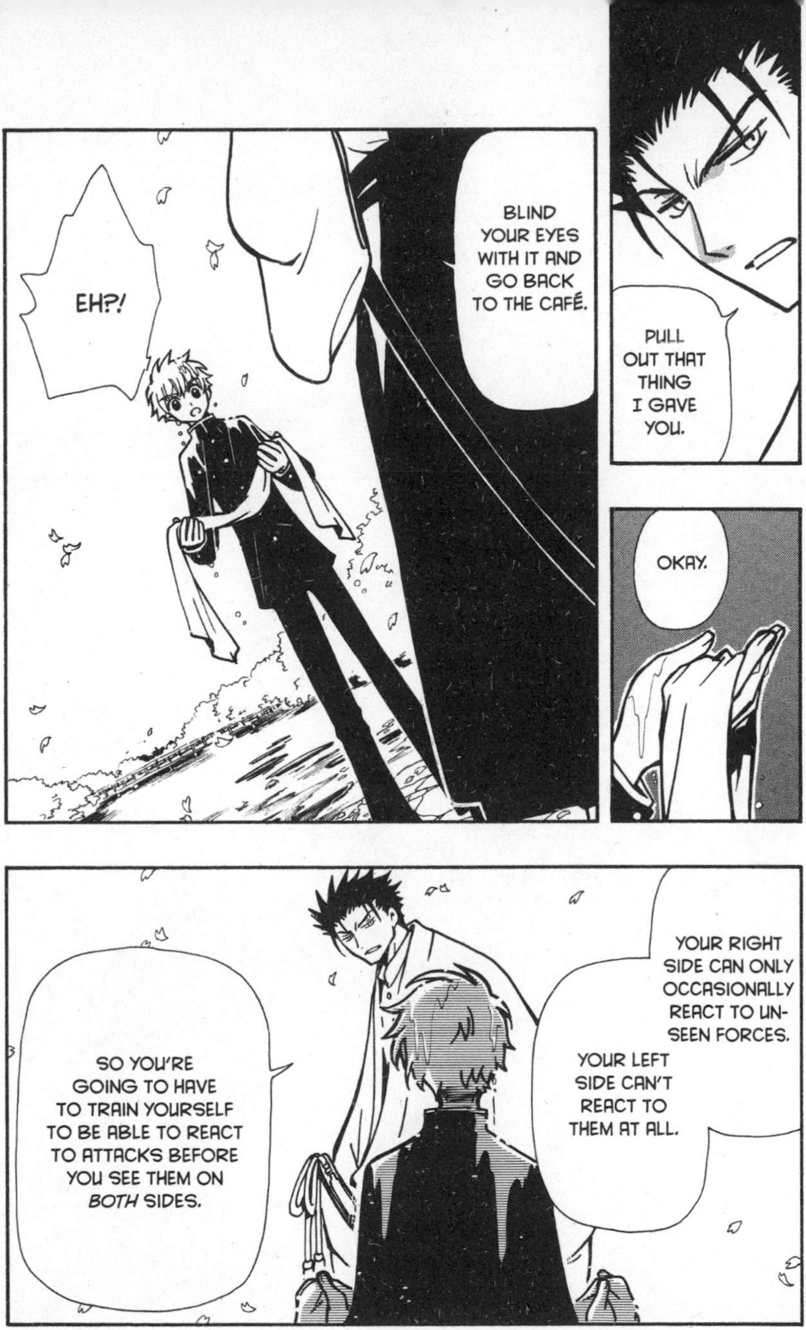
PULL OUT THAT THING I GAVE YOU.
OKAY.
BLIND YOUR EYES WITH IT AND GO BACK TO THE CAFÉ.
EH?!
YOUR RIGHT SIDE CAN ONLY OCCASIONALLY REACT TO UN-SEEN FORCES.
YOUR LEFT SIDE CAN'T REACT TO THEM AT ALL.
SO YOU'RE GOING TO HAVE TO TRAIN YOURSELF TO BE ABLE TO REACT TO ATTACKS BEFORE YOU SEE THEM ON *BOTH* SIDES.

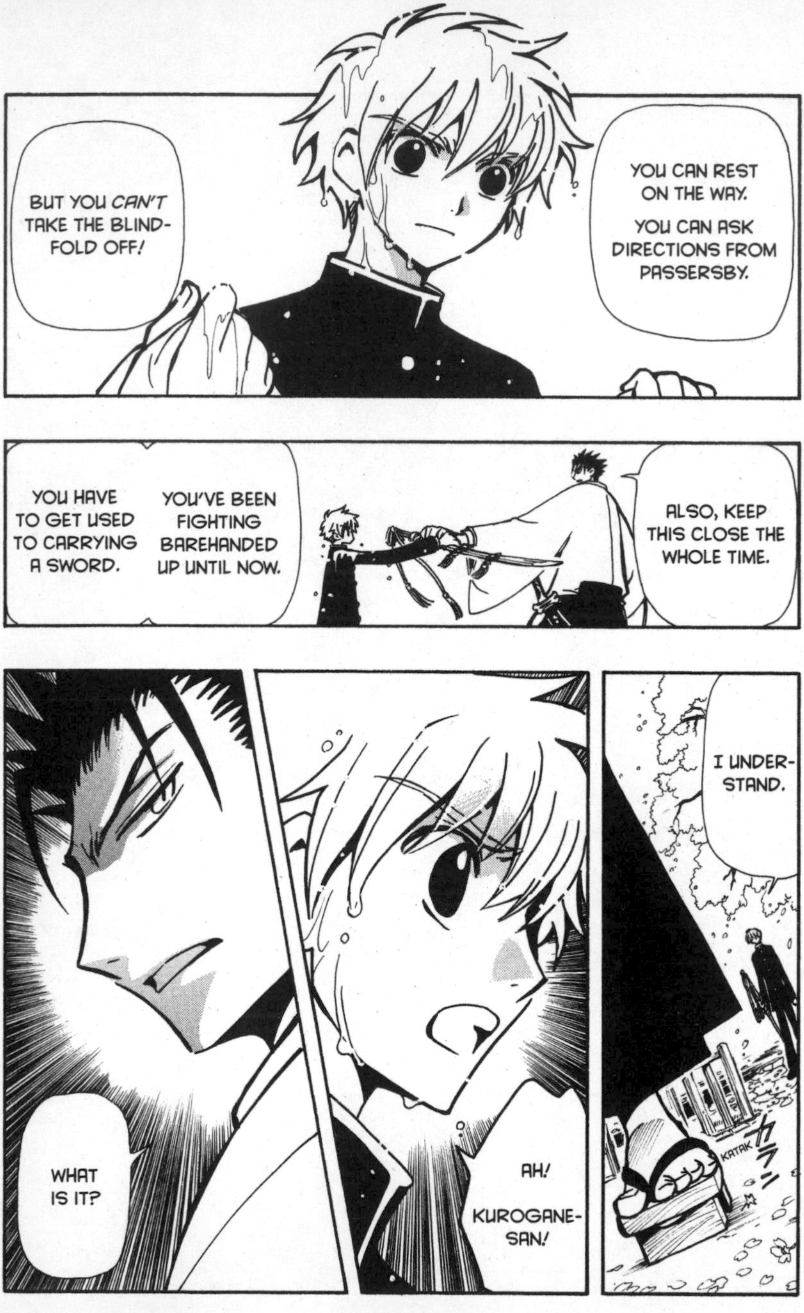
YOU CAN REST ON THE WAY.
YOU CAN ASK DIRECTIONS FROM PASSERSBY.
BUT YOU *CAN'T* TAKE THE BLIND-FOLD OFF!
ALSO, KEEP THIS CLOSE THE WHOLE TIME.
YOU'VE BEEN FIGHTING BAREHANDED UP UNTIL NOW.
YOU HAVE TO GET USED TO CARRYING A SWORD.
I UNDER-STAND.
KATAK
AH!
KUROGANE-SAN!
WHAT IS IT?

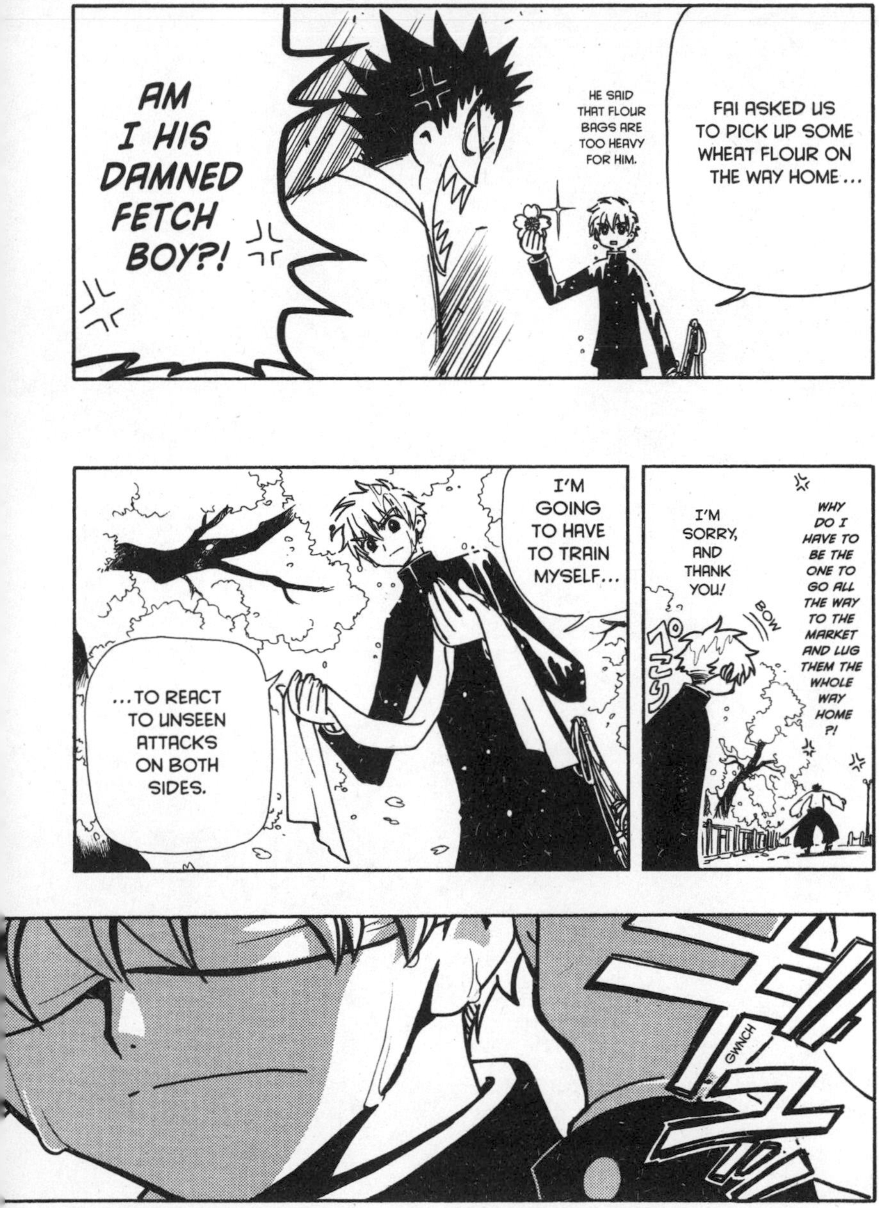
FAI ASKED US TO PICK UP SOME WHEAT FLOUR ON THE WAY HOME...
HE SAID THAT FLOUR BAGS ARE TOO HEAVY FOR HIM.
AM I HIS DAMNED FETCH BOY?!
WHY DO I HAVE TO BE THE ONE TO GO ALL THE WAY TO THE MARKET AND LUG THEM THE WHOLE WAY HOME ?!
I'M SORRY, AND THANK YOU!
BOW
I'M GOING TO HAVE TO TRAIN MYSELF...
...TO REACT TO UNSEEN ATTACKS ON BOTH SIDES.
GWNCH

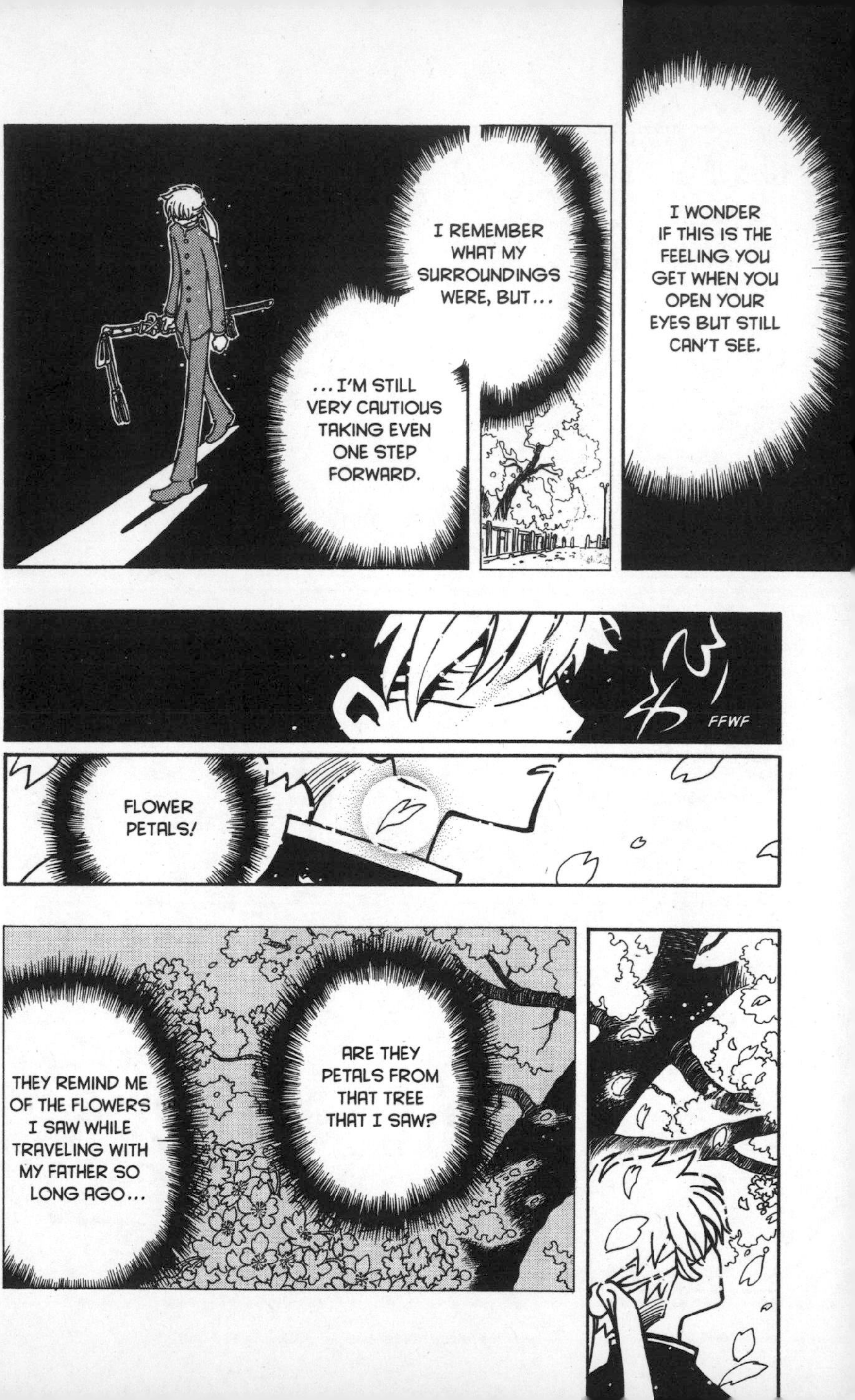
I WONDER IF THIS IS THE FEELING YOU GET WHEN YOU OPEN YOUR EYES BUT STILL CAN'T SEE.
I REMEMBER WHAT MY SURROUNDINGS WERE, BUT...
...I'M STILL VERY CAUTIOUS TAKING EVEN ONE STEP FORWARD.
FFWF
FLOWER PETALS!
ARE THEY PETALS FROM THAT TREE THAT I SAW?
THEY REMIND ME OF THE FLOWERS I SAW WHILE TRAVELING WITH MY FATHER SO LONG AGO...

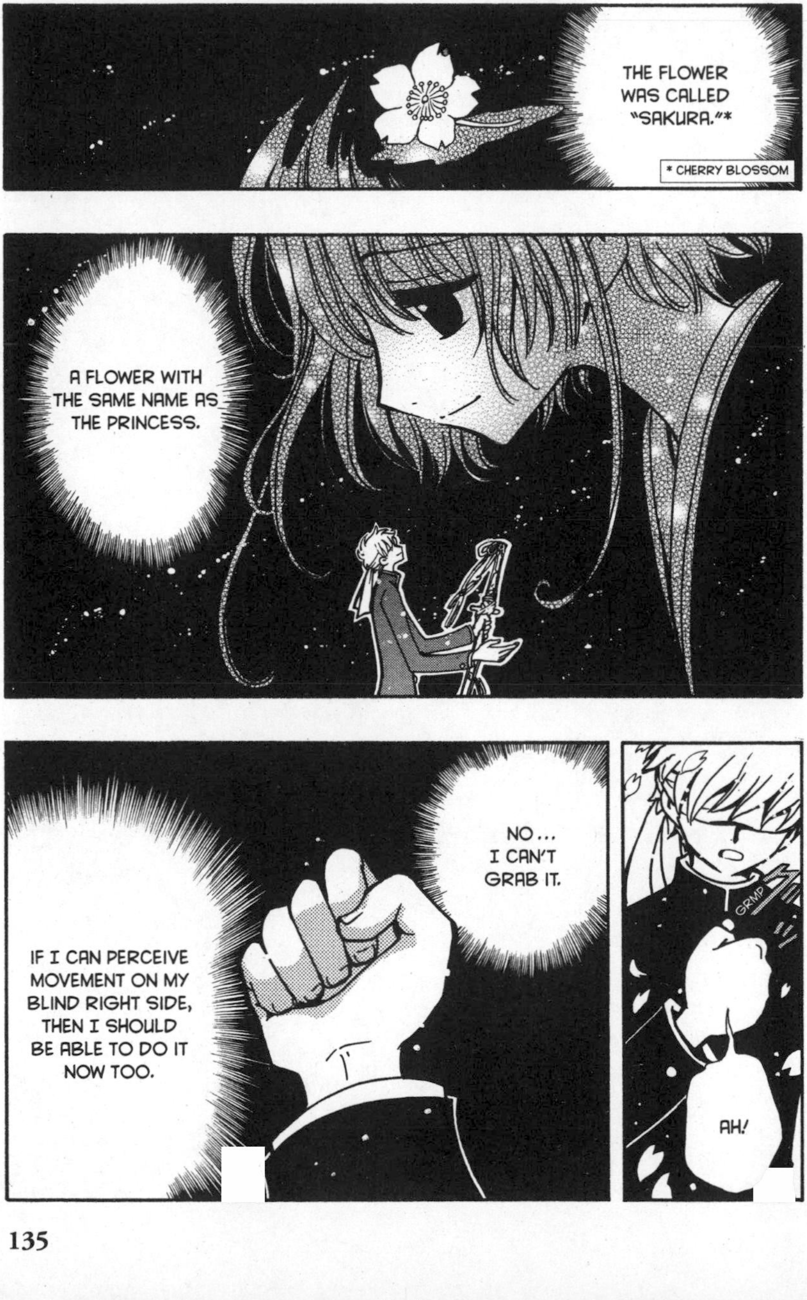
THE FLOWER WAS CALLED "SAKURA."*
* CHERRY BLOSSOM
A FLOWER WITH THE SAME NAME AS THE PRINCESS.
GRMP
AH!
NO... I CAN'T GRAB IT.
IF I CAN PERCEIVE MOVEMENT ON MY BLIND RIGHT SIDE, THEN I SHOULD BE ABLE TO DO IT NOW TOO.

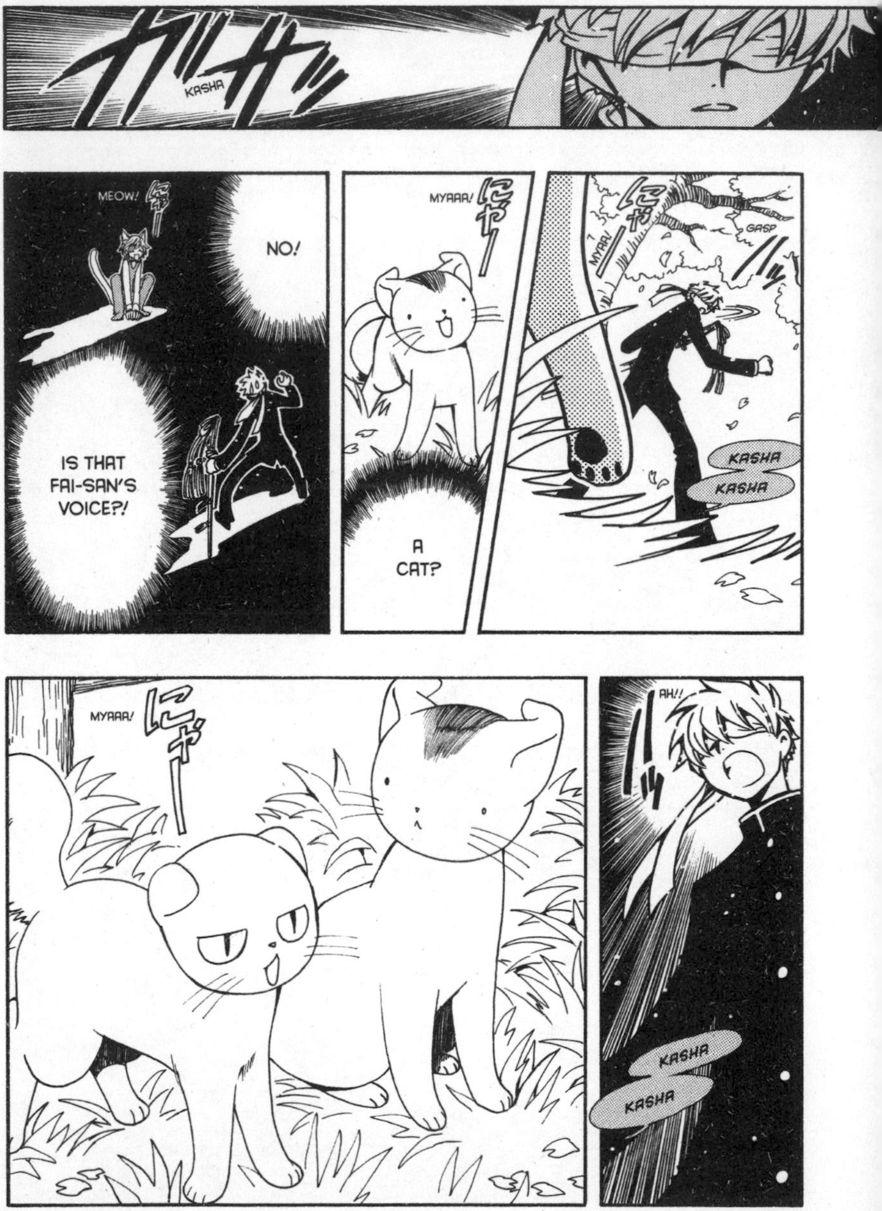
KASHA
MYAA!
GASP
KASHA
KASHA
MYAAA!
A CAT?
MEOW!
NO!
IS THAT FAI-SAN'S VOICE?!
AH!!
KASHA
KASHA
MYAAA!

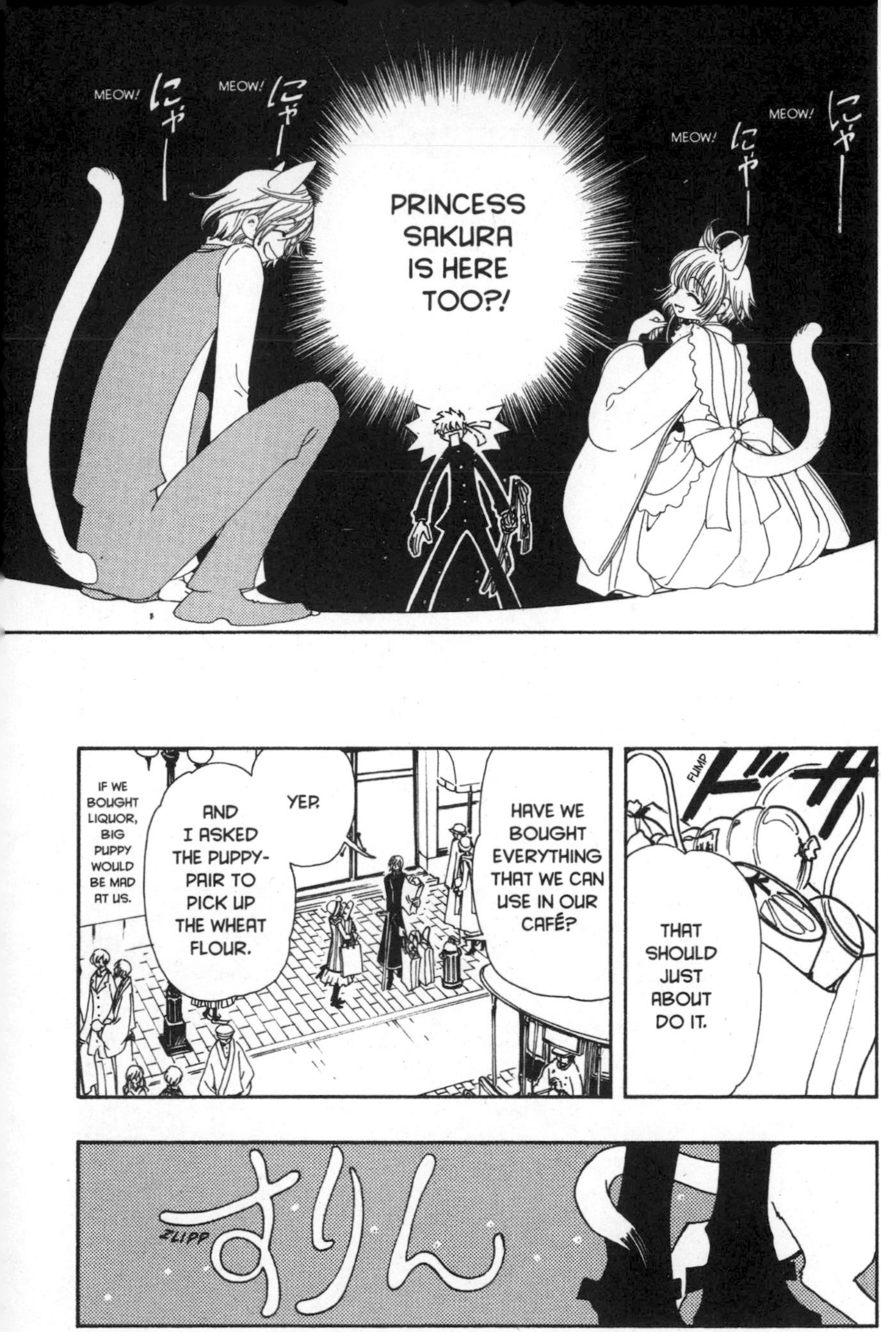
MEOW!
にゃー
MEOW!
にゃー
PRINCESS SAKURA IS HERE TOO?!
MEOW!
にゃー
MEOW!
にゃー
ドサ
FUMP
THAT SHOULD JUST ABOUT DO IT.
HAVE WE BOUGHT EVERYTHING THAT WE CAN USE IN OUR CAFÉ?
YEP.
AND I ASKED THE PUPPY-PAIR TO PICK UP THE WHEAT FLOUR.
IF WE BOUGHT LIQUOR, BIG PUPPY WOULD BE MAD AT US.
すりん
ZLIPP

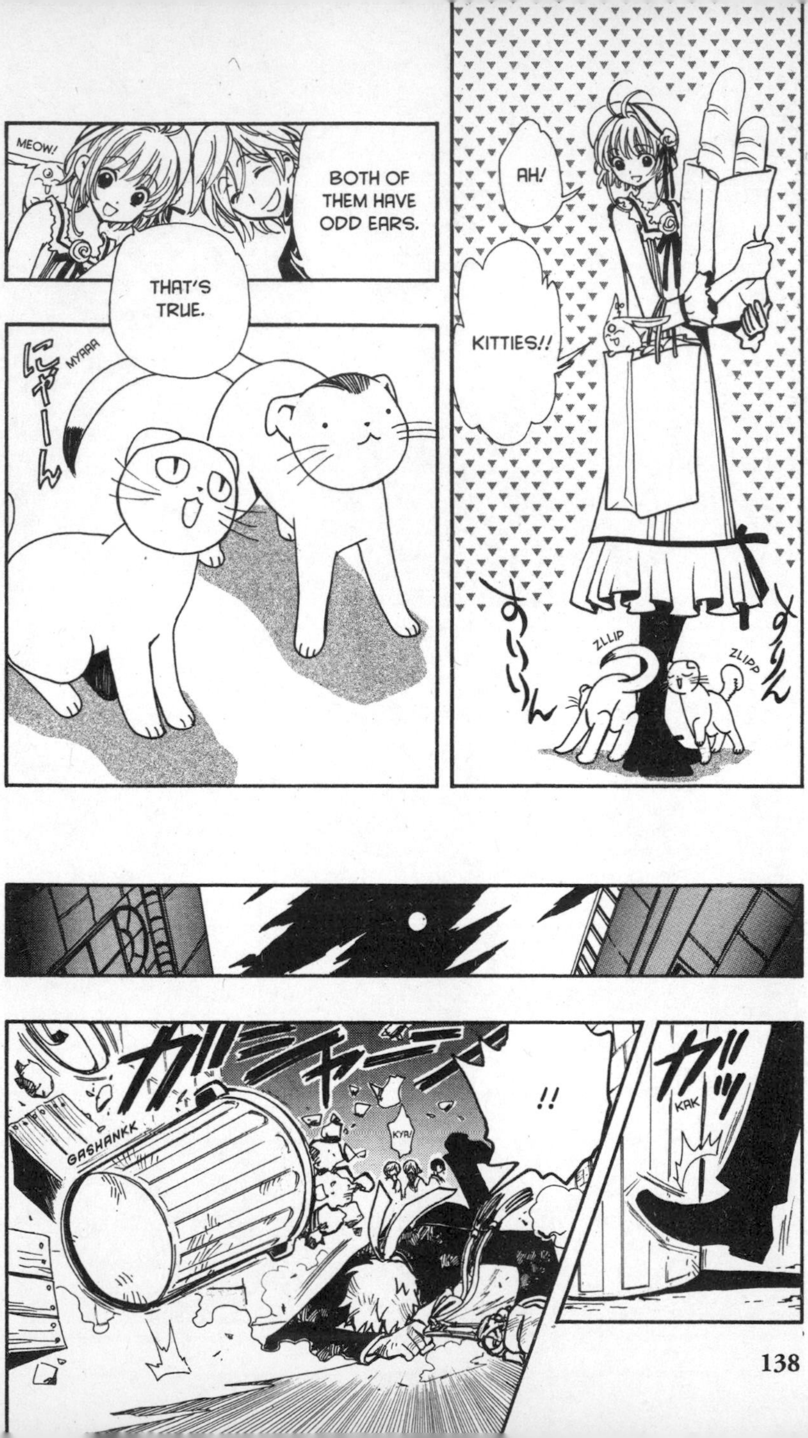

AH!
KITTIES!!
ZLLIP
ZLIPP
MEOW!
BOTH OF THEM HAVE ODD EARS.
THAT'S TRUE.
にゃーん
MYAAA
ガッ
KAK
!!
ガシャーン
GASHANKK
KYA!

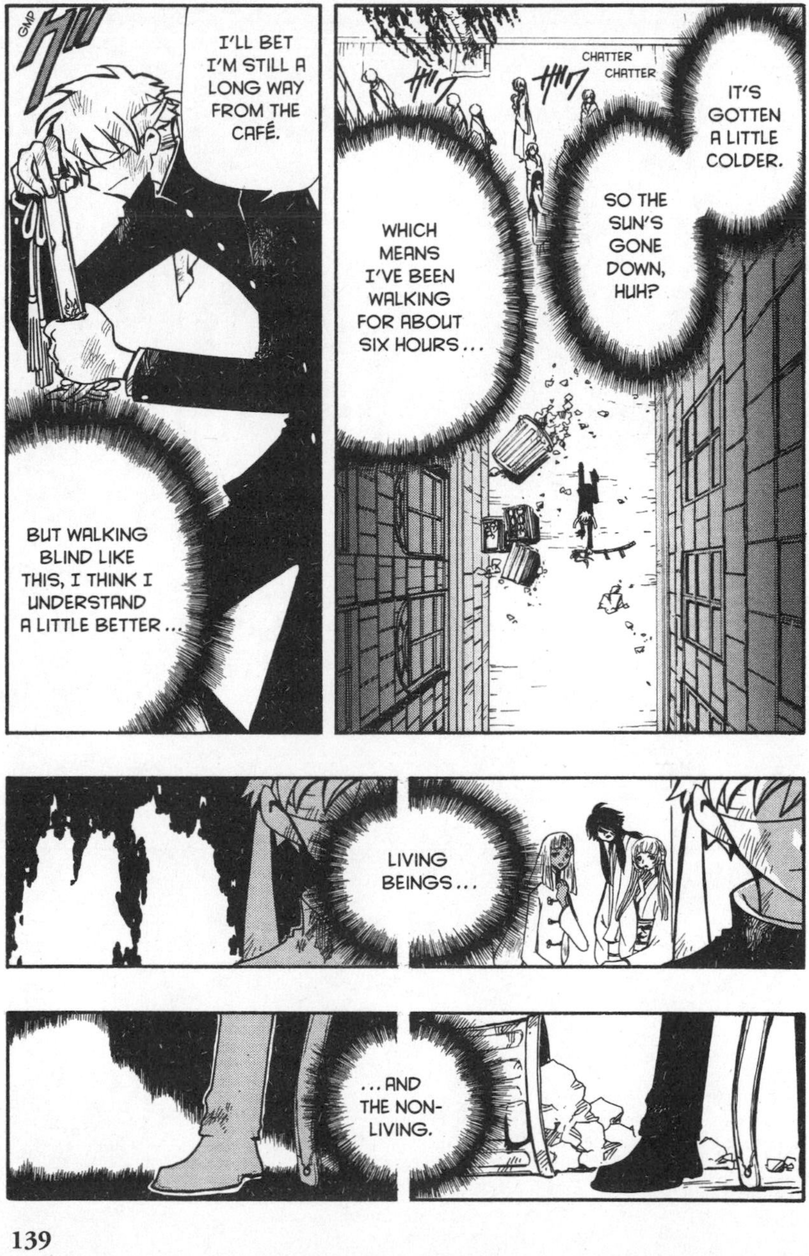
IT'S GOTTEN A LITTLE COLDER.
CHATTER CHATTER
SO THE SUN'S GONE DOWN, HUH?
WHICH MEANS I'VE BEEN WALKING FOR ABOUT SIX HOURS...
GMP
I'LL BET I'M STILL A LONG WAY FROM THE CAFÉ.
BUT WALKING BLIND LIKE THIS, I THINK I UNDERSTAND A LITTLE BETTER...
LIVING BEINGS...
...AND THE NON-LIVING.

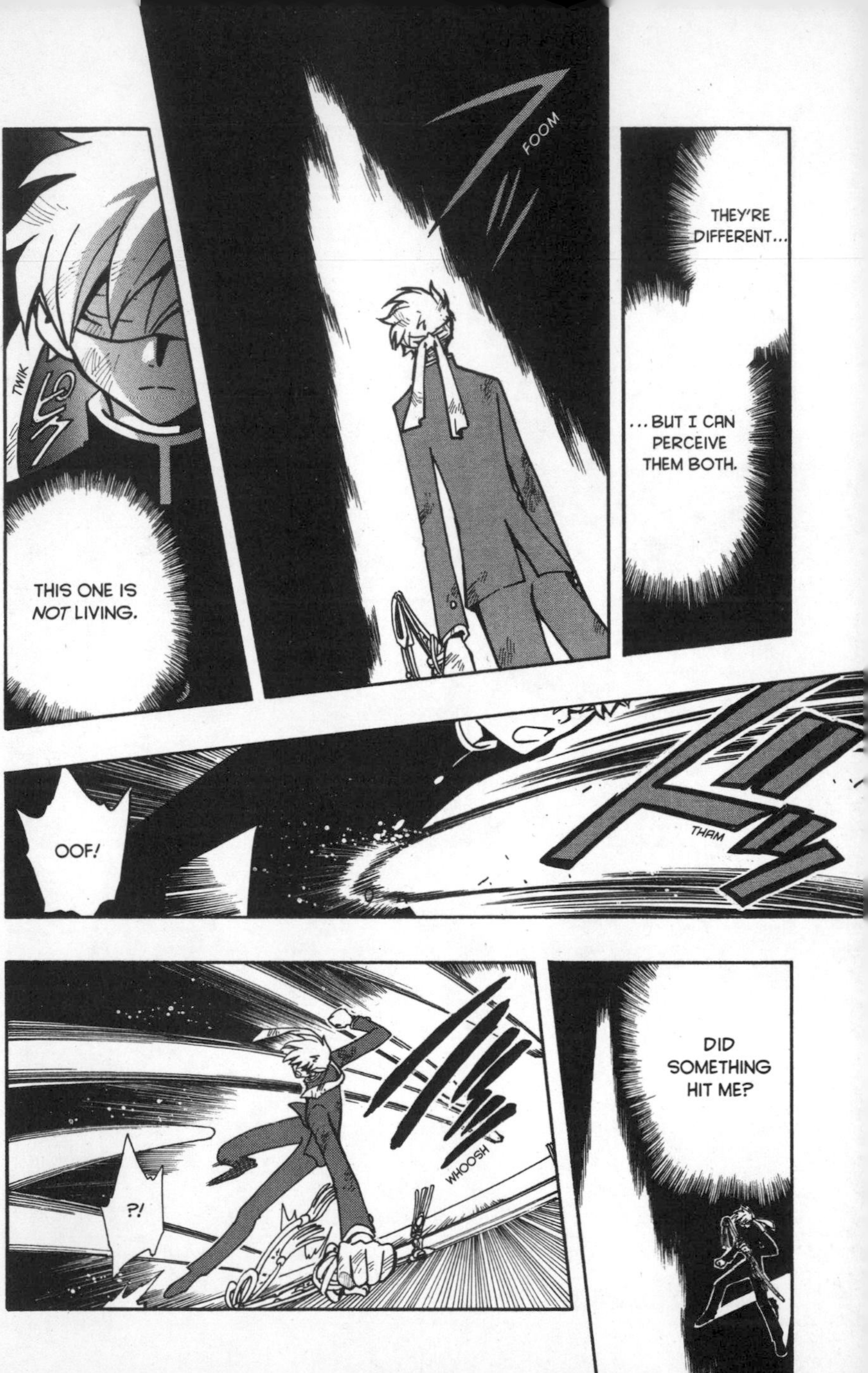
THEY'RE DIFFERENT...
...BUT I CAN PERCEIVE THEM BOTH.
FOOM
TWIK
THIS ONE IS *NOT* LIVING.
THAM
OOF!
DID SOMETHING HIT ME?
WHOOSH
?!

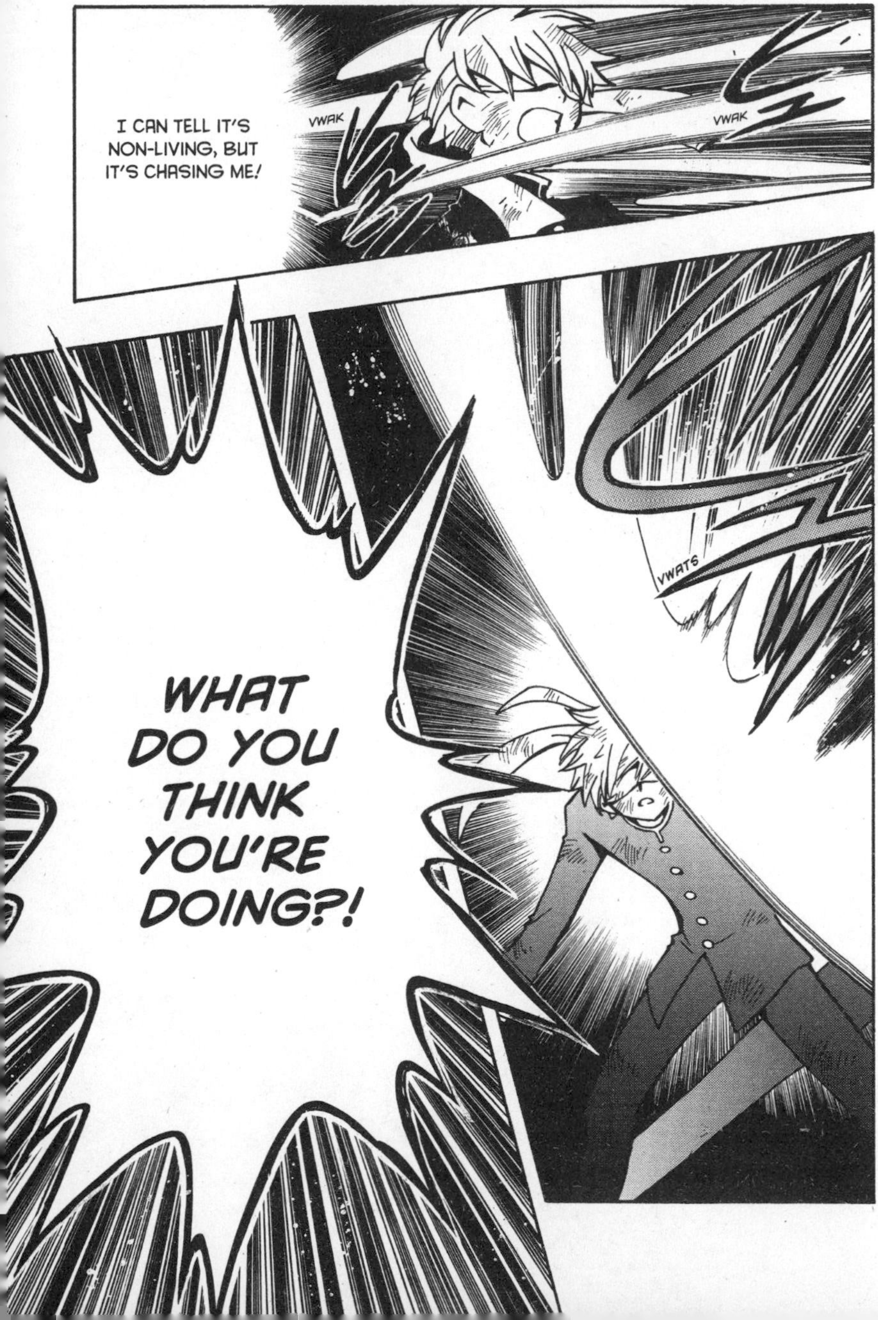
VWAK
VWAK
I CAN TELL IT'S NON-LIVING, BUT IT'S CHASING ME!
VWATS
WHAT DO YOU THINK YOU'RE DOING?!

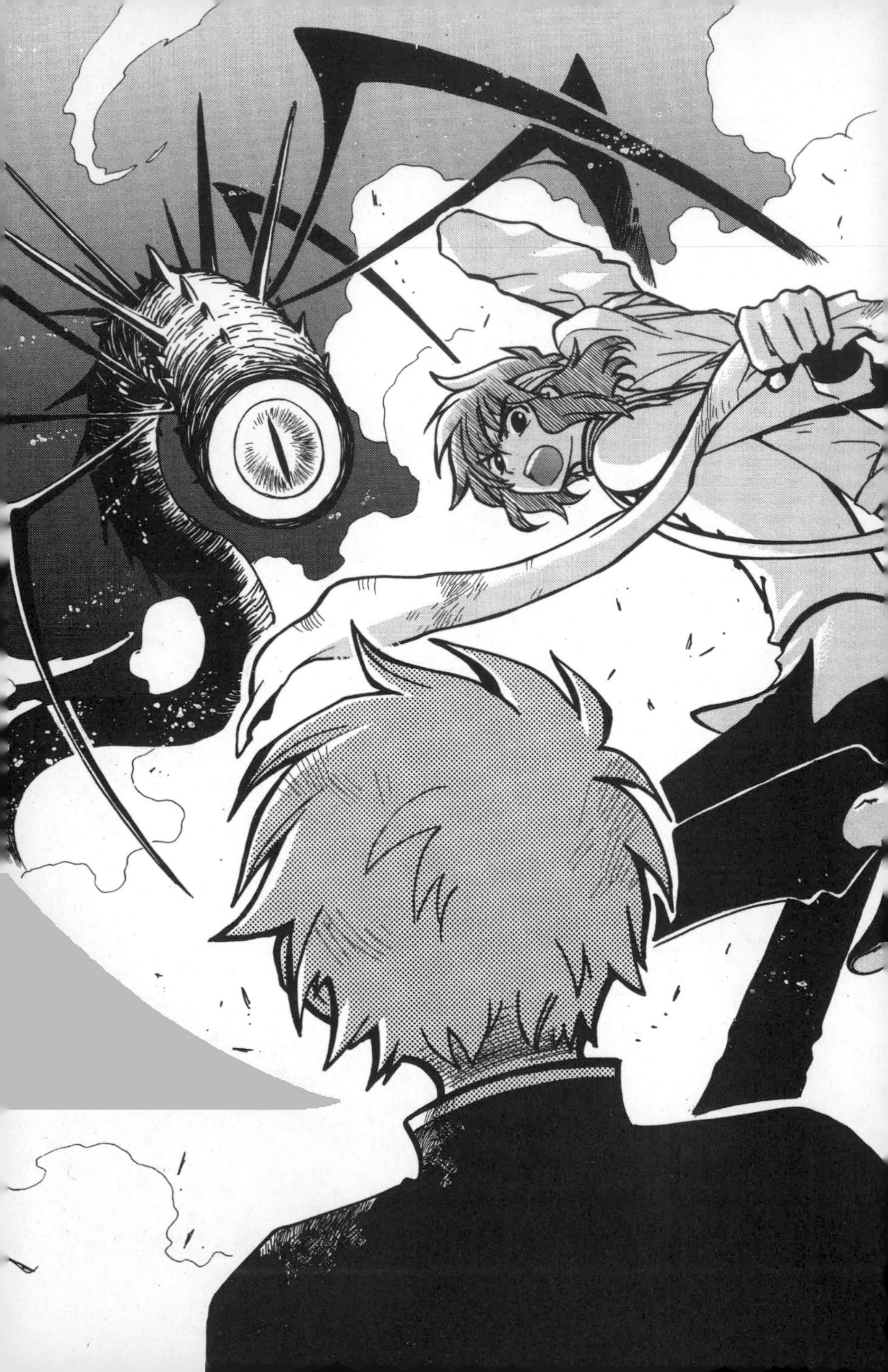

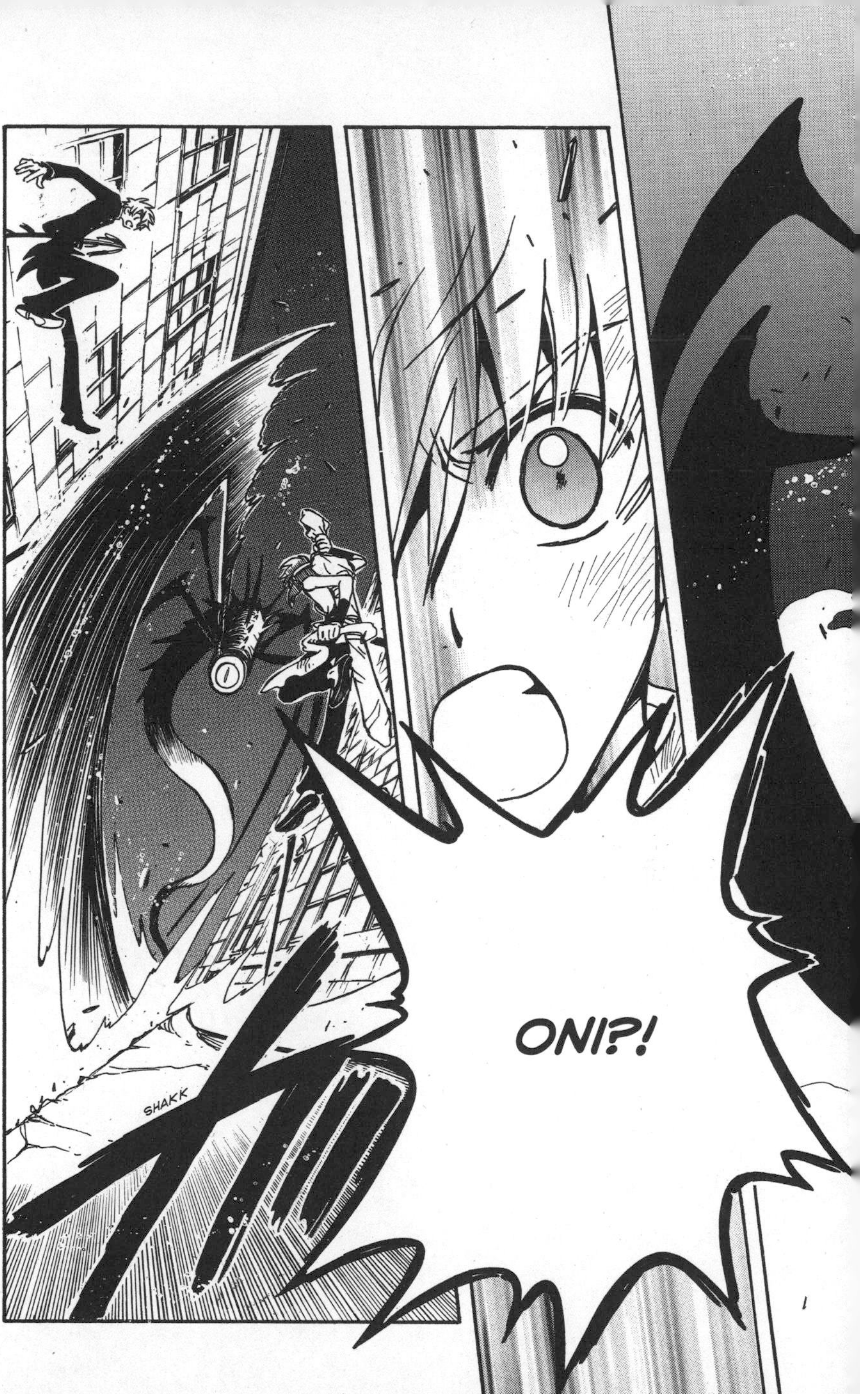
ONI?!
SHAKK

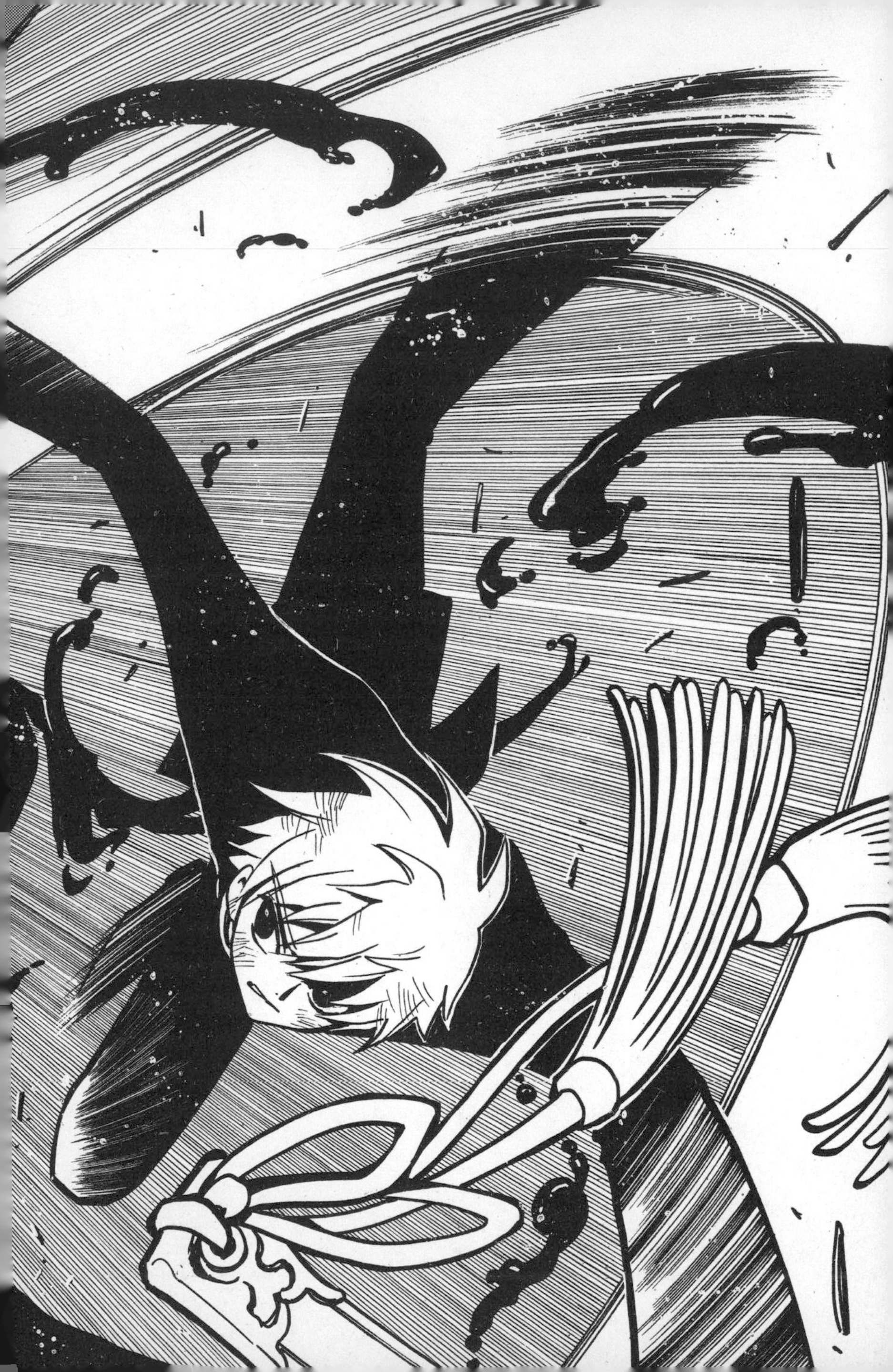

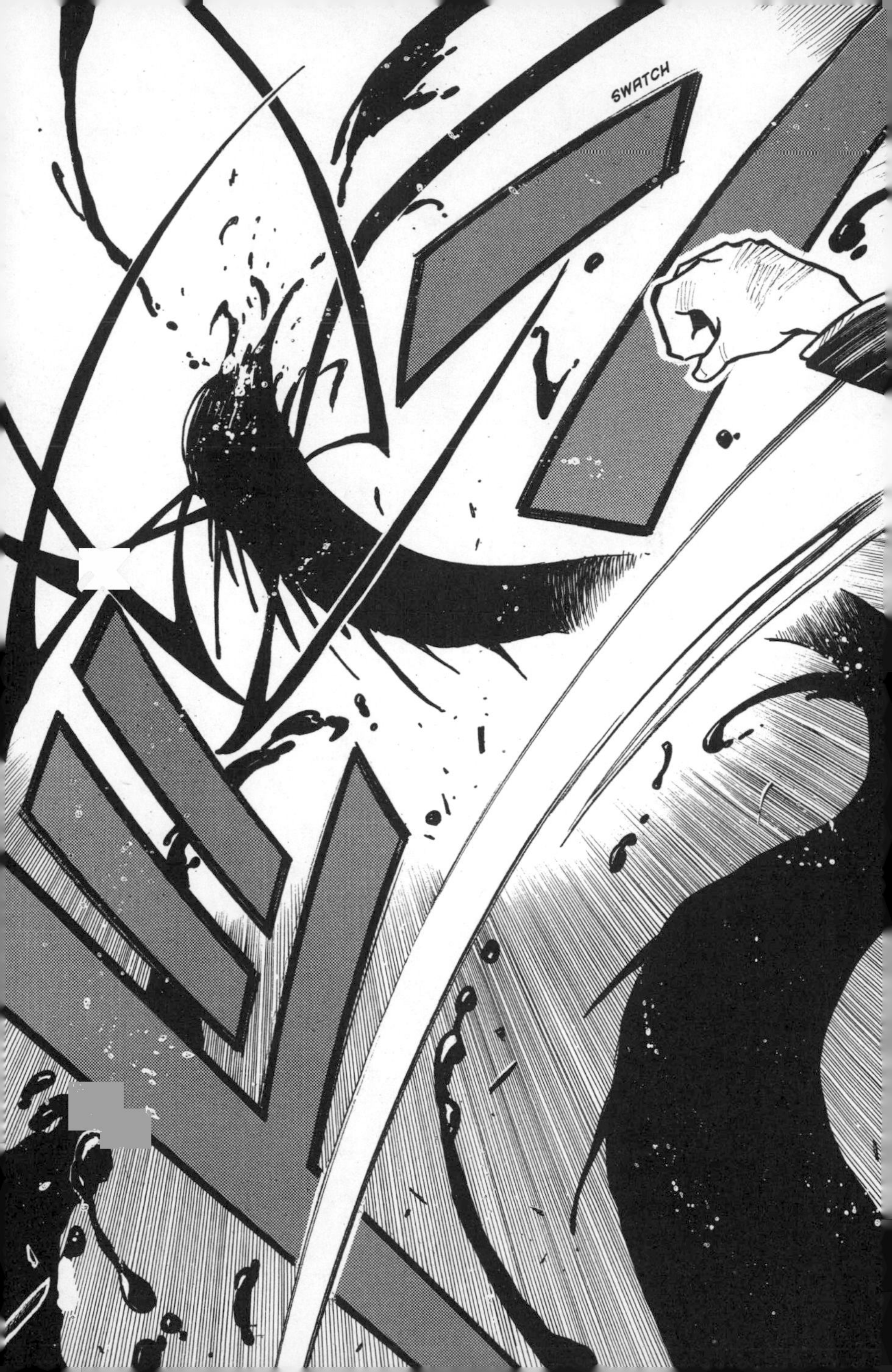
SWATCH

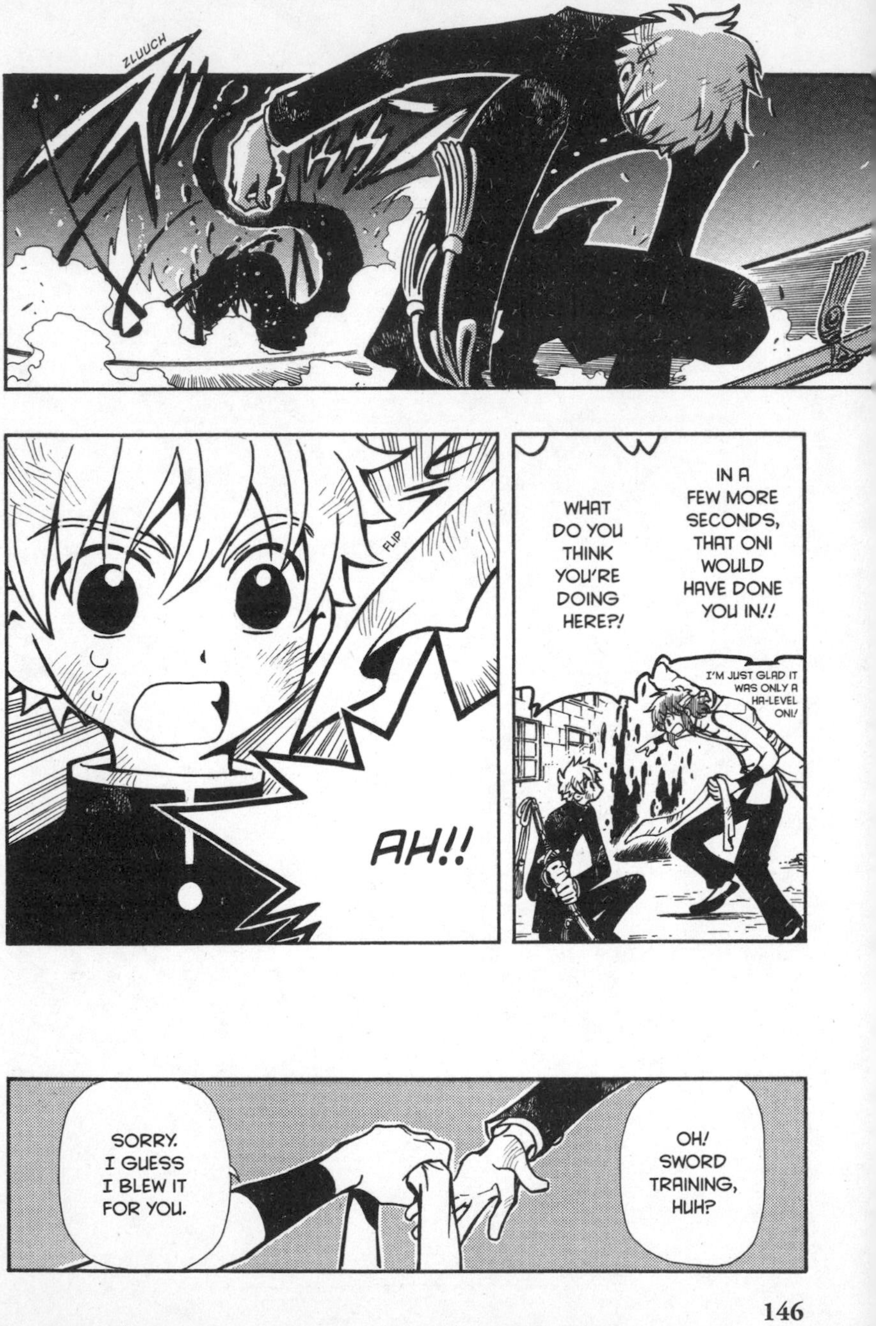
ZLUUCH
IN A FEW MORE SECONDS, THAT ONI WOULD HAVE DONE YOU IN!!
WHAT DO YOU THINK YOU'RE DOING HERE?!
I'M JUST GLAD IT WAS ONLY A HA-LEVEL ONI!
FLIP
AH!!
OH! SWORD TRAINING, HUH?
SORRY. I GUESS I BLEW IT FOR YOU.

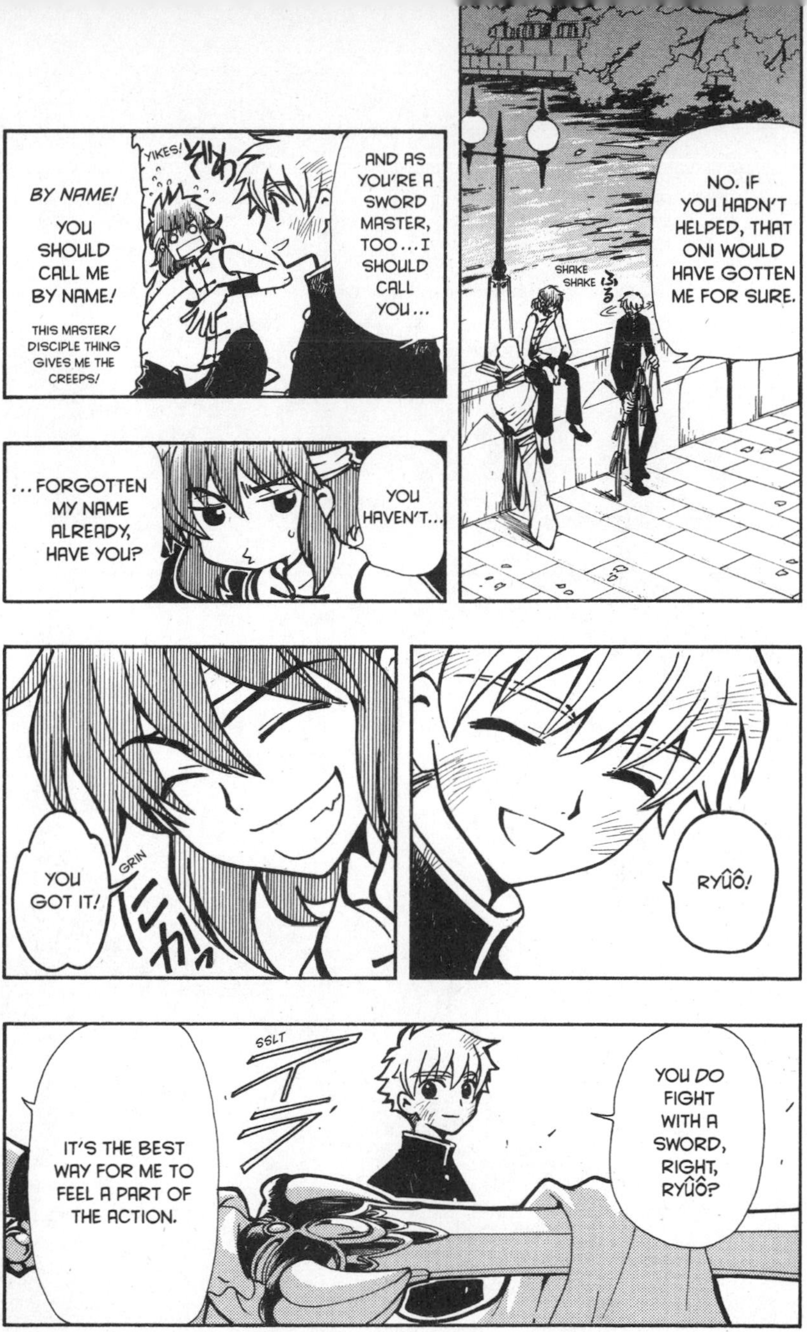
NO. IF YOU HADN'T HELPED, THAT ONI WOULD HAVE GOTTEN ME FOR SURE.
SHAKE SHAKE
AND AS YOU'RE A SWORD MASTER, TOO... I SHOULD CALL YOU...
YIKES!
BY NAME!
YOU SHOULD CALL ME BY NAME!
THIS MASTER/ DISCIPLE THING GIVES ME THE CREEPS!
YOU HAVEN'T...
...FORGOTTEN MY NAME ALREADY, HAVE YOU?
RYÛÔ!
GRIN
YOU GOT IT!
YOU *DO* FIGHT WITH A SWORD, RIGHT, RYÛÔ?
SSLT
IT'S THE BEST WAY FOR ME TO FEEL A PART OF THE ACTION.

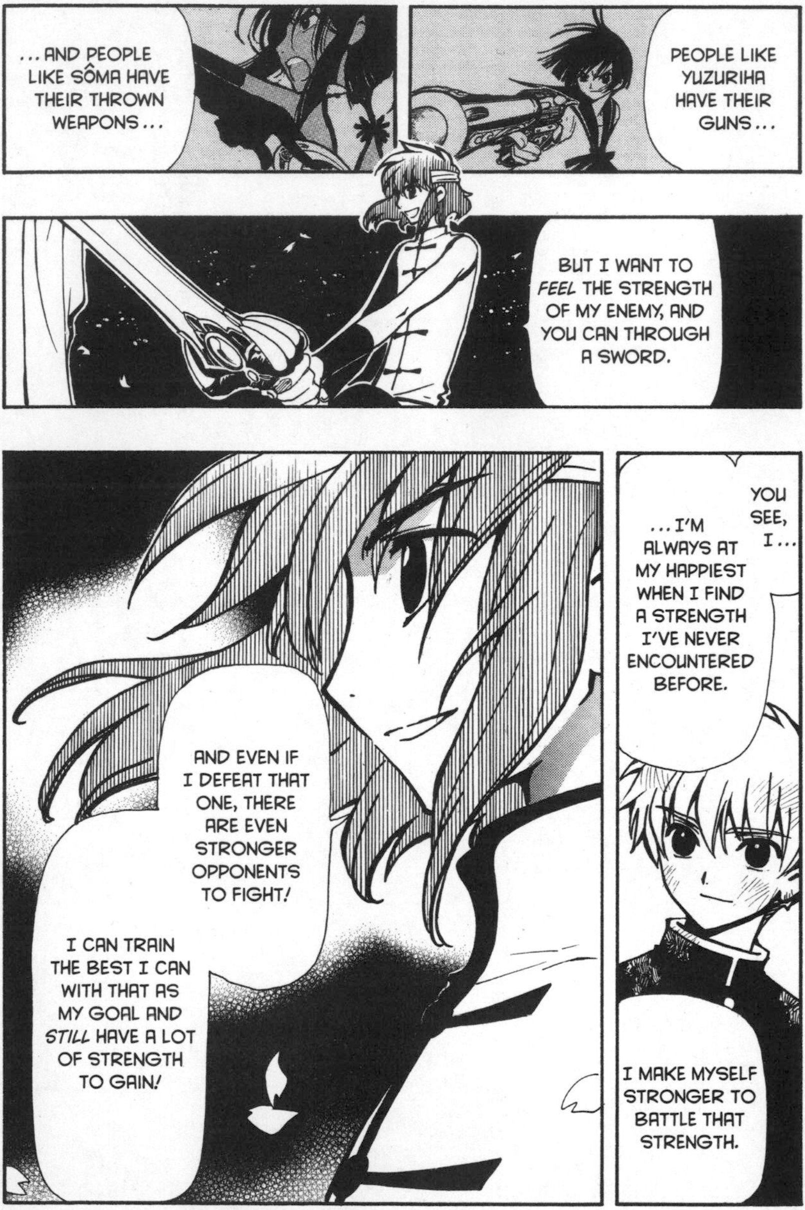
PEOPLE LIKE YUZURIHA HAVE THEIR GUNS...
...AND PEOPLE LIKE SÔMA HAVE THEIR THROWN WEAPONS...
BUT I WANT TO *FEEL* THE STRENGTH OF MY ENEMY, AND YOU CAN THROUGH A SWORD.
YOU SEE, I...
...I'M ALWAYS AT MY HAPPIEST WHEN I FIND A STRENGTH I'VE NEVER ENCOUNTERED BEFORE.
I MAKE MYSELF STRONGER TO BATTLE THAT STRENGTH.
AND EVEN IF I DEFEAT THAT ONE, THERE ARE EVEN STRONGER OPPONENTS TO FIGHT!
I CAN TRAIN THE BEST I CAN WITH THAT AS MY GOAL AND *STILL* HAVE A LOT OF STRENGTH TO GAIN!

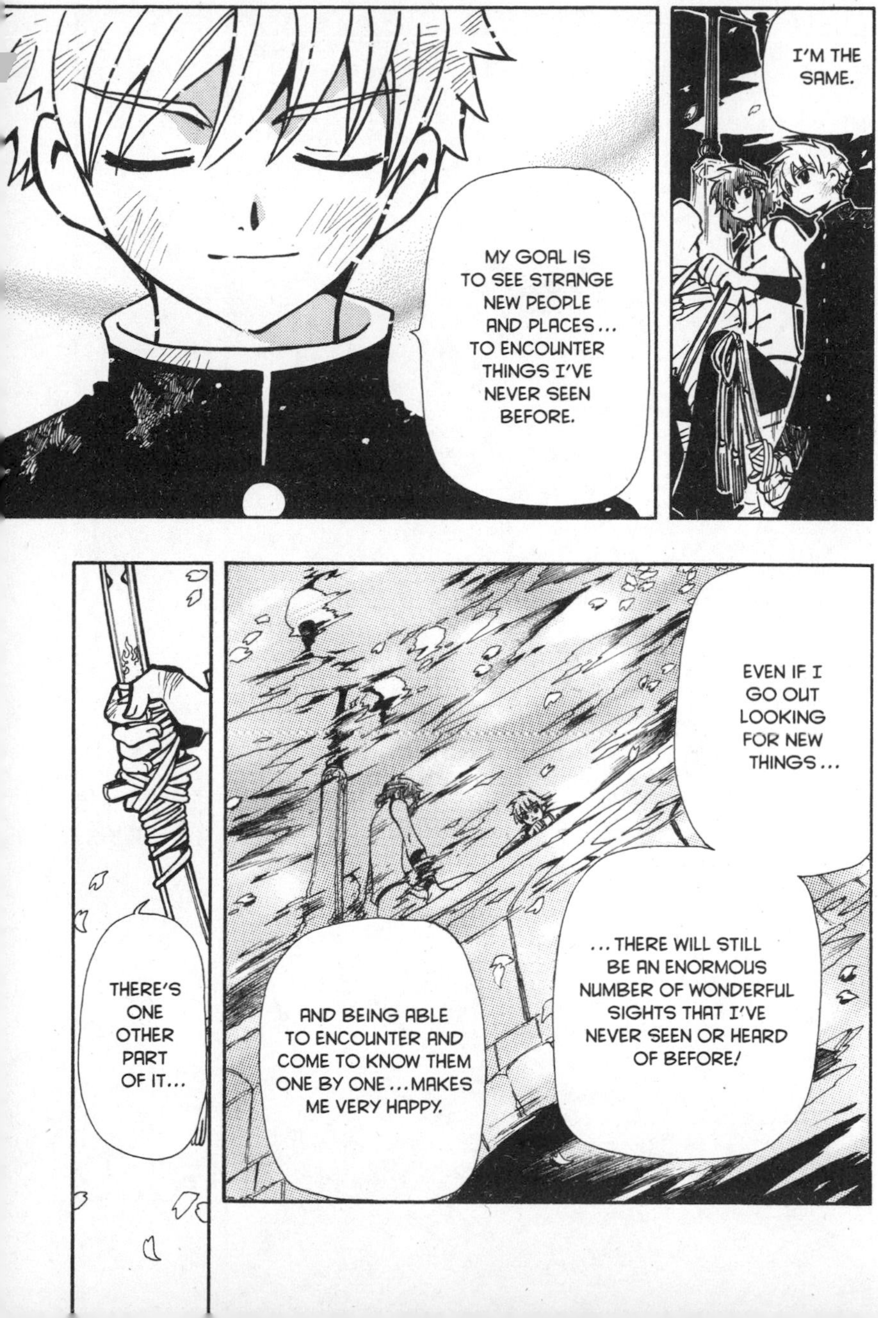
I'M THE SAME.
MY GOAL IS TO SEE STRANGE NEW PEOPLE AND PLACES... TO ENCOUNTER THINGS I'VE NEVER SEEN BEFORE.
EVEN IF I GO OUT LOOKING FOR NEW THINGS...
...THERE WILL STILL BE AN ENORMOUS NUMBER OF WONDERFUL SIGHTS THAT I'VE NEVER SEEN OR HEARD OF BEFORE!
AND BEING ABLE TO ENCOUNTER AND COME TO KNOW THEM ONE BY ONE...MAKES ME VERY HAPPY.
THERE'S ONE OTHER PART OF IT...

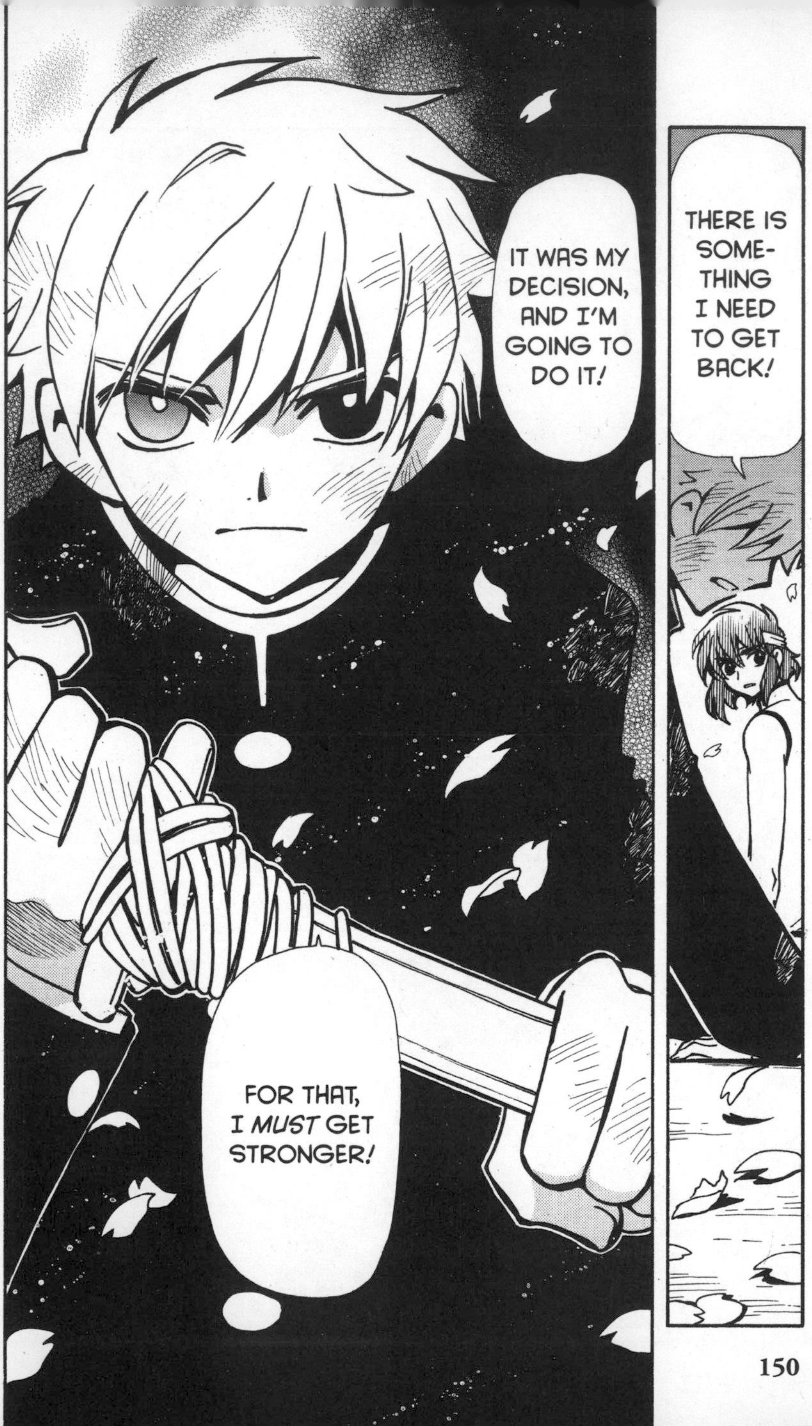
THERE IS SOME-THING I NEED TO GET BACK!
IT WAS MY DECISION, AND I'M GOING TO DO IT!
FOR THAT, I *MUST* GET STRONGER!

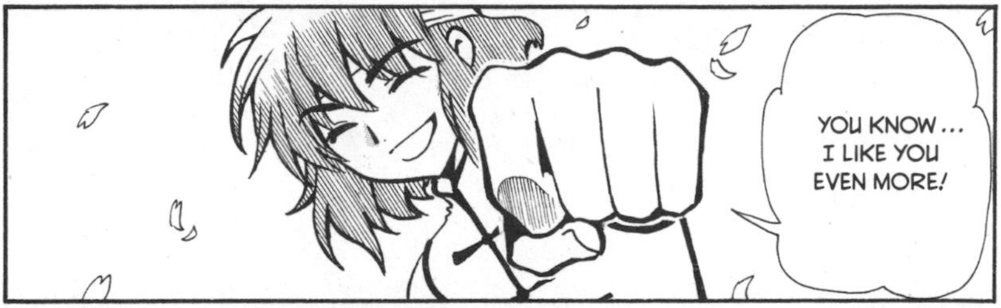
YOU KNOW...
I LIKE YOU
EVEN MORE!

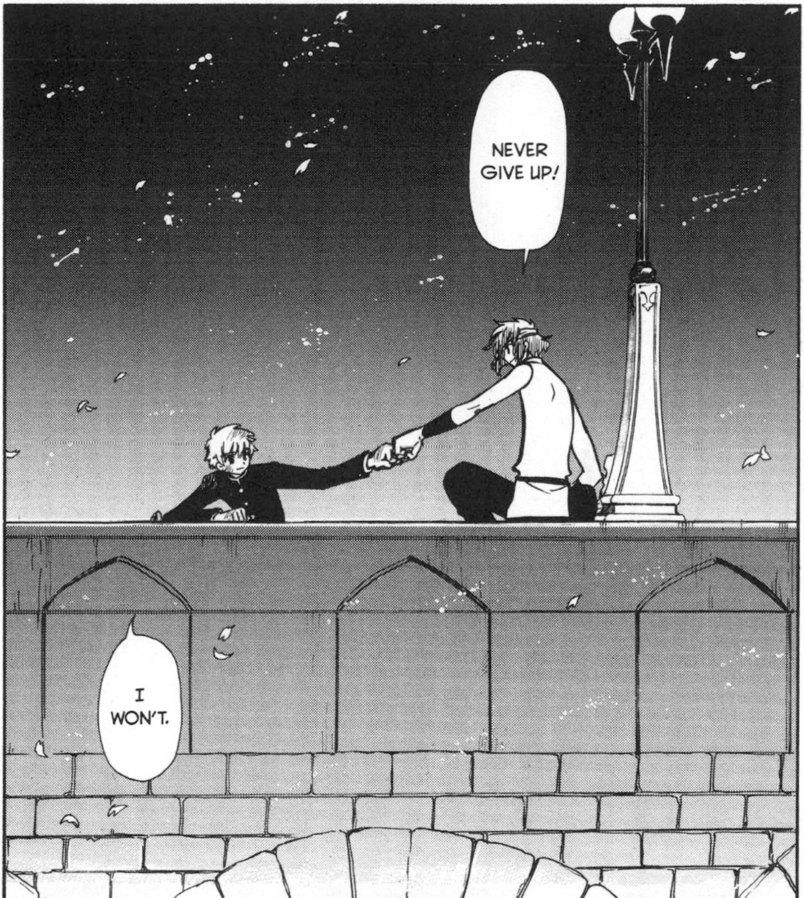
NEVER
GIVE UP!
I
WON'T.

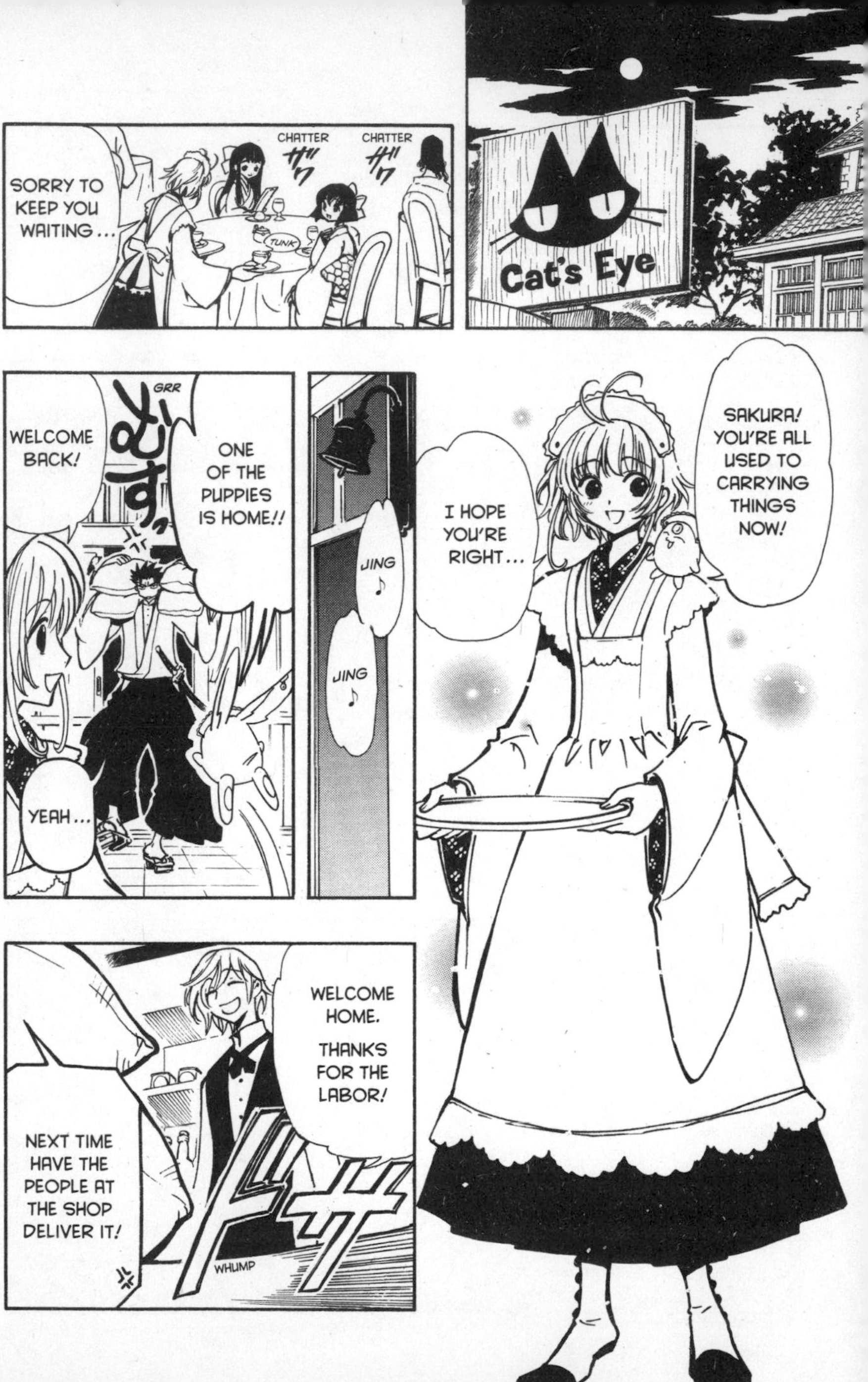
Cat's Eye
CHATTER
CHATTER
TUNK
SORRY TO KEEP YOU WAITING...
SAKURA! YOU'RE ALL USED TO CARRYING THINGS NOW!
I HOPE YOU'RE RIGHT...
JING ♪
JING ♪
ONE OF THE PUPPIES IS HOME!!
GRR
WELCOME BACK!
YEAH...
WELCOME HOME.
THANKS FOR THE LABOR!
NEXT TIME HAVE THE PEOPLE AT THE SHOP DELIVER IT!
WHUMP

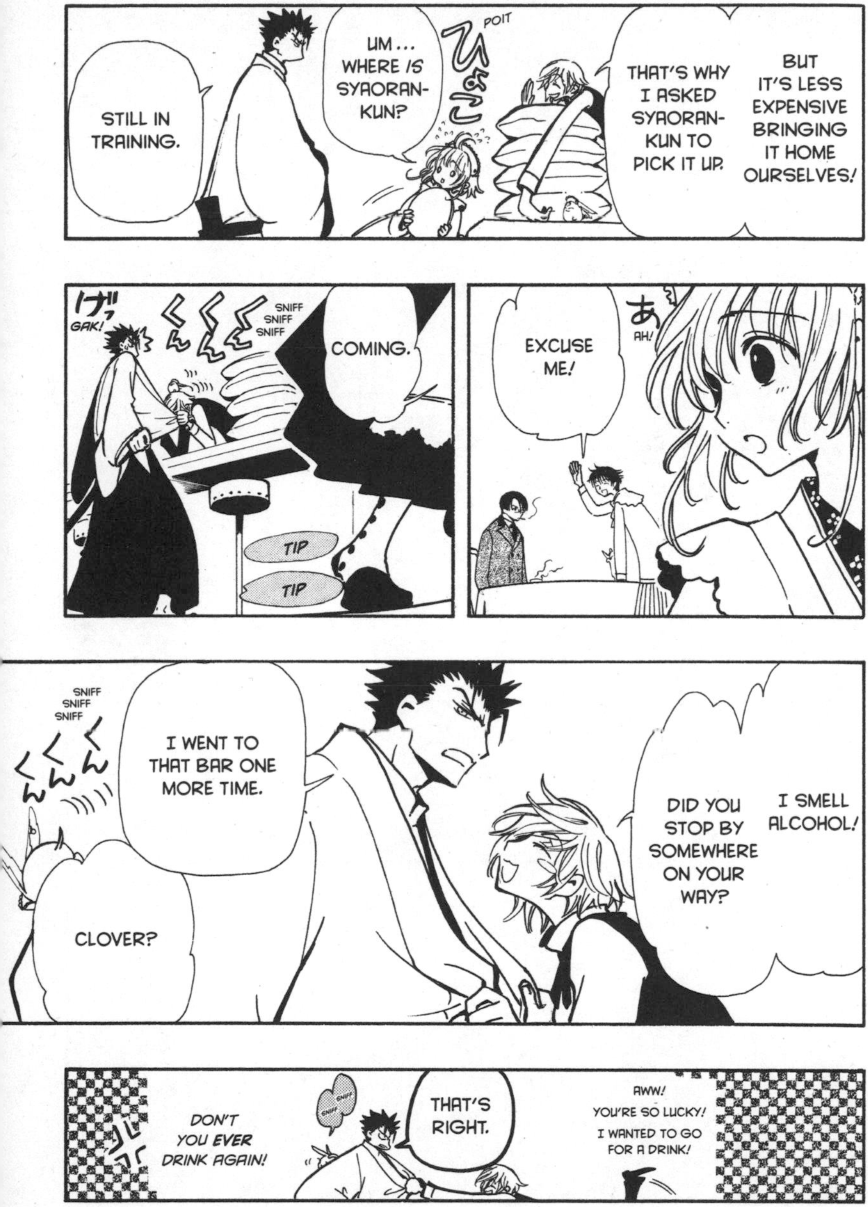
BUT IT'S LESS EXPENSIVE BRINGING IT HOME OURSELVES!
THAT'S WHY I ASKED SYAORAN-KUN TO PICK IT UP.
POIT
UM... WHERE IS SYAORAN-KUN?
STILL IN TRAINING.
AH!
EXCUSE ME!
COMING.
SNIFF SNIFF SNIFF
GAK!
TIP
TIP
I SMELL ALCOHOL!
DID YOU STOP BY SOMEWHERE ON YOUR WAY?
I WENT TO THAT BAR ONE MORE TIME.
SNIFF SNIFF SNIFF
CLOVER?
AWW! YOU'RE SO LUCKY! I WANTED TO GO FOR A DRINK!
THAT'S RIGHT.
SNIFF SNIFF
DON'T YOU EVER DRINK AGAIN!

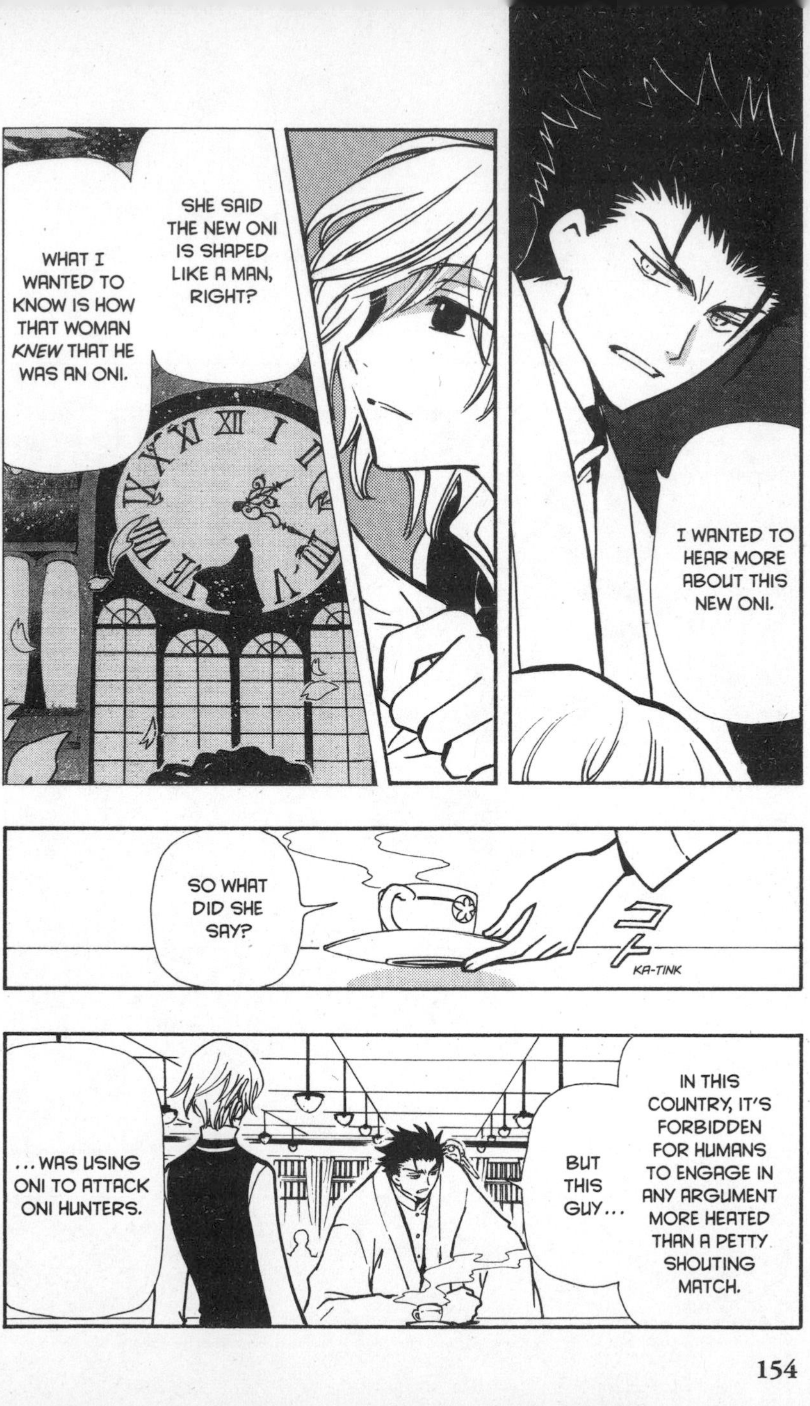
I WANTED TO HEAR MORE ABOUT THIS NEW ONI.
SHE SAID THE NEW ONI IS SHAPED LIKE A MAN, RIGHT?
WHAT I WANTED TO KNOW IS HOW THAT WOMAN *KNEW* THAT HE WAS AN ONI.
SO WHAT DID SHE SAY?
KA-TINK
IN THIS COUNTRY, IT'S FORBIDDEN FOR HUMANS TO ENGAGE IN ANY ARGUMENT MORE HEATED THAN A PETTY SHOUTING MATCH.
BUT THIS GUY...
...WAS USING ONI TO ATTACK ONI HUNTERS.

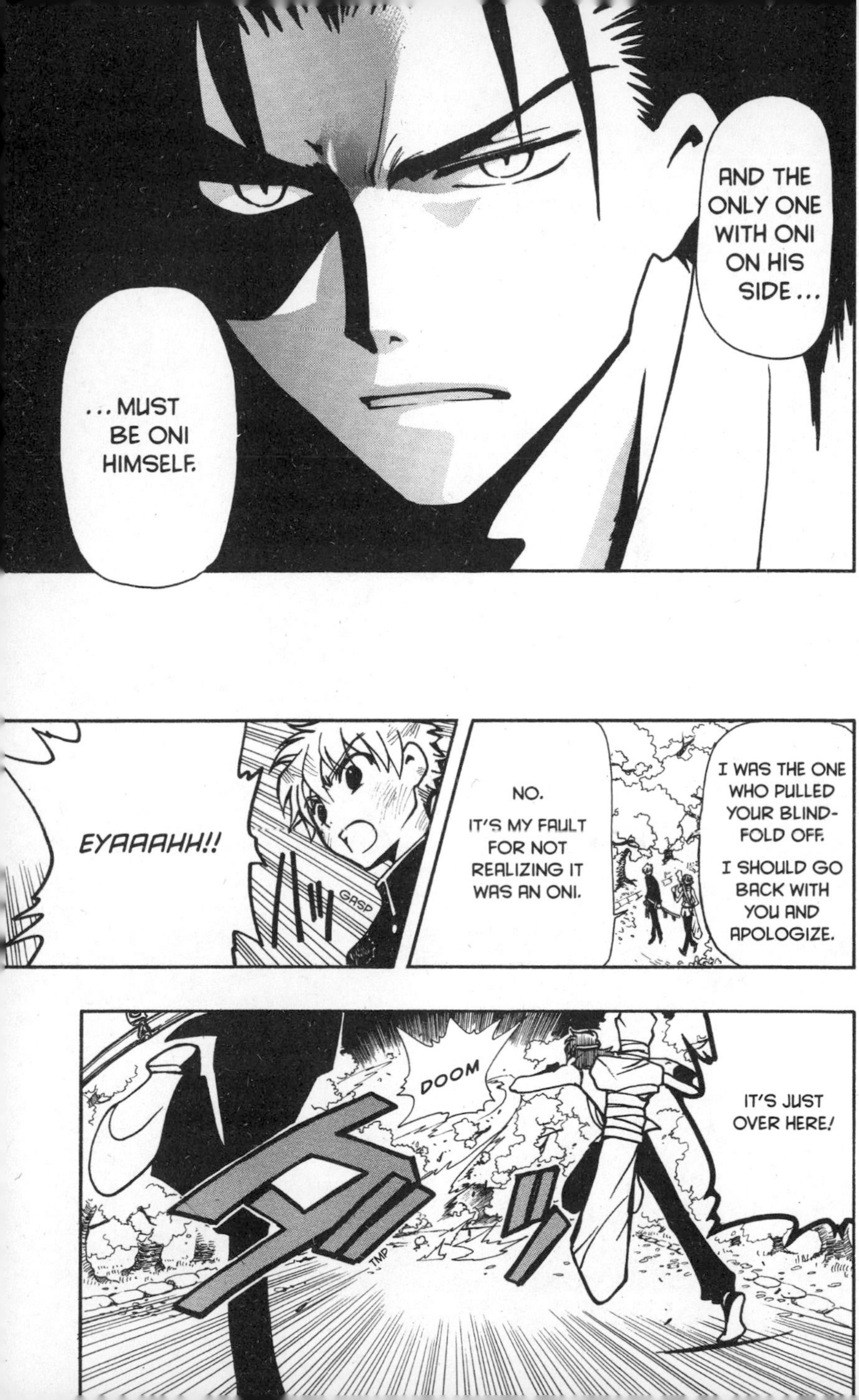
AND THE ONLY ONE WITH ONI ON HIS SIDE...
...MUST BE ONI HIMSELF.
I WAS THE ONE WHO PULLED YOUR BLIND-FOLD OFF.
I SHOULD GO BACK WITH YOU AND APOLOGIZE.
NO.
IT'S MY FAULT FOR NOT REALIZING IT WAS AN ONI.
EYAAAHH!!
GASP
IT'S JUST OVER HERE!
DOOM
TMP

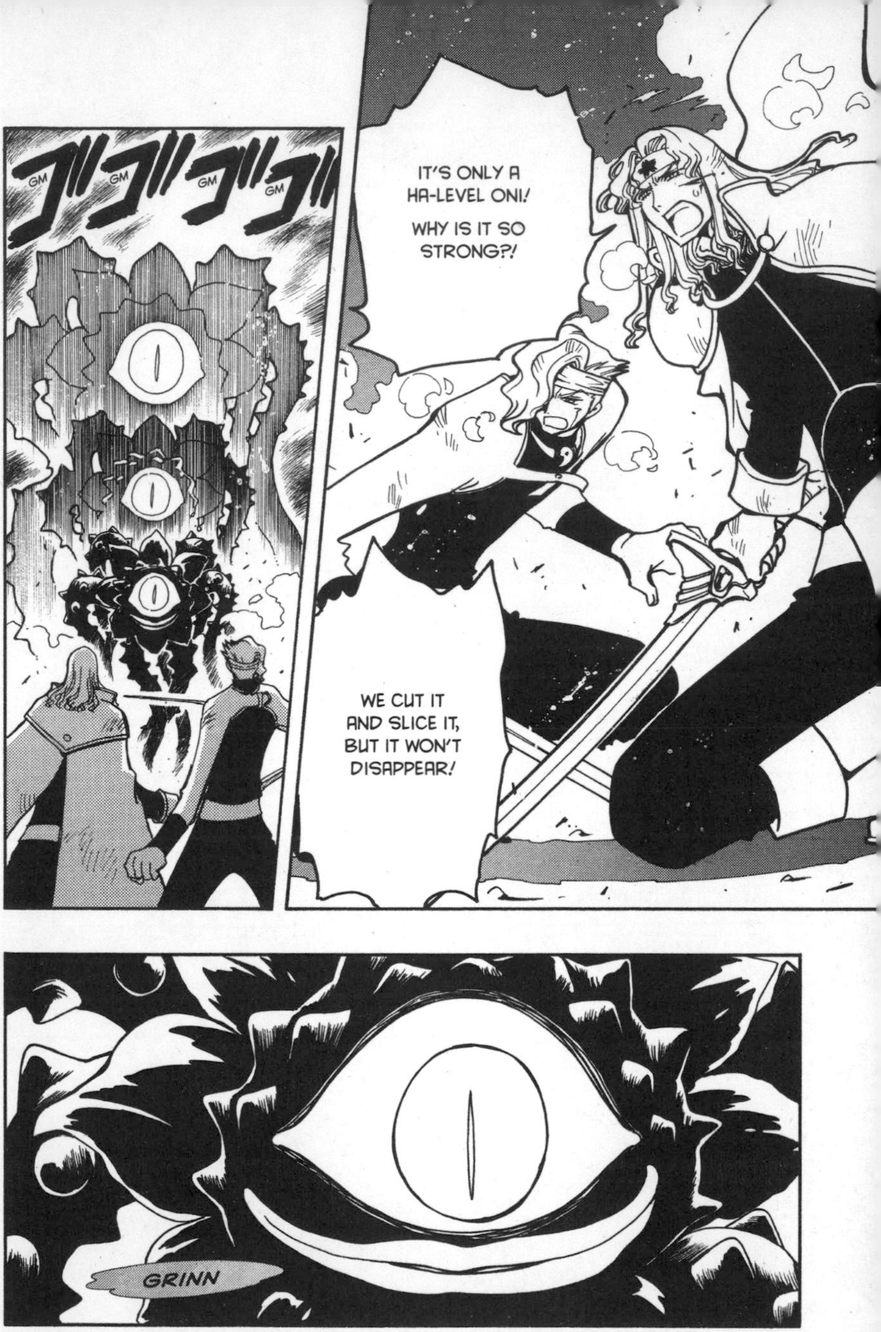
IT'S ONLY A HA-LEVEL ONI!
WHY IS IT SO STRONG?!
WE CUT IT AND SLICE IT, BUT IT WON'T DISAPPEAR!
GM GM GM GM
GRINN

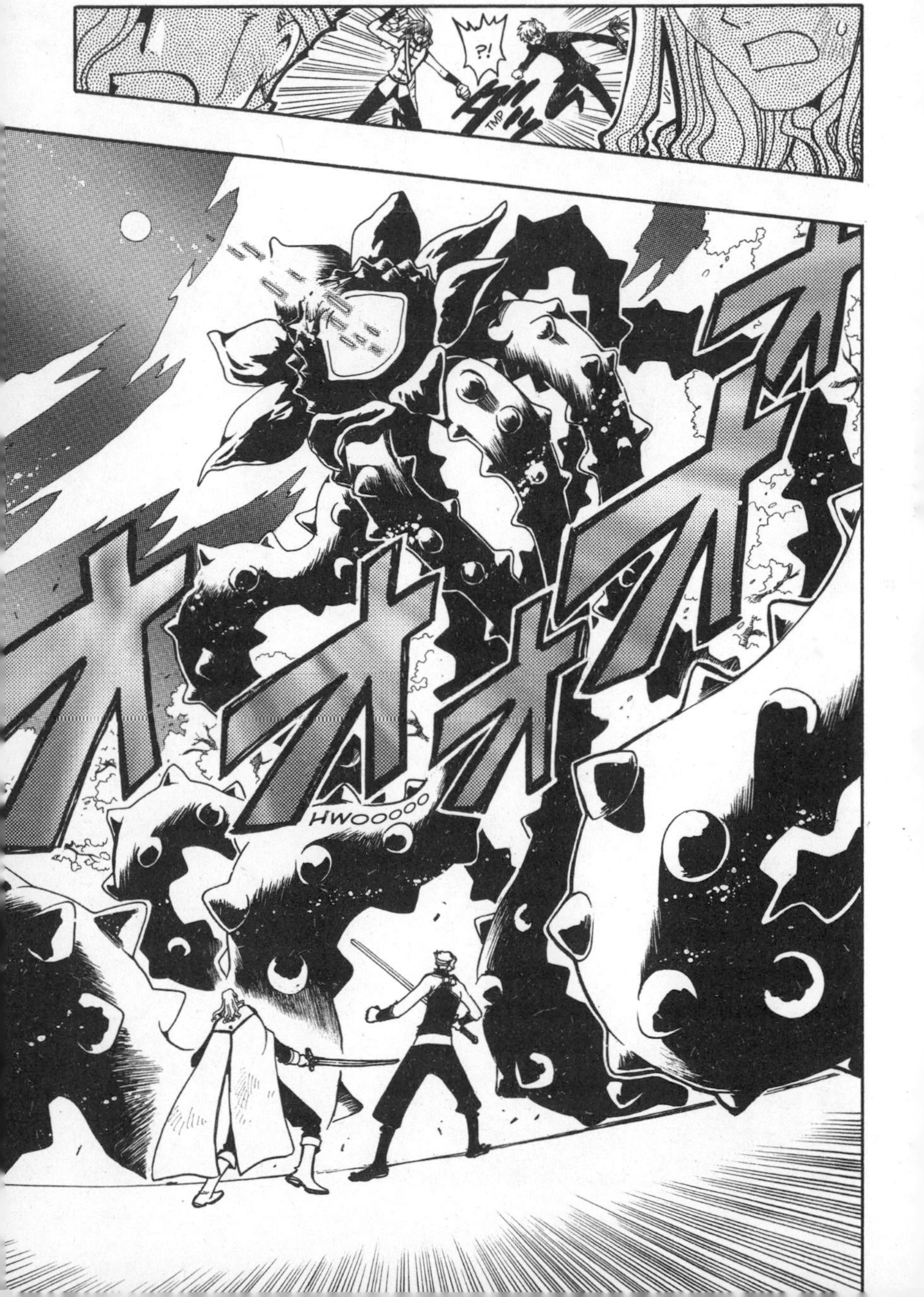
?!
TMP
HWOOOOO

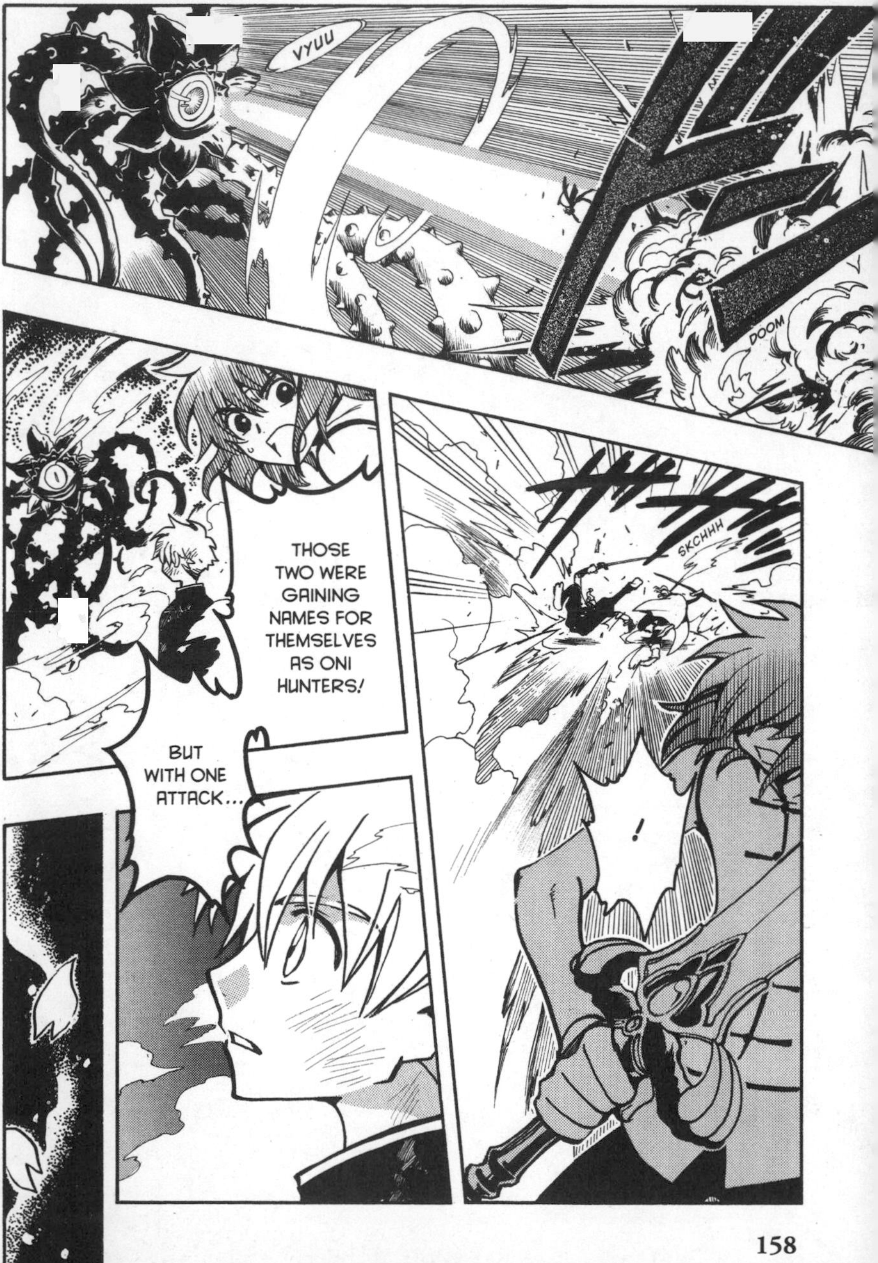
VYUU
DOOM
SKCHHH
!
THOSE TWO WERE GAINING NAMES FOR THEMSELVES AS ONI HUNTERS!
BUT WITH ONE ATTACK...

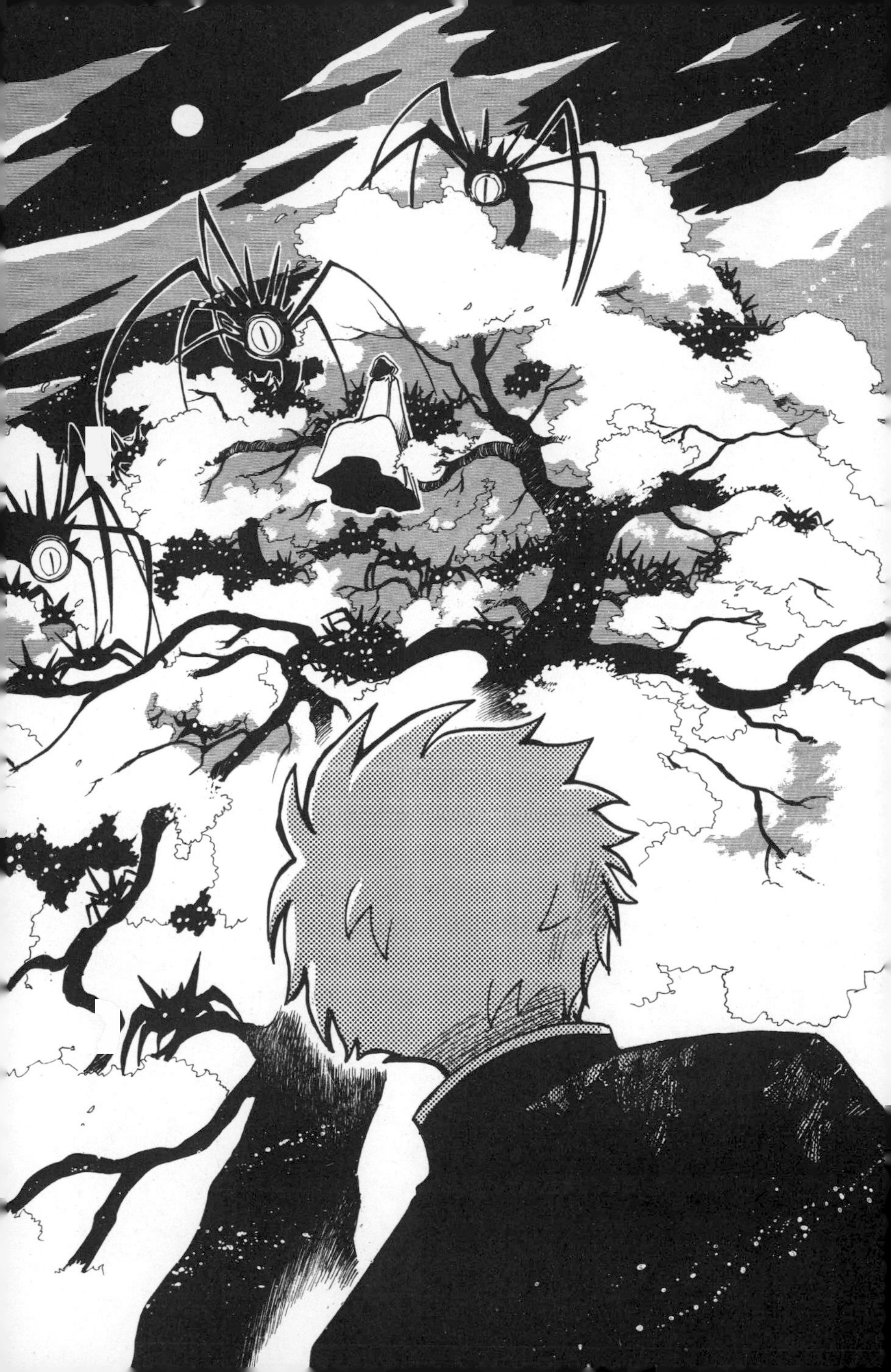

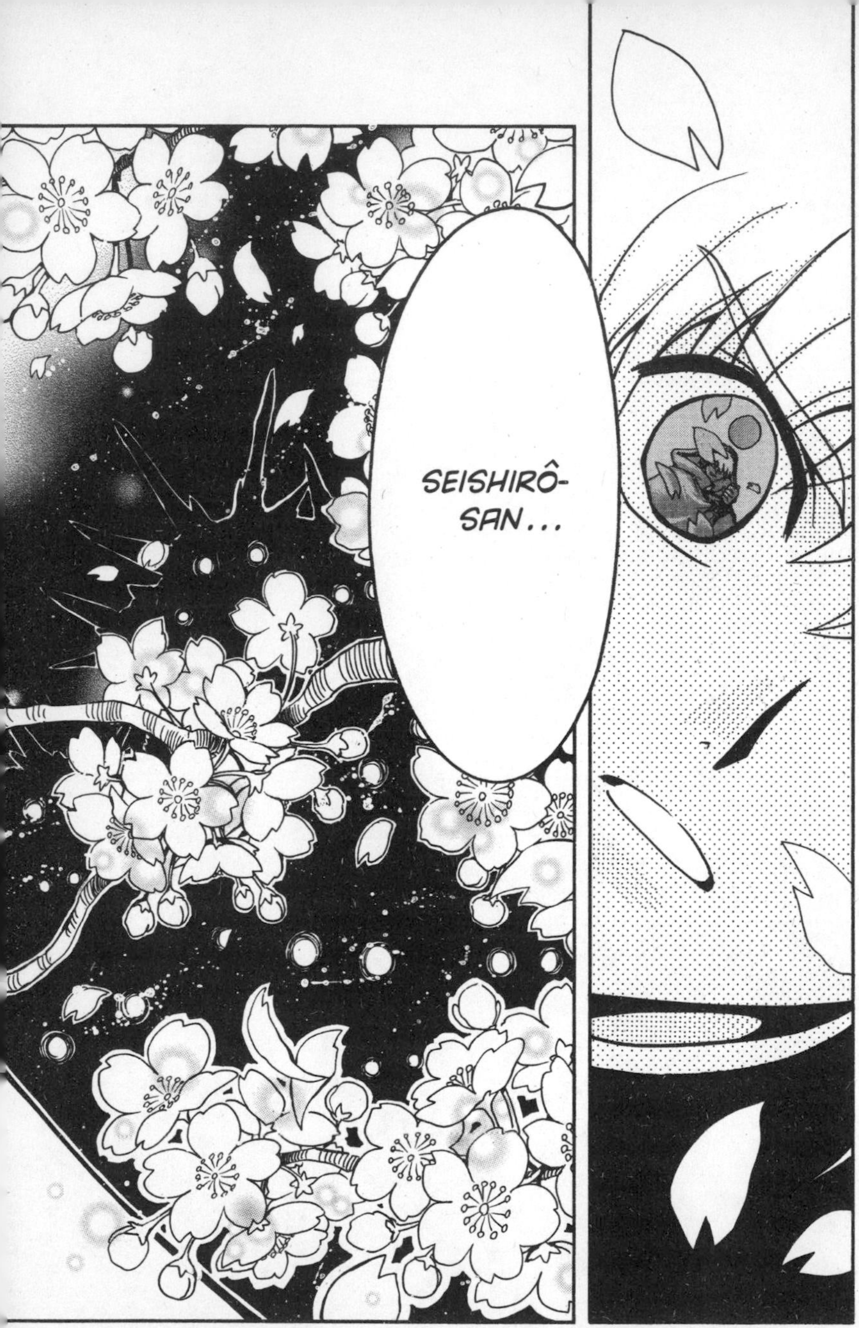
SEISHIRÔ-SAN...

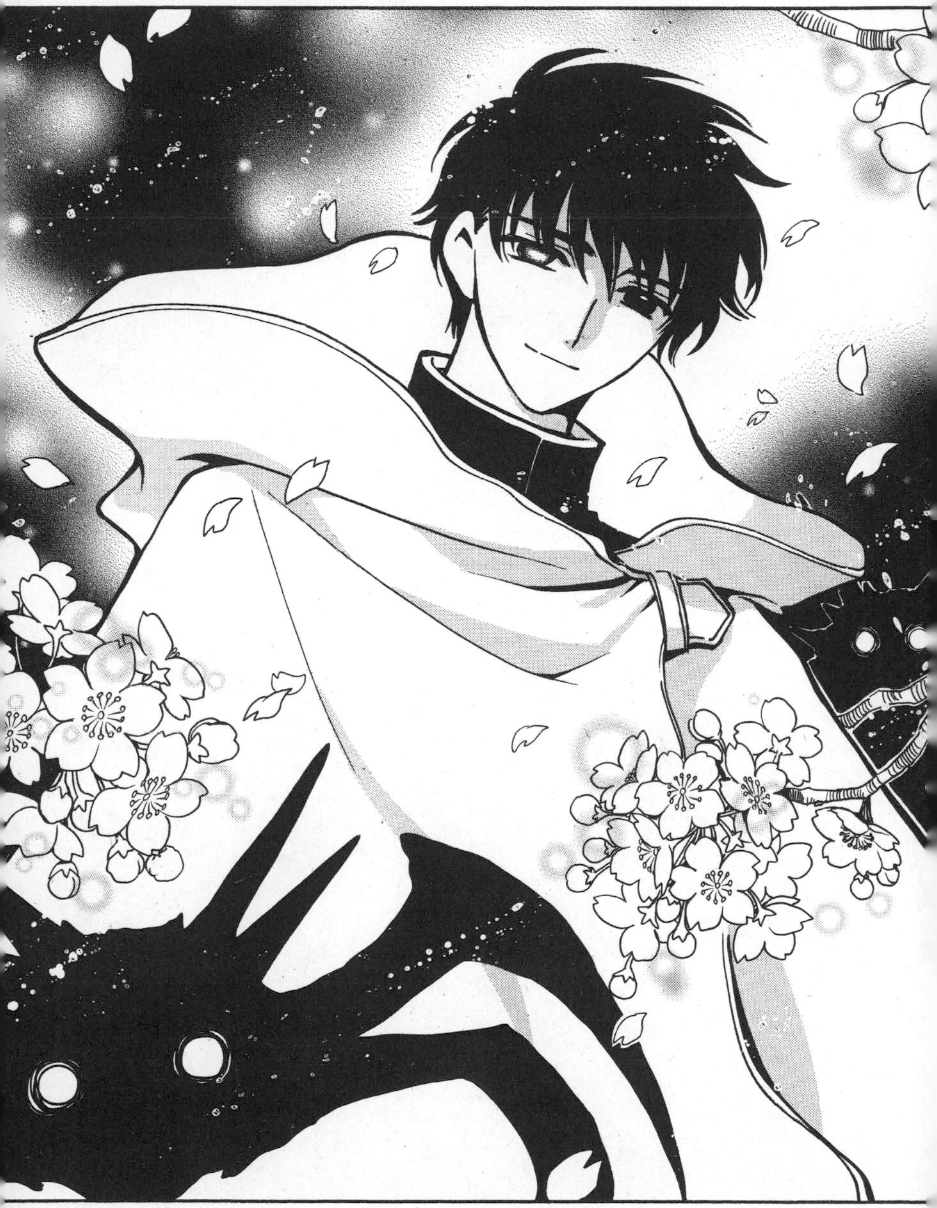

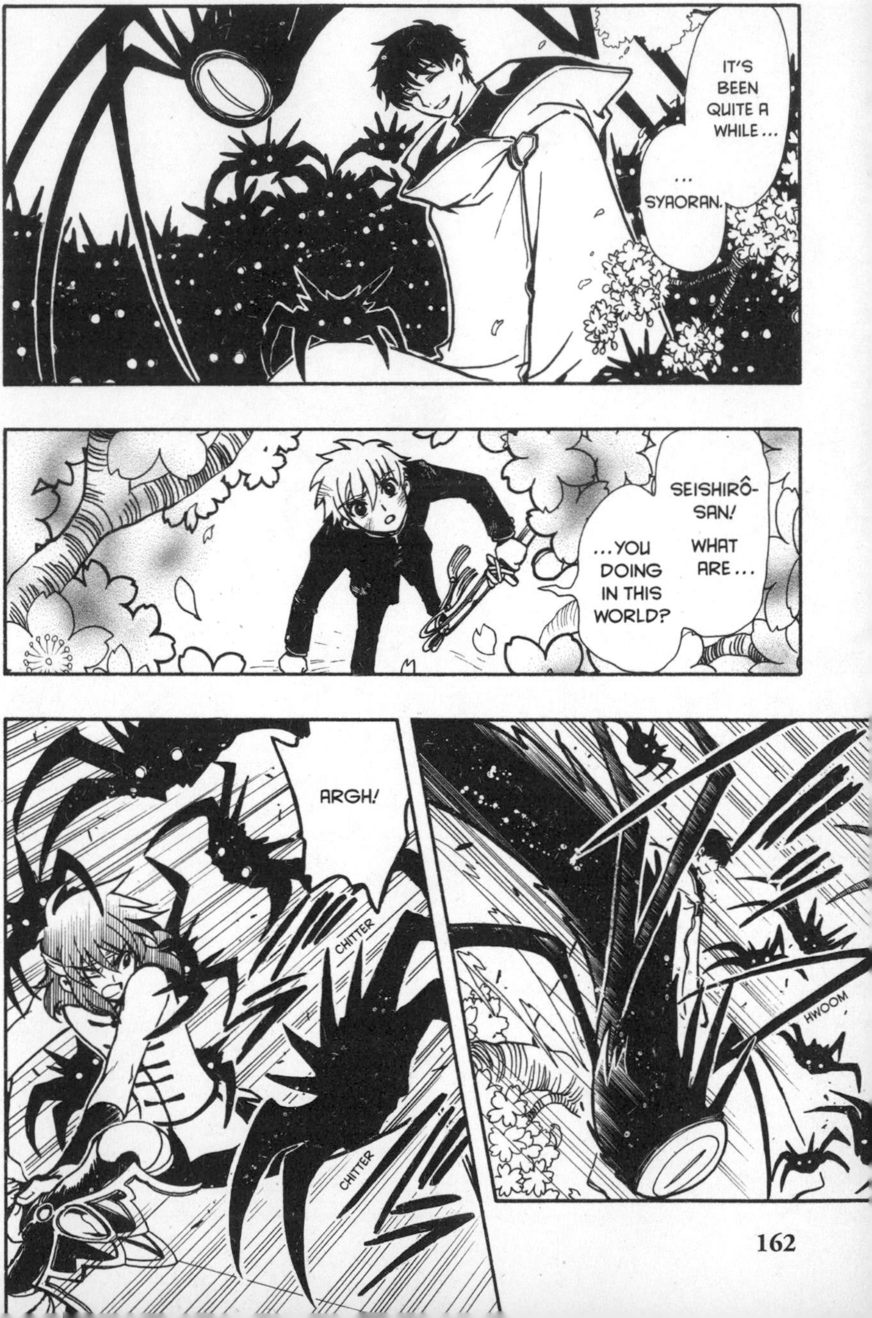
IT'S BEEN QUITE A WHILE...
...SYAORAN.
SEISHIRÔ-SAN!
WHAT ARE...
...YOU DOING IN THIS WORLD?
HWOOM
ARGH!
CHITTER
CHITTER

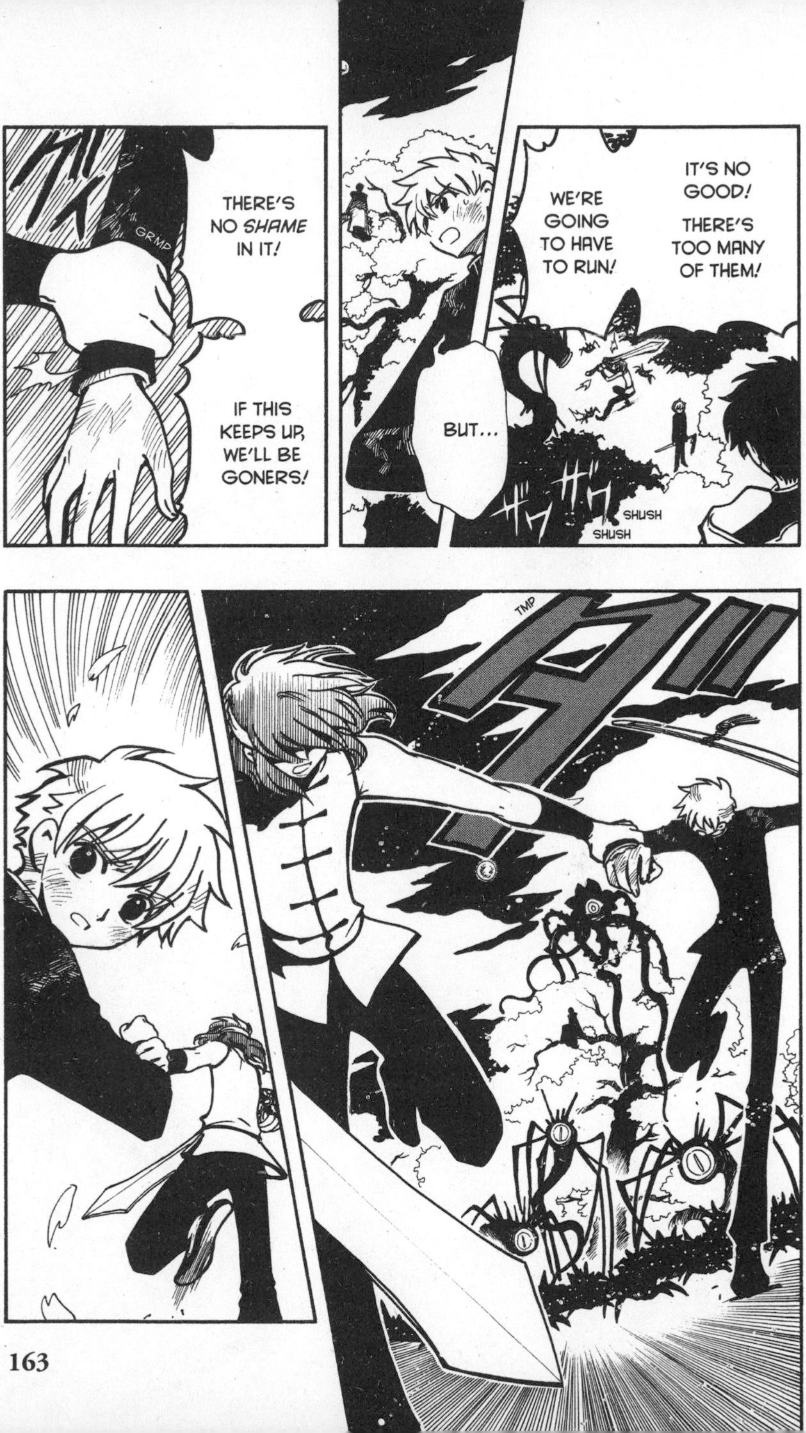
IT'S NO GOOD!
THERE'S TOO MANY OF THEM!
WE'RE GOING TO HAVE TO RUN!
SHUSH
SHUSH
BUT...
THERE'S NO *SHAME* IN IT!
GRMP
IF THIS KEEPS UP, WE'LL BE GONERS!
TMP

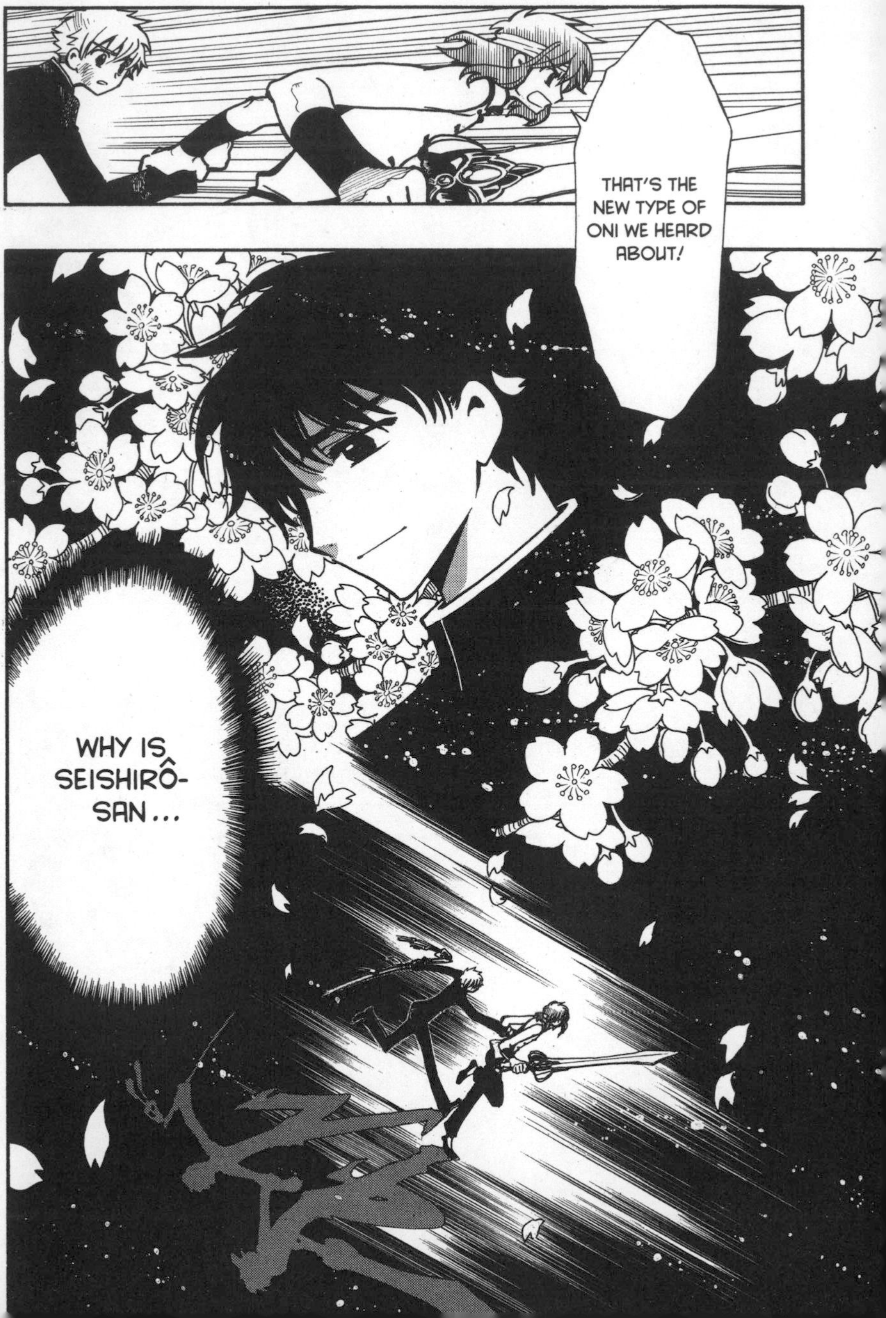
THAT'S THE NEW TYPE OF ONI WE HEARD ABOUT!
WHY IS SEISHIRÔ-SAN...

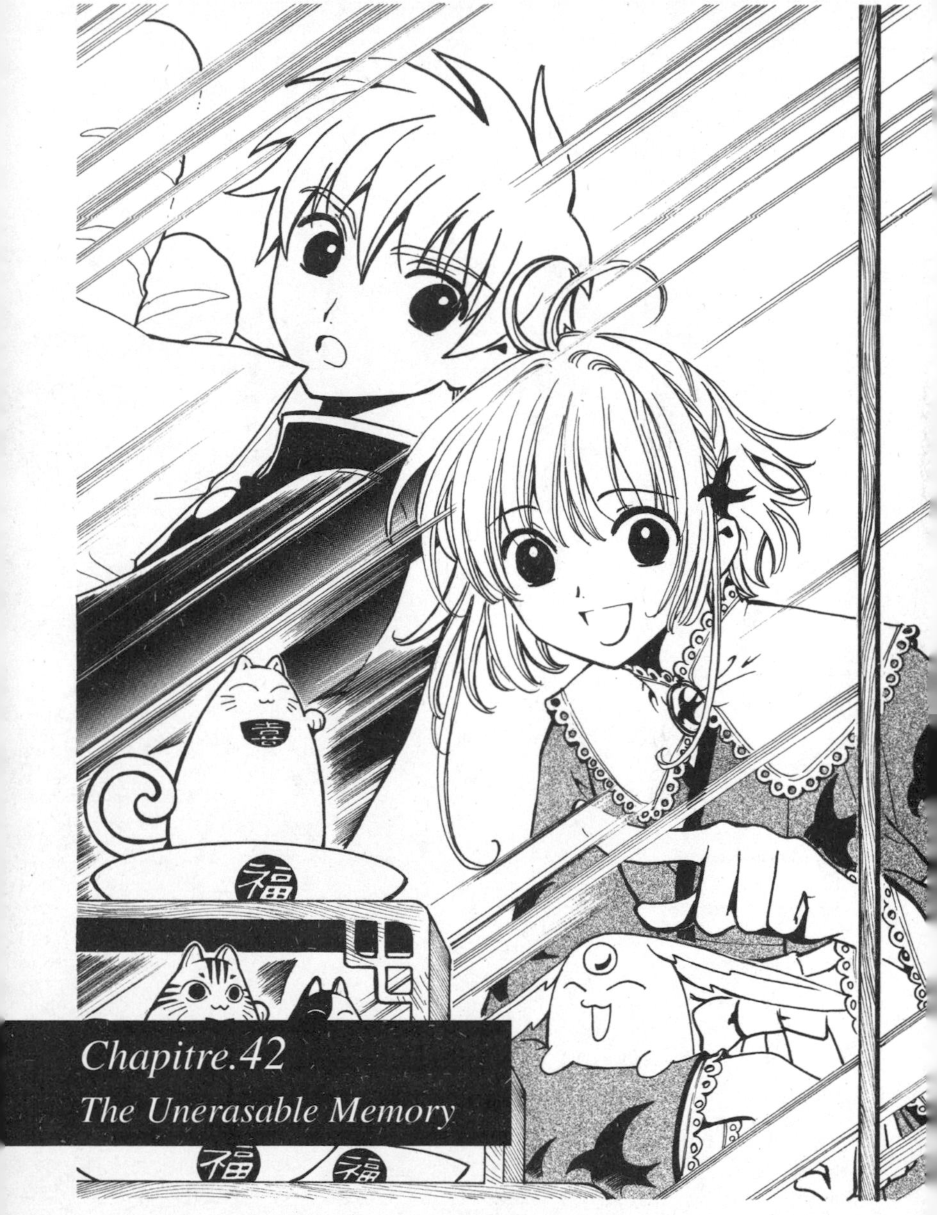
福
福
福

Chapitre.42
The Unerasable Memory

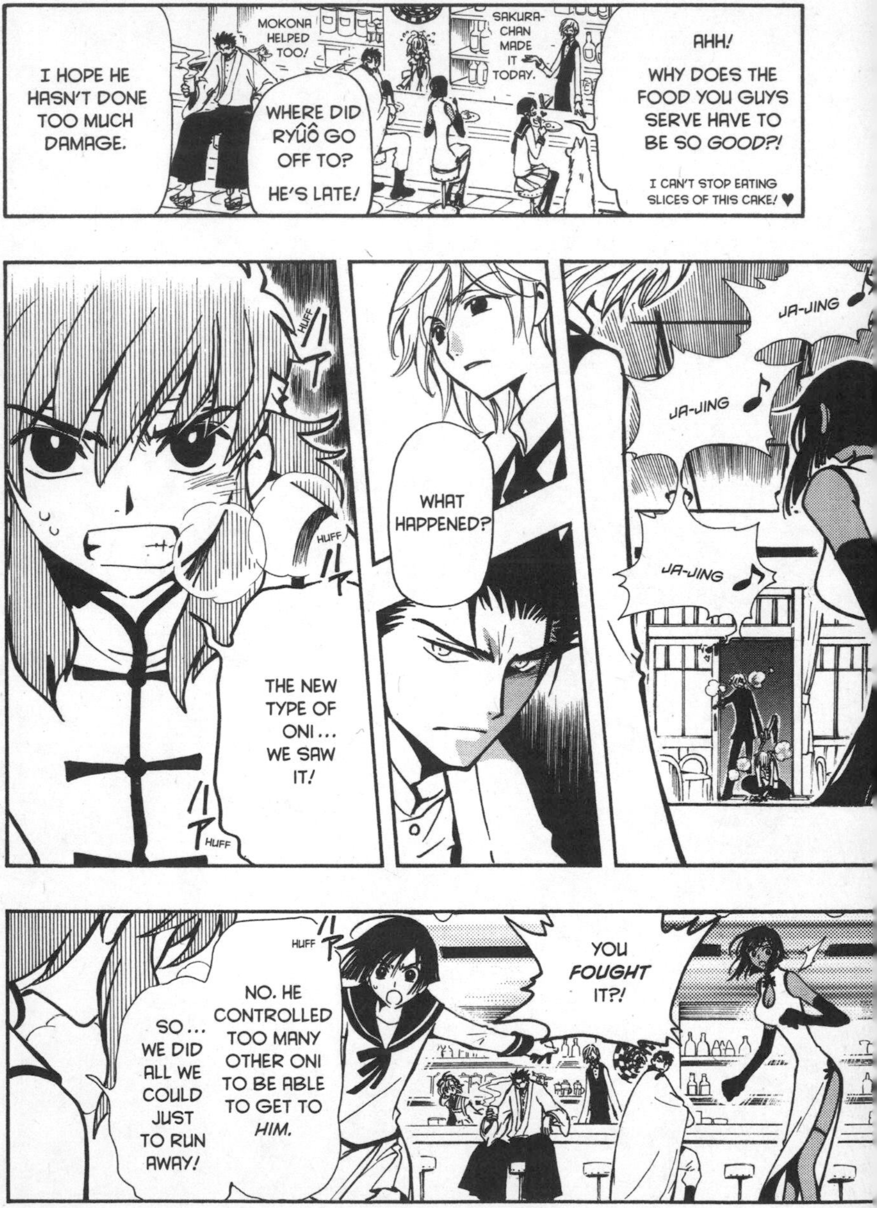
AHH!
WHY DOES THE FOOD YOU GUYS SERVE HAVE TO BE SO *GOOD*?!
I CAN'T STOP EATING SLICES OF THIS CAKE! ♥
SAKURA-CHAN MADE IT TODAY.
MOKONA HELPED TOO!
WHERE DID RYÛÔ GO OFF TO?
HE'S LATE!
I HOPE HE HASN'T DONE TOO MUCH DAMAGE.
JA-JING
JA-JING
JA-JING
WHAT HAPPENED?
HUFF
HUFF
THE NEW TYPE OF ONI... WE SAW IT!
HUFF
YOU *FOUGHT* IT?!
HUFF
NO. HE CONTROLLED TOO MANY OTHER ONI TO BE ABLE TO GET TO *HIM*.
SO... WE DID ALL WE COULD JUST TO RUN AWAY!

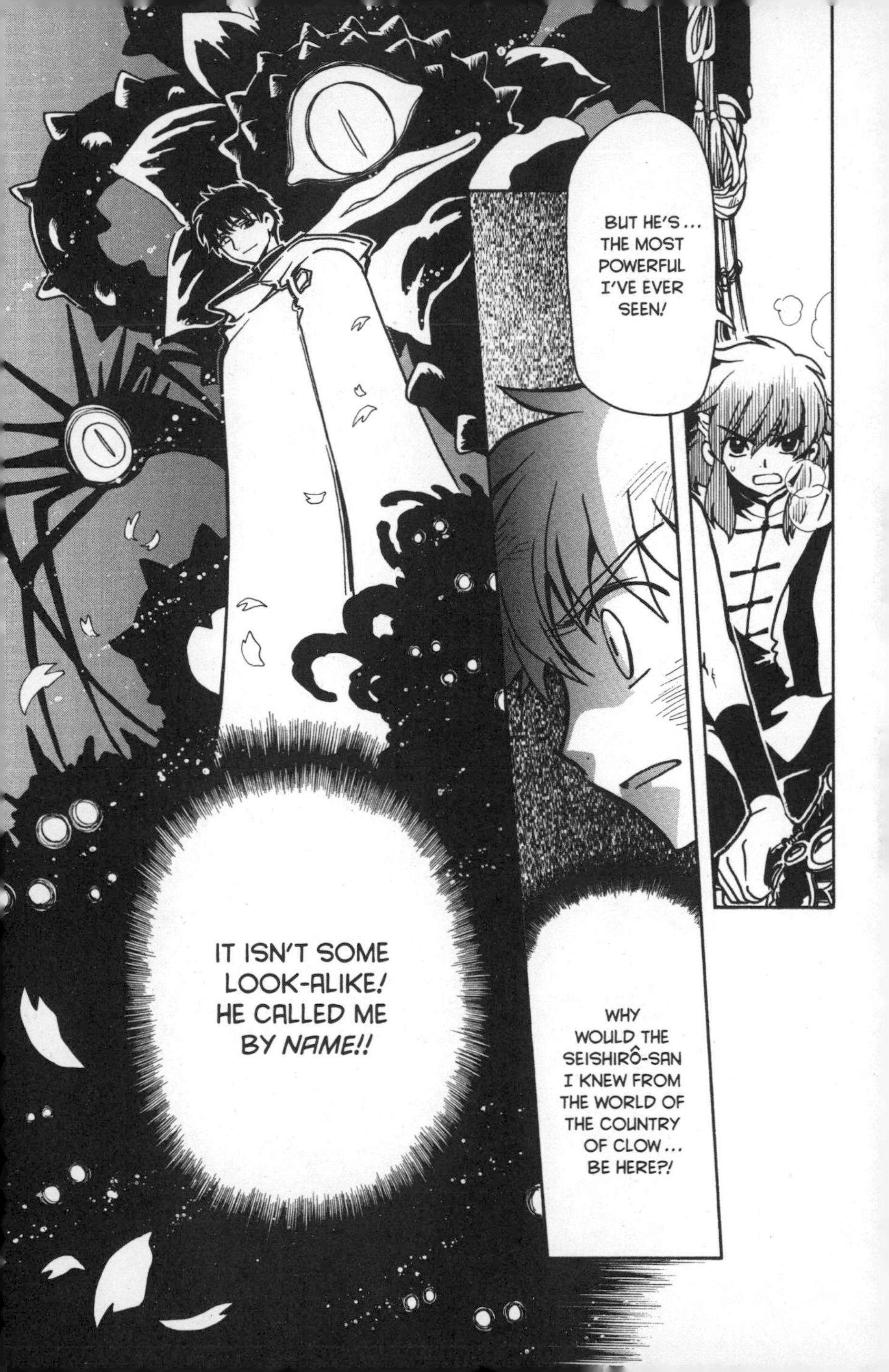
BUT HE'S... THE MOST POWERFUL I'VE EVER SEEN!
WHY WOULD THE SEISHIRÔ-SAN I KNEW FROM THE WORLD OF THE COUNTRY OF CLOW... BE HERE?!
IT ISN'T SOME LOOK-ALIKE! HE CALLED ME BY *NAME!!*

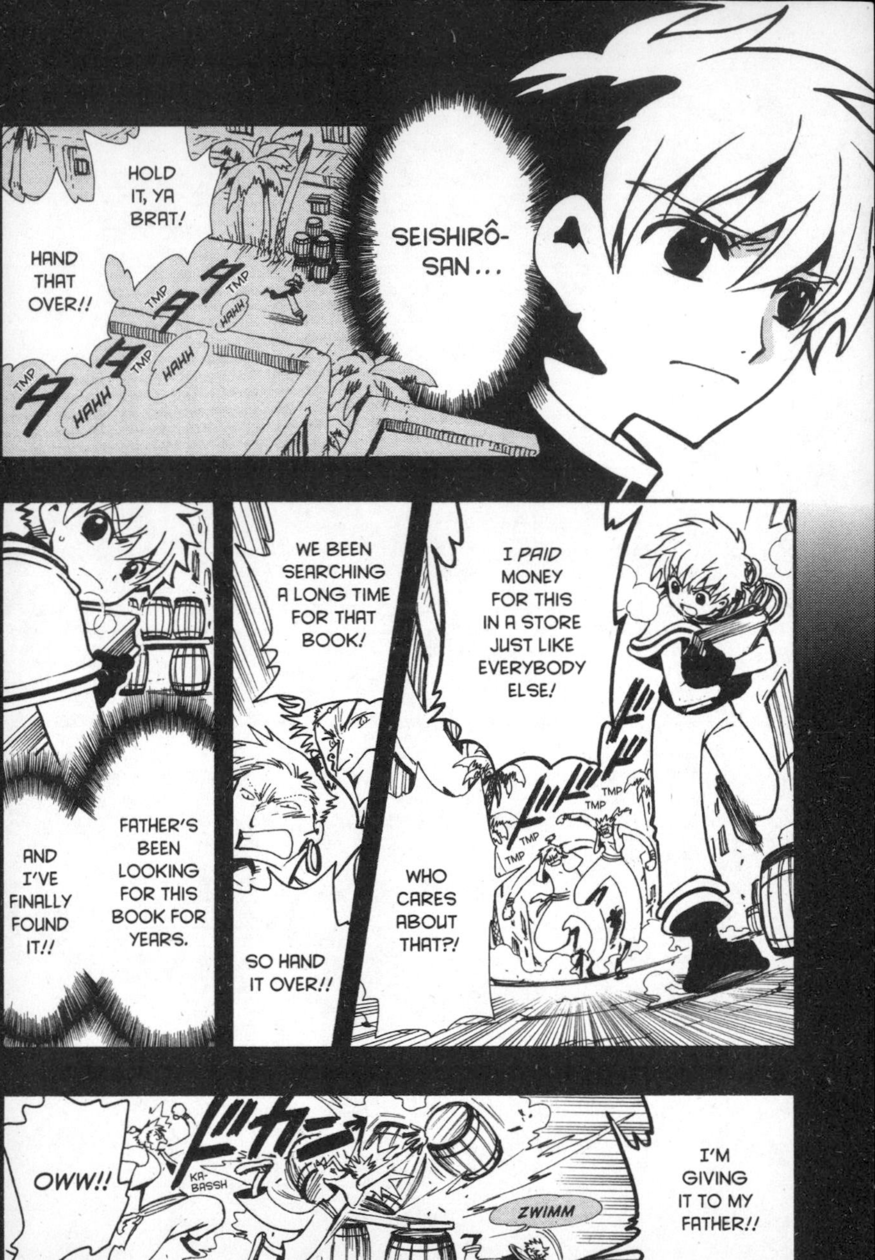
SEISHIRÔ-SAN...
HOLD IT, YA BRAT!
HAND THAT OVER!!
TMP
TMP
HAHH
TMP
HAHH
TMP
HAHH
I PAID MONEY FOR THIS IN A STORE JUST LIKE EVERYBODY ELSE!
TMP
TMP
TMP
TMP
WHO CARES ABOUT THAT?!
WE BEEN SEARCHING A LONG TIME FOR THAT BOOK!
SO HAND IT OVER!!
FATHER'S BEEN LOOKING FOR THIS BOOK FOR YEARS.
AND I'VE FINALLY FOUND IT!!
I'M GIVING IT TO MY FATHER!!
ZWIMM
KA-BASSH
OWW!!

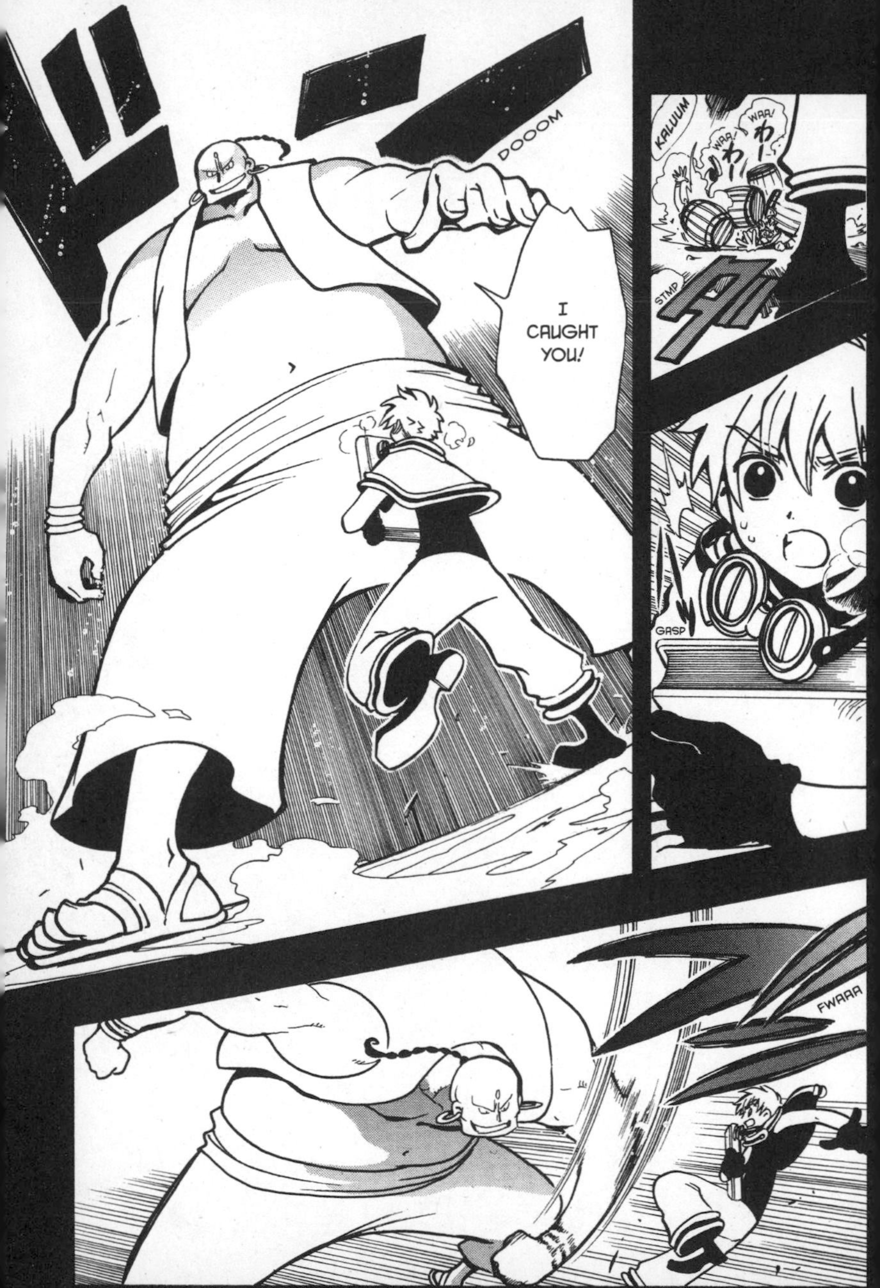
KALUUM
WAA!
わー
WAA!
わー
STMP
GASP
DOOOM
I CAUGHT YOU!
FWAAA

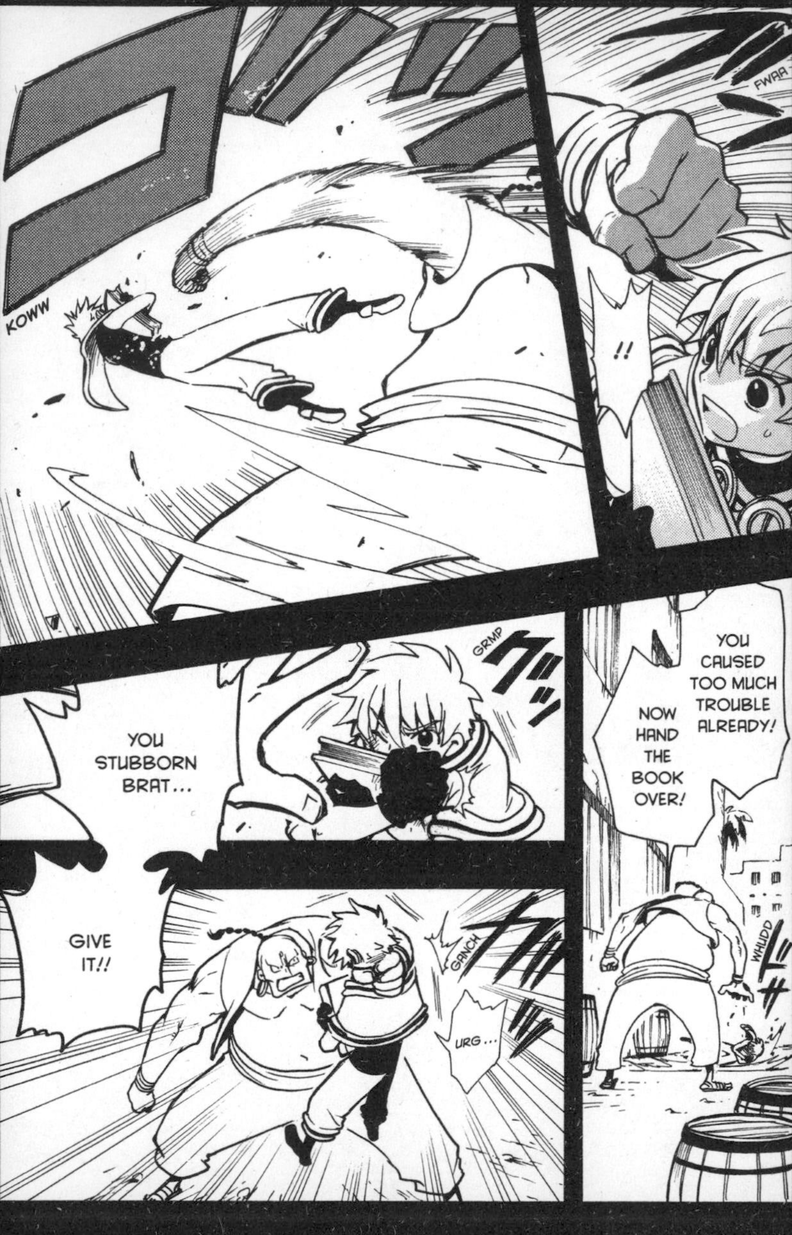
FWAA
!!
KOWW
YOU CAUSED TOO MUCH TROUBLE ALREADY!
NOW HAND THE BOOK OVER!
WHUDD
GRMP
YOU STUBBORN BRAT...
GANCH
URG...
GIVE IT!!

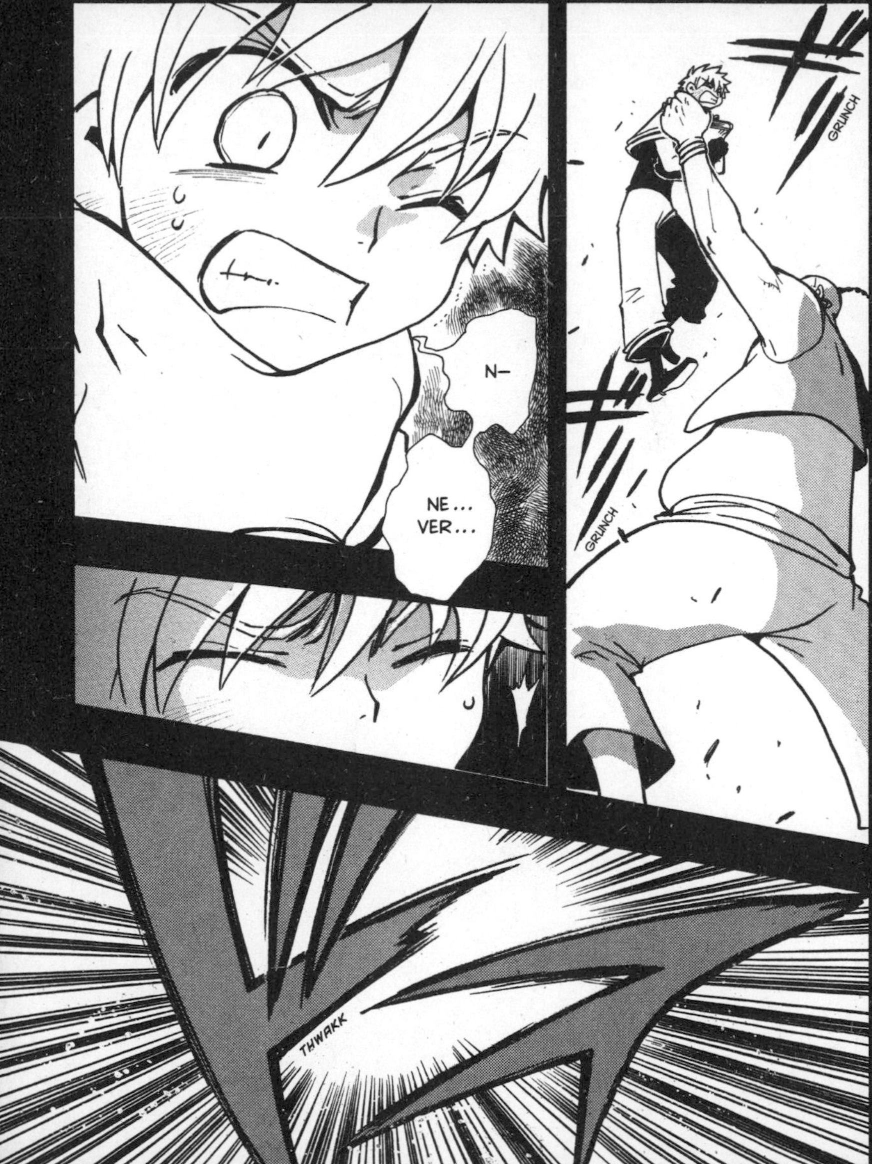
GRUNCH
GRUNCH
N–
NE...
VER...
THWAKK

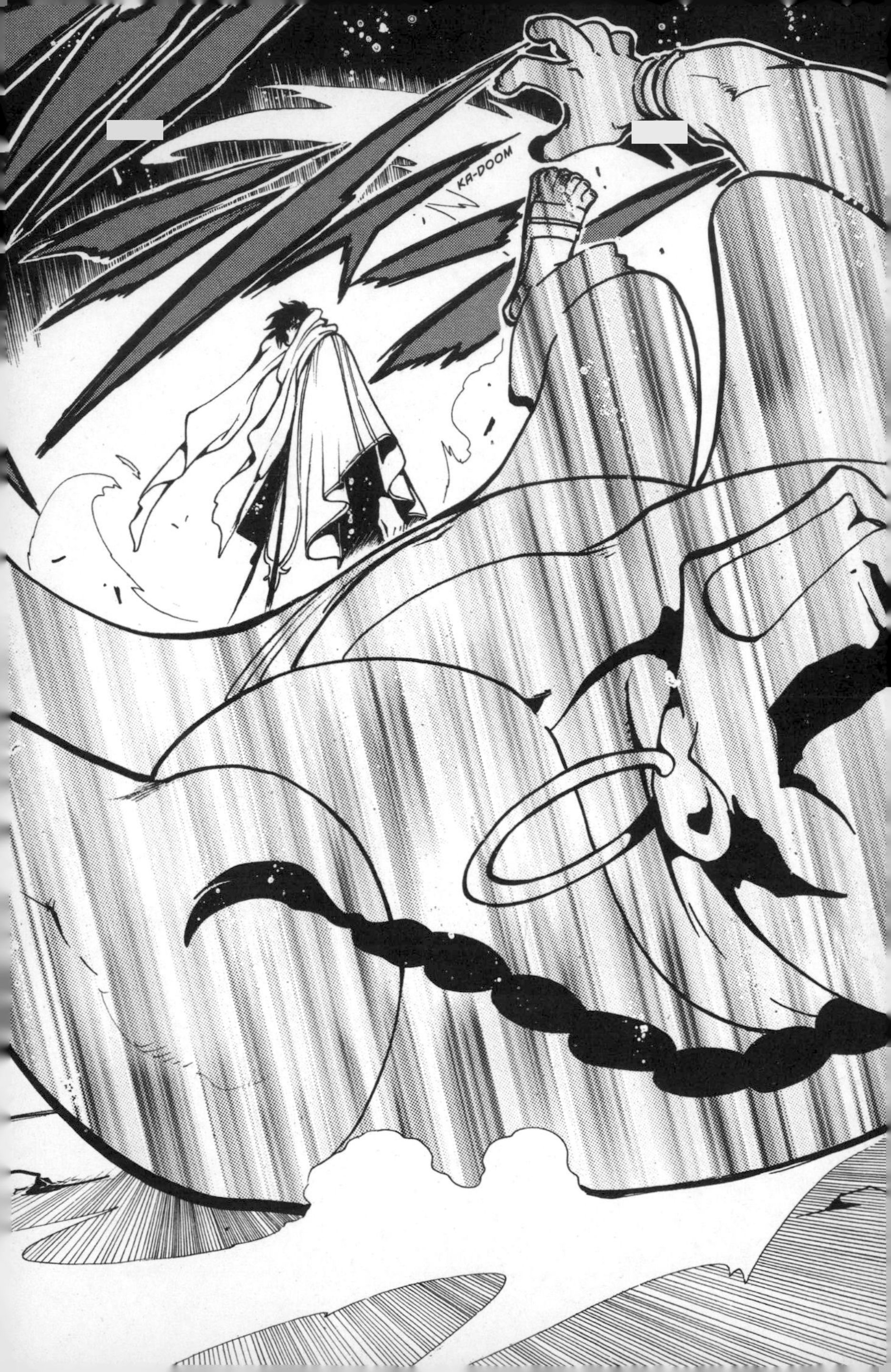
KA-DOOM

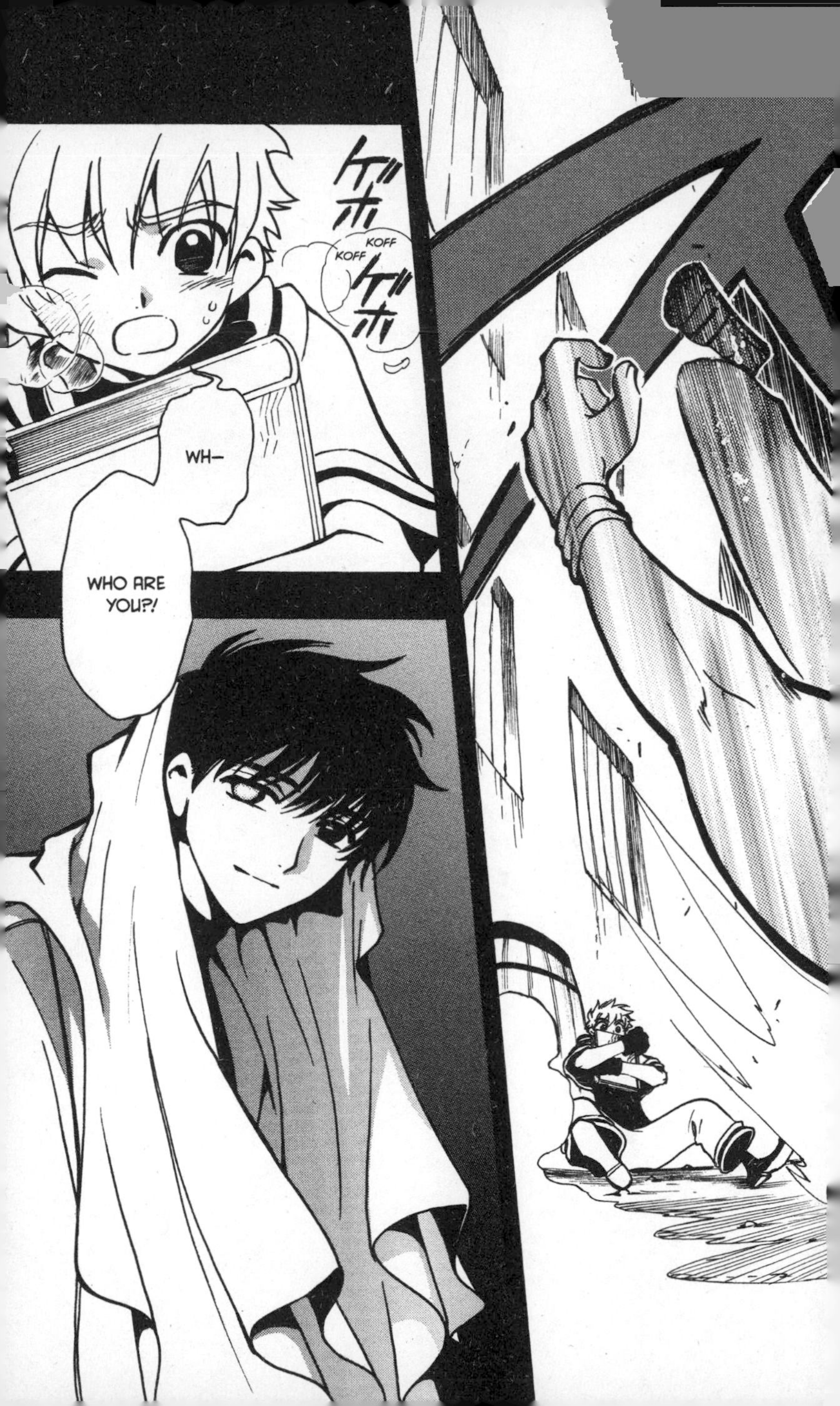
ゲホ
KOFF
KOFF
ゲホ
WH—
WHO ARE YOU?!

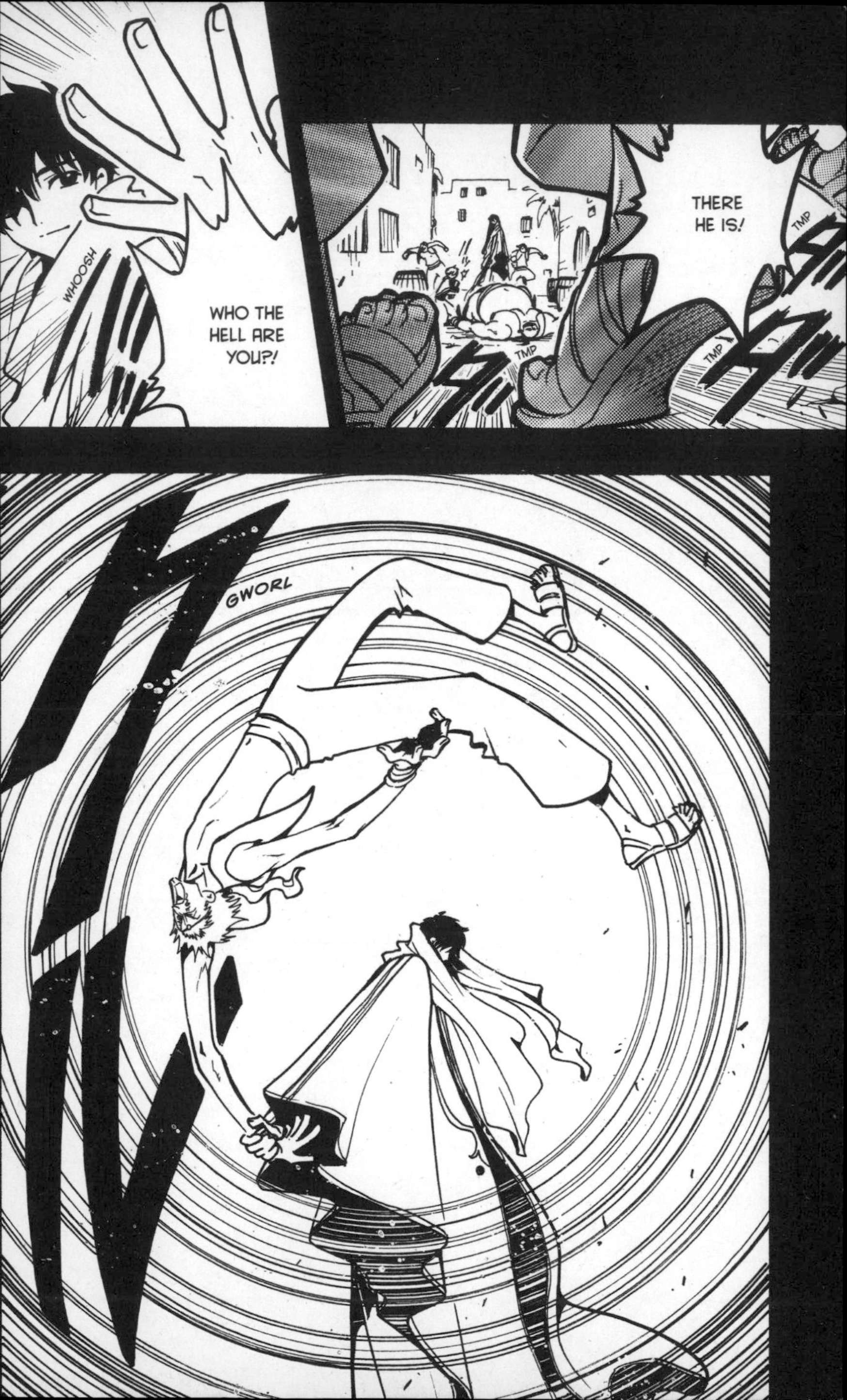
THERE HE IS!
TMP
TMP
TMP
WHOOSH
WHO THE HELL ARE YOU?!
GWORL

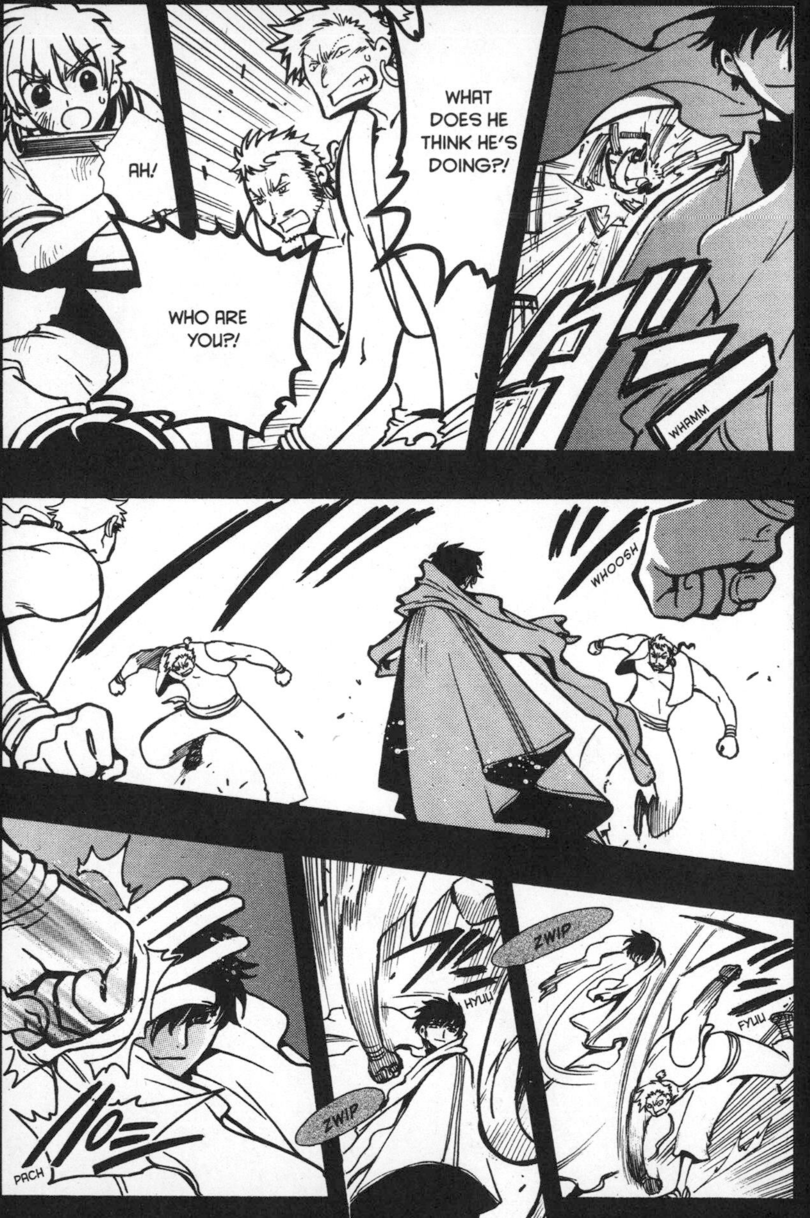
WHAMM
WHAT DOES HE THINK HE'S DOING?!
WHO ARE YOU?!
AH!
WHOOSH
FYUU
ZWIP
HYUU
ZWIP
PACH

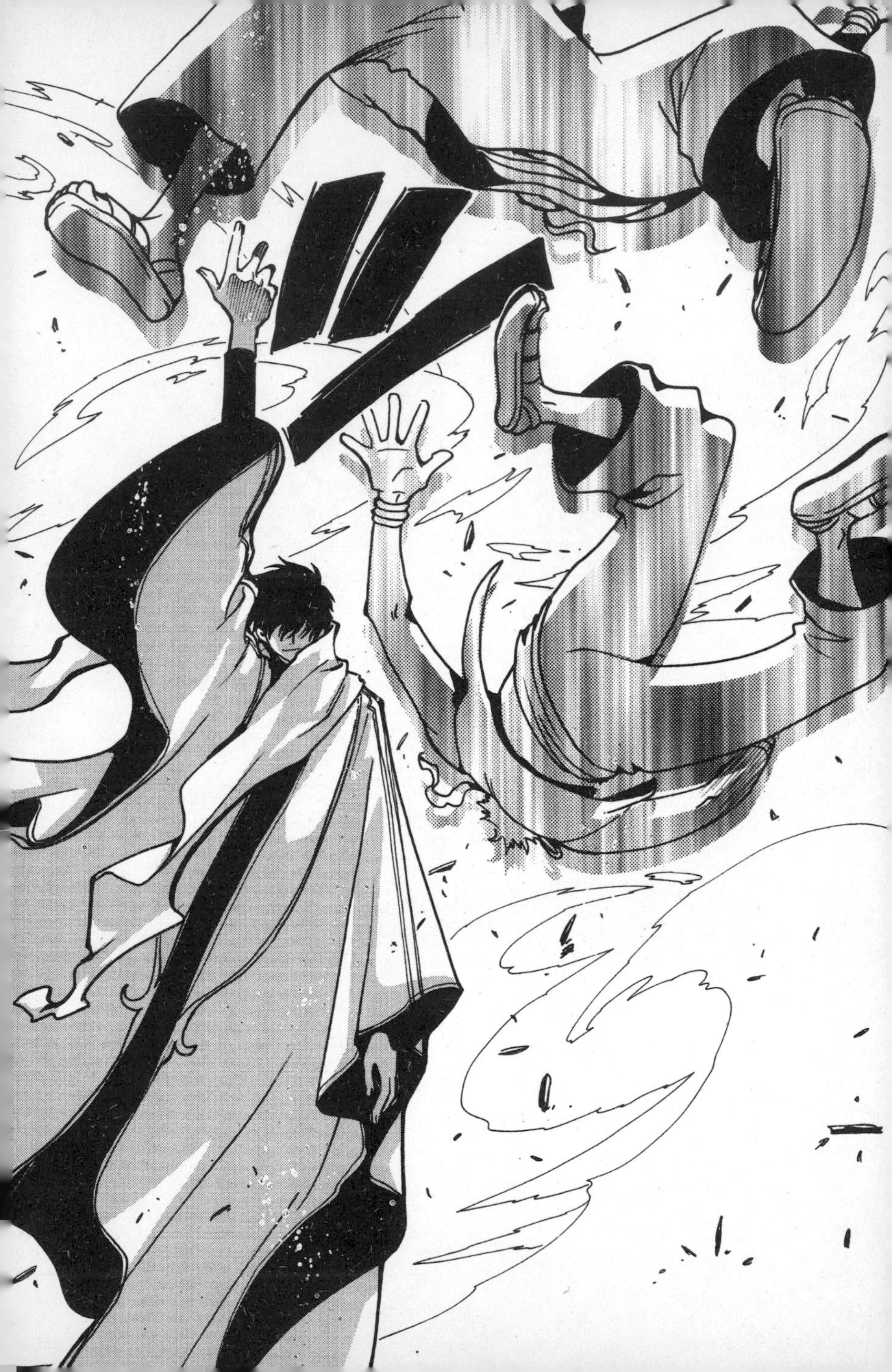

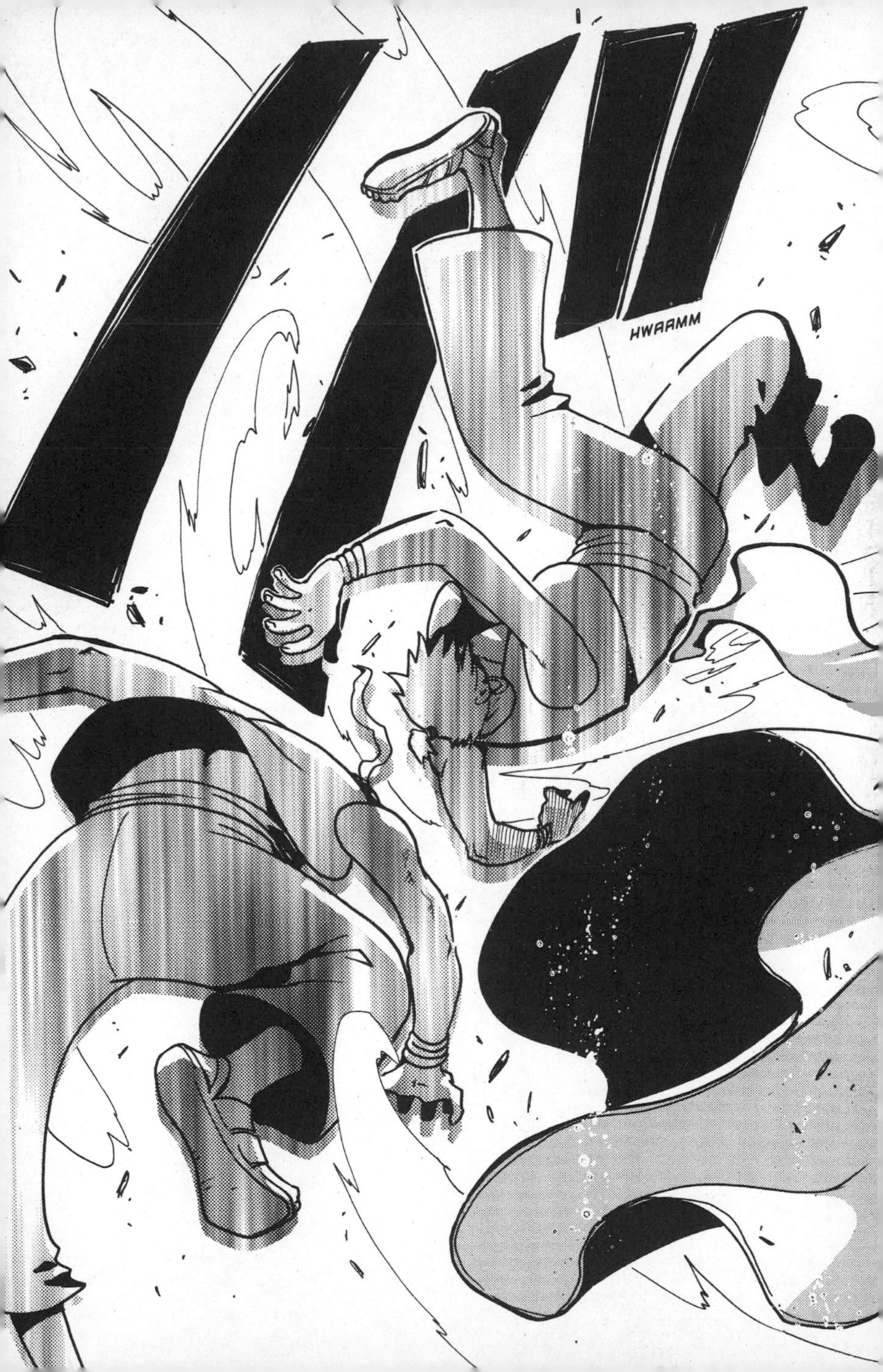
HWAAMM

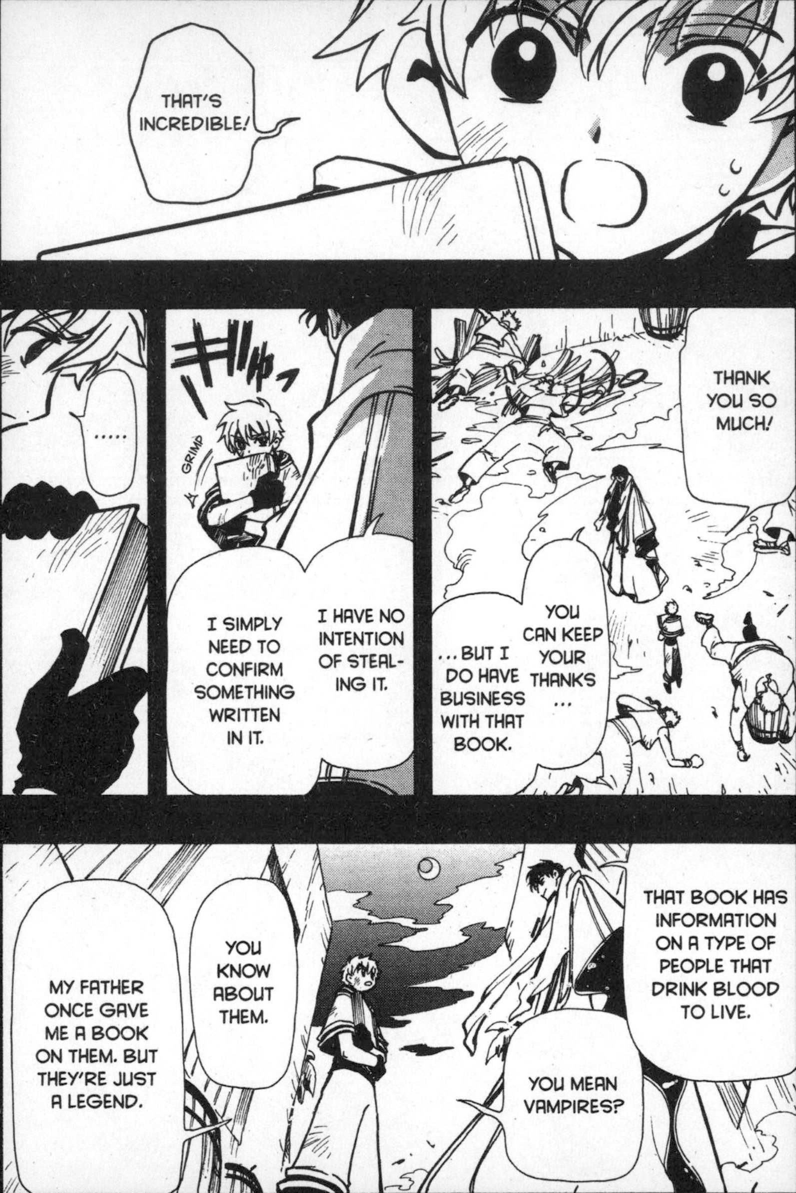
THAT'S INCREDIBLE!
THANK YOU SO MUCH!
YOU CAN KEEP YOUR THANKS ...
...BUT I DO HAVE BUSINESS WITH THAT BOOK.
GRIMP
I HAVE NO INTENTION OF STEAL-ING IT.
I SIMPLY NEED TO CONFIRM SOMETHING WRITTEN IN IT.
.....
THAT BOOK HAS INFORMATION ON A TYPE OF PEOPLE THAT DRINK BLOOD TO LIVE.
YOU MEAN VAMPIRES?
YOU KNOW ABOUT THEM.
MY FATHER ONCE GAVE ME A BOOK ON THEM. BUT THEY'RE JUST A LEGEND.

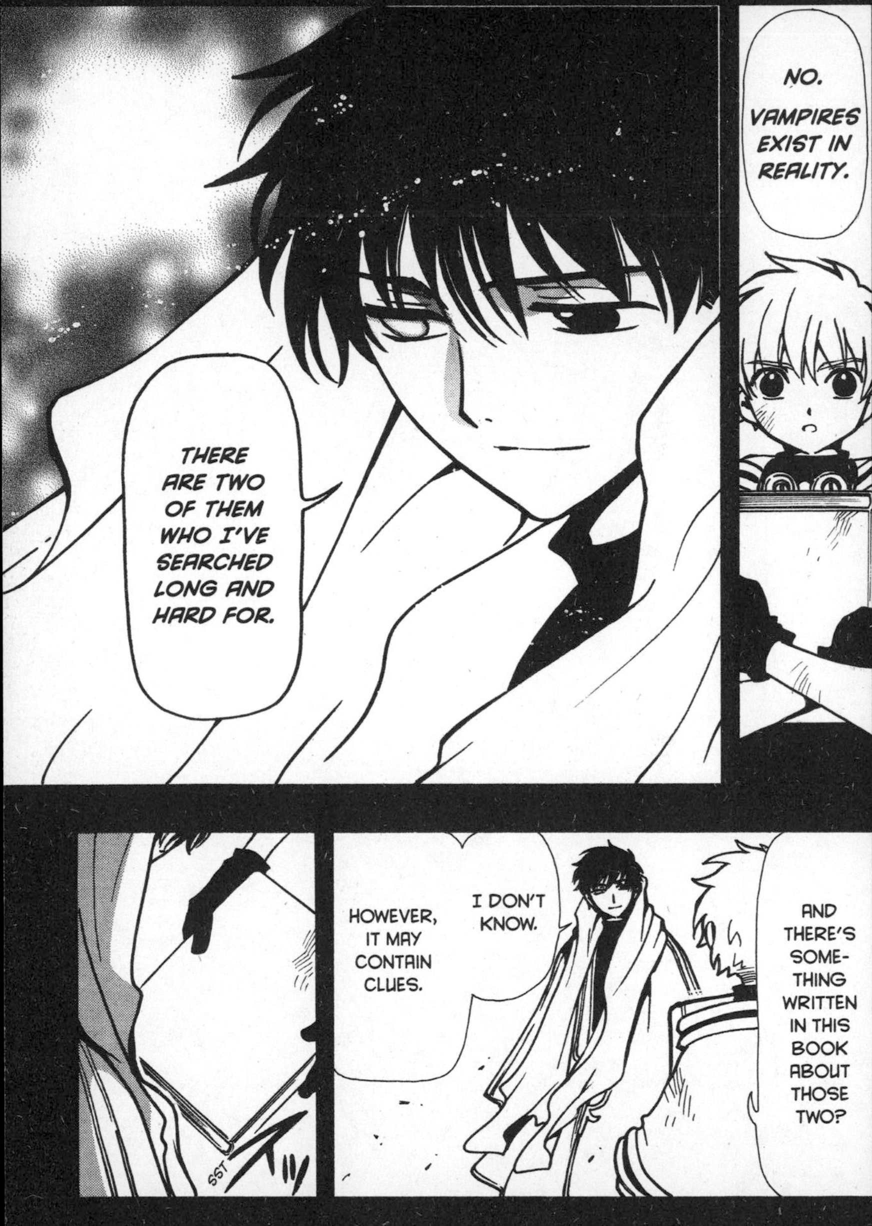
NO.
VAMPIRES EXIST IN REALITY.
THERE ARE TWO OF THEM WHO I'VE SEARCHED LONG AND HARD FOR.
AND THERE'S SOME-THING WRITTEN IN THIS BOOK ABOUT THOSE TWO?
I DON'T KNOW.
HOWEVER, IT MAY CONTAIN CLUES.
SST

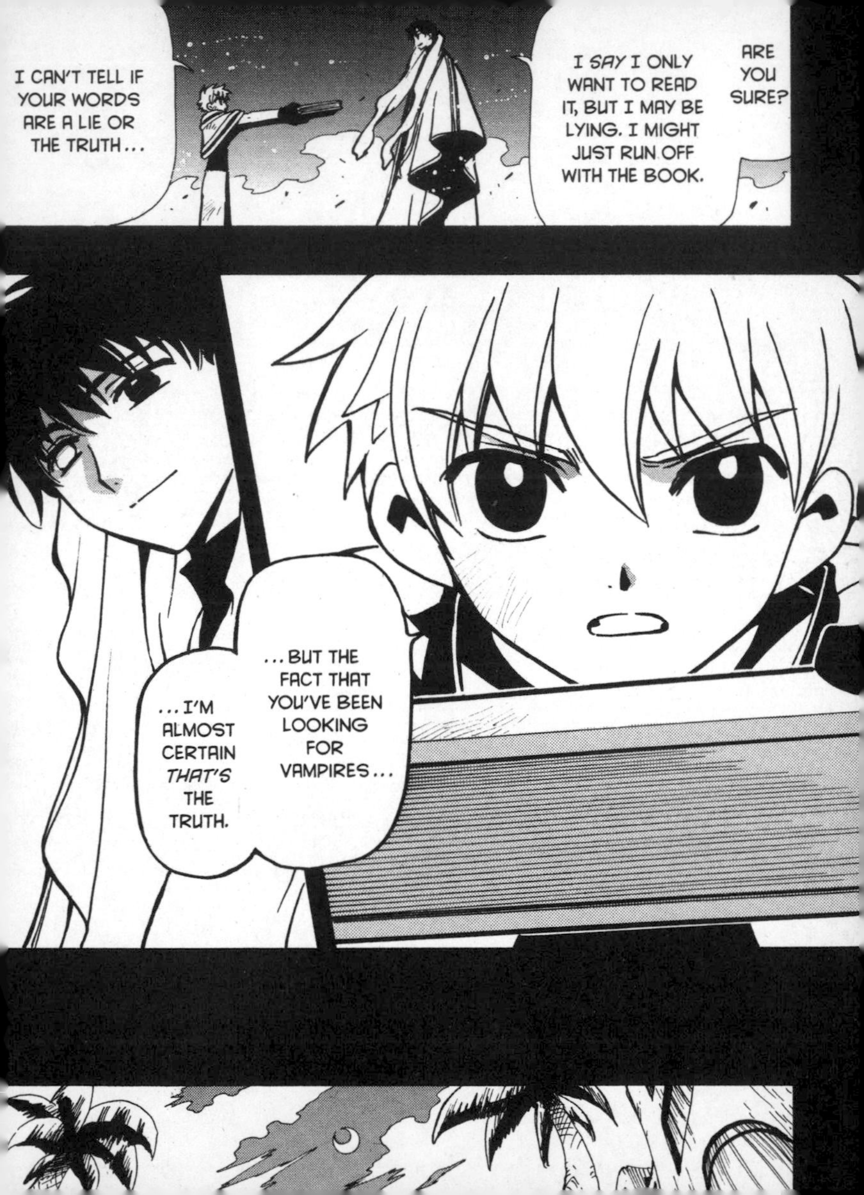
ARE YOU SURE?
I *SAY* I ONLY WANT TO READ IT, BUT I MAY BE LYING. I MIGHT JUST RUN OFF WITH THE BOOK.
I CAN'T TELL IF YOUR WORDS ARE A LIE OR THE TRUTH...
...BUT THE FACT THAT YOU'VE BEEN LOOKING FOR VAMPIRES...
...I'M ALMOST CERTAIN *THAT'S* THE TRUTH.

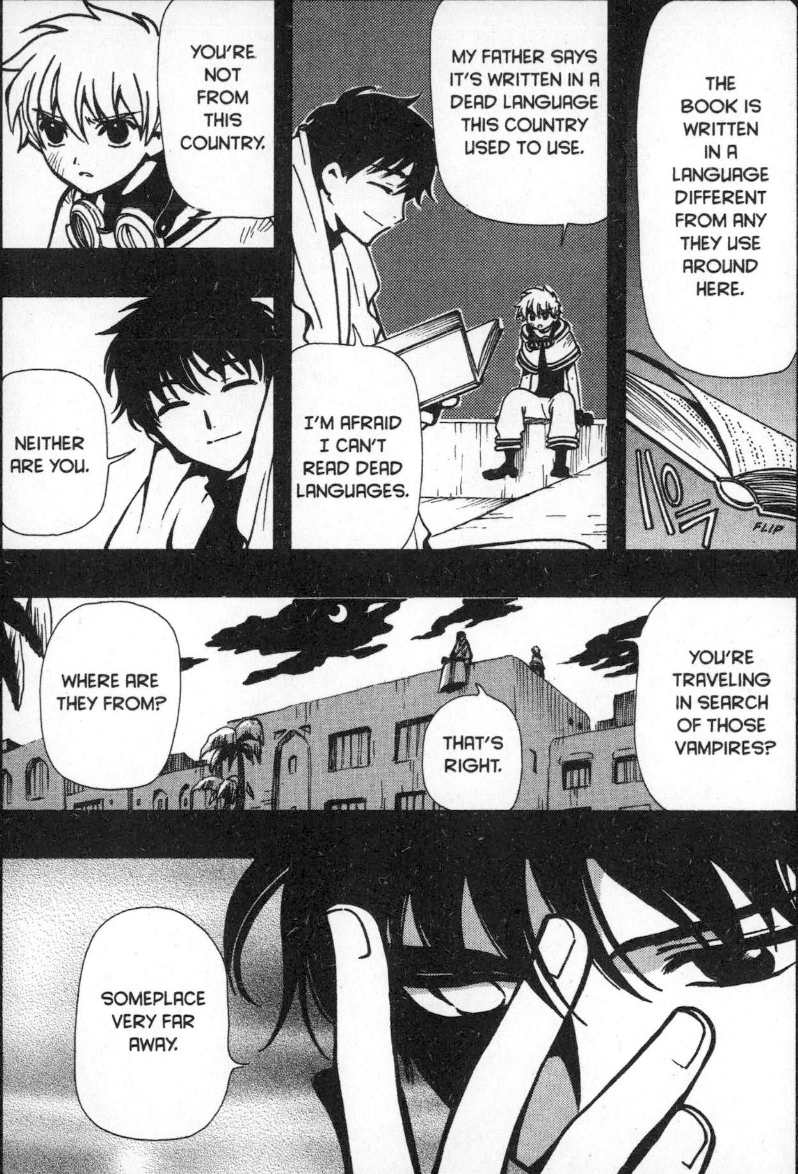
THE BOOK IS WRITTEN IN A LANGUAGE DIFFERENT FROM ANY THEY USE AROUND HERE.
FLIP
MY FATHER SAYS IT'S WRITTEN IN A DEAD LANGUAGE THIS COUNTRY USED TO USE.
I'M AFRAID I CAN'T READ DEAD LANGUAGES.
YOU'RE NOT FROM THIS COUNTRY.
NEITHER ARE YOU.
YOU'RE TRAVELING IN SEARCH OF THOSE VAMPIRES?
THAT'S RIGHT.
WHERE ARE THEY FROM?
SOMEPLACE VERY FAR AWAY.

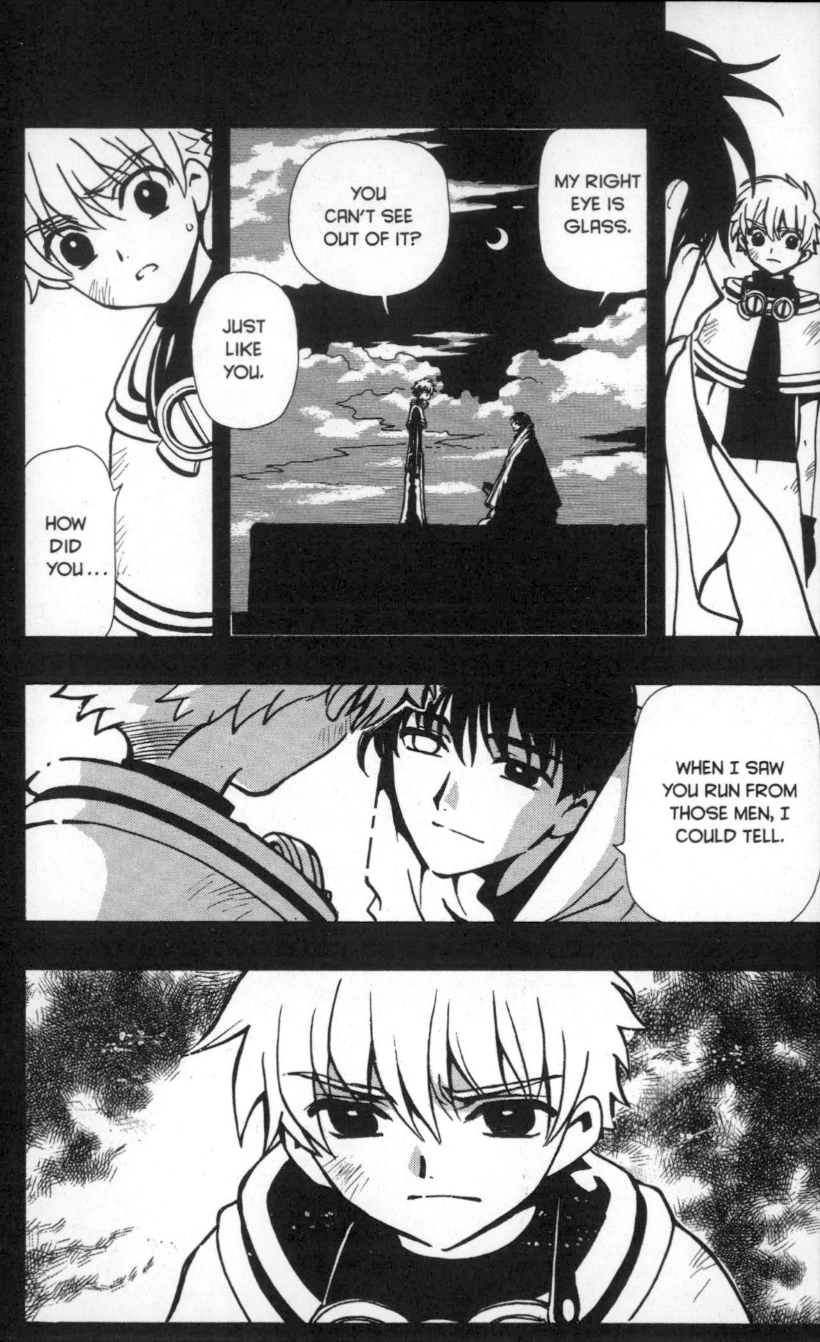
MY RIGHT EYE IS GLASS.
YOU CAN'T SEE OUT OF IT?
JUST LIKE YOU.
HOW DID YOU...
WHEN I SAW YOU RUN FROM THOSE MEN, I COULD TELL.

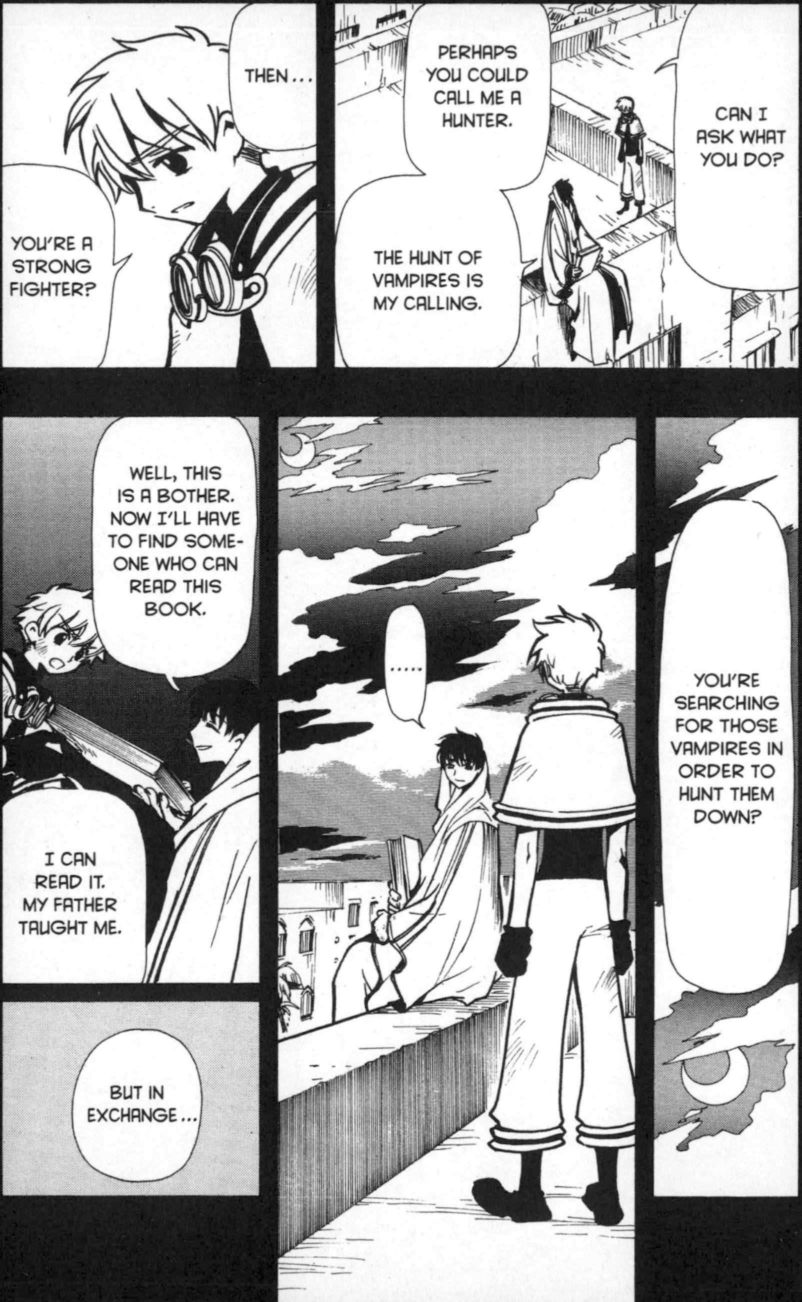
CAN I ASK WHAT YOU DO?
PERHAPS YOU COULD CALL ME A HUNTER.
THE HUNT OF VAMPIRES IS MY CALLING.
THEN...
YOU'RE A STRONG FIGHTER?
YOU'RE SEARCHING FOR THOSE VAMPIRES IN ORDER TO HUNT THEM DOWN?
.....
WELL, THIS IS A BOTHER. NOW I'LL HAVE TO FIND SOME-ONE WHO CAN READ THIS BOOK.
I CAN READ IT. MY FATHER TAUGHT ME.
BUT IN EXCHANGE...

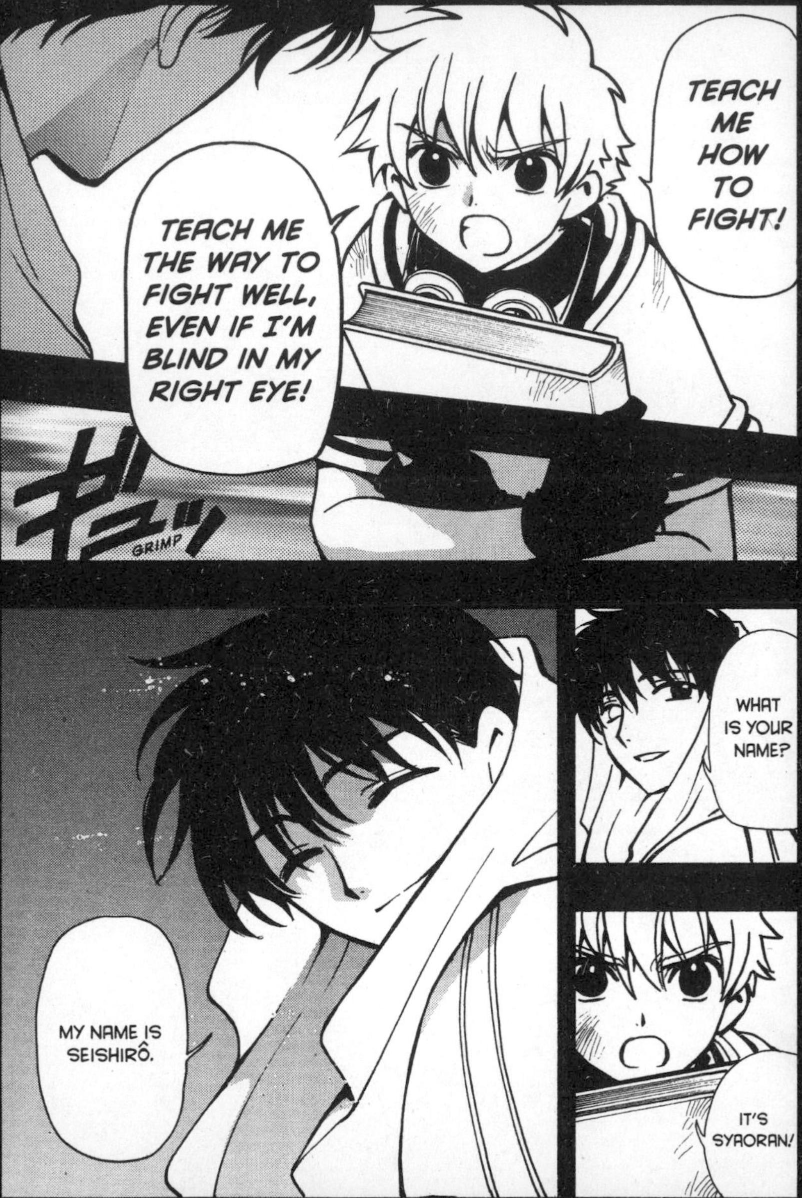
TEACH ME HOW TO FIGHT!
TEACH ME THE WAY TO FIGHT WELL, EVEN IF I'M BLIND IN MY RIGHT EYE!
GRIMP
WHAT IS YOUR NAME?
IT'S SYAORAN!
MY NAME IS SEISHIRÔ.

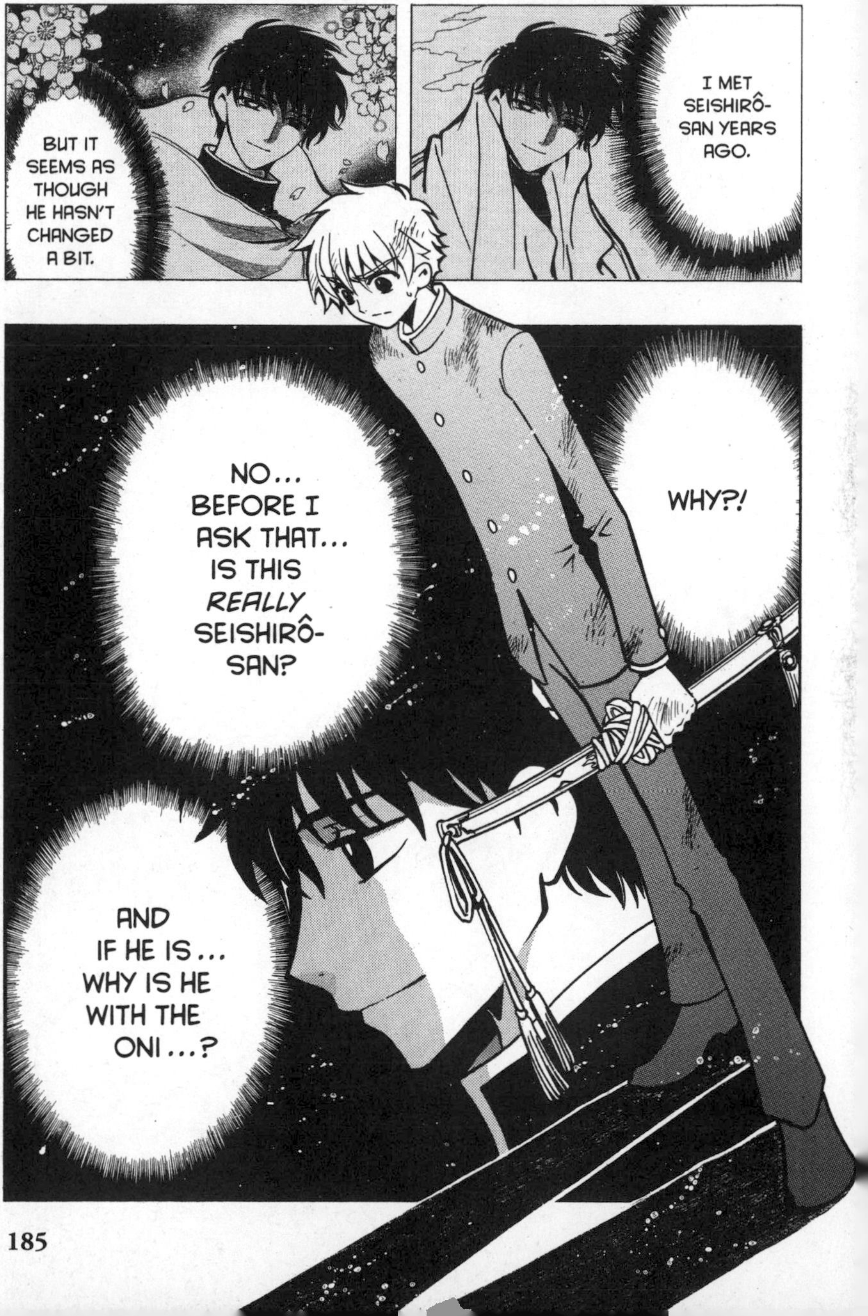
I MET SEISHIRÔ-SAN YEARS AGO.
BUT IT SEEMS AS THOUGH HE HASN'T CHANGED A BIT.
WHY?!
NO... BEFORE I ASK THAT... IS THIS *REALLY* SEISHIRÔ-SAN?
AND IF HE IS... WHY IS HE WITH THE ONI...?

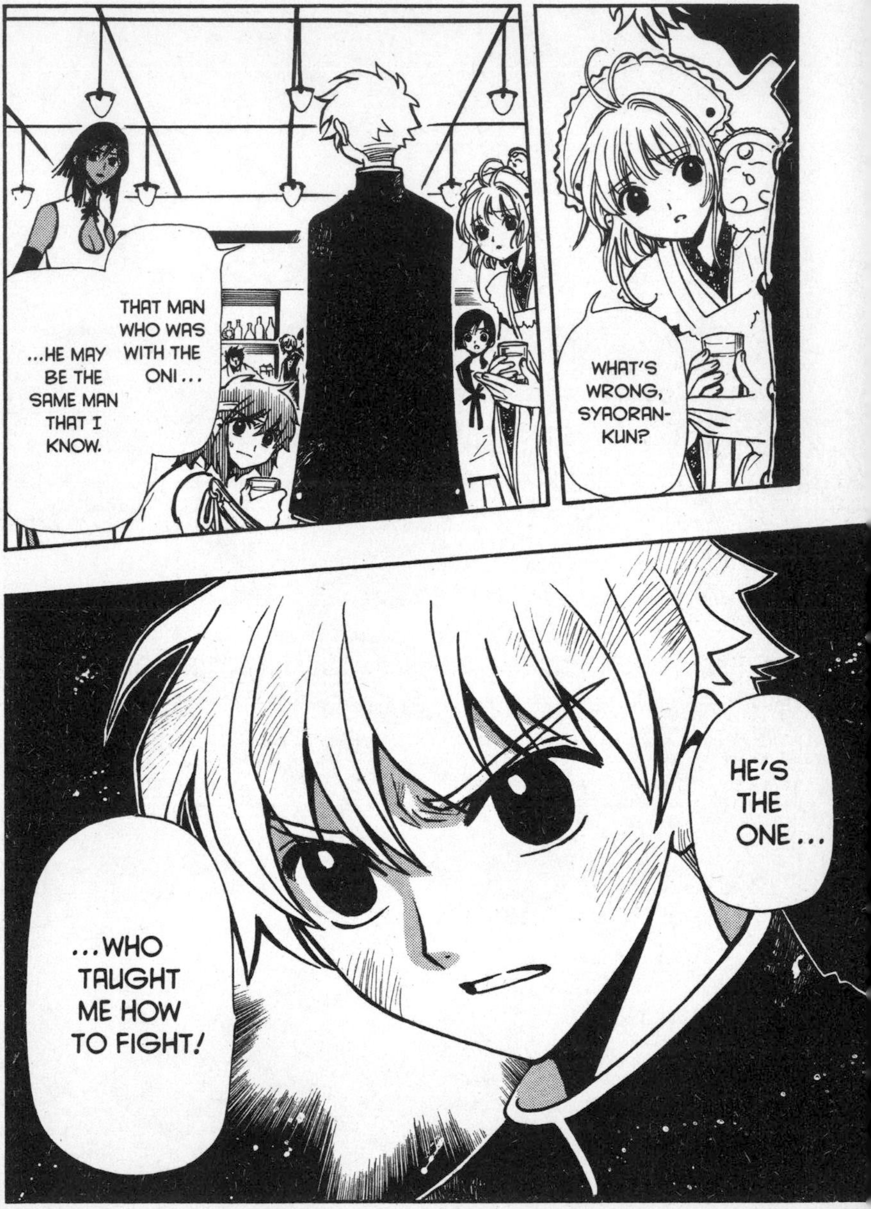
WHAT'S WRONG, SYAORAN-KUN?
THAT MAN WHO WAS WITH THE ONI...
...HE MAY BE THE SAME MAN THAT I KNOW.
HE'S THE ONE...
...WHO TAUGHT ME HOW TO FIGHT!

To Be Continued

About the Creators

CLAMP is a group of four women who have become the most popular manga artists in the United Kingdom—Ageha Ohkawa, Mokona, Satsuki Igarashi, and Tsubaki Nekoi. They started out as doujinshi (fan comics) creators, but their skill and craft brought them to the attention of publishers very quickly. Their first work from a major publisher was *RG Veda*, but their first mass success was with *Magic Knight Rayearth*. From there, they went on to write many series, including *Cardcaptor Sakura* and *Chobits*, two of the most popular manga available. Like many Japanese manga artists, they prefer to avoid the spotlight, and little is known about them personally.

CLAMP is currently publishing three series in Japan: *Tsubasa* and *xxxHOLiC* with Kodansha and *Gohou Drug* with Kadokawa.

Volumes 1—7 of *Tsubasa* and *xxxHolic* are available from Tanoshimi now.

Translation Notes

Japanese is a tricky language for most Westerners, and translation is often more art than science. For your edification and reading pleasure, here are notes on some of the places where we could have gone in a different direction in our translation of the work, or where a Japanese cultural reference is used.

Just to catch you up . . .

The country of Ôto is based on the romantic notion of early twentieth-century Japan, where the traditional feudal Japanese lifestyle still mixed with strong Western influences. The enemies, oni, are ranked in a system known to the Japanese as Iroha, a way of counting that might be compared to counting in English using "Eenie meanie minie moe," but with more historical and poetic relevance (see more on Iroha in the notes from Volume 5). The ranking of oni start with I, which is the highest, down to To, which is the lowest. Each rank has a level with 1 being the highest and 5 being the lowest. Thus we have:

Rank	
I	levels 5 to 1
Ro	levels 5 to 1
Ha	levels 5 to 1
Ni	levels 5 to 1
Ho	levels 5 to 1
He	levels 5 to 1
To	levels 5 to 1

Breakfast food, page 7

Traditional Japanese breakfast food is fish with soy sauce and rice. It wasn't until Western influences swept the country in the late 1800s and early 1900s that tastes began to change toward sweet things like jams and frosted buns in the morning.

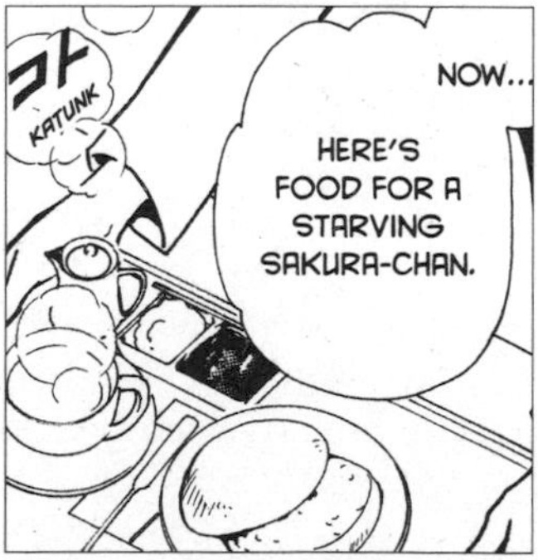

KATUNK
NOW...
HERE'S FOOD FOR A STARVING SAKURA-CHAN.

Sneezing, page 8

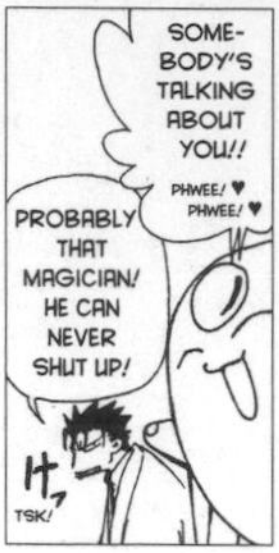
SOME-
BODY'S
TALKING
ABOUT
YOU!!
PHWEE! ♥
PHWEE! ♥
PROBABLY
THAT
MAGICIAN!
HE CAN
NEVER
SHUT UP!
TSK!

The old wives' tale goes that when you sneeze, someone is talking about you. It isn't easy to find anyone who actually believes in the saying, but the idea sure comes up in anime and manga quite a lot!

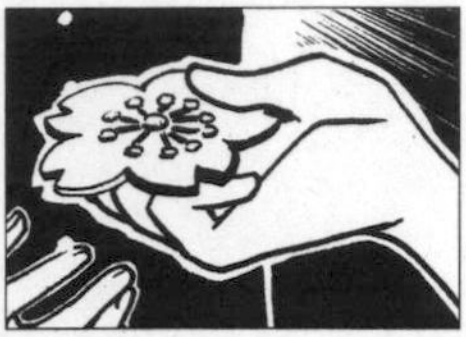

The Sakura shape, page 21

The first kanji in the spelling of the country of Ôto is the same kanji for Sakura, cherry blossom (see more on the cultural significance of the cherry blossom in the notes from Volume 5). So it is only natural that the "debit card" of Syaoran and friends would be in the shape of a cherry blossom.

Ryûô & Sôma, page 28

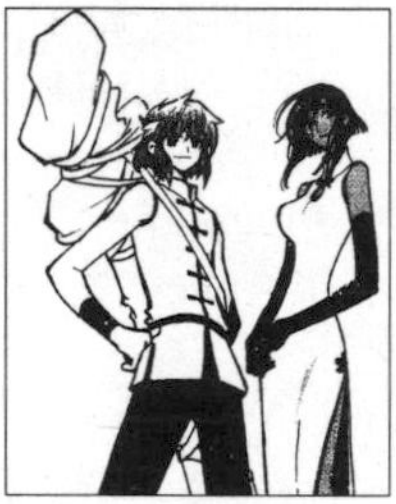

Anyone who has ever seen the anime or manga for *RG Veda* will have no problem recognizing the rambunctious attitude and ridiculously large sword of Ryûô (also spelled Ryuoh in the animated version). Sôma (also from Kurogane's world in the first volume) is the ninja servant of Kendappa, also from *RG Veda*.

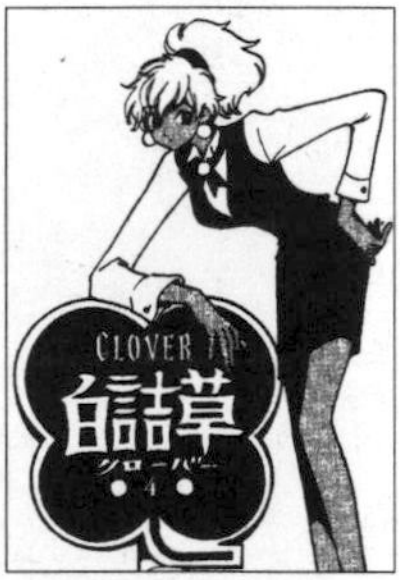
CLOVER

Caldina and the bar, page 55

The bar is obviously a reference to CLAMP's series Clover, and Caldina is borrowed from *Magic Knight Rayearth*.

Mokona coming downstairs, page 58

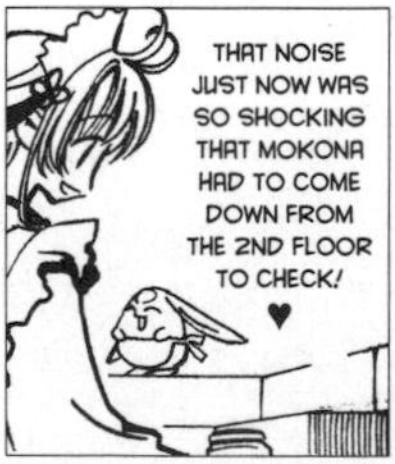
THAT NOISE
JUST NOW WAS
SO SHOCKING
THAT MOKONA
HAD TO COME
DOWN FROM
THE 2ND FLOOR
TO CHECK! ♥

Sharp-eyed readers of *xxxHOLiC* will remember a scene in *xxxHOLiC* Volume 4 when Mokona ends a conversation with Yûko to check on a noise. You've just found out what noise Mokona was checking on.

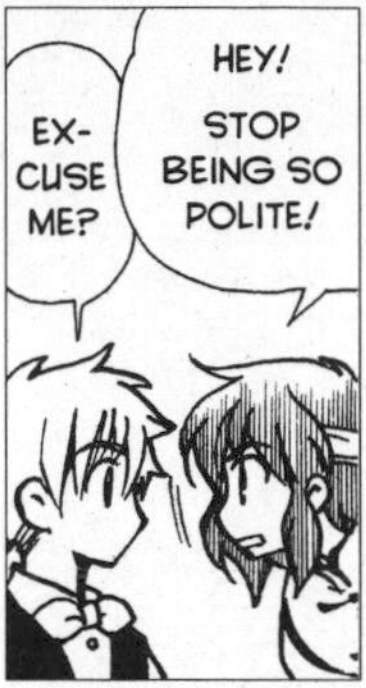
HEY!
STOP BEING SO POLITE!
EX-CUSE ME?

Polite language, page 60

There is a movement toward less formalized language among the young people of Japan, and Ryûô personifies it with his insistence that Syaoran stop using polite speech with him. Similarly in the West, we use the titles Mr., Mrs., and Ms. less now than earlier generations have, and we use first names more.

Talking like the Hanshin Republic, page 64

Caldina speaks with a "Kansai" accent (Kansai being the region encompassing the big cities of Osaka, Kyoto, Nara, and Kobe as well as the surrounding region), and since the Hanshin Republic was based on Osaka, Caldina's Kansai accent would sound like what Fai remembers from that country. The Kansai accent tends to be thought of as warm and folksy, much as the western drawl might be thought of in the United States.

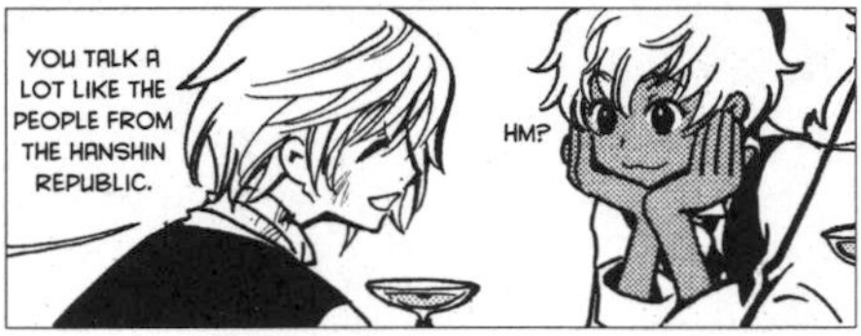
HM?
YOU TALK A LOT LIKE THE PEOPLE FROM THE HANSHIN REPUBLIC.

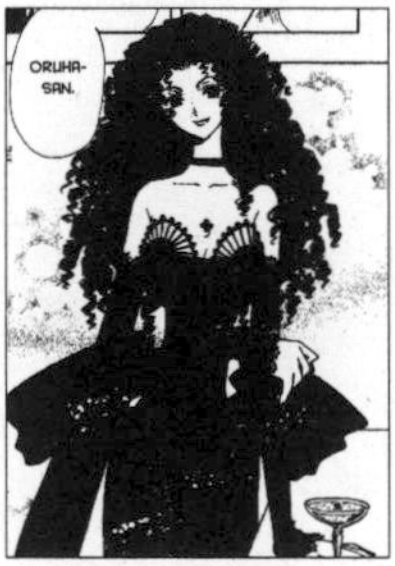
ORUHA-SAN.

Oruha, page 68

The character Ora from the manga series Clover has a crossover character in the country of Ôto by the name of Oruha. Since Ôto is based on Japan in a more traditional time, and since her name is given kanji that mean "weaved leaves"—another reference to clovers—we've decided to leave the pronunciation of her name with the more Japanese-sounding Oruha.

Polite with customers, page 72

Even though there is a move toward less formality in Japan, treatment of one's customers remains very polite and formal.

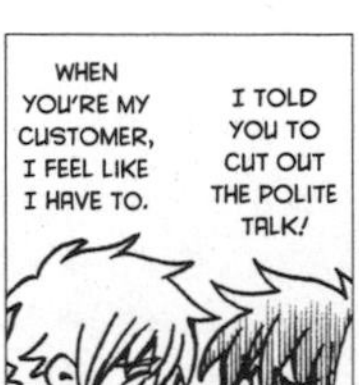
I TOLD YOU TO CUT OUT THE POLITE TALK!
WHEN YOU'RE MY CUSTOMER, I FEEL LIKE I HAVE TO.

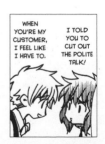

Cat's Eye, page 96

This is a reference to the witch Yûko Ishihara's (*xxxHOLiC*) love of the first hit manga series by artist Tsukasa Hojo (*City Hunter, Angel Heart*) named *Cat's Eye*. Three beautiful sisters become a group of thieves in order to steal back their father's priceless art collection stolen from them years ago—while at the same time trying to find clues to their father's disappearance. The sisters are being hunted by a young police officer who also happens to be in love with the middle sister, Hitomi. With the cat burglars "Cat's Eye" as their secret identities, their public identities are that of three sisters who run a small Tokyo café also named "Cat's Eye." The manga for *Cat's Eye* became a long-running animated TV series, and it has also spawned several popular live-action movies.

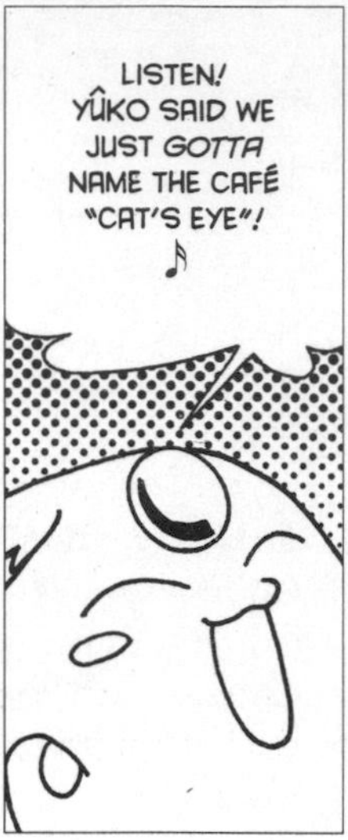
LISTEN! YÛKO SAID WE JUST GOTTA NAME THE CAFÉ "CAT'S EYE"! ♪

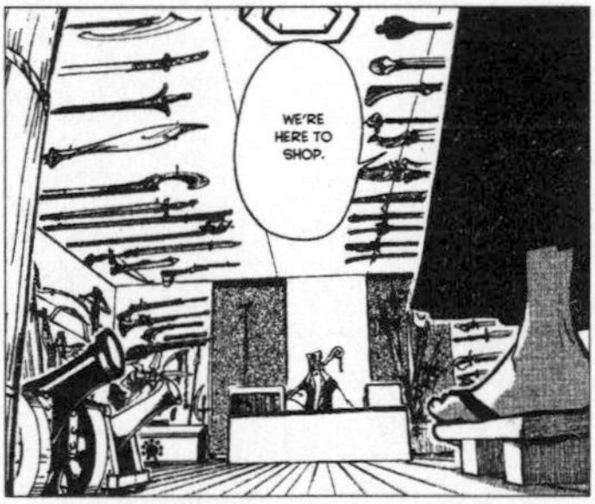
WE'RE HERE TO SHOP.

Chanan and Sanyun, page 106

Clamp fans may remember Chanan's shop from *Magic Knight Rayearth*.

The blossoming and falling of Sakura petals, page 134

Anyone who has been to one of the many cherry-tree filled parks of Japan in early spring will need no more explanation as to why the Japanese consider the cherry blossom as one of the symbols of their nation. There are few views inside or out of Japan that are quite as stunning as seeing the pale-pink petals falling like a snow flurry on the newly budding Japanese landscape.

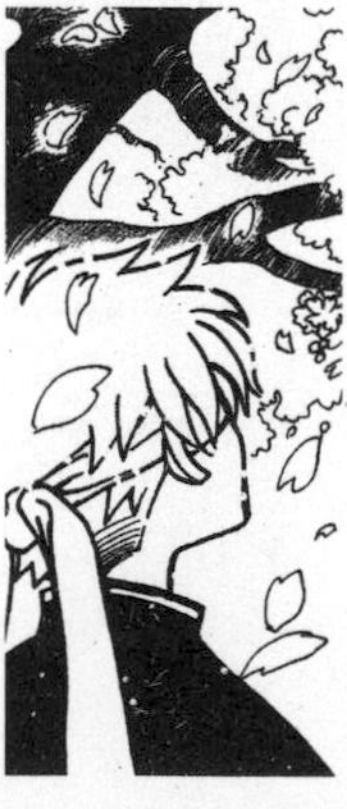

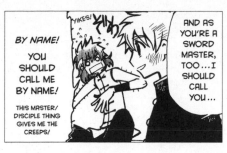

AND AS YOU'RE A SWORD MASTER, TOO...I SHOULD CALL YOU...
YIKES!
BY NAME!
YOU SHOULD CALL ME BY NAME!
THIS MASTER/ DISCIPLE THING GIVES ME THE CREEPS!

Kimi, page 147

Here's a passage that didn't quite translate. In it, Syaoran refers to Ryûô as "kimi," which translates out to "you." First of all, the Japanese very rarely use their words for "you" in conversation since all of them have strange overtones. ("Anata" is almost exclusively used these days as a name a woman calls her husband, much like "darling" or "honey" is used in North America.) Kimi has been used for addressing the emperor, and also used to address people beneath the speaker in station. Ryûô just seems to find being called "kimi" raises his hackles, so he asks Syaoran to refer to him by name rather than by pronoun. However, if Syaoran never said the word "you" to Ryûô in the English edition, the dialogue would have come out sounding unnatural. Besides, there are no bad nuances to the word "you" in English. So the translator had to borrow a different prejudice that Ryûô would certainly have—the aversion of a student to be treated as a master, especially by a friend, to make the scene work in the English version.

Seishirô, page 161

Seishirô is one of CLAMP's classic characters. He first appeared in *Tokyo Babylon*, then, along with his lifetime friend and enemy Subaru, moved to *X* (*X*/1999).

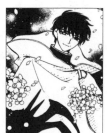

Preview of Volume 7

We're pleased to present you a preview from Volume 7. This volume is available from Tanoshimi now, here's a taste of the Japanese original.

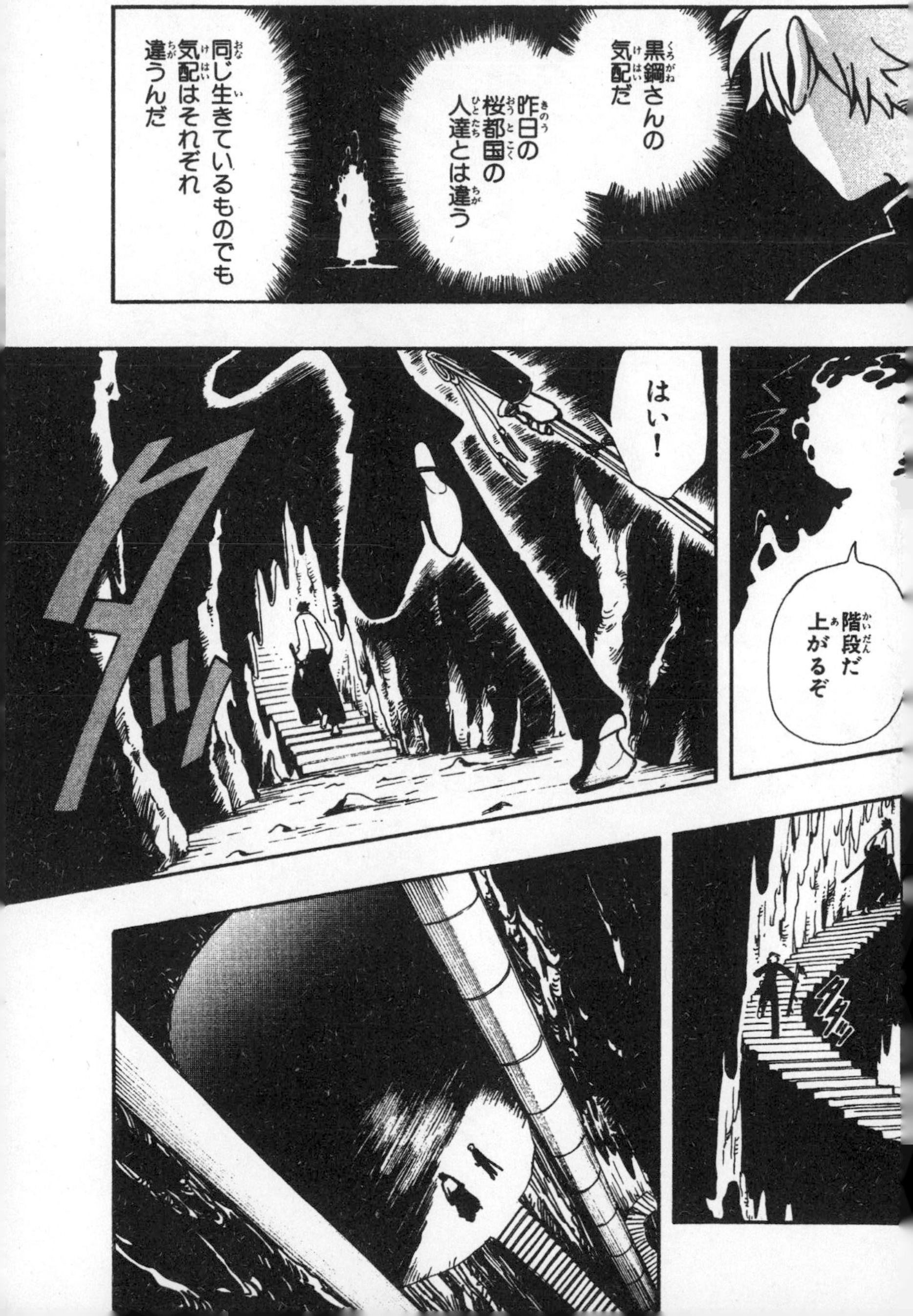
黒鋼さんの気配だ
昨日の桜都国の人達とは違う
同じ生きているものでも気配はそれぞれ違うんだ
くろ
階段だ上がるぞ
はい!
タッ
タタッ

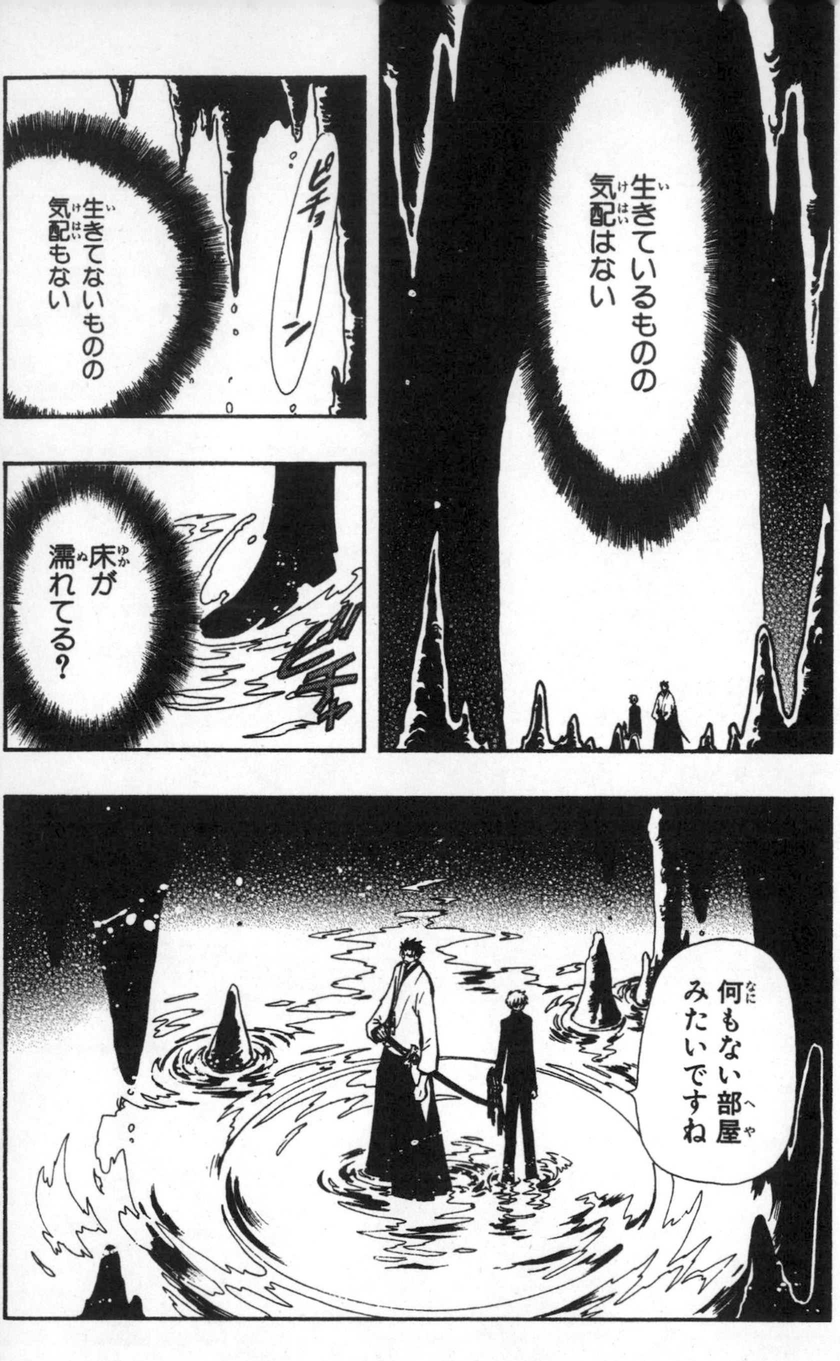
生きているものの気配はない
ピチョーン
生きてないものの気配もない
床が濡れてる？
何もない部屋みたいですね

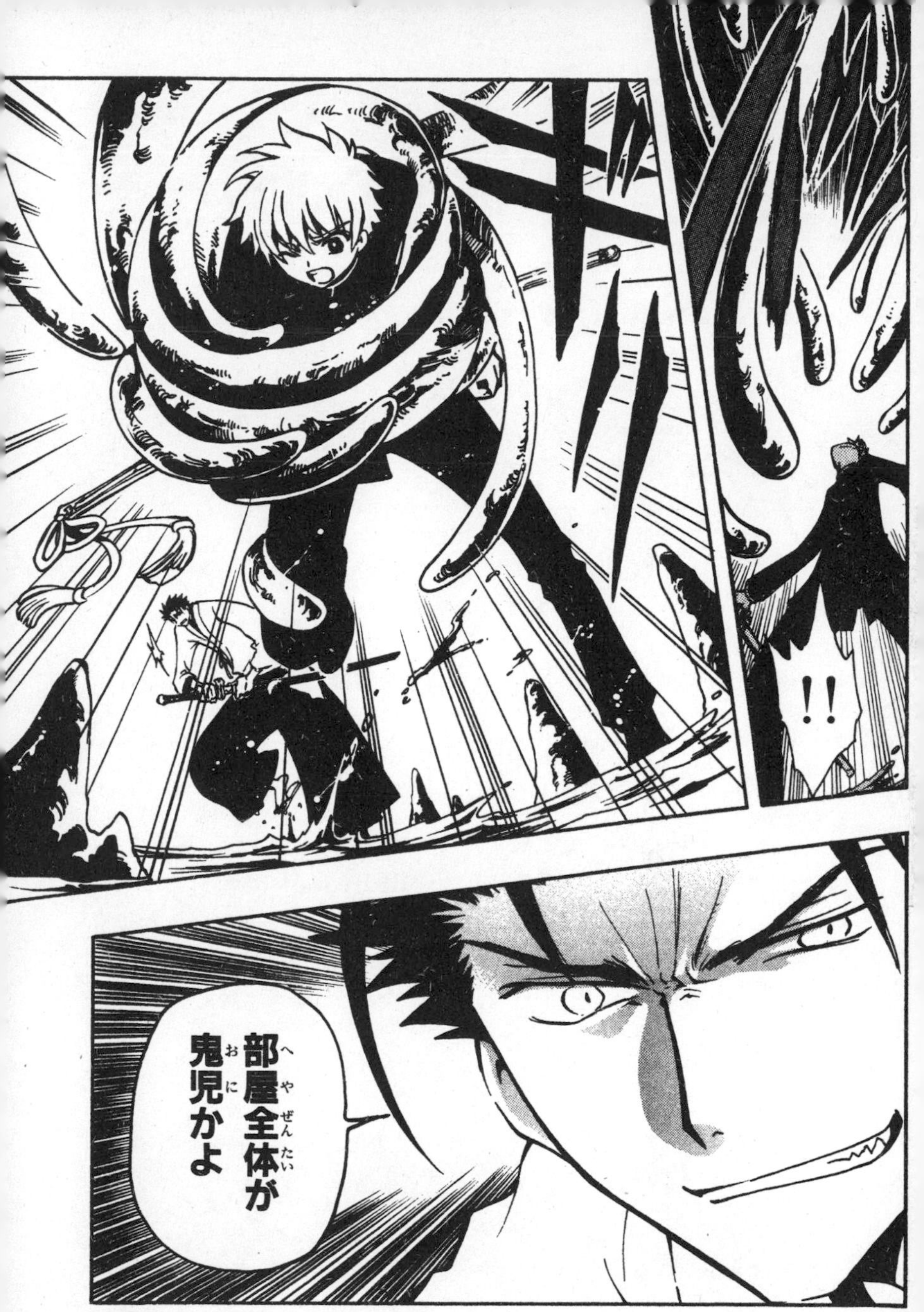
!!
部屋全体が鬼児かよ

BY OH!GREAT

Itsuki Minami needs no introduction—everybody's heard of the "Babyface" of the Eastside. He's the strongest kid at Higashi Junior High School, easy on the eyes but dangerously tough when he needs to be. Plus, Itsuki lives with the mysterious and sexy Noyamano sisters. Life's never dull, but it becomes downright dangerous when Itsuki leads his school to victory over vindictive Westside punks with gangster connections. Now he stands to lose his school, his friends, and everything he cares about. But in his darkest hour, the Noyamano girls give him an amazing gift, one that just might help him save his school: a pair of Air Trecks. These high-tech skates are more than just supercool. They'll enable Itsuki to execute the wildest, most aggressive moves ever seen—and introduce him to a thrilling and terrifying new world.

Ages: 16 +

Special extras in each volume! Read them all!

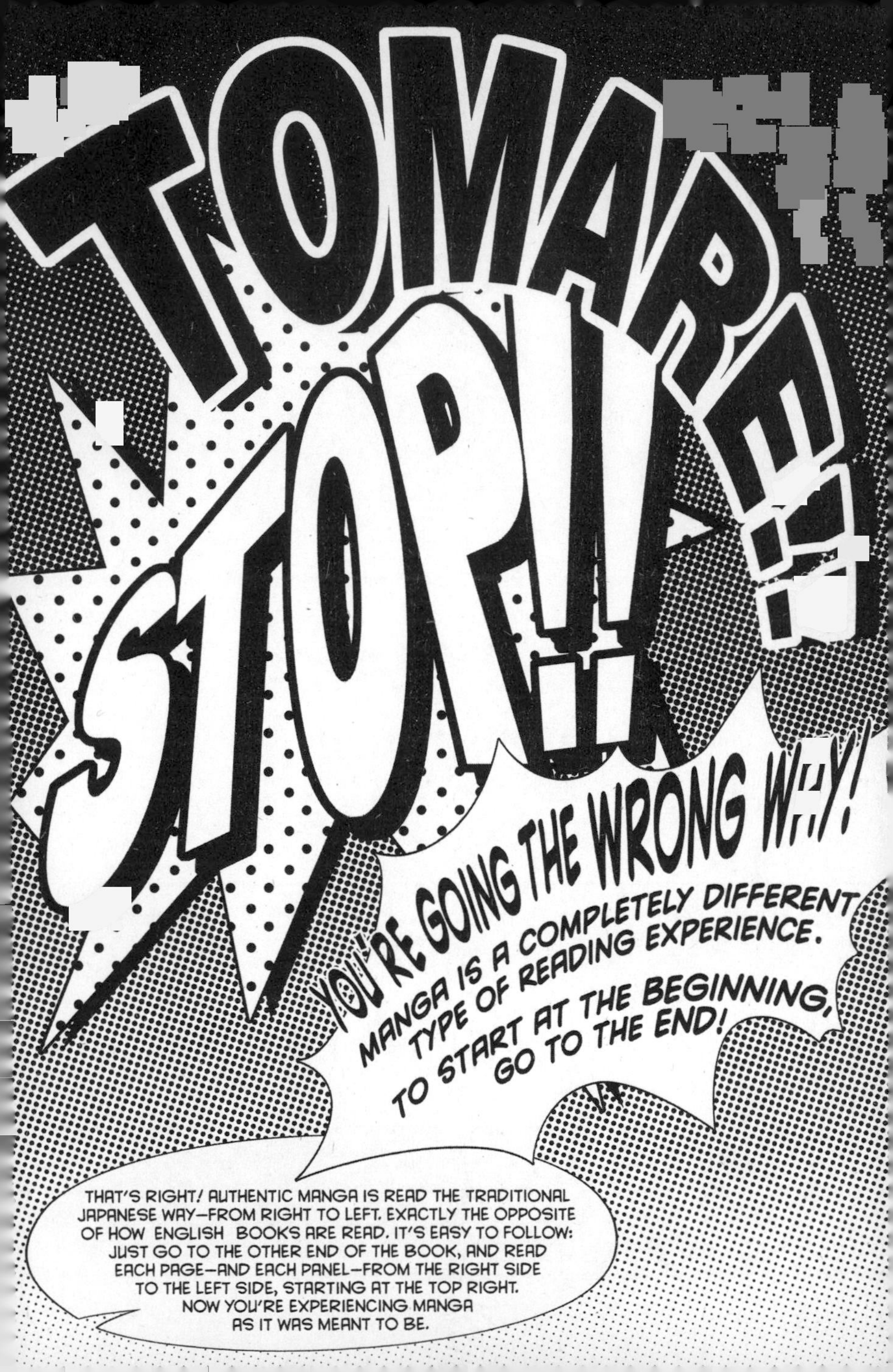
TOMARE!!
STOP!!
YOU'RE GOING THE WRONG WAY!
MANGA IS A COMPLETELY DIFFERENT TYPE OF READING EXPERIENCE.
TO START AT THE BEGINNING, GO TO THE END!
THAT'S RIGHT! AUTHENTIC MANGA IS READ THE TRADITIONAL JAPANESE WAY—FROM RIGHT TO LEFT. EXACTLY THE OPPOSITE OF HOW ENGLISH BOOKS ARE READ. IT'S EASY TO FOLLOW: JUST GO TO THE OTHER END OF THE BOOK, AND READ EACH PAGE—AND EACH PANEL—FROM THE RIGHT SIDE TO THE LEFT SIDE, STARTING AT THE TOP RIGHT. NOW YOU'RE EXPERIENCING MANGA AS IT WAS MEANT TO BE.